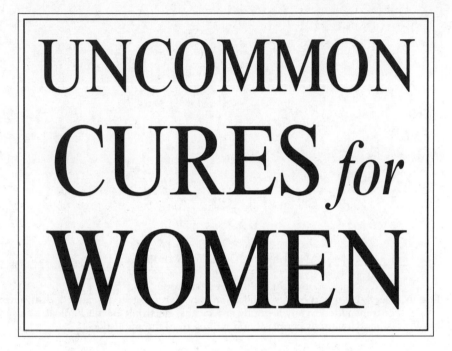

UNCOMMON CURES *for* WOMEN

Bottom Line Books
www.BottomLinePublications.com

Contents

3 • CURBING CHRONIC CONDITIONS WITHOUT DRUGS

4 • DETOX AND REJUVENATE

5 • DRUG-FREE REMEDIES FOR GOOD DIGESTION

6 • EAT WELL TO STAY HEALTHY

7 • KEY VITAMINS AND MINERALS FOR WOMEN

8 • LIFT YOUR SPIRITS, RELIEVE YOUR STRESS NATURALLY

13 • PAIN FREE NATURALLY

Preface

We are proud to bring you *Uncommon Cures for Women,* a collection of resources, news and helpful advice concerning women's health.

When you choose a Bottom Line book, you are turning to a stellar group of experts in a wide range of specialties—medical doctors, alternative practitioners, nutrition experts, research scientists and consumer-health advocates, to name a few.

We go to great lengths to interview the foremost health experts. Whether it's cancer prevention, breakthrough arthritis treatments or cutting-edge nutritional information, our editors talk to the true innovators in health care.

How do we find all these top-notch professionals? Over the past 21 years, we have built a network of thousands of leading physicians in both alternative and conventional medicine. They are affiliated with the world's premier medical institutions. We follow the latest research and we regularly talk to our advisors in major teaching hospitals, private practices and government health agencies. We also tap the resources of HealthDay, an award-winning news service devoted to consumer health issues.

Uncommon Cures for Women is a result of our ongoing research and contact with these experts, and is a distillation of their latest findings and advice. We hope that you will enjoy the presentation and glean helpful information about the health topics that concern you and your family.

As a reader of a Bottom Line book, please be assured that you are receiving reliable and well-researched information from a trusted source. But, please use prudence in health matters. Always speak to your physician before taking vitamins, supplements or over-the-counter medication…changing your diet…or beginning an exercise program. If you experience side effects from any regimen, contact your doctor immediately.

The Editors, Bottom Line Books, Stamford, Connecticut.

1

Alternative Care— What's Out There

Mayo Clinic's Top 10 Complementary Therapies

Dozens of US hospitals and major medical centers now offer complementary treatments in addition to conventional medical care*—and some of these therapies are covered by health insurance.

Problem: With so many conflicting claims being made regarding complementary therapies, how do doctors at these institutions decide which to recommend to the patients they treat? *At the world-renowned Mayo Clinic, the following four criteria are used...*

•**Is it safe?** If a complementary treatment is completely safe, then it may be worth trying, even if its effectiveness has not been proven definitively by scientific studies.

*To learn more about complementary therapies, go to *www.nccam.nih.gov*, the Web site of the National Center for Complementary and Alternative Medicine.

•**Is it standardized?** Herbs and dietary supplements are subject to limited regulatory oversight by the FDA. Therefore, these products frequently are not standardized to contain a consistent level of ingredients, potency and purity. Some herbs and dietary supplements do provide benefits, but you should work closely with a knowledgeable doctor when using them.

•**Does it meet a need that cannot be met by conventional medicine?** When it comes to stress, for example, conventional medicine includes treatments, such as anti-anxiety drugs or antidepressants, that potentially can help people. But such medications often have side effects and may not be suitable for long-term use. Complementary therapies, such as yoga,

Amit Sood, MD, associate professor of medicine at Mayo Clinic College of Medicine and director of research at the Complementary and Integrative Medicine Program at Mayo Clinic, both in Rochester, Minnesota. He is a contributor to the *Mayo Clinic Book of Alternative Medicine* (Time).

massage and meditation, can help relieve stress without the risk for serious side effects.

• **Does it positively affect not only patients, but also those with whom they interact?** The calming influence of several complementary treatments, such as meditation and music therapy, promotes a feeling of relaxation and well-being that helps bring harmony to one's interactions with family and friends. Positive, supportive relationships, in turn, are believed to help speed recovery from many types of illness.

Here is an alphabetical listing of Mayo Clinic's top 10 complementary treatments—and the research that supports their use…

BEST TREATMENTS

1. Acupuncture. In this treatment from traditional Chinese medicine, acupuncturists insert thin needles into strategic, energy-balancing points on the body. Acupuncture can prevent and treat nausea and vomiting and help relieve many types of pain, including that from osteoarthritis, low back pain, neck pain, headaches and postsurgical pain. Patients who receive acupuncture typically receive up to 12 treatments, usually given once or twice a week.

Standout scientific evidence: German researchers tracked more than 3,000 patients with hip or knee osteoarthritis and found that those receiving acupuncture experienced significantly more pain relief than those who did not receive acupuncture treatments.

2. Guided imagery. Patients imagine a beautiful, soothing environment, such as a warm beach. Guided imagery, also referred to as visualization, helps reduce anxiety in patients who become claustrophobic during magnetic resonance imaging (MRI) scans, who are having outpatient surgery without general anesthesia or who have been diagnosed with a life-threatening disease, such as cancer.

Standout scientific evidence: In a study conducted at the University of Akron in Ohio, a group of 53 women receiving radiation therapy for breast cancer either listened to guided imagery tapes once a day or did not. The women listening to the tapes felt more comfortable and less anxious, particularly during the first three weeks of treatment.

3. Hypnosis. The patient is led into a state of deep relaxation and focused attention by either a hypnotherapist or an instructional audio (self-hypnosis), and verbal suggestions are made to help relieve anxiety, pain, tension headaches and insomnia.

Standout scientific evidence: Doctors at the Mount Sinai School of Medicine in New York City analyzed 20 studies on hypnosis and surgical patients. In 89% of cases, surgical patients who were hypnotized had less pain, used less pain medication and recovered faster.

4. Massage. A massage therapist manipulates the body's soft tissue—muscle, skin and tendons—using fingertips, hands and fists. Massage treats anxiety and low back pain and improves postsurgical healing.

Standout scientific evidence: Studies conducted at the University of Miami's Touch Research Institute show that massage can help relieve back pain and strengthen the immune system in women with breast cancer by increasing levels of natural disease-fighting cells.

5. Meditation. Attention is focused on breathing and/or on a word, phrase or sound (mantra), leading to a more relaxed body and calmer mind. Doctors at the Mayo Clinic use meditation to treat patients with anxiety and high blood pressure and to help people quit smoking without medication.

Standout scientific evidence: An analysis of 20 studies on meditation found that this treatment could help patients cope with epilepsy, premenstrual syndrome (PMS), menopausal symptoms, autoimmune disease and anxiety during cancer treatment.

6. Music therapy. Many complementary medical centers employ music therapists. However, you can use music therapy on your own by listening to soothing music or your favorite tunes.

Standout scientific evidence: At Abbott Northwestern Hospital in Minneapolis, a study of 86 patients recovering from heart surgery showed that those receiving music therapy experienced less anxiety and pain.

7. Spinal manipulation. Practiced by chiropractors, osteopaths (medical doctors whose training allows them to correct structural problems in the musculoskeletal system) and physical therapists, this hands-on technique adjusts the spine to properly align the vertebrae with muscles, joints and nerves. Spinal manipulation is an accepted medical practice for low back pain, but the evidence supporting its use for other medical problems has been somewhat conflicting.

Standout scientific evidence: At the University of California, Los Angeles, School of Public Health, a study of 681 patients with low back pain showed that chiropractic care was as effective as medical care, including painkilling drugs, in relieving discomfort.

8. Spirituality. For some people, this means religious observance, prayer or faith in a "higher being." For others, spirituality can be found through a deep appreciation of nature or art or participation in a secular community.

Standout scientific evidence: Researchers in Virginia who conducted an analysis of 16 studies on illness and "religious intervention" — praying or attending religious services—found that spirituality can decrease the length of hospital stays and fever in patients with severe infections…increase immune function…help relieve rheumatoid arthritis symptoms…reduce anxiety…and improve outcomes in people with heart disease.

9. Tai chi. This gentle exercise, derived from Chinese martial arts, consists of a series of defined postures and movements performed slowly and gracefully. Medically, it is used to improve balance in older people who are prone to falls.

Standout scientific evidence: In a study of 278 elderly people at VU University Amsterdam in Amsterdam, The Netherlands, those who performed tai chi three times a week for six months had 50% fewer falls and fewer injury-causing falls.

10. Yoga. These stretching postures and breathing exercises, which originated in India, help calm body and mind. Yoga is particularly effective for stress relief, low back pain, carpal tunnel syndrome, osteoarthritis, anxiety and depression.

Standout scientific evidence: In a study conducted at All India Institute of Medical Sciences in New Delhi, 98 people with heart disease or diabetes who practiced the postures and breathing techniques of yoga had significant reductions in total cholesterol and blood sugar.

How Whole-Health Care Can Help You Feel Great …Live Longer

Henri Roca, MD, medical director, Greenwich Hospital Center for Integrative Medicine, Greenwich, Connecticut. He is a diplomate of both the American Academy of Family Practice and the American Board of Holistic Medicine and serves on the Louisiana State Board of Medical Examiners Complementary and Alternative Medicine Advisory Board.

Think of your health as a pot on the stove that's about to come to a boil. Conventional medicine would try to slam a lid on the pot and hold it down tight. That may work at first, but unless the heat is also turned down, the pressure under the lid will build up and the pot will boil over anyway. What alternative therapies try to do is reduce the intensity of the flame under the pot. In both cases, we're trying to keep the pot from boiling over.

The difference is that with integrative medicine, we're trying to keep that flame turned way down and keep it from bringing the pot to a boil at all.

This combination of conventional medicine and alternative treatments works so well that today many hospitals (including the one where I work) offer integrative medicine centers. When we incorporate alternative treatments, we're looking at ways to help people with certain lifestyle issues that are out of balance and will eventually cause illness. We're looking at the whole person—mind, body and spirit.

CREATING BALANCE

Our goal is to bring balance back—instead of allowing an imbalance to continue until it develops into serious symptoms. Through poor eating habits, lack of exercise and exposure to chemicals (pesticides and added hormones) in the air we breathe, water we drink and food we eat, we put a huge burden on the body. By

3

using integrative medicine, we can reduce that burden and help the body detoxify.

How it works: By supporting the liver, the kidneys and the intestines. If any of these organs don't function correctly, we will develop serious disease sooner or later.

Do you suffer from such common disorders as acid reflux, stomach ulcers, obesity, diabetes, menstrual irregularities, skin rashes, allergies, asthma or digestive problems? Many of my patients do. All those diagnoses are related, because the human system is a web of interactions and no single diagnosis can stand alone. Instead of giving someone three or four or 10 diagnoses with three or four or 10 pills to treat them, we work to bring that entire system back into balance. *Treatments I use include...*

• **Herbal product**

• **Biofeedback or other types of mind-body techniques, such as visualization**

• **Meditation or techniques involving deep breathing**

• **Traditional Chinese Medicine, such as acupuncture**

• **Homeopathy**

There's no single best treatment that works for everyone. We look closely at the patient as an individual and choose treatments based on what is most likely to be effective for him/her. *But there are some important general guidelines that may apply to you...*

CHRONIC DISEASES

When we have situations in life that impact our bodies significantly, such as chronic disease or stress, our nutrients are used up very quickly. We need to replenish them—if we don't, then chronic diseases worsen or we develop new disease.

Examples...

• **Depression often occurs after a person has been under significant stress that continues over a long period.** Under these circumstances, by replenishing basic nutrients necessary to create natural mood-regulating chemicals in the brain, we can potentially diminish depression symptoms. We don't automatically put any depressed person on an antidepressant medication. Sometimes we do so in conjunction with vitamin therapy, but the goal is to eventually lower the medication dosage or stop it altogether.

• **High blood pressure (hypertension) can be caused by a magnesium deficiency.** In that case, we might prescribe medication to lower blood pressure but also recommend a diet with more magnesium (or use magnesium supplements).

WHEN TO CHOOSE ALTERNATIVE THERAPIES

Conventional practitioners worry that by using alternative methods, some patients will end up delaying treatment until the condition has worsened...or even until it's "too late" in the case of life-threatening conditions. That's a valid concern, but rarely do I ever tell anyone that it's appropriate to use only conventional medicine or only an alternative approach.

Emergencies: When there's a truly dangerous medical condition—for example, blood pressure that's so high that the patient is in serious danger of having a heart attack or stroke...or a serious bacterial infection needing antibiotics...or cancer that might respond to chemotherapy, radiation and/or surgery—then conventional medicine, through the emergency room if necessary, is definitely the way to go.

But what if your blood pressure has just begun to increase? Then you could choose standard blood pressure medication to protect yourself from complications and worsening disease...and use an integrative approach to rebalance the system and turn off the fire. The ultimate goal is to reduce the medication dose or to stop the drugs completely.

In the case of a life-threatening illness, such as cancer, alternative therapies are not cures. Instead, integrative medicine focuses on supporting the person through the conventional treatment process and can be very effective in helping with the pain, fatigue and nausea associated with chemotherapy and radiation treatments. Similarly, integrative medicine can be very helpful for treating chronic diseases, such as multiple sclerosis, where fatigue is a big problem. Integrative medical doctors are board-certified by the American Board of Holistic Medicine. You can find a doctor near you by checking its Web site, *www.holisticboard.org.*

RELAX!

The most difficult thing for my patients to do is to prioritize their lives so that they have time for a different kind of therapy—relaxing. Yes, relaxing can be therapeutic. But it doesn't mean watching TV or reading a book. It means sitting in a place of silence and meditating.

Why this so important: Focused relaxation reduces stress, and if there is one single thing I see that causes a tremendous amount of disease, it's stress, whether related to work, family, money or some combination.

Because of stress, people make poor diet choices, drink too much alcohol, take illegal drugs and don't get enough exercise. Stress is the underpinning of the current epidemic of obesity, among other health problems. By making the time for focused relaxation, you can reduce your stress level—and improved health will follow.

Healing Outside the Box Of Mainstream Medicine

Mark A. Stengler, NMD, naturopathic medical doctor in private practice, Encinitas, California...adjunct associate clinical professor at the National College of Natural Medicine, Portland, Oregon...author of *The Natural Physician's Healing Therapies* (Bottom Line Books).

Almost invariably, new patients tell me, "Conventional medicine is not helping me. I'm here to try something different." Americans are waking up to the fact that most diseases can be helped or healed through natural medicine. Yet success requires that patients and their doctors "think outside the box" of mainstream medicine.

Healing sometimes takes more than an open mind, however. I'm often impressed by my patients who demonstrate dedication to a new lifestyle...perseverance despite setbacks...and courage to combat a discouraging prognosis. Here are the stories of four patients from whom I've learned invaluable lessons. I hope you find them inspiring, too.

LISTEN TO YOUR BODY

"I've lost track of how many different doctors I've seen in the past three years," said Nancy, 39, a real estate agent and mother of four. "They never agree on what's wrong, other than to imply that my problems are in my head. But I believe in listening to my body—and it's telling me that something isn't right."

Nancy had a daunting list of two dozen symptoms, including relentless fatigue, widespread muscle pain, dry skin, hair loss, weight gain, hypoglycemia (low blood sugar), recurring respiratory infections, dizzy spells, panic attacks and heart palpitations. Her various medical doctors had run numerous blood tests and other laboratory analyses over the years, but the results had always been "normal." Several times Nancy was offered antidepressants, which she refused. "I'm not sick because I'm depressed—I'm depressed because I'm sick," she told me.

Instead of trying to treat Nancy's symptoms one by one, I looked for a connection among her seemingly disparate problems—and recognized that many of them suggested low thyroid function. I ordered a blood test for free T3, the most specific marker of thyroid function available. (T3 is one of the thyroid hormones, and the "free" level is the amount not bound to protein and therefore available for use by the body's cells.) This test is not routinely ordered by most doctors, though I think it should be used more often.

The test confirmed that Nancy's free T3 level was low. I prescribed Armour Thyroid, a brand of natural thyroid hormone in tablet form that contains T3 and a blend of other thyroid hormones found in the human body. Most thyroid prescriptions do not contain T3, but instead contain only T4, a less potent and less effective thyroid hormone.

The results were fantastic. Within one week, Nancy's fatigue had eased and her mood had improved. Over the next three months, her energy level returned to normal...muscle pain disappeared...respiratory infections cleared up...weight and blood sugar stabilized...skin and hair condition improved...and mood lifted. Nancy said, "I can hardly believe how well I feel from just one simple type of treatment."

Self-help strategy: Before seeing a dozen different specialists for a dozen different symptoms, consult a holistic doctor. He/she will evaluate you as a whole person, rather than as a collection of problematic body parts—and may identify a single root cause behind all your symptoms. A good holistic doctor also will acknowledge that you know your own body best and will take all your concerns seriously.

HELP CELLS TO HELP THEMSELVES

A dedicated farmer and proud new grandparent, David was devastated when his oncologist reported that his prostate cancer had spread to his breastbone and that chemotherapy could not help. In an attempt to keep the cancer from spreading further, David underwent radiation treatments. He also received injections of drugs to reduce his body's production of testosterone and estrogen, since these hormones are associated with prostate cancer. Despite these measures, his prognosis was bleak. "Get your affairs in order," his doctor advised. "You've got about 12 months." David was 55 years old.

Though he had never given credence to alternative medicine, David decided that he had nothing to lose. At his son-in-law's urging, he came to see me.

I emphasized the need for David to help his cells detoxify—to release toxins that could be causing the cancer and to minimize the harmful side effects of the radiation treatments. I also recommended that we stimulate his immune system so that it could more effectively combat the disease.

First line of defense: A detoxifying diet.

Although he had been a lifelong beef lover, frequent beer drinker and occasional cake baker, David immediately gave up red meat, alcohol and sugary foods, and greatly increased his intake of nutritious vegetables and fish. He also began taking daily supplements of cancer-fighting vitamin C and selenium... the herbal detoxifiers dandelion root, burdock root and milk thistle...and various natural immune boosters, including echinacea and Oregon grape root.

The nutrients did their job better than David had dared to hope. He is now cancer-free—10 years after his doctor had predicted his im-

minent demise. David remains conscientious about his detoxifying diet-and-supplement regimen. "It's the reason I'm here today," he says, "watching my grandson grow up."

Self-help strategy: By detoxifying the body, it's often possible to fight serious diseases at the most basic cellular level. By being open-minded about alternative therapies, you expand your treatment options and optimize healing.

SAY NO TO DRUGS...AND
YES TO NUTRITION

Victor, 12, was in trouble at school. For years, the boy's behavior had caused problems in the classroom, and recently his restlessness and outbursts had worsened. His grades, never good, had dropped perilously close to failing. After Victor's pediatrician diagnosed attention deficit hyperactivity disorder (ADHD), the school psychologist and principal pressured the boy's parents, warning, "If Victor does not go on ADHD medication, he will be asked to leave the school."

But Victor's mother stood firm—"Those drugs can have serious side effects. We need to explore all other options first." That's when the family contacted me.

I shared the family's concerns about ADHD drugs, such as *methylphenidate* (Ritalin) and *amphetamine/dextroamphetamine* (Adderall XR), which can cause nausea, loss of appetite and stunted growth...headaches, dizziness and tics...insomnia and fatigue... irritability and mood swings...and heart palpitations, blood pressure changes and an increased risk of heart attack. We agreed to try nutritional therapies first and to use drugs only as a last resort.

Fortunately, we had summer vacation to address Victor's problems. The boy's diet was already good—but nonetheless, I suspected a deficiency of essential fatty acids (EFAs), which are vital structural components of cell membranes that affect the health of the brain, nervous system and cardiovascular system.

The clue: Victor's skin was extremely dry. EFA deficiency is a common cause of dry skin, and studies show that EFA supplementation improves mood and focus in some children with ADHD.

To boost Victor's intake of EFAs, I started him on daily supplements of fish oil (Nordic Naturals ProDHA, 800-662-2544, *www.nordic naturals.com*) and evening primrose oil. In addition, I prescribed the homeopathic remedy *Lycopodium clavatum*, made from club moss, to improve mood and concentration. I also had Victor take daily supplements of *phosphatidylserine*—a nutrient essential for the normal functioning of brain cell membranes and naturally found in soy, rice, fish and leafy green vegetables.

Victor was tested by a child psychologist before starting his treatment with me and again after 10 weeks. To the psychologist's amazement, Victor improved so markedly that he was no longer considered to have ADHD. During the ensuing school year, his teachers reported that Victor's behavior was exemplary. When I asked the boy during a follow-up visit, "How are your grades?" he grinned from ear to ear as he answered, "I made the honor roll!"

Self-help strategy: Many behavioral problems result from biochemical imbalances. Before resorting to drugs, investigate potential side effects—and explore natural alternatives that can safely restore the body's proper balance.

PERSEVERANCE PAYS OFF

Turning 40, Joanne laughed at the idea of a midlife crisis. She was happily married and had a busy, successful medical practice as a doctor of chiropractic. Life was good, and the future looked bright.

But then Joanne began to experience recurring pain in her bladder and the surrounding pelvic area, plus a frequent and urgent need to urinate. Her doctor diagnosed interstitial cystitis (IC), a condition that affects more than 700,000 people in the US (primarily women), yet is still not well understood. Joanne tried every treatment her doctors could suggest —including the prescription drug *pentosan polysulfate* (Elmiron), which is intended to repair the bladder lining, and a surgical procedure called bladder distension, which stretches the bladder by filling it with gas or water to increase its capacity—but nothing brought relief.

After five years, Joanne was in such severe and incessant pain that she could no longer see patients, take care of her two-year-old or find any pleasure in sex. Compounding her problems, she also experienced an early menopause, with symptoms that included dozens of hot flashes a day, frequent insomnia and severe fatigue, heart palpitations, anxiety, mood swings and trouble concentrating.

As I took her medical history, I noticed that her IC symptoms had eased during her pregnancy. This suggested that her IC was connected to her hormone balance and that menopause was aggravating the condition. Blood and saliva tests confirmed that she had a deficiency of estrogen, progesterone and thyroid hormones.

Finding the root of Joanne's problem was easier than treating it. For seven months, we used a trial-and-error approach, looking for a precise mix of hormone replacement therapies to alleviate her IC and menopausal symptoms. Finally, we hit upon the solution—a mix of an *estriol* (estrogen) vaginal cream…an estrogen/progesterone combination transdermal (skin) cream…and oral thyroid hormone tablets. Two months later, Joanne's pelvic pain and urinary urgency were gone, her menopausal symptoms had abated, and her sex life was back on track. "I'm enjoying being a mom," she reported, "and I may reopen my chiropractic practice. I've got my life back!"

Self-help strategy: Joanne deserves credit for her patience as we worked to figure out the best treatment for her individual needs. Too many people give up if they don't find a quick fix. For health problems—as with most of life's challenges—perseverance is the key to finding a solution.

WHEN YOU NEED SUPPORT

Facing a medical problem? Reach out for help. These organizations can provide physician referrals…information on conditions, treatments and research…and/or emotional support.

COMPLEMENTARY AND ALTERNATIVE MEDICINE

•**American Association of Naturopathic Physicians,** 866-538-2267, *www.naturopath ic.org*.

- **American Association of Acupuncture and Oriental Medicine,** 866-455-7999, *www. aaaomonline.org.*

- **American College for Advancement in Medicine,** 800-532-3688, *www.acamnet.org.*

- **North American Society of Homeopaths,** 206-720-7000, *www.homeopathy.org.*

MAINSTREAM MEDICINE

- **American Autoimmune Related Diseases Association,** 800-598-4668, *www.aarda.org.*

- **American Cancer Society,** 800-227-2345, *www.cancer.org.*

- **American Diabetes Association,** 800-342-2383, *www.diabetes.org.*

- **American Heart Association,** 800-242-8721, *www.americanheart.org.*

- **American Lung Association,** 800-586-4872, *www.lung.org.*

- **National Alliance on Mental Illness,** 800-950-6264, *www.nami.org.*

More from Mark A. Stengler, NMD...

How to Find a Good Holistic Doctor in Your Area

Finding a holistic doctor is easier than ever, but finding a good one is a different matter. When I was in college, alternative medicine was in its infancy, and naturopaths were scarce. (I had to drive three hours to the nearest one!)

Today, things are different. Alternative and complementary medicine have become big business, and many conventionally-trained physicians have jumped on the bandwagon. While some of these doctors are quite good, many others have only the most basic knowledge of alternative and natural therapies—not nearly enough to treat people with chronic illnesses.

Example: A prominent hospital in the San Diego area has what they call, an "integrative center," but several of its practitioners dispense little more than multivitamins and coenzyme Q10 supplements. Many of my patients tried this center before they found me, and I wouldn't want you to get similar poor results before you find good care.

GETTING STARTED

Searching professional associations can be a good place to start because they specify which treatment modalities a particular provider offers.

Example: If you want a doctor who does nutritional therapies, homeopathy, or oxygen therapies, these membership directories will often tell you...

- **American Association of Naturopathic Physicians,** 866-538-2267 or *www.naturo pathic.org.*

- **International College of Integrative Medicine,** 419-358-0273 or *www.icimed.com.*

- **American College for Advancement in Medicine,** 800-532-3688 or *www.acamnet.org.*

The downside is that directories don't necessarily tell you whether the doctor is any good. Membership in an association doesn't guarantee a great practitioner—only that he or she has met certain standards and pays annual dues.

WHAT HELPS

The best way to find a good holistic doctor is to talk to people who see one regularly. A great place to get recommendations is your local health food store. Ask your fellow customers and store workers about their experiences. After you've spoken to five or ten people, you'll start hearing the same one or two doctor's names that are the ones you should call.

Once you're at the doctor's office, you can gauge how good he or she is by asking the following magic question, "What are the root causes of my condition, and how shall we address them?" Mediocre holistic doctors will look at your symptoms and prescribe their remedies (just like conventional physicians who prescribe drugs). Superior practitioners look for the root cause of your condition to achieve true healing.

HOW TO CHOOSE AN ACUPUNCTURIST

Make sure the acupuncturist you choose has graduated from an accredited school and has at least two years' experience. You can find practitioners by contacting the American Association of Acupuncture and Oriental Medicine (866-455-7999, *www.aaaomonline.org*). Confirm a practitioner's certification through the National Certification Commission for

Acupuncture and Oriental Medicine (904-598-1005, *www.nccaom.org*).

Be wary of conventional physicians who practice acupuncture. MDs are not required to complete the same three-or-four-year program as licensed acupuncturists. Many MDs by law have done nothing more than take a few weekend courses to learn 10 or 15 pressure points, instead of hundreds. The best way to find a good acupuncturist is through recommendation from another patient.

The Essential Guide to Acupuncture: Calm Your Qualms About This Ancient Healing Practice

Effie Poy Yew Chow, PhD, RN, founder and president of East West Academy of Healing Arts in San Francisco (*www.eastwestqi.com*). A California-licensed acupuncturist, qigong grandmaster and registered psychiatric nurse, she was appointed by President Clinton to the original 15-member White House Commission on Complementary and Alternative Medicine Policy.

Acupuncture has been practiced in Asia for more than 5,000 years, but only recently has Western medicine begun to acknowledge this ancient healing therapy. Just over a decade ago, the FDA reclassified acupuncture needles from "experimental" status to "medical device." Around the same time, a consensus panel of the National Institutes of Health (NIH) found acupuncture to be an effective treatment for post-operative dental pain, chemotherapy-induced nausea and several other conditions.

Since then, people in the US have increasingly embraced acupuncture as an alternative or complementary therapy for numerous common ailments—and many health insurance companies now cover it. *What acupuncture can do for you...*

HOW IT WORKS

The human body has 12 major energy meridians (pathways), each corresponding to a different organ system. Flowing through this network is the body's *qi* (pronounced chee), or life force. Health problems result when there is too much or too little qi in specific places.

Example: If qi flow is excessive, a woman may be congested, feverish or unable to sleep. If qi flow is insufficient, she may lack energy, feel chilly or catch a cold.

Acupuncture often eases arthritis, asthma, migraine and many other conditions (see the list at the end of this article). The practitioner inserts very fine needles into the skin at one or more of about 1,000 specific points. This either calms the flow of excessive energy or stimulates the point if the qi is blocked.

Among Western researchers, the most widely accepted theories are that acupuncture triggers the release of pain-relieving brain chemicals called endorphins...helps release substances that transmit nerve impulses to the brain...and/or stimulates the immune system.

To date, one of the largest and most rigorous trials on acupuncture in the US was an NIH study in 2004 involving 570 participants. The study evaluated acupuncture's usefulness in treating osteoarthritis of the knee.

Results: After receiving 23 acupuncture sessions over 26 weeks, participants showed, on average, 40% more improvement in pain plus significantly more improvement in movement and function compared with a control group that received sham acupuncture. (In sham treatments, fine needles are inserted but not in the appropriate points.)

WHAT TO EXPECT

Before seeing an acupuncturist for a health condition, it is best to have a diagnosis from a medical doctor or naturopathic doctor. This helps the acupuncturist provide appropriate complementary treatment. However, even if a doctor has not been able to diagnose your problem, acupuncture still may correct the underlying cause or causes of your symptoms. For instance, I had a patient with severe asthma plus unexplained joint pain and digestive problems. Within two weeks of her first acupuncture session, her symptoms were gone and she was able to discontinue her many medications.

Your acupuncturist also will want as complete a picture of you as possible—including your health history and medications...diet and supplement use…exercise and sleep patterns…relationships, emotional state and stress level. Healing is most complete when a patient takes responsibility for her own health—so getting stuck with needles is only part of the process. You may be advised to adjust your diet and lifestyle, keep a journal of your feelings and/or take steps to reduce stress.

At the start of every session, the acupuncturist checks the pulse points that correspond with the various meridians and examines your tongue color and coating, which provide clues to imbalances in qi flow. Then, depending on where the needles need to go, you'll lie face-down, faceup or on your side during treatment.

DOES IT HURT?

Many people hesitate to try acupuncture for fear that it will hurt. In fact, the needles are so fine that they cause little pain. You may feel a brief uncomfortable sensation—like a pinprick or small electric shock—from the electromagnetic force or "energy grabbing" of the needle. This is called *dur-qi* and it subsides within seconds, and then you may feel a wave of calmness. If you do feel a strong reaction when a needle goes in, it may mean that you have a lot of qi blockage. The needle disperses that blockage, so with each treatment, discomfort lessens.

Note: The needle should not cause prolonged discomfort. If it does, tell the practitioner so he/she can make adjustments.

The number of needles varies with the condition being treated, your individual needs and the practitioner's training. Needles may be inserted just a tiny fraction of an inch or as deep as an inch or more. They may be left in place for a few minutes, a few hours or even a few days.

A session usually lasts 20 to 60 minutes and costs from $60 to $100 or more, depending on the practitioner and location. Patients generally have a total of six to 10 sessions, going once or twice weekly at first and then gradually increasing the time between appointments as their symptoms improve. Patients may notice improvement during a session, hours after a session or sometimes only after a number of sessions.

Safety: When done by a qualified practitioner, acupuncture is safe for most people.

The practitioner should swab treatment sites with disinfectant, then use sterile, single-use, disposable needles. Occasionally, patients experience very slight bleeding or bruising at a needle site.

Warning: Extra caution must be used when acupuncture is done on patients who have a bleeding disorder or who take a blood thinner. Acupuncture should not be used during pregnancy because there is a slight risk of miscarriage.

Best: Verify that your acupuncturist is certified by the National Certification Commission for Acupuncture and Oriental Medicine (904-598-1005, *www.nccaom.org*)…or by your state's licensing authority. For state-by-state information, contact the American Association of Acupuncture and Oriental Medicine (866-455-7999, *www.aaaomonline.org*).

PROBLEMS OFTEN TREATED WITH ACUPUNCTURE

Acupuncture may ease many conditions, including…

- **Anxiety**
- **Arthritis**
- **Asthma**
- **Back pain**
- **Bladder infections**
- **Blood sugar imbalances**
- **Bursitis**
- **Carpal tunnel syndrome**
- **Dental pain**
- **Depression**
- **Fibromyalgia** (widespread muscle and joint pain)
- **Headache and migraine**
- **Insomnia**
- **Menopausal hot flashes**
- **Menstrual cramps**
- **Postoperative nausea**
- **Sciatica**
- **Seizures**
- **Sinus problems**
- **Stress**
- **Tendinitis**

Acupuncture Zaps Surgical Pain

Tong J. Gan, MD, professor and vice chairman, department of anesthesiology, Duke University Medical Center, Durham, North Carolina.

Kenneth Levey, MD, director, New York Center for Pelvic Pain and Minimally Invasive Gynecologic Surgery, and clinical assistant professor, obstetrics and gynecology, New York University School of Medicine, New York City.

David P. Martin, MD, department of anesthesiology, Mayo Clinic, Rochester, Minnesota.

American Society for Anesthesiology meeting, San Francisco.

Powerful opioids taken after surgery can have powerful side effects, but new research finds that using acupuncture before and during an operation cuts a patient's need for the painkillers.

"From a pain perspective, you can reduce the amount of morphine that the patient uses and improve the quality of analgesia and pain control," said lead researcher Tong J. Gan, MD, a professor and vice chairman of anesthesiology at Duke University Medical Center, in Durham, North Carolina.

Morphine is a type of opioid, a category of potent painkillers that often produce side effects, such as nausea and vomiting.

THE STUDY

In a study, Dr. Gan's team analyzed data taken from 15 small, randomized clinical trials looking at the use of acupuncture to reduce postoperative pain.

The analysis found that acupuncture received 30 minutes before and during surgery, could reduce common side effects of morphine experienced by eight out of 10 patients. It reduced post-op itchiness by 30%, nausea by 50% and dizziness by 60%, Dr. Gan said, in part because it lessened the need for morphine.

ACUPUNCTURE ALSO REDUCES URINARY RETENTION

One expert said Dr. Gan's finding that adjunctive acupuncture can reduce urinary retention by 3.5 times is especially important.

"The risk reduction is huge," said Kenneth Levey, MD, a clinical assistant professor of obstetrics and gynecology at New York University School of Medicine in New York City. Urinary retention is not only uncomfortable for the patient but the use of a catheter to relieve it increases the risk of infection, he said.

ACUPUNCTURE IN THE OPERATING ROOM

The studies also show that acupuncture could be of benefit following many types of surgeries, said Dr. Gan. Chinese acupuncture was the style used in the studies he reviewed, but similar effects would occur with other styles and whether needles, electrical or manual acupuncture were used, Dr. Gan speculated.

Adjunctive acupuncture is "not widely used because people need to be educated," Dr. Gan said. To use it, surgeons need training but they don't "need to know every acupuncture point. Only a few are important points to relieve this discomfort."

Dr. Gan said he uses acupuncture in about 20% to 30% of the surgeries he's involved with. He said that few patients decline to use adjunctive acupuncture, and when they do, it's usually because they have little knowledge of it.

Acupuncture "is becoming increasingly accepted by both physicians and patients," added David P. Martin, MD, an anesthesiologist at the Mayo Clinic in Rochester, Minnesota. He said the technique could be helpful whether it is used to lower morphine doses or other opioid painkillers, or whether it is used to relieve nausea.

He questioned, however, how widely acupuncture could be used during operations because "acupuncture needles tend to get in the way" in crowded operating room conditions.

"For optimum pain control with minimum side effects, opioids plus acupuncture are the way to go and hopefully will become more widely accepted," Dr. Levey added.

For more information on acupuncture, visit the Web site of the National Center for Complementary and Alternative Medicine at *http:// nccam.nih.gov/health/acupuncture.*

Are Acupuncture Needles Painful?

Joan-Ellen Macredis, ND, LAc, licensed acupuncturist in private practice, Stamford, Connecticut.

U sually not. The goal of acupuncture, which is a key component of Traditional Chinese Medicine, is to treat illness by correcting imbalances in the flow of energy. To do this, the acupuncturist inserts needles in acupuncture points along meridians, or energy pathways, in the body. Acupuncture needles, which are disposable and made of stainless steel, are about the width of a human hair. Most practitioners use sterile plastic tubes to guide the needles into the acupuncture point, making insertion relatively painless. And even if you feel the insertion, you usually don't feel the needles once they're in. The number of needles used during a treatment depends on the condition and the patient's overall health. Acupuncture is typically performed with the patient lying flat on his/her back or stomach. Treatment lasts 20 to 40 minutes.

To find a licensed acupuncturist in your area, contact the National Certification Commission for Acupuncture and Oriental Medicine (904-598-1005, *www.nccaom.org*).

Acupuncture Lessens Knee Pain Due to Arthritis

I n a recent study of osteoarthritis patients with knee pain, those who received acupuncture 12 times in eight weeks experienced less pain and more functionality eight weeks after the treatment than those who received "sham" acupuncture or none at all. One year after treatment, both groups fared the same.

Claudia Witt, MD, deputy administrative director, project coordinator, complementary medicine, Institute for Social Medicine, Epidemiology, and Health Economics, Berlin, Germany, and leader of a study of 294 people with knee osteoarthritis.

Do-It-Yourself Acupressure—Relief From Headache, Nausea, Insomnia and More

Guanhu Yang, PhD, a licensed acupuncturist (LAc) at the Acupuncture Wellness Center of Mason in Mason, Ohio, the Integrative Center in Blue Ash, Ohio. *www.acupuncturecincinnati.com.*

A cupressure is similar to acupuncture but uses no needles, just hands—so you can treat common discomforts yourself. According to Traditional Chinese Medicine, it stimulates points along meridians (energy channels) to eliminate unhealthful blockages of *qi*—the energy life force that flows through the body. In Western terms, stimulating these points may

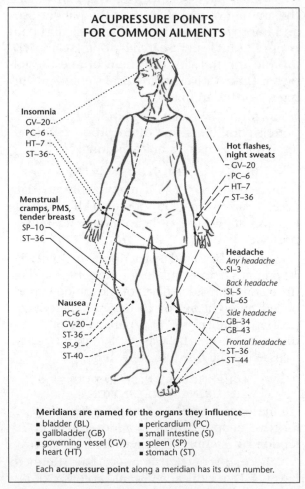

ACUPRESSURE POINTS FOR COMMON AILMENTS

Insomnia
GV–20
PC–6
HT–7
ST–36

Hot flashes, night sweats
GV–20
PC–6
HT–7
ST–36

Menstrual cramps, PMS, tender breasts
SP–10
ST–36

Headache
Any headache
SI–3

Back headache
SI–5
BL–65

Nausea
PC–6
GV–20
ST–36
SP–9
ST–40

Side headache
GB–34
GB–43

Frontal headache
ST–36
ST–44

Meridians are named for the organs they influence—
■ bladder (BL)   ■ pericardium (PC)
■ gallbladder (GB)   ■ small intestine (SI)
■ governing vessel (GV)   ■ spleen (SP)
■ heart (HT)   ■ stomach (ST)

Each **acupressure point** along a meridian has its own number.

release endorphins, natural opiates that reduce pain and relax muscles. *What to do…*

• **Stand,** sit or lie down.

• **Beginning on either side of your body,** apply pressure to each of the designated spots for your ailment, in any order, holding each spot for 30 to 60 seconds. Repeat on the other side.

• **Use your thumb to apply firm,** steady but not forceful pressure.

• **Slowly inhale as you press and exhale as you release.** This further promotes nervous system responses that alleviate qi-blocking tension.

• **If symptoms do not abate,** repeat the cycle two or three times.

• **To help prevent symptoms,** do acupressure every day upon awakening and at bedtime.

• **Avoid pressing on any recent injury,** cut or varicose vein.

Illustration by Shawn Banner.

Relief at Your Fingertips: Acupressure Helps Arthritis, Back Pain, Colds, Insomnia, More

Michael Reed Gach, PhD, founder of the Acupressure Institute in Berkeley, California. He is author of self-healing instructional DVDs and CDs and many books, including *Acupressure's Potent Points* (Bantam), *Acupressure for Lovers* (Bantam), *Arthritis Relief at Your Fingertips* (Warner) and coauthor of *Acupressure for Emotional Healing* (Bantam). *www.acupressure.com.*

You've probably heard of acupuncture, but there's something similar that you can do yourself—no needles involved—called acupressure. Acupressure can alleviate many physical, mental and emotional problems in only a few minutes—and it is free.

Acupressure involves stimulating acupoints on the body with fingertips or knuckles and is based on the principles of acupuncture, an ancient healing technique used by practitioners of Traditional Chinese Medicine (TCM). The acupoints often have ancient descriptive names, such as "Joining the Valley" and "Mind Clearing." Acupressure increases blood flow to the treated area and triggers the release of endorphins, pain-relieving brain chemicals.

ACUPRESSURE BASICS

Unless otherwise noted, use your middle finger, with your index and ring fingers for support. Firmly and gradually, apply stationary pressure directly on the acupoint for three minutes.

• **Firmly means using an amount of pressure that causes a sensation between pleasure and pain**—pressure that "hurts good." If the pressure is applied too fast or too hard, the point will hurt. If the pressure is too soft, you won't get the full benefit.

• **Gradually means moving your finger into and out of the point in super-slow motion.** Applying and releasing finger pressure allow the tissue to respond and relax, promoting healing.

• **Stationary means you are not rubbing or massaging the area.**

• **Directly means at a 90-degree angle from the surface of the skin.** If you are pulling the skin, the angle of pressure is incorrect.

• **When you apply pressure,** lean your weight toward the point. If your hands are weak or it hurts your fingers when you apply pressure, try using your knuckles. You also can use a tool, such as a golf ball or pencil eraser.

• **Breathe slowly and deeply while you apply pressure.** This helps release pain and tension.

Once you've mastered the basics, use them with the techniques that follow for various health problems. Unless otherwise noted, daily acupressure sessions, three times a day, are the best way to relieve a temporary or chronic problem.

ARTHRITIS PAIN

Joining the Valley is a truly amazing acupoint because it can relieve arthritis pain anywhere in the body.

Location: In the webbing between the thumb and index finger, at the highest spot of the muscle when the thumb and index finger are brought close together.

What to do: Rhythmically squeeze the acupoint. As you're squeezing, place the side of your hand that is closest to the little finger on your thigh or a tabletop. Apply pressure in the webbing as you press downward. This allows you to angle more deeply into the point, increasing the benefits.

Also good for: Headache, toothache, hangover, hay fever symptoms, constipation.

Caution: This point is forbidden for pregnant women because its stimulation can cause premature contraction in the uterus.

MEMORY PROBLEMS

The Mind Clearing acupoints are for improving recall instantly—for example, when you have forgotten a name or gone to the supermarket without your shopping list.

Location: One finger width (about one-half inch) directly above the center of each eyebrow.

What to do: Gently place your right thumb above your right eyebrow and your middle fingertip above the eyebrow on the left side. Hold very gently. You should feel a slight dip or indentation in the bone structure—the acupoints on both sides are in the dip. Press the indentation very lightly, hold and breathe deeply. After a minute or two, you'll experience more mental clarity and sharper memory.

LOWER BACK PAIN

To help prevent and relieve lower back pain, practice this exercise for one minute three times a day. You can do it standing or sitting.

Location: Place the backs of your hands against your lower back, about one inch outside the spine.

What to do: Briskly rub your hands up and down—about three inches up and six inches down—using the friction to create heat in your lower back.

If you're doing the technique correctly, you'll need to breathe deeply to sustain the vigorous rubbing, and you'll break out in a slight sweat.

Also good for: Food cravings, especially sugar cravings, chronic fatigue, sexual problems, chills, phobias and fibromyalgia symptoms.

EMOTIONAL UPSET

The Inner Gate acupoint can reduce emotional upset—such as anxiety, depression and irritability—in two to three minutes.

Location: On the inner side of the forearm, three finger widths up from the center of the wrist crease, in between two thick tendons.

What to do: Place your thumb on the point and your fingers directly behind the outside of the forearm between the two bones. Squeeze in slowly and firmly, hold for two to three minutes, breathing deeply. Repeat on the other arm for the same amount of time.

Also good for: Carpal tunnel syndrome, insomnia, indigestion and nausea.

COLDS AND FLU

If you think you're about to get a cold or flu, stimulating the Heavenly Rejuvenation acupoint may prevent infection.

Location: On the shoulders, midway between the base of the neck and the outside of the shoulders, one-half inch below the top of the shoulders, just above the tip of the shoulder blades.

What to do: There are two ways to stimulate this point...

Curving your fingers, hook your right hand on your right shoulder and your left hand on your left shoulder. You also can use your fingers on your opposite shoulder, which may be easier. With your fingertips, firmly press the point and take three slow, deep breaths.

If you don't have the flexibility to perform the first technique...lie down on your back, on a firm mattress or carpeted floor, with your knees bent and feet on the floor as close to your buttocks as possible. Bring your hands above your head, and rest the backs of your hands on the floor beside or above your head. Inhale and lift up your pelvis, pressing your feet against the floor to assist the lift. The higher your pelvis, the more weight will be transferred onto your shoulders, stimulating the acupoint. Hold this posture for one minute, taking long, slow, deep breaths, with your eyes closed. Lower your pelvis, and rest for three minutes.

Also good for: Nervous tension, stiff neck, high fever, chills, shoulder aches as well as irritability.

INSOMNIA

The acupoints Calm Sleep and Joyful Sleep—on the outer and inner ankles—can help relieve insomnia. Use these acupressure points whenever you want to deeply relax and sleep better.

Location: Calm Sleep is in the first indentation below the outer anklebone. Joyful Sleep is directly below the inside of the anklebone, in a slight indentation.

What to do: Place your thumb on one side of your ankle and your fingers on the other, and press firmly. If you're on the right spot, it will be slightly sore. Hold for two minutes, breathing deeply. Repeat on the other ankle. Do this again if you still are having trouble sleeping or if you wake up.

HEADACHES

The acupoints Gates of Consciousness relieve a tension headache or migraine.

Location: Underneath the base of your skull to either side of your spine, about three to four inches apart, depending on the size of your head.

What to do: Using your fingers, thumbs or knuckles, press the points under the base of your skull.

At the same time, slowly tilt your head back so that the angle of your head relaxes your neck muscles. Press forward (toward your throat), upward (underneath the base of your skull) and slightly inward, angling the pressure toward the center of your brain. Continue to apply pressure for two minutes. Keep your breathing even and relaxed.

Also good for: Neck pain, insomnia, high blood pressure.

Massage Essentials

Ben E. Benjamin, PhD, massage practitioner in Cambridge, Massachusetts. His books include *The Ethics of Touch* (Sohnen-Moe Associates) and *Exercise Without Injury* (MTI).

Body massage is available at many health clubs and spas as well as medical centers and hospitals. Most massages last 30 to 60 minutes with prices ranging from about $50 to $150 per hour. Health insurance may cover all or part of the cost of massage therapy with a doctor's referral.

WHO SHOULD AVOID MASSAGE

Massage is generally considered safe for most people. However, massage should be avoided by people who have deep vein thrombosis, bleeding disorders, fever, varicose veins, osteoporosis, a recent fracture, open wounds or who have had recent surgery (unless approved by a physician).

CHECK WITH YOUR DOCTOR

Until recently, many medical experts warned cancer patients to avoid massage for fear of stimulating growth or spread of a malignancy. Now, this belief has been debunked and massage is generally considered safe for cancer patients, who often experience energy-boosting and/or stress-relieving benefits.

If you have cancer, however, you should still check with your doctor before you receive massage. In some cases, it can damage tissue that is fragile due to treatments such as radiation and/or chemotherapy.

CHOOSING A THERAPIST

When selecting a massage therapist, choose someone who is licensed by his/her municipality or state and certified by a national certifying agency. These qualifications will ensure that the practitioner has at least 500 hours of training. You can also seek a referral from the American Massage Therapy Association, 877-905-0577, *www.amtamassage.org*…or the Associated Bodywork & Massage Professionals, 800-458-2267, *www.abmp.com*.

Surprising Ways a Chiropractor Can Help You Feel Better

Karen Erickson, DC, chiropractor in private practice in New York City and spokesperson for the American Chiropractic Association. She is author of several academic texts on the role of chiropractic in integrative health care and is on the board of trustees at New York Chiropractic College, New York City.

Well-designed studies have shown that chiropractic care (often just called "chiropractic") is at least as effective —and sometimes more effective—than conventional medicine for treating certain types of physical complaints.

Emerging research indicates that chiropractic affects more than just the spine and surrounding muscles. It has been used to successfully treat a variety of conditions, including digestive complaints and ear infections.

Ways chiropractic can help…

DIGESTIVE DISORDERS

A survey of 1,494 patients found that 22% reported digestive relief following chiropractic treatments, even though the majority had never mentioned digestive issues to their chiropractors.

Many of the spinal nerves that are affected by chiropractic manipulation control digestive functions. Patients who undergo routine manipulations may experience changes in their levels of digestive fluids, the speed at which food moves through the intestinal tract or the strength and/or frequency of intestinal contractions.

We're often told by patients that manipulations for, say, neck or low-back pain not only helped their musculo-skeletal complaints but also resulted in improvement in constipation, irritable bowel syndrome and other digestive issues.

Digestive problems need to be medically diagnosed first, but the most effective treatments involve an integrative approach, which can include chiropractic. I often get referrals from medical doctors of patients with constipation, colitis or irritable bowel syndrome.

Help for colic: A study published in *Journal of Manipulative and Physiological Therapeutics* found that colicky babies treated with chiropractic cried about three hours less daily than they did before, compared to a one-hour reduction in those given the drug *dimethicone,* a standard treatment. The manipulations given to children are very gentle. Many have a reduction in colic after just one or two treatments. Look for a chiropractor who specializes in children's problems.

TENSION HEADACHE

The headaches that we all get from time to time often are related to the cervical spine in the neck. Known as cervicogenic headaches, these occur when vertebral misalignments cause muscle tightness or spasms. The tension begins in the neck but can radiate through the occipital nerves that rise upward from the base of the skull.

A study that compared patients receiving chiropractic care for tension headaches with those who were treated with the antidepressant *amitriptyline* showed reduction in both the frequency and pain intensity of these types of headaches. Most important, the chiropractic patients sustained these improvements after the treatment period, unlike patients who were treated with medication.

In a typical treatment, the chiropractor attempts to realign the cervical joints by manipulating the neck and head. The main goals of the treatment, apart from adjusting the vertebrae, are to increase the range of motion, relax the surrounding muscles and decrease pain and inflammation.

People who have only recently started getting headaches often will improve after one or two sessions with a chiropractor. Those who have suffered from headaches for years probably will require multiple treatments before they start to notice a significant improvement.

Also important: The chiropractor will take a detailed history to learn why there is excess misalignment in the neck. This usually is due to lifestyle issues. For example, many of us look down at our computer monitors, which puts excessive tension on the neck. Raising the monitor to eye level can correct this. Women may be advised to carry a handbag rather than a heavy shoulder bag. Cradling your phone between your neck and shoulder also can cause problems. If you often find yourself doing this, get a headset.

It's not clear if chiropractic is as effective for migraines, but preliminary research suggests that chiropractic manipulations may affect nerves that control vascular expansion and contraction, a key component of migraines.

EAR INFECTIONS

Some adults and virtually all children accumulate fluids in the eustachian tube, the passage between the throat and middle ear. The fluid is a perfect medium for viruses and bacteria, which can cause otitis media, an infection or inflammation of the middle ear.

Many studies have shown that chiropractic can relieve and prevent ear infections without antibiotics. The treatments, which include chiropractic adjustment and massage of the lymph nodes along the neck and around the ear, help drain excess fluid. The adjustment helps regulate the nervous system, which in turn helps drain the eustachian tube and promotes long-term drainage.

SINUSITIS

People with chronic sinusitis (inflammation of the mucous membranes in the sinuses) rarely get long-term relief from antibiotics or other types of conventional medicine, such as antihistamines and decongestants. Chiropractic can sometimes relieve all or most of the typical symptoms, such as facial pain and nasal congestion.

People with chronic sinusitis often have a misalignment in the cervical vertebrae. Chiropractic adjustments may help sinuses drain more efficiently. The treatment for sinusitis also includes applying pressure to the sinuses near the eyebrows and on either side of the nose.

REPETITIVE STRESS DISORDERS

Most repetitive stress injuries, including tennis elbow, are caused by tendinitis, an inflammation of the fibrous tissue that connects muscles to bones. Carpal tunnel syndrome, another type of repetitive stress injury, is caused by nerve inflammation in the wrist.

Doctors usually treat these conditions with anti-inflammatory drugs, including steroid in-

jections in severe cases. For carpal tunnel syndrome, surgery to "release" pressure on the nerve is sometimes recommended.

Chiropractic, a more conservative approach, is effective for virtually all types of repetitive stress disorders. Manipulations to realign joints and improve range of motion can reduce pressure on tendons and nerves. The movements also improve lymphatic drainage, which reduces inflammation, improves circulation and accelerates healing.

To find a chiropractor: Go to the American Chiropractic Association Web site, *www.acatoday. org,* and click on "Patients" then "Find a Doc."

Qigong for Beginners

Roger Jahnke, OMD, a board-certified doctor of oriental medicine and author of *The Healer Within* (Harper-SanFrancisco). He is director of the Institute of Integral Qigong and Tai Chi and CEO of Health Action Synergies, both in Santa Barbara, California. *www.instituteof integralqigongandtaichi.org.*

The Chinese wellness system *qigong* (chee-GONG) combines four ancient practices, all meant to harness the body's self-healing powers. The basics are easy to learn and easy on the body, and they can be done at home. Here are samples of qigong movements and methods. Practice each daily to generate vitality and promote healing.

BODY MOVEMENT

Slow, gentle exercises build awareness of posture…increase strength, endurance and flexibility…and unlike vigorous exercises, do not cause injury or consume internal resources (such as energy) to fuel muscles.

• **Gentle bending of the spine.** Stand with the feet shoulder-width apart, knees slightly bent. Inhaling, raise arms above the head, elbows slightly bent and palms facing skyward…tip head back and tilt the pelvis, arching back slightly. On the exhalation, bend the elbows and bring arms down in front of you, hands fisted and pressed together...tuck chin to chest, tilt the pelvis under and round your back. Repeat five to 10 times.

BREATH PRACTICE

Deep breathing sends more oxygen-rich blood toward tissues...and "pumps" lymph fluid through the lymphatic system, a major part of the immune system.

●**Gathering breath.** Sit with hands in your lap. Inhaling through the nose, move hands outward and upward, scooping up healing energy, until hands are just above face level, palms toward you, with elbows slightly bent. Exhaling slowly,  bring hands toward you, then downward past the chest and navel. Repeat five to 10 times.

MASSAGE

Reflexes refer to areas of the body that are separated physically, yet linked via acupuncture and energy channels. Self-massage of points on the hands, ears and feet has a healing effect on the organs, joints or tissues to which these reflexes connect.

●**Healing hand massage.** Grasp your left hand with your right hand, thumb against the palm and fingers on the back of the hand. Starting gently and gradually increasing the pressure, knead your left hand, including fingers and wrist. Spend extra time on any sore points—these areas are linked to body functions and organs that are not operating optimally. Continue for three to five minutes, then switch hands.

MEDITATION

Stress overstimulates the nervous system and exhausts the adrenal glands (which secrete stress hormones). Meditation counteracts stress, enhancing healing brain chemicals and hormones.

●**Qigong meditation.** Stand, sit or lie comfortably. Inhale fully, imagining you are drawing in *qi* (vitality) from the universe through hundreds of energy gates (acupuncture points) all over your body's surface. Exhale slowly, visualizing healing resources circulating inside

you. Continue for five to 15 minutes, mentally directing the healing flow to wherever your body needs it most.

Illustrations by Shawn Banner.

Tai Chi Helps You Stay Young and Vital

Mark A. Stengler, NMD, naturopathic medical doctor in private practice, Encinitas, California...adjunct associate clinical professor at the National College of Natural Medicine, Portland, Oregon...author of *The Natural Physician's Healing Therapies* (Bottom Line Books).

Roger Jahnke, OMD, a board-certified doctor of oriental medicine and author of *The Healer Within* (HarperSanFrancisco). He is director of the Institute of Integral Qigong and Tai Chi and CEO of Health Action Synergies, both in Santa Barbara, California. *www.instituteof integralqigongandtaichi.org.*

Tai chi is great for stress reduction—and for maintaining muscle tone and balance. To give you an idea of what tai chi is like, tai chi expert Roger Jahnke, OMD, describes easy-to-do beginner exercises. Dr. Jahnke trains teachers of tai chi at the Institute of Integral Qigong and Tai Chi. You can stand up and start moving right now! You'll find out immediately how great tai chi can make you feel.

Try these beginner exercises...

EXERCISE 1—RAISE HANDS

(This exercise also can be performed in a seated position with only the arm movements.)

Try: 10 repetitions 1 to 2 times daily.

Helps: Develop a calm awareness of the body. Builds leg and arm strength.

1. Stand with feet shoulder-width apart or slightly wider (toes pointing forward). Bend your knees slightly. Don't let your knees extend past the front of your toes.

2. Rest your palms on the front of your thighs. Inhale as you straighten your legs (don't lock them). Keep your fingers slightly down (so that your wrists are bent) as you let your arms float up to shoulder level.

3. Bend your knees and let your arms float down—fingers pointed up—as you bend your elbows and sink further into the bent-knee position. Then slowly straighten your wrists so that your outstretched hands (palms facing down) are aligned with your arms.

4. Exhale as you slowly sink down, bending your knees as much as is comfortable. Keep your palms parallel to the ground as you come back to the starting position.

EXERCISE 2—SWAYING BEAR

(If this exercise is difficult, try it holding on to a chair. When you get stronger, you can try it without the chair.)

Try: 10 repetitions on each side.

Helps: Develop a sense of balance and strengthen the leg muscles.

1. Stand with your feet a little wider than shoulder-width, toes facing forward. Bend your knees slightly.

2. Place your hands at your sides (at waist level) with your palms facing down and your elbows bent. Imagine your arms floating on top of water.

3. Very, very slowly shift your weight from side to side, keeping your knee over your foot and not bending your knee past your toes.

Slowly shift to the right by bending and putting your weight onto your right leg—then slowly shift back and put more weight onto your left leg. Go to the point where the other leg is straight but not locked. As you advance, you can take a wider stance and bend your knees farther.

WHAT YOU MIGHT NOT KNOW ABOUT TAI CHI

• **It can improve immune function.**

• **It can reduce pain and safely increases movement in people with arthritis.**

• **It reduces risk of falling by nearly 50%** in people age 65 and older by improving one's balance.

• **Its slow, gentle movements and the sensation of slowing down**—some have even said that it feels as though you are moving through water—increase energy.

Get Hypnotized, Get Healthier

Benjamin Kligler, MD, MPH, associate professor of family and social medicine at Albert Einstein College of Medicine, vice chair of the department of integrative medicine at Beth Israel Medical Center and research director of the Continuum Center for Health and Healing, an integrative medicine practice, all in New York City. *www.healthandhealingny.org.* Dr. Kligler, who is certified in Ericksonian hypnotherapy, is author of *Curriculum in Complementary Therapies* (Montefiore Medical Center).

Hear the word "hypnosis" and you may think of a stage show—a guy in a turban dangling a pocket watch and making you cluck like a chicken or behave in some other silly and uncharacteristic way.

This is not at all what modern hypnotherapy is like.

Reality: Ericksonian hypnosis (named after American psychiatrist Milton Erickson, who pioneered the techniques used today) is a collaboration between you and a trained health-care practitioner that can help you achieve specific health goals.

Hypnotherapy does not use commands, such as, "Now you will do what I say." Instead, the practitioner offers gentle, nonauthoritative suggestions when you are in a highly relaxed state. The idea behind hypnosis is that there is no separation between body and mind—so you can access the healing potential of the unconscious mind to move yourself in a healthful direction. Unlike classical hypnosis, which works on only a small subset of highly suggestible people, Ericksonian hypnosis can help almost anyone—though it is most effective for those who are motivated and accepting of treatment.

HELP FROM HYPNOSIS

Research shows that hypnotherapy helps treat a variety of physical and psychological problems, including…

- **Anxiety**
- **Chronic pain**
- **Insomnia**
- **Irritable bowel syndrome** (recurring bouts of diarrhea and/or constipation)
- **Menopausal hot flashes**
- **Nausea**
- **Overeating**
- **Phobias,** such as claustrophobia or fear of flying
- **Sugar addiction**
- **Tobacco addiction.**

Examples: One study found that a single 15-minute hypnosis session significantly decreased pain and anxiety in women undergoing breast cancer surgery—and, for unknown reasons, also shortened the procedure time in the operating room. In another study, 68% of women with menopausal hot flashes showed reduced symptom severity and frequency, as well as decreased insomnia, after hypnosis.

How it works: Everybody has chatter in the conscious mind that can get in the way of healthful behaviors, such as controlling consumption of sweets or not panicking in an elevator. Hypnosis quiets the conscious mind so your unconscious can come in and say, "Wait a minute, we're trying to be healthier here"—making it easier to turn down that donut or stay calm in the elevator. Hypnosis relieves physical symptoms, such as pain or hot flashes, by reducing stress hormones that contribute to physical ailments.

Hypnosis by itself does not cure the problem —rather, it creates a heightened state of awareness that opens the way for your own willingness to bring about the desired changes. Hypnotherapy can focus on symptom reduction …strategies for coping with stress…resolution of personal problems…as well as personality development.

WHAT TO EXPECT IN TREATMENT

Typically, the first session with a hypnotherapist lasts one hour. During this visit, the practitioner asks questions about your particular problem—when symptoms began, other treatments you have tried, how the issue affects your life and stress level. Because hypnotherapy is highly individualized, this information helps determine the most appropriate treatment for you. Hypnosis may or may not be done during this first session.

A course of hypnotherapy generally ranges from three to eight sessions, with each weekly hypnosis session lasting about 30 to 40 minutes. Sometimes patients return months or years later for a "booster" session.

During a session, you sit on a comfortable chair or couch in a quiet and softly lit room. Usually your eyes are closed, but you can hear everything around you.

Speaking in a soothing voice, the practitioner leads you into an induction, a trancelike state of deep relaxation. One common technique is the body scan. The practitioner asks you to focus on your feet, relaxing the muscles there. Next you focus on feeling the relaxed sensation in your ankles, your calves, your knees. Over five to 10 minutes, the practitioner guides you to relax your entire body.

While you are in a state of deep relaxation, the practitioner makes therapeutic suggestions, prompting your unconscious mind to deal more effectively with your health issue. The practitioner does not say something like, "You will not be afraid of the airplane," but rather, "You may find yourself feeling much more relaxed on the airplane than you have in the past." Suggestions are tailored to the specific problem and person. The process generally is pleasant and completely safe. You do not reveal personal secrets or do anything that you don't want to do.

After the therapeutic suggestions, the practitioner typically brings you back to your normal state of consciousness by saying, "I'm going to be quiet now, and over the next few minutes, you can gradually bring yourself back to the room." You may or may not consciously remember what was said to you during hypnosis…you may come to the end of a session thinking that it lasted just a few minutes, when in reality it lasted half an hour.

Over the following few days or weeks, you may notice that your symptoms are improving —for instance, you sleep better, feel less nauseous or fearful, or find it easier to resist cravings for cigarettes.

HYPNOTHERAPY HOMEWORK

The practitioner may assign you some simple self-hypnosis techniques to do on your own. For instance, if you are seeking to change a habit, such as compulsive overeating, self-hypnosis helps you handle cravings as they arise. These techniques typically include physical strategies, such as pressing two fingers together as a reminder of how to reach the relaxation state…or taking a series of deep breaths while focusing on a certain calming image or phrase.

For a physical problem, such as irritable bowel syndrome, the practitioner may tape-record an in-office hypnosis session and have you listen to it at home. As you reexperience the state of deep relaxation again and again, not only your mind but your entire body benefits—making your gut less susceptible to digestive upsets.

Finding a practitioner: In addition to being a licensed doctor, psychologist or social worker, a qualified practitioner should have about one year of hypnotherapy training. To ensure that your practitioner has met educational standards and training requirements in clinical hypnosis, you may want to verify that he/she is certified through the American Society of Clinical Hypnosis (630-980-4740, *www.asch.net*).

Hypnotherapy costs about $125 to $300 per session. Although many insurance companies do not cover hypnosis per se, you may be able to collect under a mental-health benefit if your psychotherapist or integrative physician includes hypnosis among the treatments offered.

Drug-Free Ways to Reduce Blood Pressure

Mind–body therapies reduce high blood pressure as effectively as medication does. They can be used alone or as an adjunct to traditional drug therapy.

Helpful: Do yoga, meditate and/or visualize a relaxing scene. As with drugs, sustained results require regular use.

Ather Ali, ND, MPH, assistant director of Integrative Medicine Research at the Yale-Griffin Prevention Research Center, Derby, Connecticut, and leader of a review of 12 studies, presented at a meeting of the American Public Health Association.

Amazing Healing Power Of Pets

Bernie Siegel, MD, a pioneer in mind-body medicine and founder of the support group Exceptional Cancer Patients, Woodbridge, Connecticut. *www.ecap-online. org.* He is author of many books and tapes, including the best-seller *Love, Medicine and Miracles* (Quill) and the children's book *Smudge Bunny* (H.J. Kramer), the story of Dr. Siegel's beloved pet rabbit.

Pets—cats, dogs, rabbits, horses, birds, etc.—are good for our health. Pet owners make fewer doctor visits, have shorter hospital stays and take less medication than people who don't own pets. *Pets even help prevent and relieve the following medical conditions…*

•**Cardiovascular disease.** A researcher at Brooklyn College in New York studied 369 people who had suffered heart attacks. Dog owners were eight times more likely to survive for one year after a heart attack than those who didn't have dogs—and it wasn't because they were walking their dogs and exercising more. Increased survival rates were based on owning a dog, not on any other physical, psychological or social factors.

•**High blood pressure.** In another study, half of a group of stockbrokers with high blood pressure were instructed to get a cat or dog. Six months later, both groups pretended to have a brief discussion with an angry client who had lost a lot of money in the stock market. On average, those with pets experienced only half the rise in blood pressure as those without pets.

•**Arthritis.** At the Missouri Arthritis Rehabilitation Research and Training Center at University of Missouri–Columbia, pets such as dogs are recommended to help patients increase their daily movement—one of the best ways to manage the disease and minimize disability.

•**Cancer.** At the Mayo Clinic, an oncologist tells many of his new patients to acquire a pet to reduce the devastating emotional impact of a cancer diagnosis. In a Canadian study, children hospitalized for cancer who spent time with a dog experienced less emotional distress and adapted better to the rigors of treatment.

•**Alzheimer's disease.** Studies show that when animals are present, Alzheimer's patients are more positive and alert. In one study, Alzheimer's patients at a resident facility ate more and gained weight after aquariums were installed. In another study, patients at a facility had fewer behavioral problems one month after a dog became a resident.

MIND/BODY CONNECTION

Petting an animal is soothing to mind, body and spirit. You become focused on loving and being loved. This increases levels of the mood-improving brain chemical serotonin. Interacting with a pet even increases oxytocin, a hormone generated in high levels during pregnancy and lactation. Dozens of animal studies link higher levels of oxytocin with lower blood pressure, lower cortisol (a hormone associated with stress), positive social interaction, increased pain tolerance and faster wound healing.

•**Pets can even lengthen life.** In a study of nursing homes, when pets were part of the program, mortality rates were 25% lower than at facilities that didn't include pets.

•**Dogs also encourage us to exercise.** If there's one thing that every doctor agrees on, it's that exercise is good for you. And because pets are such great icebreakers, you're more likely to meet and talk with other people. That extra sociability is beneficial, too.

LEARN FROM YOUR PET

Pets can teach you a lot about health and healing. *They are great role models for...*

•**Recovery.** Pets ask for what they need. They take naps when they're tired. Pets instinctually know how to survive.

•**Self-love.** Maimonides, the 12th-century philosopher and physician, said that if we took care of ourselves as well as we do our animals, we would suffer fewer illnesses. Notice how much you care for and love your pet. Love and care for yourself at least that much.

For more information: The Healing Power of Pets by Marty Becker (Hyperion)...*God's Messengers: What Animals Teach Us About the Divine* by Allen Anderson (New World Library)...*Animals as Teachers and Healers* by Susan Chernak McElroy (Ballantine)...*Kindred Spirits* by Allen M. Schoen (Broadway).

How Music Can Improve Your Health

Suzanne B. Hanser, EdD, chair of the music therapy department at Berklee College of Music in Boston and past president of the American Music Therapy Association and the World Federation of Music Therapy. She is a research associate at the Dana-Farber Cancer Institute, an affiliate of Harvard Medical School, also in Boston, where she investigates medical applications of music therapy.

Everyone knows the soothing effect of listening to a favorite piece of music. But until recently, there was little scientific evidence to support its effectiveness in helping to combat specific health problems.

Now: A growing body of research has found that music can affect key areas of the brain that help regulate specific physiological functions necessary for good health. The best choice of music and the time spent listening depends on an individual's needs and preferences. *Medical conditions that can be improved by listening to appropriate music...*

HIGH BLOOD PRESSURE

The hypothalamus helps control the autonomic nervous system, which regulates our breathing, heartbeat and other automatic responses in the body. It also is linked to emotional activity.

How music helps: When a person listens to music that stimulates positive memories and/or images, the activity of the hypothalamus helps slow a person's heart and respiration rates as well as blood pressure.

Scientific evidence: In a study published in the *British Journal of Health Psychology,* 75 adults performed a stressful three-minute math problem. Afterward, they were randomly assigned to sit in silence or listen to classical, jazz or popular music. Those who heard classical selections had significantly lower systolic (top number) blood pressure levels. Blood pressure did not significantly improve in people who listened to the other selections.

What to do: Observe how you respond to different types of music. Match your state of mind to the tempo and dynamics.

Example: If you are agitated, listen to something with a strong, fast beat, then gradually switch to slower and softer music. This can reduce stress and lower blood pressure.

INSOMNIA

Although healthy adults typically fall asleep within 30 minutes, adults age 50 and older often have more trouble falling—and staying—asleep.

How music helps: Soft, restful music can act as a sedative by reducing the amount of the stress-related neurotransmitter noradrenaline that circulates in the bloodstream.

Scientific evidence: Sixty people ages 60 to 83 who reported sleep difficulties took part in a study at Tzu Chi General Hospital in Taiwan. After three weeks, researchers found a 35% improvement in sleep quality, length of sleep, daytime dysfunction and sleep disturbances in subjects who listened to slow, soft music at night. The most effective types of music used in the study were piano versions of popular "oldies," New Age, harp, classical and slow jazz.

What to do: Make sure your bedroom temperature is comfortable, then lie in bed at your usual bedtime, with the lights out (light interferes with the production of the sleep hormone melatonin) and your eyes closed while listening to music. Experiment with different types of music until you discover what's relaxing for you. (Earphones are optional.) If you wake during the night, try listening to music again.

PAIN

Listening to music does not eliminate pain, but it can help distract your brain by creating a secondary stimulus that diverts your attention from the feeling of discomfort.

Scientific evidence: In a 14-day study published in the *Journal of Advanced Nursing,* 66 older adults with osteoarthritis pain sat quietly for 20 minutes daily, while another group listened to music. Those who listened to music reported a significant decrease in pain.

What to do: For pain reduction, it's important to identify music that engages you—that is, it should elicit memories and/or make you want to tap your foot, sway or even dance. Singing, which requires deep breathing, or using a simple percussion instrument (such as chimes or a drum), which does not require playing specific notes, also helps.

Spiritual Awakenings: Life-Changing Stories From a Top Doctor, an NBA Champ and More

Phil Bolsta, a freelance writer and author of *Sixty Seconds: One Moment Changes Everything* (Atria). He teaches a class in the healing power of affirmations at Pathways, a Minneapolis-based health-crisis resource center. His Web site is *www.bolstablog.com.*

Reports of spiritual visions would be easy to dismiss as hallucinations and fabrications except that many of these experiences have been reported by credible, successful people who have nothing to gain by lying.

Writer Phil Bolsta has spoken with dozens of prominent people who have had spiritual encounters. He has discovered that these encounters often occur during times of personal crisis, when people are willing to drop their intellectual armor and open their minds to the possibility of a spiritual world around them. Spiritual encounters often trigger deep, positive changes in the character, attitude and behavior of those who experience them, and they frequently lead to a strengthening of religious faith.

True stories of spiritual awakenings from five well-respected sources...

A SHARED VISION IN DEATH

• **Joan Borysenko, PhD. Best-selling author and former Harvard Medical School instructor.**

Joan Borysenko was sitting at her dying mother's bedside in 1988 when she had a clear and profound vision. Borysenko saw herself giving birth to a child—but in her vision, she also was the baby being born.

Borysenko had not always seen eye-to-eye with her mother, but this vision of childbirth instantly reframed the relationship in her mind. Just as her mother had given physical birth to her, Borysenko now believed that she was giving birth to her dying mother's soul as it departed the world. In a flash, Borysenko understood that the problems she had had with her mother over the years were not problems at all. Though the experiences were difficult at the time, they helped shape Borysenko into the very special person she had become.

When the vision ended, Borysenko found herself back in her mother's hospital room. She saw that her mother had passed away in her sleep. To Borysenko, it appeared that the objects in the hospital room were interconnected and made of energy and light. Before Borysenko could say a word about her vision, her then-20-year-old son, Justin, also in the hospital room, said, "Mom, the whole room is filled with light. Can you see it?"

She could.

DISCOVERING UNEXPECTED STRENGTH

• **Wayne Dyer, PhD. Best-selling author who is known as the "father of motivation" for his inspirational writings and speeches.**

Wayne Dyer is not a world-class athlete, yet one day in October 2000, Dyer performed a feat of strength that should not have been possible.

Dyer was leading a tour group through a castle in San Damiano, Italy, that once had been home to a convent set up by St. Francis of Assisi. In Dyer's group was a young man with muscular dystrophy who could walk only with the help of leg braces. A few steps up a narrow three-flight staircase, this young man realized that his leg braces made it impossible for him to climb any farther. He could not turn back either, because a long line behind him blocked his way.

Dyer offered to carry the man, forgetting for the moment about his own physical condition. Dyer was then 60 years old and suffered from significant knee and leg problems. The man he had offered to carry up three very steep flights of stairs weighed nearly 200 pounds.

After only a few steps, Dyer could feel his knees crumble under him. At that moment, he experienced a vision of St. Francis and felt a surge of energy like he never had before. Dyer virtually ran up the remaining two-and-a-half flights and was not even winded when he reached the top.

To Dyer, the incident confirmed that there is a supreme, benevolent intelligence that governs everything around us.

FINDING ONE'S REWARD

• **Tom Gegax. Founder and chairman emeritus of the Tires Plus chain.**

In 1989, Tom Gegax's life was falling apart. He had been diagnosed with cancer, his 25-year marriage had ended and his company was struggling. Gegax decided that he needed to spend some time thinking. Fearing that his busy everyday life in America made such quiet reflection impossible, he decided to do this thinking in the Greek Islands. He had heard that Greece had a terrible phone system and reasoned that it would be the ideal place to avoid interruptions.

After several blissful days of quiet meditation, Gegax woke suddenly at 3:00 in the morning. He saw a bright, glowing treasure chest on the pillow next to him. The chest looked very real, and Gegax felt certain that he was awake. After about 10 seconds of staring, Gegax tried to touch the chest, but it disappeared as he reached for it.

Everything seemed bright and magical to Gegax for the remainder of this retreat. His senses were heightened, and he felt that he was experiencing life at a deeper level than ever before. The meaning of the vision was clear to Gegax—there were immense treasures to be found in stepping back from his hectic life.

Gegax soon regained his health, remarried and built his business, Tires Plus, into the largest independent tire-store chain in the country. (He sold the company to Bridgestone/Firestone in 2000.) He continues to find time for quiet reflection.

THE CALMING SPIRIT

• **Trent Tucker. One of basketball's most accurate three-point shooters during his 11 years in the NBA.**

Early in his career, Trent Tucker rarely got off the New York Knicks' bench. The young Tucker was on the bench during a 1983 game in Madison Square Garden when fellow Knick Ray Williams sprained his ankle. With Williams hurt, the Knicks had to depend on Tucker. There was no way to know how the unproven player would handle the pressure.

Suddenly Tucker felt a presence. He looked up and saw a spirit shaped like a cloud coming down an arena aisle at the opposite end of the court. Tucker sensed that this was a higher force, a positive force. The spirit removed all of the tension and apprehension from him, leaving him in a state of sudden and unexpected calm.

The spirit then spoke to him, saying, "I'm here. I'm going to support you. You have done what you were supposed to do. It's time to go out and play now. Your time has come."

Tucker began to establish himself as a quality NBA player that day. Perhaps more important, the experience gave him a new perspective. Ever since then, Tucker has not let minor problems bother him. He understands that his life is not all about him. A quarter-century later, Tucker still credits his arena vision with broadening his horizons and making him a better man. After retiring from basketball, he founded the Trent Tucker Non-Profit Organization to give back to his community.

INTERPRETING THE MESSAGE

• **Dean Ornish, MD. Clinical professor of medicine at the University of California, San Francisco, and the author of several best-selling health and diet books.**

Back in the early 1970s, Ornish was a freshman in college struggling with his grades. The harder the young Ornish pushed himself to do well in his classes, the more sleep-deprived and depressed he became and the more his grades suffered.

One day, Ornish experienced what he considered to be a spiritual vision, the message of which was, "Nothing can bring lasting happiness." This seemingly hopeless message made Ornish even more depressed. He withdrew from college and considered suicide.

Ornish then met a spiritual leader called Swami Satchidananda, who had helped his sister cure her migraine headaches. The swami was speaking to a group at Ornish's parents' home. Remarkably, the swami's first words to Ornish were "Nothing can bring lasting happiness."

Though Ornish had earlier taken these exact words as a bleak message, the swami saw them as a cause for joy. Nothing can bring lasting happiness, he explained to Ornish, but you have happiness already until you disturb it. Just stop chasing all the things that you believe will make you happy.

Ornish returned to college and graduated first in his class. When he felt angry, afraid, anxious or depressed, he no longer saw it as a problem—he saw it as a helpful warning that he was looking in the wrong places for peace and happiness. Pain was not punishment, he realized. It was just information.

2

Beautiful Skin, Teeth, Hair and Nails

My Rules for Natural Skin Care

Americans spend up to $5 billion a year on skin-care products, but, in my opinion, many of these lotions, balms and gels are not necessary. *Here's a natural approach that not only helps keep your skin supple and vibrant, but also improves your overall health...*

1. Hydrate. For skin to function properly as a protective layer and a vehicle for eliminating toxins, the body must be hydrated. With dehydration, the skin loses its "turgor," or fullness, and begins to sag. For good skin health, consume one-half ounce of water per pound of body weight daily. (Some of this can come from herbal tea.) You will need more water if the temperature is above 90°F or if you are perspiring a lot.

2. Use a dry brush. Using a natural bristle brush or loofah (the dried interior of fruit from the loofah plant)—both are available at most drugstores—brush your skin with small,

circular motions for two minutes before getting into the shower or bath several times a week. Dry brushing improves circulation to your skin and removes old, dead skin cells.

3. Take cod-liver oil. My favorite omega-3 fish oil choice for people who have skin conditions is cod-liver oil. It not only contains essential fatty acids necessary for healthy skin, but also vitamins A and D, which are both fundamental to good health.

Daily dose: 1,500 mg in capsule or liquid form, taken with a meal. Be sure the label says the oil has been purified—and consult your doctor before exceeding 10,000 international units (IU) of vitamin A daily from all supplement sources.* If you have skin problems and

*Pregnant or lactating women should check with their doctors before using cod-liver oil.

Jamison Starbuck, ND, naturopathic physician in family practice in Missoula, Montana. She is a past president of the American Association of Naturopathic Physicians and a contributing editor to *The Alternative Advisor: The Complete Guide to Natural Therapies and Alternative Treatments* (Time-Life).

already take fish oil, check the label to determine the fish source. If it's not cod, consider switching.

4. Reduce your toxic load. The skin is an organ that, like the liver, kidneys and lungs, helps excrete toxins. The health of your skin declines in proportion to the amount of toxic substances you ingest through medication and food and/or are exposed to via pollution, herbicides and household chemicals. Don't smoke, and don't allow others to smoke in your home. Use natural-based cleaning products, such as baking soda and vinegar. Consider buying a high efficiency particulate air (HEPA) filter, available at most home stores, for your home and/or office.

5. Eat turmeric. Curry, the traditional Indian dish, is often made with turmeric, which contains curcumin, a substance that has antioxidant, anti-inflammatory and anticancer properties. Curcumin may help prevent acne and sun damage.

Caution: If you have a stomach ulcer, avoid curry.

6. Choose the right sunscreen. Use a sunscreen that contains zinc oxide as its main sun-blocking agent, as well as vitamins E and C and the mineral selenium, and has a sun protection factor (SPF) of 15 or higher. Researchers have found that sunscreens containing these antioxidants are more likely to prevent skin damage than sunscreens without these protective compounds.

Antioxidant Creams That Fight Aging

Mark A. Stengler, NMD, naturopathic medical doctor in private practice, Encinitas, California...adjunct associate clinical professor at the National College of Natural Medicine, Portland, Oregon...author of *The Natural Physician's Healing Therapies* (Bottom Line Books).

Anti-aging creams are big business in both the cosmetic and natural-health industries. Everyone wants healthy, youthful-looking skin. My patients, particularly women, often ask me about natural anti-aging creams for the face and neck.

ANTIOXIDANTS FOR DAMAGE CONTROL

When it comes to anti-aging products, some of the most popular natural creams contain *antioxidants*, nutrients that neutralize harmful molecules called free radicals. We associate antioxidants with foods, particularly fruits and vegetables, that can reduce *oxidative* stress (an increase in cell-damaging free radicals caused by stress, eating fried and processed foods, and breathing pollutants) and subsequent inflammation.

The same idea applies when these nutrients are in topical form—what is good inside the body also is good outside. Our skin incurs oxidative damage from excessive sun exposure and through *glycation*, a process in which dietary sugar alters the molecular structure of collagen and other skin components. Eventually, in the course of normal aging, these factors overwhelm the skin's natural antioxidant capability. It stands to reason that adding antioxidants back to the skin might help preserve and restore youthfulness.

Many doctors are surprised to learn that a great deal of research has been published demonstrating the effectiveness of several antioxidants used in topical solutions. Contrary to moisturizers that provide on-the-surface fixes (such as mineral oil, which slows evaporation of water from the skin), antioxidant creams work at the cellular level, making lasting changes to the skin and reducing wrinkles and blemishes. As with many products on the market, the potency of antioxidant creams varies.

For best results, try products that contain one or two of the antioxidants noted below (or try the products I recommend below). Give the product a chance to work. Don't expect any changes in a week. Instead use it for six to 10 weeks. Then check to see whether there is a noticeable improvement in the quality of your skin. Look to see if blemishes have diminished and if your skin is softer, clearer or more radiant. If there is no improvement, try a different anti-aging cream formulation.

Bonus: These natural skin ingredients are all considered very safe. If any product causes skin irritation or redness, stop using it and try another.

TO ENHANCE MOISTURE CONTENT

•**Vitamin C.** This well-known antioxidant was one of the first to be used in anti-aging creams. A Brazilian study last year showed that vitamin C (*ascorbic acid*) and several of its derivatives enhanced skin moisture content when it was applied daily for four weeks. A review of studies conducted by a US researcher concluded that vitamin C is effective for treating photoaging (sun damage) and that combining it with other vitamins (A, B-3 and E) is more effective than using individual compounds.

Good brands: Avalon Organics Vitamin C Renewal Facial Cream (888-659-7730, *www.avalonorganics.com*, $21.99 for two ounces) ...or MyChelle Dermaceuticals, The Perfect C Serum, All Skin Types (800-447-2076, *www.mychelle.com*, $44.25 for 0.5 ounce). These products may seem expensive, but they last for a long time because you apply just a pea-size dab at a time.

Best for: Dry, sun-damaged skin.

TO RESTORE ELASTICITY

•**Green tea.** When ingested, green tea protects us against illness, including cardiovascular disease, diabetes and even some cancers. So it isn't surprising to find out that it also can help the skin.

A study conducted at Emory University found that an eight-week regimen of a topical cream containing 10% green-tea extract and a 300-mg twice-daily green-tea oral supplement resulted in tissue improvements that could be seen under a microscope, although the improvements were not visible to the naked eye. Researchers noted that it may take longer than eight weeks to see visible improvements.

Good brands: Green Tea Skin Natural Anti-Aging Cream (781-326-1700, *www.greenteaskin.com*, $19.95 for 1.7 ounces).

Plus: Take 600 mg daily of an oral green-tea supplement.

Best for: Wrinkles, age-related loss of skin elasticity.

TO SMOOTH WRINKLES AND IMPROVE SKIN HEALTH

•**Coenzyme Q10 (CoQ10).** This natural substance exists in every cell of the body and is a popular ingredient in anti-aging creams. Several studies indicate that it may be able to enhance the skin's ability to combat signs of aging at the cellular level—for example, making skin cells look younger. At an American Academy of Dermatology meeting, researchers reported that CoQ10 cream seemed to reduce fine wrinkles around the eyes without harmful side effects, such as itching.

Good brands: Avalon Organics CoQ10 Wrinkle Defense Night Creme (888-659-7730, *www.avalonorganics.com*, $25.99 for 1.75 ounces)...or Botanic Spa CoQ-10 Plus Wrinkle Cream (800-644-8327, *www.botanicchoice.com*, $19.99 for two ounces).

FOODS FOR YOUR SKIN

Choosing the right foods can help protect your skin. Review your diet, and add as many foods as possible that are rich in carotenoids, disease-fighting plant chemicals. These fat-soluble pigments are powerful antioxidants and protect against damaging UV rays.

•**Lycopene** is the carotenoid that has been shown to offer the most protection. Tomatoes, especially tomato sauce (heat releases the lycopene), are a rich source of lycopene. Other carotenoid-rich foods include peaches, watermelon, carrots, broccoli and spinach.

Carotenoids also are available in supplement form. Take a mixed carotenoid complex formula containing 25,000 IU daily. These supplements are commonly available at health food stores.

•**GliSODin** is a supplement that helps prevent sunburn and sun allergy (flushing of skin due to sun exposure). GliSODin is a vegetarian form of the antioxidant enzyme *superoxide dismutase* (SOD). SOD prevents cell damage by neutralizing harmful free radical molecules. GliSODin is manufactured by Bluebonnet (800-580-8866, *www.bluebonnetnutrition.com*). A bottle of 60 100-milligram (mg) capsules can be purchased at health food stores for about $20. Take 500 mg daily during the summer or year-round, if you like. GliSODin should not be used by people who are allergic to gluten, pregnant women or children under age 12.

Eat Your Way to Beautiful Skin

Nancy Appleton, PhD, retired nutritional consultant now in San Diego, California, and author of Lick the Sugar Habit (Avery) and Stopping Inflammation (Square One).

Diet and other lifestyle choices are clearly reflected in your face and skin, the body's largest and most protective organ. Take care of yourself, and your skin will show it. Eat poorly, smoke and skimp on sleep, and your skin will be worse for wear. Your skin's condition is, in some ways, a barometer of the health of your entire body.

RECIPE FOR HEALTHY SKIN

Proper nutrition will keep you glowing and rosy, as will getting enough sleep, regular exercise and fresh air (but not too much sun)... keeping your worries under control...and avoiding negative habits such as smoking and overindulgence in alcohol. While this sounds simple, it is important to keep in mind that your skin needs proper nourishment to ensure proper function. It is not just a shell that keeps your insides in. Your skin is a functioning body organ.

What you should eat and drink for healthy skin...

STAY AWAY FROM SUGAR

According to Nancy Appleton, PhD, retired nutritional consultant now in San Diego, California, and author of *Lick the Sugar Habit* (Avery) and *Stopping Inflammation* (Square One), sugar has a major impact on the skin. In young people, it upsets digestion, which can lead to inflammatory skin problems such as acne and rashes. In older people, sugar makes the skin age more rapidly by changing the structure of collagen, a protein that is the building block of skin. As the structure of the skin changes, wrinkles become increasingly apparent.

CUT BACK ON SATURATED FAT AND FRIED FOODS

A high-fat diet may contribute to the development of skin cancer, according to researchers at Baylor College of Medicine in Houston, Texas. In a two-year study of 76 skin cancer patients, half followed their usual diet (about 40% fat) while half adopted a low-fat diet (20% fat). In the months that followed, researchers found that low-fat dieters developed an average of only three new precancerous lesions (called *actinic keratoses*), while high-fat dieters developed an average of 10. To cut back on saturated fat in your diet, eat more fish instead of red meat, and remove the skin from poultry.

In Dr. Appleton's opinion, the problem is not so much in fatty foods but in how they are prepared. She says that the real culprits are *acrylamides*—the carcinogenic chemical by-products of cooking carbohydrates at high temperatures. Frying, barbecuing, baking and smoking foods leads to the formation of acrylamides. Highly processed foods, such as french fries and chips, are also high in these carcinogens and should be eaten very sparingly, if at all. It's easy to cut back on acrylamides by poaching rather than grilling fish and by eating boiled potatoes instead of fried.

IDENTIFY AND AVOID FOOD ALLERGENS

Foods that some people can handle with no problem can cause food sensitivities in others, observes Dr. Appleton. She explains that when the gut fails to fully digest hard-to-process foods, such as simple sugars, fried foods and hydrogenated fats, partially digested food particles enter the bloodstream. The body reacts to these particles as foreign invaders, with the immune system establishing inflammation around them in an effort to protect the body. When this reaction takes place on the skin, inflammatory skin problems such as pimples and rashes result. Inflammation can occur anywhere—and in multiple locations—in the body, where it manifests itself in different ways. In the case of acne, hair follicles become clogged with substances such as sebum (oil) and *P. acnes* bacteria. *P. acnes* produce large amounts of inflammatory enzymes called *porphyrins*, and white blood cells rush in to protect the body. The result is inflammatory acne, characterized by pimples, pustules, blackheads and whiteheads. According to Dr. Appleton, the good news is that when you stop eating reactive foods, such as sugary junk foods, fried foods and overly processed products, these symptoms will go away.

EAT MORE NUTRIENT-RICH FRUITS AND VEGETABLES

Your skin will benefit from eating a wide range of fruits and vegetables…especially, as Dr. Appleton points out, if you eat them instead of sugary and fried foods. For optimal skin health, plenty of nutrient-rich vitamins and minerals are a must, and a lack of A, B or C vitamins can lead to dry skin and rashes. Fruits and vegetables are also rich in antioxidants, which can prevent the oxidation of free radicals that leads to inflammatory skin problems.

DRINK PLENTY OF FLUIDS

To cleanse your body of toxins, it's important to drink plenty of fluids. The standard recommendation is eight glasses of water (or other healthy liquids such as herbal teas or fresh juices) daily. This flushes toxins out of the bowel, kidneys and liver, and keeps the skin supple and hydrated.

Note: Make sure that your drinking water is of high quality. Contaminants such as lead and bacteria can harm the skin and may even increase cancer risk. If you have concerns about water purity, install a filter.

MONITOR YOUR DAIRY INTAKE

Word comes from Boston's Harvard School of Public Health that milk—rather than greasy foods or chocolate—is the most likely dietary contributor to severe teenage acne. While researchers do not go so far as to recommend that teens eliminate dairy from their diets, they recommend moderating their consumption of milk. Also keep in mind that there are other rich sources of calcium, including canned salmon, sardines, tofu and green vegetables, such as broccoli and collard or turnip greens.

All in all, the same balanced diet that benefits your health overall will keep your skin in tip-top shape, too.

The Anti-Wrinkle Vitamin

When dietary data for 4,025 women was analyzed in a recent study, those with high intakes of vitamin C and the essential fatty acid linoleic acid had fewer wrinkles than women with lower intakes.

Theory: Vitamin C is an important component in collagen synthesis (which keeps skin supple), and linoleic acid promotes normal skin structure.

For younger-looking skin: Eat vitamin C–rich fruits and vegetables, such as oranges and broccoli, and foods high in linoleic acid, such as soybeans and sunflower oil.

Maeve C. Cosgrove, PhD, research scientist, Corporate Research, Unilever Colworth Science Park, Bedford, UK.

Face-Lift in a Jar?

Heather Woolery-Lloyd, MD, director of ethnic skin care, University of Miami, Department of Dermatology and Cutaneous Surgery.

A fish extract may provide help for sagging facial skin. It is known as *2-dimethylaminoethanol* (DMAE), a substance found in fish and used in over-the-counter skin products. In the body, DMAE helps form a neurotransmitter that makes muscles contract. Some people think that DMAE creams increase facial muscle tone. There is no convincing evidence from placebo-controlled, double-blind studies to support this theory—though "open label" studies (in which researchers and participants are aware of the treatment being given) concluded that DMAE improved skin appearance.

Another theory is that DMAE reduces wrinkles by plumping up skin. In lab experiments, DMAE made skin cells swell—yet a three-month clinical trial found no difference in the effects of DMAE versus a placebo.

Bottom line: DMAE products are safe—but you may get equally good results from a good moisturizer with sunscreen.

Banish Morning Wrinkles

Is your face creased with wrinkles when you wake up?

Cosmetic pencils and creams sold as "line erasers" are widely available and will help improve the appearance of these wrinkles for an hour or so. But that's only a temporary solution.

These facial creases—which are caused by sleeping with your face pressed into your pillow—eventually will become permanent if the skin is folded the same way every night over a long period. The best way to prevent these lines altogether is to sleep on your back.

Helpful: Buy a U-shaped cushion—often sold to make airline travel more comfortable—and sleep with the back of your neck nestled into it. This should help to keep your face crease-free.

Neal B. Schultz, MD, assistant clinical professor of dermatology at Mount Sinai School of Medicine, assistant adjunct physician at Lenox Hill Hospital and owner of Neal Schultz MD PLLC, all in New York City.

The Mask of Plastic Surgery

Lauren Zander, life coach, the Handel Group (*www.handelgroup.com*).

A recent morning news program featured an interview with a mature woman who had endured a terrible year with a divorce and a death in the family. It was truly very tragic for her. A year after all of the tragedy, she had felt that she had overcome her pain thanks to a face-lift and cosmetic dental work. She seemed happy and said she felt more confident. Perhaps she was, but can altering the outside actually help her better handle these very serious life challenges?

Aging and appearance has become such a peculiar issue in our culture. With mass media's worship of the young, nubile and wrinkle-free, getting older has become almost a character flaw—to be delayed and, for many, denied whenever possible. It's hardly a surprise, then, that the popularity of plastic surgery and cosmetic techniques has soared both among the young and, more to the point, the old hoping to look young.

This begs the question: Does all this attention to the outside prevent people from looking at what is happening internally?

Life coach Lauren Zander, of the Handel Group (*www.handelgroup.com*), helped bring clarity and focus to the issue. Zander first pointed out that this focus on appearances reaches beyond cosmetic changes—many people today are primarily focused on the outward appearance of their lives. Rather than trying to keep up with the Joneses, they are trying to be the Joneses. They show off the "quality" of living that they have achieved through their home, clothes, cars, vacation choices, even the restaurants they patronize—all kinds of external factors that people feel make them worthy.

Attention to living a nice life is important and can be rewarding as well as fun...but when attention to physical or material measures takes priority over the emotional and spiritual aspects of life, it becomes dangerous—it is now an attempt to draw meaning from things that are not intended to provide it...or to hide behind them. This brings us back to the potential problem with plastic surgery, says Zander.

She is completely in favor of cosmetic surgery if, she says, it makes people feel better about a specific trait that they feel has held them back or gotten in their way of relaxing and being fully confident. But if the goal of surgery is to paint over feelings of not being good enough inside, the "solution" will be feeble and short lived and the emotional problems will soon rear their head again. Indeed, when people fixate on cosmetic changes—or for that matter any external alteration or possession—as "The Answer," they are courting trouble.

For example, a woman might decide she needs a face-lift to make herself prettier so that her marriage will be better. She is now stuck in the idea that an external change is the answer, which prevents her from looking inside where she is likely to find a real (however scary) solution to her unhappy marriage.

THE BEAUTY OF AGING

This perversion of focusing on a youthful appearance permeates the aging issue. Aging and all that it entails happens to everyone who lives, but some people attempt to sneak away from the feelings and fears by fixating instead on the youthful looks the surgeon, or hair dresser, or new clothes, or sports car can give them. "They focus on how great they look and this grants them, they think, permission not to experience the feelings about getting old," says Zander.

With their identity now centered on their external presentation, the question becomes, what are these people missing in their internal relationship with themselves? Are they afraid to be with themselves? Do they not like what they see? Are they afraid of what they see? In their determination to stay "young," are they throwing away the opportunity to evolve and develop pride and true acceptance of themselves, whatever their age? Are they not facing their fears of aging? Of dying?

FINDING A WHOLE NEW MEANING OF SELF

Aging offers people the opportunity to find new and deeper meaning in themselves and life. Without the familiar reassurance of looking as they did in youth, people are forced to decide whether to make themselves miserable about their lined face and sun-blotched hands, or to go deep within themselves to investigate and take pride in their real sense of self-worth and personal identification. It is an opportunity to stop looking in the mirror and instead reflect on the accomplishments of their lives…the sense of self…the people they've touched…and the big and small ways they have impacted the world around them.

No one else can decide that for another. Everyone must venture into the deeper feelings and inner happiness and the experience of being alive and, yes, of getting old.

As a society we have backed ourselves into a corner on this aging thing, hiding behind another surgery to deny a little while longer the reality of accumulating years, or in the case of the woman on television, perhaps hiding behind her fears of being alone or of dealing with loss. It is time for people to come out into the open to demonstrate the grace and wisdom of age, says Zander. Getting old is part of the cycle of life and can, indeed should, be a spiritual experience. Aging is a rite of passage and the challenge before us as we grow old is to explore the personal meaning of that rite of passage—to live it, to enjoy it, to fully experience it.

What's Great About Wrinkles

Tamara Eberlein, editor, Bottom Line's *Daily Health News* E-letter. Boardroom Inc., 281 Tresser Blvd., Stamford, Connecticut 06901.

When the bouncer said, "ID, please," my jaw dropped. Sure, the bar was dark—but I was 46 years old at the time! Then I grinned…at which point, seeing the crinkles around my eyes, he waved me in. It was fun being carded—yet I wouldn't trade my wrinkles for the flawless face of a 20-year-old. *Very good reasons…*

• **Eye crinkles are attractive.** Yale researchers digitally altered a woman's photo in a variety of ways—adding or removing wrinkles, reshaping the eyelids or brows. Participants then identified the emotions that the faces portrayed. Photos that mimicked the effects of surgical eyelid tucks were judged to make the woman look more surprised, fearful, tired and/or sad…whereas crows' feet (wrinkles at the eyes' outer corners) made her look happier. Happiness is an attractive feature—so crow's feet are attractive, too.

• **Wrinkles are a sign of wisdom.** It takes life experiences to make us comfortable in our own skin, points out Karen Kaigler-Walker, PhD, a professor of marketing and psychology at Woodbury University in Burbank, California, and author of *Positive Aging* (Red Wheel). She says, "With maturity, challenging situations become easier…we learn which battles are worth fighting and when to walk away… we feel less fearful of being judged and freer to be ourselves."

To me, the knowledge that comes with age is more precious than a smooth complexion. That's something to smile about—no matter how long it's been since I was carded.

Compound in Berries May Lessen Sun Damage

Federation of American Societies for Experimental Biology, news release.

You probably already knew that berries are nutritious. But new research shows that a compound found in nuts, berries and other fruits might help prevent wrinkles and repair skin damage caused by the sun.

THE STUDY

Researchers in Korea applied *ellagic acid*, an antioxidant found in raspberries, strawberries, cranberries and pomegranates, to human skin cells in the lab and to the skin of hairless mice that had been exposed to strong, ultraviolet rays.

In the human cells, ellagic acid reduced the inflammatory response and the destruction of collagen, both major causes of wrinkles.

Researchers had a similar result in 4-week-old mice, which are often used in dermatology studies because their skin is similar to that of humans.

For eight weeks, 12 hairless mice were exposed three times a week to increasing ultraviolet radiation. The exposure would have been strong enough to cause sunburn and skin damage in humans, according to the researchers, from Hallym University in South Korea.

Half of the exposed mice were given daily topical applications of ellagic acid, even on the days in which they did not receive UV exposure. Ellagic acid was not applied to the other mice.

The mice that did not receive ellagic acid developed wrinkles and thickening of the skin that indicates sun damage.

The mice that received the ellagic acid showed less wrinkle formation. The study was presented at the Experimental Biology meeting in New Orleans.

HOW IT WORKS

In human skin cells, ellagic acid protects against ultraviolet damage by blocking production of *matrix metalloproteinase* enzymes that break down collagen and reduce the expression of ICAM, a molecule involved with inflammation.

For more on preventing sun damage, visit the Web site of the American Academy of Family Physicians, *http://familydoctor.org*, and search "prevent sun damage."

Green Tea Combats Skin Cancer

Polyphenols, a type of antioxidant found in green tea, protect skin from the sun's damaging ultraviolet radiation and help prevent the formation of skin tumors.

Best: Drink five to six cups of green tea a day—the fresher, the better. Fresh green tea leaves have a light yellow or green color. A brownish hue indicates that the tea has undergone oxidation, which destroys antioxidants. Tea bags and loose leaves are better than instant and bottled teas.

Santosh Katiyar, PhD, professor of dermatology, University of Alabama, Birmingham, and leader of a study of green tea and skin tumor development in mice, published in *The Journal of Nutritional Biochemistry*.

Drivers' Skin Cancer Risk

Ellen Marmur, MD, vice chair, cosmetic and dermatologic surgery at the Mount Sinai Medical Center in New York City. She is skin health editor of *Your Health Now*.

You might think there's no reason to worry about the sun's harmful rays when you are driving. But science says otherwise, as a recent study from Saint Louis University made clear. Researchers there evaluated data from 1,047 people with skin cancer and discovered that 53% of them had skin cancers on the left side of the body. When researchers looked at cancers that were only on the arms, hands, head and neck, they found more cancers on the left side (the side that is exposed while driving), especially in men. Researchers speculate that people who drive frequently may be more apt to have left-side cancers.

GLASS NOT A BARRIER FOR SKIN CANCER

Ellen Marmur, MD, vice chair, cosmetic and dermatologic surgery at the Mount Sinai Medical Center in New York City, explains that for a long time, people assumed that the glass in cars blocked all ultraviolet (UV) rays. Now we know that while glass blocks most of UVB rays, it only filters less than half of UVA rays, leaving people vulnerable to damage from the sun. Until recently, it was believed that UVB rays were the main cause of skin cancer—but recent research proved that to be wrong as well, with UVA rays equally potent and dangerous, says Dr. Marmur.

All windshield glass is laminated to prevent shattering. As a result, it blocks more UVA rays than the glass in side windows, but still allows 20% of rays through. That plus the rays from the side windows adds up to a considerable amount of exposure. Convertible drivers—even those whose top-down days were years ago—have yet another skin cancer concern, says Dr. Marmur, which is skin cancer on the scalp. Hair offers some protection, but not much. Drivers who rest their left arm on the window ledge risk sun damage, too.

PROTECT YOURSELF

Tinted windows, popular in some areas of the country, have more protection than clear ones, says Dr. Marmur, but even better protection is available from special films that can be applied to clear or tinted glass to reduce UVA rays. Check with your car dealer or local garage for more information. Go to *www.skincancer.org* and type "UV film" in the search bar for a list of recommended products. However, she still advises everyone to wear sunblock or protective clothing when in the car for extended periods of time and, of course, keep the windows closed to avoid direct sun exposure. She reminds everyone to do a body check—including the scalp—each month, looking for any changes on the skin, and to see a dermatologist once a year for a full body check.

Easing Stasis Dermatitis

Mark A. Stengler, NMD, naturopathic medical doctor in private practice, Encinitas, California...adjunct associate clinical professor at the National College of Natural Medicine, Portland, Oregon...author of *The Natural Physician's Healing Therapies* (Bottom Line Books).

Stasis dermatitis results when poor circulation through the small blood vessels known as capillaries prevents the skin from receiving adequate oxygen. Nutrients and waste products accumulate in the tissues, and that is what causes the inflammation and sometimes itching, tingling, soreness, skin ulceration, and swollen ankles. It is common for people with stasis dermatitis to have varicose veins and poor blood flow from the legs to the heart.

Applying moisturizing creams, especially those with vitamin E, can help heal skin ulcers. However, stasis dermatitis is more than skin deep and so is best treated by taking herbs that will improve circulation.

I recommend horse chestnut and butcher's broom—1,000 milligrams (mg) of each in capsule form daily. I also recommend 100 mg of Pycnogenol, a natural antioxidant that improves circulation. Also, simple everyday solutions can be helpful. When you are sitting at home, raise your legs above heart level to improve circulation, and talk to your doctor about wearing support hosiery.

My Favorite Natural Treatments For Itching

Jamison Starbuck, ND, naturopathic physician in family practice in Missoula, Montana. She is a past president of the American Association of Naturopathic Physicians and a contributing editor to The Alternative Advisor: The Complete Guide to Natural Therapies and Alternative Treatments *(Time-Life).*

The causes of itching are so varied that there is at least one associated with nearly every letter of the alphabet—starting with allergies, bug bites, contact dermatitis (from such things as soap or chlorine), drug reactions (antibiotics and painkillers are common culprits), eczema, fungus, gallbladder disease and hives. Exposure to poison ivy, oak or sumac is another common cause. Unfortunately, the instinctive desire to scratch an itch can exacerbate the underlying problem. Many people scratch their skin raw in an effort to get relief. *Natural medicines that gently—yet effectively—treat the most common causes of itching are much better options...*

• **Chamomile tea.** For itching due to insect bites, eczema, hives or poison ivy, oak or sumac, use two tea bags per 12 ounces of water and let it steep for six minutes. Soak sterile gauze or clean cotton cloth in the tea, and apply compresses for 15 minutes to the itchy area several times per day.

• **Calendula and comfrey salve.** These plants are common ingredients in topical salves that often include vitamins A and E in an olive oil base. This salve works best for dry, scaly rashes that result from contact dermatitis, fungus or eczema. For a moist, itchy rash with oozing

*Pregnant or lactating women should consult their physicians before trying herb-based products.

clear or yellow fluid (such as that caused by insect bites or poison ivy, oak or sumac), use a tea or tincture preparation of calendula only. Apply the tea in a compress or pour or spray it on the area.

• **Oatmeal.** This paste made from rolled oats is best for itching caused by hives or insect bites.

What to do: Fill a muslin or cotton bag with one cup of raw, rolled oats. Attach the bag to the spout of your bathtub and let the water flow through the bag as you fill a tub with warm (not hot) water. Lie in the oatmeal water for 20 to 30 minutes several times a day until the itch is gone. An oatmeal bath product, such as Aveeno, also can be used. For poison ivy, oak or sumac, use a compress of the oatmeal water.

• *Grindelia* **ssp (gumweed).** This is my favorite remedy for itching caused by poison ivy, oak or sumac. Wash the plant oil from the skin with soap and water, then apply a lotion or tincture of grindelia three times daily for several days.

• **White vinegar.** Itching caused by sunburn, bug bites or yeast responds well to white vinegar. Dilute vinegar with an equal amount of water and test a small area first to make sure the vinegar solution does not sting. Dab it on the skin or apply it with a compress. If tolerated, the diluted vinegar can be applied to itchy areas several times a day.

• **Water.** It's surprising how often simply drinking one-half ounce of water per pound of body weight daily can heal troublesome dry, itchy skin, which can result from inadequate hydration.

If itching is accompanied by a fever or if you notice skin discoloration or red or purple streaking near a bite, or if you have confused your medications, are urinating frequently, are having shortness of breath or are in significant pain, see your doctor. These could be signs of an infection, a reaction to medication or a medication overdose.

When Eczema Is Not Eczema

Mark A. Stengler, NMD, naturopathic medical doctor in private practice, Encinitas, California...adjunct associate clinical professor at the National College of Natural Medicine, Portland, Oregon...author of *The Natural Physician's Healing Therapies* (Bottom Line Books).

Living with eczema (dermatitis) is its own special torture. In many people, the chronic skin condition causes nearly incessant itching along with telltale unsightly red or sometimes brown rashes on the arms, face and neck, including in the folds of skin of knees and elbows. Worse, it is a lifelong condition—eczema has no known cure and the few treatments for it may only be marginally helpful. And so when a 53-year-old carpenter and painter called Mark A. Stengler, ND, a naturopathic physician in private practice in Encinitas, California, for a consultation about the eczema that he had had for more than two decades, he had little hope.

The man's work exposed him to chemicals practically every day. It was hardly surprising that many of the specialists he saw over the years pointed to the patient's livelihood as the trigger for his eczema flare-ups and the reason why the condition became so intense at times. Indeed, the itching was often so bad that he got little sleep at night and the rash had grown to cover much of his body. He reported that his previous doctors had prescribed numerous different topical steroid ointments in an attempt to stem the chronic itching—but nothing really helped.

After meeting with him, Dr. Stengler figured that the man's toxicity was so deep, he needed some cleansing from the inside out. And so, to counteract any toxic residue that could result from frequent exposure to chemicals, Dr. Stengler put him through a detoxification program with liver-cleansing herbs, purified water and the like. Surprisingly, this didn't help much. Although the skin had the appearance of eczema, Dr. Stengler decided to look past the decades-long diagnosis to see what else it might be and what might possibly be an underlying cause.

A WHOLE DIFFERENT CAUSE

Eczema is sometimes associated with allergies or reactions to a variety of foods with milk, peanuts, soy, fish and tree nuts (walnuts, cashews) leading the pack. But there is another reaction to food that has been associated with a form of dermatitis as well—that is an intolerance to gluten, the protein found in many grains including wheat, barley and rye. (At one time oats were also on the gluten list, but some researchers now feel that oats may not produce a reaction.) Complicating the picture further, the gluten-associated rash is not actually eczema. This condition, which looks strikingly like eczema, bears the name *dermatitis herpetiformis*. In spite of the name, this has nothing at all to do with the herpes virus. It does, however, have everything to do with celiac disease, or gluten intolerance.

CONSIDER GLUTEN INTOLERANCE

Celiac disease is also a lifelong condition with symptoms that can surface in a number of different ways—from few symptoms at all to severe gastrointestinal distress, including diarrhea, abdominal pain, gas and bloating. In fact, celiac sufferers occasionally become seriously malnourished because the small intestine loses its ability to absorb nutrients, although many do not exhibit symptoms. Celiac disease can develop in childhood, but dermatitis herpetiformis is more apt to surface starting in the 20s or after. It occurs more frequently in men.

UNLOCKING THE PUZZLE

Dr. Stengler tested his patient for antibodies to gluten in the digestive tract through a stool test. Having such antibodies reveals the presence of a gluten intolerance. The antibodies tested extremely high. Consequently, Dr. Stengler put his patient immediately on a strict gluten-free diet with no foods containing wheat, rye or barley and allowed him to eat oats only occasionally. After six weeks of faithfully following this diet, the decades-old eczema-like disorder disappeared completely. In this particular case, Dr. Stengler's patient's skin should stay like this as long as he adheres to his gluten-free diet. He should be able to sleep peacefully without the itching that plagued him previously and continue his work around chemicals without any effect on his skin.

CONCLUSION

Dr. Stengler points out that although just less than 1% of the population is affected by celiac disease, some researchers estimate it is largely underdiagnosed and that many more people suffer from gluten intolerance. This disorder can cause a host of other problems, including, as we have seen, skin rashes and digestive distress, but it might also be behind other chronic conditions, including headaches, fatigue, mood swings, depression and joint pain.

Consequently, Dr. Stengler advises anyone struggling with problems such as these, who do not respond well to mainstream short-term treatment, to consider the possibility of gluten intolerance. The way to tell? Do not eat any foods containing wheat, barley or rye for a minimum of two weeks, he says, and see how you feel. In many cases, this small change in diet can make a big difference in how you feel. You can also visit a holistic doctor for gluten intolerance/sensitivity testing.

RESCUE YOUR WINTER SKIN

By the time February rolls around, your skin has been contending with months of dry indoor heating and bitter outdoor air. (Even in temperate climates, temperature dips take a toll.) Dryness, flaking and cracking may have set in—and more extreme problems can arise, such as eczema and other types of inflammation. *Natural solutions to help you well past the cold weather...*

●**Skip long showers and baths.** Lengthy exposure to hot water strips away the skin's natural moisture. Limit showers and baths to no more than five minutes.

●**Use mild soaps.** Commercial products may contain harsh, drying chemicals. Try mild soaps with *Calendula officinalis* (marigold), a botanical that promotes healing.* One popular brand is made by Weleda (800-241-1030, *www.usa. weleda.com*). Scented soaps can irritate sensitive skin. Until spring, consider switching to an unscented soap, such as Dove Sensitive Skin Unscented Beauty Bar.

*Pregnant or lactating women should consult their physicians before trying herb-based products.

●**Apply a moisturizer with a humectant.** Moisturizing is a must. Look for lotions that contain humectants, such as *glycerine*, *sorbitol* and *alpha-hydroxy acids* that attract moisture to the skin.

Good choice: Aveeno Skin Relief Moisturizing Cream (available in drugstores and at *www.drugstore.com*).

●**Relieve the driest patches.** For especially distressed areas, such as fingertips, that are cracked, painful, even bleeding, apply topical creams. Try salves or creams made by Burt's Bees (800-849-7112, *www.burtsbees.com*).

●**Take oral supplements for severely dry skin.** For excessive discomfort, including itchiness or cracking, I recommend fish oil—1,500 milligrams (mg) of combined *eicosapentaenoic acid* (EPA) and *docosahexaenoic acid* (DHA)—plus 1,000 mg of *gamma linoleic acid* (GLA). Together, they help the skin retain moisture.

Steps to Prevent Chronic Dry Skin

Marianne N. O'Donoghue, MD, associate professor of dermatology at Rush University Medical Center, Chicago, and dermatologist in private practice for more than 30 years in Oak Brook, Illinois.

Eczema, the chronic, dry skin condition that afflicts 15 million Americans, accounts for at least 20% of my practice, especially in winter, when the humidity is low. Men and women of all ethnic groups are equally vulnerable to the disease, but children under the age of six are slightly more likely to develop it.

The term *eczema* is broadly used to describe a variety of noncontagious conditions characterized by dry, red, scaly, itchy patches on the skin. It most often targets the arms and legs.

There are many different types of eczema, and the disorder can have many causes and occur in many forms. The most common kind of eczema—atopic dermatitis—is caused by an allergic reaction. It usually occurs in people who have a family history of hay fever, asthma or other allergies. I recently treated a little girl whose eczema was made worse because she was allergic to the nickel snaps on the front of her pants.

Eczema cannot be cured—but it can be controlled. *Here's how...*

PREVENTION

If you're prone to eczema, don't wait for a flare-up to take these steps, especially in the winter...

• **Use mild cleansers.** Use bar soaps that are meant for the face on your entire body. They are gentler on the skin. Good brands include Dove, Aveeno, Basis, Oil of Olay and Camay. Avoid antibacterial soaps and deodorant soaps, all of which aggravate eczema.

• **Lubricate skin twice a day.** Emollients are necessary to decrease the loss of water from the skin and prevent it from becoming too dry. Lotions won't do the trick. They are too watery and won't seal in moisture as ointments will. I recommend Vaseline Petroleum Jelly and Aquaphor to my patients.

• **Take no more than one shower a day.** People who shower at home, then go to the health club and take a second shower, particularly during the winter, are going to have more trouble with eczema than people who shower just once a day. It's even better not to shower daily—three or four times a week is optimal. And when you shower or bathe, make sure the water is lukewarm, not hot. Hot water dries out the skin more than cooler water.

• **If you swim in a pool for exercise,** be sure not to shower before getting in the pool. After getting out, rinse only long enough to get the chlorine off—and don't use soap.

• **Avoid animals.** Many people are allergic to the shed skin—the dander—of animals, such as cats, dogs and rabbits. Animal dander floats in the air and gets on furniture and clothes. Without even touching an animal, you still can come in contact with its dander.

• **Watch what children eat.** Children under the age of six who have eczema should avoid orange juice, egg whites and peanuts—including peanut products, such as peanut butter and foods that contain even traces of peanuts. Children usually outgrow these allergies, and adults usually don't have to worry that something they eat will trigger their eczema.

Acne Prevention

Mark A. Stengler, NMD, naturopathic medical doctor in private practice, Encinitas, California...adjunct associate clinical professor at the National College of Natural Medicine, Portland, Oregon...author of *The Natural Physician's Healing Therapies* (Bottom Line Books).

Acne affects more than 85% of adolescents and young adults. Hormonal changes cause glands of the skin to produce more oil, which clogs hair follicles. This sets the stage for the overgrowth of bacteria and yeast on the skin, leading to acne. Natural treatments are helpful.

Facial washes containing tea tree oil, available at health-food stores, can destroy bacteria and fungi associated with acne. Wash the face with a gentle, unscented soap in the morning, and use a tea tree oil facial rinse—such as Desert Essence Thoroughly Clean Face Wash—at night.

Taking 500 milligrams (mg) to 750 mg of the herb chasteberry helps balance hormones in the body, which in turn reduces the production of facial oils. Fish oil is also useful, since it reduces skin inflammation. A daily dose of 1,000 mg of combined EPA and DHA is probably right for most adolescents. Ask your doctor. To help heal the skin, take 30 mg to 50 mg of zinc and 2 mg of copper daily until acne is gone. Limit processed foods (including soda, candy, white bread and chips)...get more fiber from vegetables and fruits...and drink plenty of water. These dietary habits will moderate blood sugar levels, reducing inflammation.

More from Mark A. Stengler, NMD...

Cures for Cold Sores

They swell up...blister...scab. Cold sores that sprout on or near the lips are a year-round annoyance. Sun exposure increases their frequency. Other triggers include stress... a cold or fever...menstruation...and irritation, such as severely chapped lips.

The cause of most cold sores is a virus—herpes simplex type 1. (Type 2 typically causes genital herpes but also can cause cold sores.) The herpes simplex type 1 virus is spread by person-to-person contact, including kissing or touching someone else's cold sore or saliva. Once in your body, the virus never goes away, which means that you will be forever vulnerable to cold sores.

Note: Those who have strong immune systems are less susceptible to cold sores.

Several natural substances may help heal or prevent cold sores...

•*L-lysine.* This amino acid can prevent a cold sore outbreak or reduce its severity. Take 1,000 milligrams (mg) three times daily without food as soon as you feel a cold sore developing. Take it until the problem has resolved. If prone to outbreaks, you can use L-lysine preventively (500 mg to 1,000 mg twice daily without food) for two to three months and then again as needed. There are no side effects. Avoid foods such as nuts and egg yolks that are high in the amino acid *L-arginine*, which can cause cold sores.

•**Balms.** Natural balms can soothe the pain of cold sores and speed up healing. Look for balms with these ingredients—*aloe vera...zinc sulfate...lemon balm.* Apply to the cold sore four times daily. Although these ingredients are safe, they can cause a reaction (usually redness in the area). If you are sensitive to one ingredient, try a product with another ingredient. Protect your lips from the sun with a sunblock balm.

Natural Ways to Keep Your Teeth Healthy

Jamison Starbuck, ND, naturopathic physician in family practice in Missoula, Montana. She is a past president of the American Association of Naturopathic Physicians and a contributing editor to *The Alternative Advisor: The Complete Guide to Natural Therapies and Alternative Treatments* (Time-Life).

Dental health may seem, at first glance, to have little to do with your overall physical health. But that's not true. For example, an increasing body of scientific evidence links dental conditions to heart disease, diabetes and even certain types of cancer. *Areas of dental health that my patients ask about most often...*

•**Periodontal disease.** According to the National Institutes of Health, 25% of Americans over age 65 have lost all of their natural teeth. Much of this is due to periodontal disease— including inflammation of gums (gingivitis) and/or bones around the teeth (periodontitis). For the most part, periodontal disease is preventable, but you may have to do more than just brush and floss.

To fight periodontal disease, you need a strong immune system, a limited amount of harmful bacteria in the mouth and healthy gum tissue. The standard advice is to avoid tobacco as well as sugary foods and beverages—and brush two to three times daily and floss once daily. You will have even greater success if you also use a daily regimen of 1,500 milligrams (mg) of vitamin C...20,000 international units (IU) of vitamin A*...60 mg of the antioxidant CoQ10...and one-half cup of antioxidant-rich berries, such as blueberries and blackberries (fresh or frozen), or purple grapes. These nutrients help you maintain a strong immune system and healthy gums.

•**Fluoride.** For years, we've been told that fluoride hardens tooth enamel, thereby reducing tooth decay that can lead to cavities. However, some research indicates that this mineral may not reduce cavities or fight harmful bacteria in the mouth and actually may increase the risk for hip fracture. Fluoride also has been linked to osteosarcoma (bone cancer) in teenage boys who were exposed to the mineral during childhood. Instead of using fluoride in toothpaste and other dental products, I recommend a regimen that includes good dental hygiene (as described above)...and the use of xylitol, a safe, plant-derived sugar product. Xylitol is available in toothpastes and chewing gums that are sold at health-food stores and pharmacies.

A study published in the *Journal of the American Dental Association* found that xylitol reduces levels of harmful bacteria in the mouth and discourages the formation of cavities. While cavity risk is greatest in children (whose teeth are still forming), some adults are also in jeopardy—especially smokers, older adults, people with dry mouth syndrome, which of-

---

*Pregnant women and people with liver disease should not exceed 5,000 IU daily.

ten results from Sjögren's syndrome (an auto-immune disease)...radiation therapy to the head or neck...or medication side effects.

•**Mercury fillings.** This is a controversial issue. While the American Dental Association has stated that amalgam (mercury-containing) fillings are not dangerous, mercury toxicity may lead to neurologic problems, such as memory loss, and autoimmune disease, such as lupus. My approach is to test mercury levels (via a urine sample) in patients who have many of these fillings as well as symptoms, such as chronic fatigue and pain. If levels are high, I recommend removing amalgam fillings and replacing them with non-mercury material, such as composite resin.

Whiter Teeth

Mark A. Stengler, NMD, naturopathic medical doctor in private practice, Encinitas, California...adjunct associate clinical professor at the National College of Natural Medicine, Portland, Oregon...author of *The Natural Physician's Healing Therapies* (Bottom Line Books).

There are several natural options when it comes to whitening teeth. I contacted David Banks, DDS, a holistic dentist in San Marcos, California. He explains that most darkening of teeth is due to the accumulation of stains over time.

First: Brush with a quality low-abrasion toothpaste.

His favorites: PerioPaste by Bio-Pro, which contains antibacterial herbs and essential oils, such as peppermint, calendula flower and olive leaf (800-650-9060, *www.naturaldentalhealth. com*) and PowerSmile Enzyme Brightening Oral Pre-Rinse by Jason Naturals, with papaya and pineapple enzymes (866-595-8917, *www.jason-personalcare.com*). Both contain *calcium carbonate, sodium bicarbonate* and *colloidal silica*—low-abrasion tooth-cleaning compounds that help with stains. Beyond that, if you want still whiter teeth, a bleaching process may be necessary.

Best: Have your dentist perform an in-office procedure, which limits the duration of exposure to the bleaching chemicals.

To Protect Teeth and Gums

Replace your toothbrush if the bristles are frayed or point outward—usually after three or four months.

That's when the brush becomes less effective at removing plaque and may start to irritate gums. Get rid of the toothbrush immediately if the bristles smell or have changed color or if you have had an infection or any systemic disease that can be transmitted by blood or saliva, such as hepatitis or tuberculosis. It is not necessary to disinfect a toothbrush—but do store it in an area where it can dry between uses to reduce bacteria.

Matthew Messina, DDS, in private practice, Cleveland, and spokesman, American Dental Association.

A Tooth-Friendly Snack

Are raisins good for your teeth? In a recent study, *oleanolic acid*, a plant chemical found in raisins, was shown to inhibit the growth of two species of oral bacteria. *Streptococcus mutans* causes cavities, and *Porphyromonas gingivalis* is associated with gum disease. This finding refutes the long-standing belief that raisins promote tooth decay.

Christine D. Wu, PhD, professor, periodontics department, University of Illinois at Chicago College of Dentistry.

More from Christine D. Wu, PhD...

Freshen Your Breath with a Cup of Tea

Polyphenols found in green and black tea inhibit growth of odor-causing bacteria. Drinking one to two cups of tea a day can help keep your breath fresh.

Banish Bad Breath

Violet I. Haraszthy, DDS, PhD, associate professor of oral biology and restorative dentistry, University of Buffalo School of Dental Medicine, Buffalo, New York, and leader of a study on bad breath.

I f a whiff of your breath makes others wince, it may be more than a social problem—often it suggests a medical problem, too. Here's what you need to know about halitosis, or bad breath.

•**Occasional bad breath** typically results from diet.

What to do…

•Minimize food odors with herbs. Onions, garlic, cabbage and spices contain strong-smelling compounds that break down during digestion, are absorbed into the bloodstream and travel to the lungs. To reduce production of smelly intestinal gases, along with the offending foods, swallow one of the following—one-eighth teaspoon of dried caraway seeds (chew them first)…six ounces of hot water mixed with one-quarter teaspoon of powdered caraway…one caraway capsule…or one parsley oil capsule.

•Mask the smell. For a quick temporary fix, chew a clean mint leaf or sprig of fresh parsley, or suck on a sugar-free breath mint.

•**Chronic halitosis** usually is caused by bacteria in the mouth. *Fixes…*

•Prevent dry mouth. Saliva helps flush out bacteria. Cut back on alcohol and caffeine, which are dehydrating…drink more fluids…chew sugarless gum or suck on sugarless hard candy to stimulate saliva production. Antihistamines, antidepressants, blood pressure drugs and diuretics contribute to dry mouth, so ask your doctor about alternatives. Use a humidifier in your bedroom, especially if you are a nighttime mouth-breather.

•Clean your tongue. The tongue's surface has tiny protuberances called *papillae* that create havens for bacteria. Use a tongue scraper ($10 or less at drugstores) once a day…or try the Colgate 360 toothbrush, which has soft tongue-cleaning knobs on the back of the head.

•Use antibacterial mouthwash. Good nonprescription antibacterials include *zinc*, found in TheraBreath Plus and Tom's of Maine Natural Tartar Control Mouthwash…or *chlorine dioxide*,

found in ProFresh. *Avoid:* Mouthwashes with alcohol, such as Listerine, which are drying.

•Try antimicrobial toothpaste. The only toothpaste with the effective antimicrobial *triclosan* is Colgate Total. *Also important:* Floss teeth daily!

•**Disease-related bad breath** may stem from a dental problem or from a systemic (body-wide) medical condition. *Solutions…*

•See your dentist. When plaque-filled pockets form between teeth and gums, trapped bacteria create foul odors. Your dentist may recommend a cleaning, antibiotics and/or surgery. *If that does not fix the problem…*

•See your primary care doctor. Do not wear cologne or scented lotion to your appointment—these mask odors that could help your doctor make a diagnosis. *Warning signs:* Diabetes makes breath smell overly fruity…gastric cancer produces a fecal odor…kidney disorders create an ammonia-like smell…liver problems lead to fishy breath…lung disease causes a putrid smell…postnasal drip leads to sulfurous breath. *Good news:* When the underlying disorder is addressed, breath freshens up, too.

Beauty Fixes from Your Kitchen

Mark A. Stengler, NMD, naturopathic medical doctor in private practice, Encinitas, California…adjunct associate clinical professor at the National College of Natural Medicine, Portland, Oregon…author of *The Natural Physician's Healing Therapies* (Bottom Line Books).

Joan Wilen and Lydia Wilen, folk-remedy experts based in New York City and authors of many books, including *Bottom Line's Healing Remedies* (Bottom Line Books, 800-678-5835, *www.bottomlinepublications.com*).

Y ou don't need to go to the pharmacy to find powerful cures for everyday ailments. The answers could be in your kitchen. Joan and Lydia Wilen have been collecting, researching and testing folk remedies for more than two decades—and all their remedies have been reviewed for safety by medical doctors, naturopathic doctors and other experts.

Bonus: You might even save a few pennies in the process—having to turn no further than your own kitchen. If you have an existing health condition, check with your physician before trying any of these remedies.

DANDRUFF
Thyme

We all have dead cells that fall from our scalp as new cells come in. But some people have a greater number of cells falling that are bigger and easier to see. Dried thyme can help get rid of dandruff. Boil one cup of water, and add two heaping tablespoons of dried thyme to the cup. Let it simmer for seven to 10 minutes. Use a strainer to collect the thyme, and get rid of it. Let the tea cool. Wash your hair with a regular shampoo. While your hair is still damp, gently massage the cooled tea into your scalp. Do not rinse.

SAFER SHAMPOOS AND MORE

Many of the health and beauty products we use every day contain trace amounts of toxic substances. Nearly 90% of the 10,000+ chemicals used in these products have not been evaluated for safety by a publicly accountable institution. *Examples…*

•**Coal Tar** is the anti-itch, antiflake ingredient in some shampoos for dandruff and psoriasis, and a color agent in many hair dyes. In 1994 the FDA warned that coal tar was a possible carcinogen. Further study revealed that low concentrations are not cancerous, but a California law requires that products containing more than 0.5% coal tar must include a warning label. Check hair-color ingredient lists for *FD&C Blue 1*, *Green 3* or *Yellow 5 & 6*, as well as *D&C Red 33*.

•**Phthalates** are chemicals used as softening agents in perfumes, nail polish, shampoos, conditioners, baby lotions and wipes. A study published in *Environmental Health Perspectives* linked phthalates to genital abnormalities developed in utero, and animal studies have shown phthalates to be cancerous. Avoid products with "fragrance," because there is no way to tell if this includes phthalates, which help scents to last longer. Look for natural fragrance agents, such as essential oils of mint or lavender.

•**Parabens** are chemicals used as preservatives in lotions, shampoos, shaving creams, toothpastes and more. Animal studies have shown that parabens mimic estrogen in the body and can disrupt hormone balance. Watch for *methyl-*, *propyl-*, *ethyl-* and *butyl-* on labels, and opt for products marked "paraben-free."

Healthy alternative: Many brands sold in natural-food stores are free of these additives. Good choices include Aubrey Organics, Avalon Organics, Burt's Bees and Light Mountain. Consider that one in four women uses at least 15 personal-care products daily, according to the Environmental Working Group, and it makes sense to consider nature-based varieties.

More from Mark A. Stengler, NMD…

Help for Brittle Fingernails

Splitting fingernails can be caused by repeated and prolonged exposure to water. They also can indicate several different internal imbalances but not any specific medical conditions. Imbalances include deficiencies of nutrients, such as amino acids, calcium, vitamin D, biotin (a form of B vitamin) and silica. These deficiencies may occur because of poor digestion and poor absorption of nutrients from foods and supplements. Although testing for nutritional deficiencies is always optimal, most doctors don't offer this kind of testing. For patients over age 50, who are likely to have low stomach acid, which can inhibit the absorption of nutrients, I prescribe *betaine hydrochloride* supplements that mimic stomach acid. Taken with meals, they improve the absorption of nutrients. For younger patients who have more normal stomach acid levels, digestive enzymes taken with meals can be quite helpful.

Best: Work with a nutrition-oriented physician to determine the cause.

3

Curbing Chronic
Conditions Without Drugs

The Diabetes Miracle

Type 2 diabetes is one of the many chronic diseases that often can be managed entirely without medication, particularly when it is diagnosed at an early stage.

Among people with insulin resistance, a precursor to diabetes, nearly all can reverse it with the same changes. Even with longstanding diabetes, many patients can discontinue most of their insulin/oral drugs when they make significant dietary and other lifestyle changes.

CATCH IT EARLY

About 24 million Americans have type 2 diabetes (once known as adult-onset diabetes), and at least 57 million have prediabetes, an intermediate condition in which levels of fasting glucose (blood sugar) are between 100 milligrams per deciliter (mg/dL) and 125 mg/dL.

What they have in common: An inability to effectively utilize insulin, the hormone produced by the pancreas that allows glucose to move from the bloodstream into the cells.

Most people with diabetes are first diagnosed via a fasting blood sugar test. But by the time glucose levels are high, the disease already has progressed—and the cells that produce insulin may have suffered irreversible damage.

Better: The fasting serum insulin test.

Cost: About $50 (which may be covered by insurance). High levels of insulin indicate insulin resistance, a condition that precedes sharply elevated glucose.

Anyone with diabetes risk factors, including obesity, high blood pressure, elevated cholesterol or a waist circumference of more than 40 inches in men or 35 inches in women, should have the fasting serum insulin test.

Those who have diabetes or are at risk for diabetes should consider making the following lifestyle changes. People sometimes complain

Stuart A. Seale, MD, medical director of Lifestyle Center of America, a diabetes center in Sedona, Arizona. He also is lifestyle educator and staff physician for the Stopping Diabetes Program in Sedona. He is coauthor, with Franklin House, MD, and Ian Blake Newman, of *The 30-Day Diabetes Miracle* (Perigee). *fullplateliving.org* about the "restrictive" nature of the changes needed to control diabetes. It does take some effort, but far less than dealing with the complications of the disease—which may include blindness, nerve damage and amputation.

NEAR-VEGETARIAN DIET

One study found that 21 of 23 patients were able to discontinue oral diabetes drugs after switching to a mainly meatless diet—of those on insulin, 13 out of 17 were able to quit taking the insulin.

A plant-based diet is high in fiber, which slows digestion and the rate of glucose absorption into the blood. This causes the pancreas to secrete less insulin, and it makes cells more sensitive to insulin's effects. People who consume little or no meat also tend to have lower cholesterol and blood pressure—important for minimizing the cardiovascular complications of diabetes.

The Diabetes Prevention Program study found that people at risk for developing type 2 diabetes who exercised regularly and ate a Mediterranean-style diet—mainly fruits, vegetables, legumes (beans, lentils) and whole grains, with only small amounts of meat a few times a month—decreased their risk of developing diabetes by 58%. In contrast, trying to prevent diabetes by using the popular medication metformin lowered the risk of developing diabetes by 31%.

CARBOHYDRATE COUNTING

Carbohydrate counting is among the most effective ways to control diabetes. *Main steps…*

• **Calculate net carbohydrate.** This is the amount of carbohydrate in a food minus fiber content. One cup of Kashi GoLean cereal, for example, has 30 grams (g) of total carbohydrates, but because this includes 10 g of fiber, the net carbohydrate is actually 20 g. You can find all of this information on food labels.

• **Identify "carbohydrate choices."** One carbohydrate choice equals 15 g of net carbohydrates.

Example: A slice of whole-wheat bread is one carbohydrate choice (about 15 g of net carbs).

• **Eat 9 to 13 carbohydrate choices daily for optimal control.** Most people should have three to five carb choices for breakfast.

Sample breakfast: One cup of old-fashioned oatmeal with milk or milk alternative, such as soy milk (two carbohydrate choices)…one cup of berries (one carb choice)…egg or tofu scramble with vegetables, such as mushrooms, bell peppers and onions (one carb choice)…one slice of toast with nut butter (one carb choice).

• **Have three to five carbohydrate choices at lunch and zero to three at supper.** Eating lighter at night helps stabilize overnight and morning blood sugar levels.

Carbohydrate counting is confusing initially, but people quickly memorize the carbohydrate contents of the foods that they tend to eat most often.

Helpful: I advise patients to eat meals at the same time every day…and to eat about the same portion sizes to keep blood sugar levels stable.

GLYCEMIC INDEX

Some carbohydrates elevate blood glucose almost instantly—others much more slowly. The Glycemic Index (GI) is a measure of how quickly carbohydrates elevate glucose. A lower number indicates a slower glucose rise—and better glucose control.

Example: White bread has a GI of 73. It is transformed very quickly into glucose, which causes blood sugar levels to surge. A serving of carrots, on the other hand, has a GI of 32. The glucose conversion happens slowly, which causes steadier levels of blood glucose.

Recommended: Mainly consume foods with GIs of less than 55. Foods that are minimally processed, such as legumes and whole grains, generally have lower GI numbers. (See *www.glycemicindex.com* for a complete guide to the Glycemic Index.)

Helpful: Above-ground vegetables, such as grains and leafy greens, typically have lower GIs than below-ground vegetables, such as potatoes and radishes. Fruit from the temperate climates, such as apples, pears and peaches, have lower GIs than tropical fruits, such as bananas.

Also, if you feel like eating a food with a high GI (such as white bread), combine it with a low-GI food, such as peanut butter, to reduce the glucose surge.

POSTMEAL EXERCISE

Exercise helps people lose weight, which improves insulin sensitivity and reduces cardiovascular risk factors.

Even without weight loss, exercise is very effective for managing diabetes, particularly when you exercise after meals. Exercise after meals makes it easier for muscle cells to absorb glucose from the blood.

Patients who check their blood sugar two hours after eating, then test it again after a brisk 20-minute walk, typically see a drop of at least 30 points.

Strength training also is helpful. People who lift weights or engage in other forms of resistance exercise (such as push-ups) two or three times a week have an increase in muscle tissue, which increases metabolism and insulin sensitivity.

LOWER STRESS

In an emergency, the body releases cortisol. This is the "fight-or-flight" hormone that increases blood glucose to produce a quick surge of energy. Unfortunately, the same thing happens in people with daily stress. Their cortisol—and glucose—remains at chronically high levels, making diabetes more difficult to control.

Stress management is critical if you have diabetes. Most people find that a daily walk keeps them calmer. In addition, hobbies are a good way to defuse tension and stress. Others learn to meditate or practice yoga. Whatever you find relaxing, make time for it at least a few times a day.

Weight Loss a Big Help For Those with Diabetes

Mark H. Schutta, MD, medical director, Penn Rodebaugh Diabetes Center, University of Pennsylvania Health System, Philadelphia.

I n study after study we learn more about how chronic diseases overlap and how one can lead to another. This is especially true of diabetes, which for many people is followed by kidney and/or cardiovascular disease and often other problems. While adequate control of diabetes requires careful monitoring of blood glucose levels to keep them as close to normal as possible, a new study indicates that the amount of fat people have in their cells may also be a key factor in preventing diseases related to diabetes.

FAT KILLS CELLS

One of the critical elements in scientific research of disease is the concept of cell death (apoptosis). All cells die but not all die as planned. This is especially evident in cancer cells, where cancerous cells do not die like "normal cells."

Scientists at Washington University School of Medicine in St. Louis investigated the role excess fat might have in the process of cell death. They discovered through studying cells in culture tissues and in rodents that cells can become overloaded with saturated fat and this situation results in an overproduction of the protein EF1A-1. This protein is abundant and normal in the body and indeed necessary for a number of cellular activities, including protein synthesis and maintaining the cell's internal support structure.

However, when EF1A-1 increases substantially, as it does in the presence of excess cellular fat, it appears to turn on the cells and cause them to die.

The theory that has emerged from these studies is this: If insulin-producing cells in the pancreas are jammed with too much saturated fat (and so too much EF1A-1), these vital pancreatic cells end up dying. This likely contributes to the development of diabetes. This study also suggests that the same pattern of cell death takes place in cardiac muscle cells when they have a concentration of saturated fat and this might well contribute to the association of diabetes and cardiac disease.

NEED MORE RESEARCH

Endocrinologist Mark H. Schutta, MD, medical director of the Penn Rodebaugh Diabetes Center at the University of Pennsylvania Health System in Philadelphia, weighed in on the studies. He describes the information from them as interesting and intriguing, but he adds that until we have additional research to back this up, the theory of saturated fat-induced protein causing apoptosis remains speculative.

Of course, just because there is more research to be done, that doesn't mean it isn't a warning signal worthy of heeding. Dr. Schutta observes how this study underscores once again the ill effects of obesity and the dangers of the typical American diet. The study team used the saturated fatty acid palmitate in the research—the major component of palm oil and one of the most common saturated fats in processed foods.

Among his patients, Dr. Schutta says, there are some who are genetically predisposed to insulin problems, but there are many others whose diets are a strong contributory factor. He estimates that although his entire patient group receives extensive information and advice about weight loss and a healthful lifestyle, only 10% to 20% of patients actually go on to make these changes.

FEWER POUNDS, SO MANY BENEFITS

Admittedly, losing weight is especially difficult for people with diabetes—the disease itself predisposes people to excess weight because diabetes makes it more difficult to metabolize fats efficiently. Nevertheless, it is of the utmost importance for people with diabetes and those who have become insulin resistant to lose weight. Weighing less improves metabolism of fats, insulin sensitivity and can even lower blood pressure. Being lighter also increases energy, which in turn makes exercising easier.

Interestingly, it doesn't take a lot of weight loss to improve health among people with diabetes. Dr. Schutta says that his patients assume when he tells them they need to lose weight that he is recommending they get back to what they weighed in their youth. But in fact, this isn't so. A weight loss of just 5% to 7% of a person's current weight is all that is necessary to make a substantial difference. This holds true for both those considered obese, with a body mass index (BMI) of 30 or above, and those with the all-too-typical extra 10 pounds to lose. This doesn't require any kind of dramatic dieting—just a healthful approach that includes protein, fruits (though no fruit juice because of its high sugar content), vegetables and whole grains—and getting rid of those saturated fats.

Popular Foods Increase Diabetes Risk

Among middle-aged nondiabetic people, those who ate the most red meat, refined grains, fried potatoes, tomato-based items (lasagna, enchiladas), eggs and cheese were four times more likely to get type 2 diabetes within five years than those who ate the least of these—regardless of body weight.

Best: Eat fruits, vegetables, whole grains, low-fat dairy and beneficial fats (olive oil, nuts).

Angela D. Liese, PhD, professor, department of epidemiology and biostatistics, University of South Carolina, Columbia, and leader of a study of 880 people.

Coffee Dramatically Drops Diabetes Risk

Rob M. van Dam, PhD, adjunct associate professor, department of nutrition, Harvard School of Public Health, Boston.

Recently, coffee has been linked to a reduced risk for liver cancer. There is more good news for latte lovers from researchers at the Harvard School of Public Health (HSPH)—they found that people who drink coffee on a regular basis experience a substantially lower risk for type 2 diabetes.

These findings appeared in the *Journal of the American Medical Association* (JAMA).

ABOUT THE STUDY

In a retrospective review of nine studies of coffee consumption and type 2 diabetes risk, Harvard researcher Rob M. van Dam, PhD, and his colleagues in Boston looked at 193,473 regular coffee drinkers who experienced 8,394 cases of type 2 diabetes. They excluded from consideration studies that involved type 1 diabetes, animals or short-term exposure to coffee or caffeine.

Next, researchers calculated the relative risk of type 2 diabetes in relation to how many daily cups of coffee the participants consumed. *It turned out that the more coffee, the better…*

• **The risk for diabetes was lowest in people who consumed the most coffee each day (six or more cups).**

• **Those who drank four to six cups daily also faced a lower risk for diabetes** (about 30% reduction in risk) as compared with people drinking little or no coffee.

These numbers did not differ significantly according to sex, obesity or geographic region (which in this case meant the US and Europe). However, Dr. van Dam adds that the results were rather diverse in the lowest consumption category. He would not be surprised if future studies that are able to measure coffee consumption more precisely find a lower diabetes incidence for any amount of coffee.

MORE COFFEE, LESS DIABETES

These current findings serve to underscore the results of an earlier HSPH study in 2004, in which men who drank more than six cups of coffee a day reduced their risk of type 2 diabetes by more than 50% in comparison with men who did not drink coffee…and women by 30% in comparison with women who were not coffee drinkers. This beneficial effect was observed independent of lifestyle choices such as smoking, exercise and obesity.

Scientists don't know exactly how coffee works to cut diabetes risk. Paradoxically, caffeine reduces insulin sensitivity and raises blood sugar in the short term—both no-nos for diabetes. However, Dr. van Dam emphasizes that coffee is a complex beverage that contains numerous chemical compounds and minerals, which may have both helpful and harmful impacts on the body. Components other than caffeine—such as the antioxidants chlorogenic acid and magnesium—actually improve sensitivity to insulin and thus help lower diabetes risk. In animal studies, *trigonelline* and *lignans,* also found in coffee, improved glucose levels. Dr. van Dam adds that additional studies

on effects of coffee components in humans are clearly needed.

WHAT ABOUT DECAF?

For those of us who prefer decaf, coffee still packs some protection against type 2 diabetes. Although the effect appears to be more modest, some of this discrepancy may be attributed to study limitations. Decaffeinated coffee consumption was substantially lower than caffeinated coffee consumption, and this may have affected the estimates, explains Dr. van Dam. He points out that it is easier to detect larger contrasts in consumption than smaller differences. In addition, one can expect some misclassification when you ask for the amount of coffee people consume (change over time, differences in strength and cup size, etc.).

Dr. van Dam notes that in a recently published study on coffee consumption and C-peptide concentrations (a marker for insulin resistance), the association was actually similar for decaffeinated and caffeinated coffee consumption. He adds that it is currently unclear whether caffeine has detrimental effects on insulin sensitivity over the long term, because only short-term studies have been conducted. Nor is it clear if non-coffee sources of caffeine would have similar effects.

THE JOLT OF JAVA

Other trials have already lined up in coffee's favor, demonstrating that it can lower the risk of liver problems, gallstones, colon cancer and Parkinson's disease. Of course, there's also a downside to coffee (which pregnant women, children and people with colitis, hepatitis and other dietary challenges should not drink), such as jitteriness, insomnia and a rapid heartbeat. (Coffee stimulates liver function, which in healthy people is fine in moderation, but those with active liver disease may experience a worsening of symptoms when they consume coffee.)

Promising as it seems, Dr. van Dam and his colleagues do not go so far as to recommend drinking coffee to prevent type 2 diabetes. They emphasize that while coffee consumption may contribute to the reduction of risk for diabetes, it cannot replace the myriad health benefits of diet, exercise and weight management.

Many people stop drinking coffee because they think this is good for their health. Now coffee drinkers can take comfort in knowing that their daily jolt of java not only gets them up and moving, it also provides a health benefit.

Great News! Chili Peppers Lower Insulin Levels

Madeleine J. Ball, MD, professor and head of the School of Human Life Sciences, University of Tasmania, Australia.

Accaccording to an important recent study from Australia, chili peppers may actually help improve health by affecting the hormone insulin that controls blood sugar.

Madeleine J. Ball, MD, one of the researchers from the study at the University of Tasmania, says that both some small animal and human studies have indicated that consumption of meals containing chili peppers or chili seasoning might increase both calorie burning and fat burning. What the researchers wanted to find out was whether the consumption of chili also affects insulin levels after a meal.

CHILI AND INSULIN

As it turns out, it does. "The subjects had similar blood sugar levels after eating the bland meals and the chili containing meals," Dr. Ball tells us, "but their insulin levels were different." Why does this matter? Because chronically high levels of insulin can be a risk factor for metabolic syndrome, heart disease, diabetes and obesity. "Chili is probably having some effect on the ability of the body to clear—or remove—insulin from the bloodstream," Dr. Ball says.

Though blood sugar went up about the same in all test subjects regardless of whether they were fed chili-containing meals or bland meals, those who ate the chili-containing meals had less insulin in their bloodstream according to post-eating measures. The implication? The chili lowered the insulin-induced cortisol response to the meal, which promoted a more stable blood sugar level. Interestingly, the results were more pronounced in those with a higher BMI (body mass index).

CAPSAICIN'S HEAT

The chili preparation used in the study consisted of 30 grams a day of a chili blend that consisted of 55% cayenne chili plus a few other ingredients—such as water and sugar. Dr. Ball believes that capsaicin was responsible for the effect—the compound responsible for the heat or pungency in chili peppers. Capsaicin is also the active ingredient in pepper spray. While it's responsible for the burning heat you feel when you eat a really hot chili pepper, it also has significant health benefits. "We suspect it has significant antioxidant and anti-inflammatory properties," Dr. Ball says, which could also be important in reducing atherosclerosis.

More studies will no doubt come on capsaicin. In the meantime, go ahead and enjoy chili.

Unbelievable! Pollutants Raise Risk of Diabetes

Duk-Hee Lee, MD, PhD, professor of epidemiology, School of Medicine, Kyungpook National University in South Korea. She has written extensively about the relationship of persistent organic pollutants (POPs) and diabetes.

Rick Relyea, PhD, ecologist, University of Pittsburgh, Pennsylvania.

The following almost reads like a detective story and sets the stage for what's to come...

A few years ago a story came out about how the population of gray tree frogs was being decimated by the use of a common pesticide, *carbaryl*. But the makers of carbaryl insisted it wasn't harming the frogs. They had numerous studies showing that if you take the little creatures and put them in a lab setting and expose them to the pesticide, nothing happens.

But still, the tree frogs were dying. And the environmentalists were positive it had something to do with their continued exposure to this pesticide.

FROGS RELEVANT TO DIABETES?

Rick Relyea, PhD, an ecologist from the University of Pittsburgh, in Pennsylvania, discovered that carbaryl was less harmful to frogs in the unnaturally tranquil setting of the lab (at least it was less likely to kill them). But most tree frogs don't live in a lab, they live in the wild. And in the wild there are constant dangers from predators. When tree frog tadpoles were exposed to a predator, the predator emitted a chemical cue that resulted in a stress response in the gray tree frog—a stress response just like we get when we're caught in traffic or miss a deadline. Expose a stressed frog to the pesticide and you've got a dead frog. The combination of the two—physiological stress and a low-level pesticide, neither of which has a significant impact on survival alone—was lethal for a majority of the gray tree frog tadpoles.

"In other species such as bullfrog tadpoles, carbaryl became up to 46 times more deadly with the addition of predator cues. Moreover, this phenomenon has since been observed with both insecticides and herbicides, suggesting that it may be a quite common phenomenon," says Dr. Relyea.

The take-home point is that elements in the environment often interact with elements of our own physiology to cause serious problems. New research is emerging that suggests we may be seeing exactly the same phenomenon with diabetes.

AN INTERESTING TRAIL OF BREADCRUMBS

We've long known that obesity is a major risk factor for diabetes. But now it appears that exposure to pollutants can seriously aggravate the risk, and—in combination with obesity—may be associated with the increased risk of becoming diabetic. A recent study in the journal *Diabetes Care* looked at the connection between six persistent organic pollutants (known as POPs) and diabetes…and what they found was dramatic.

The prevalence of diabetes increased by 14- to 38-fold as the concentrations of the sum of the six POPs increased, irrespective of participants'

weight, says lead researcher Duk-Hee Lee, MD, PhD, assistant professor of epidemiology at the School of Medicine, Kyungpook National University in South Korea. Her team divided the 2,016 subjects into groups comparing five levels of pollutants. Group 1 had the lowest levels and group 5 had the highest levels. Compared with group 1 (which had a .4% incidence of diabetes), group 2 had a 6.7% incidence of diabetes, while group 5 had an astonishing 25.6% incidence of the disease (groups 3 and 4 ranged in between). Dr. Lee notes that while obesity remains a risk factor for type 2 diabetes, the obese and overweight people with very low concentrations of POPs had a much lower incidence of diabetes. Could obesity and pollutants interact to cause diabetes in much the way that the pesticide and stress interacted to cause the death of frogs?

"It's our hypothesis that obesity might be only weakly associated with diabetes among people with very low serum concentrations of POPs," Dr. Lee says. She explains that while her research concentrated on only six specific pollutants out of about 50 POPs identified in the National Health and Examination Survey, there was a striking connection between the blood concentrations of these six toxins and the prevalence of diabetes. This is not the first time that such a connection has been demonstrated. Earlier research from Sweden also found that exposure to POPs may contribute to the development of type 2 diabetes. And earlier research also demonstrated that exposure to at least one toxin—a dioxin called *TCDD*—increases the risk of diabetes and insulin resistance. It's believed that these toxins may interfere with glucose metabolism.

POPS ARE EVERYWHERE

POPs include certain chemical byproducts, PCBs and certain insecticides that have been linked to cancer, neurobehavioral impairment, endocrine problems and reproductive disorders. Previous researchers looked at special populations that are occupationally or accidentally exposed to high levels of these pollutants —for example, Vietnam veterans. (The US Department of Veterans Affairs includes type 2 diabetes in its list of presumptive diseases associated with exposure to the dioxin-containing

Agent Orange.) But Dr. Lee's study is the first to examine the cumulative effect of most commonly detected POPs among a random low-level exposure in the general population. The six toxins in the study are found in the environment, and move through the air and water to accumulate in the environment.

Dr. Lee points out that pollutants by themselves do not necessarily cause diabetes, and expresses caution about jumping to strong conclusions based on one or two studies. "Plenty of people have exposure to these pollutants and don't get diabetes," she explains. "But the strong connection between high levels and increased incidence is very hard to ignore, as is the fact that there are such low levels of diabetes among those with low levels of exposure, even among the overweight and obese." Could genes be a factor? "It's prudent to act as if everyone is at risk, regardless of genetic makeup," she advises.

How do we get exposed to these chemicals in the first place? "Exposure to POPs comes mostly from fatty animal food consumption," Dr. Lee tells us.

When asked what protective measures people might take, Dr. Lee answers concisely: "A low intake of animal foods and a higher intake of plant foods may be beneficial. Aside from trying to avoid POPs, preventing obesity is still very important because the toxicity of POPs appeared to synergistically increase the risk of type 2 diabetes among obese persons."

Arsenic in Water Linked To Diabetes

About 13 million Americans live in areas where arsenic levels in the water supply exceed EPA standards.

Study: Participants with type 2 diabetes had 26% more arsenic in their urine than those without diabetes.

Best: Have your water tested. If arsenic is above 10 micrograms per liter, install a filter that removes arsenic on your home's main waterline.

Ana Navas-Acien, MD, PhD, associate professor, Johns Hopkins Bloomberg School of Public Health, Baltimore, and leader of a study of 788 people.

Saliva Test Could Monitor Type 2 Diabetes

Paturi V. Rao, MD, departments of endocrinology and metabolism and medicine, Nizam's Institute of Medical Sciences University, Hyderabad, India.

Charles F. Burant, MD, PhD, professor, internal medicine, University of Michigan, Ann Arbor.

Umesh Masharani, MD, professor, clinical medicine, University of California, San Francisco.

Scientists say they are on the verge of developing a saliva test for monitoring type 2 diabetes, a test which might someday replace invasive blood tests.

For the first time, researchers from Oregon and India have identified proteins in saliva that appear more frequently in people with diabetes than in nondiabetics. Using these proteins, they are working to develop a test to monitor and perhaps diagnose the condition.

The report was published in the *Journal of Proteome Research*.

THE STUDY

For the study, Paturi V. Rao, MD, from the departments of endocrinology and metabolism and medicine at Nizam's Institute of Medical Sciences University in Hyderabad, India, and colleagues analyzed saliva samples from people with and without type 2 diabetes. Their goal was to find proteins associated with the blood sugar disease.

The researchers found 65 proteins that occurred twice as frequently in the people with diabetes than in those without the condition.

LESS PAINFUL WAY TO TEST GLUCOSE

Using these proteins, Dr. Rao's team hopes to develop a noninvasive test for diabetes screening, detection and monitoring.

Dr. Rao's group thinks the pain involved with current diabetes monitoring causes many people with diabetes to be lax in monitoring their condition. A noninvasive test could make it easier and less painful for patients to keep track of their blood sugar levels.

"As recent studies have shown that early and multifactorial intervention in diabetes prevents cardiovascular complications and mortality, advances in understanding molecular aspects of preclinical diabetes will further facilitate accurate diagnosis and early intervention," said the authors.

EXPERT COMMENTARY

Diabetes expert Charles F. Burant, MD, PhD, a professor of internal medicine at the University of Michigan, isn't convinced that a test using proteins in saliva is needed.

Dr. Burant noted that diabetes and prediabetes already have an accurate marker—glucose. "Thus, this is interesting biochemistry and raises questions why these changes occur, but the clinical utility is unclear," he said.

Umesh Masharani, MD, professor of clinical medicine at the University of California, San Francisco, doesn't think this approach is going to replace current blood tests any time soon.

"I think this is an interesting and novel approach," Dr. Masharani said. "I do not think this approach will be used in the diagnosis or treatment of diabetes any time in the near future. It is interesting, I think, for research studies in diabetes."

LEARN MORE

For more about type 2 diabetes, visit the American Diabetes Association Web site, *www.diabetes.org/diabetes-basics/type-2*.

Stop Diabetes Before It Starts

Michael Hirt, MD, founding medical director, Center for Integrative Medicine, Encino-Tarzana Regional Medical Center, California and associate clinical professor, University of California, Los Angeles (UCLA). *www.drhirt.com*.

There are some illnesses that it seems you just "can't help." Then there are some that can be helped but require commitment on the part of the sufferer. Such is the case with type 2 diabetes. It is also the case with prediabetes, which affects nearly 60 million Americans, in which a person has elevated glucose levels but is not yet classified as diabetic. Much to the frustration of doctors, many people dismiss the impact of diabetes because some of its risks, including kidney failure, blindness, amputation and death, are felt in the long term, not in the short term.

While diabetes is definitely no fun to live with, it is often very manageable. There are a number of medications for diabetes, and many patients have progressed to the point that they must take them, but there are also vitamins and other supplements that address the particular problems. Michael Hirt, MD, former medical director of the Center for Integrative Medicine at Encino-Tarzana Regional Medical Center, California, reviewed the protocol for them.

FREE-RADICAL ATTACK

The main issue for people with diabetes is that high blood sugar levels cause dysregulated oxidative reactions in the body. This process can accelerate internal aging, resulting in such things as more rapidly hardening arteries and increased cardiovascular disease risk. To combat the free radicals contributing to this oxidation, it is necessary to take more antioxidants than diet alone commonly provides. Dr. Hirt recommends 1,000 milligrams (mg) a day of vitamin C (the long-acting one that lingers in the system) also known as Ester-C …and 200 mg to 300 mg a day of alpha-lipoic acid. This little known antioxidant is one of the most powerful, in part because it is the only one that can deactivate free radicals in both fat and water, giving much more bang for the buck. Studies show that alpha-lipoic acid has beneficial effects on the long-term nerve damage that often occurs in diabetes. Research also suggests that it helps improve insulin sensitivity.

EAT AND DRINK WISELY

A surprising aid to helping stabilize blood sugar is undoubtedly in your kitchen already— cinnamon. Dr. Hirt reports that researchers discovered this while testing people with diabetes to see how common foods affected their blood sugar levels. For some reason, patients' sugar levels didn't rise as anticipated when they ate apple pie. Ultimately, the researchers found that it was the cinnamon in the pie that helped prevent a rise. He recommends having one-half to one teaspoon a day, sprinkled over cereal, yogurt, fruit or other food or beverages of your choice.

Dr. Hirt adds that tea made from an ayurvedic herb called *Gymnema silvestre* seems to lower blood sugar and help pancreas cells work more efficiently.

MANAGING WEIGHT

An ongoing problem for diabetics is weight. One reason, of course, is that excess weight is a risk factor for developing the disease. In fact, 80% of people with diabetes are overweight. But as a double whammy, insulin—used to treat diabetes—can cause weight gain. Dr. Hirt says that he hasn't seen anything surefire to address this problem, but chromium picolinate may help. Being deficient in chromium, a trace element, can cause insulin resistance and increase blood glucose. According to the USDA Human Nutrition Research Center, diabetics who are chromium deficient significantly reduce fasting blood glucose levels by taking chromium picolinate. There are actually other more efficient delivery systems for chromium than the picolinate salt used in research. Consult your naturopathic physician or pharmacologist for other options for you.

Always discuss every medicine you take or are considering with your physician. Doctors must have this overview information in general, and in the case of diabetes, it is especially critical.

The reason: One substance might offset or enhance the effectiveness of another and at the very least your doctor may want to alter the dosages of your medication or supplementation. Be aware that diabetics should also avoid taking unprescribed glucosamine, a popular supplement used as a remedy for osteoarthritis. According to a report from the National Institutes of Health National Center for Complementary and Alternative Medicine presented at the 2004 American Diabetes Association meeting, glucosamine can make insulin resistance worse.

Dr. Hirt also strongly urges those with diabetes to make any necessary changes in lifestyle to bring about better health. He explains that diabetes is a disease of poor nutrition and lack of exercise—both situations that people have the power to turn around. Eat well, exercise regularly, take your multivitamin once a day in addition to the other supplements you need and, he says, you should be able to greatly improve or even eliminate adult-onset, or type 2 diabetes.

Herbal Remedy Could Halt Peanut Allergy

Xiu-Min Li, MD, associate professor, pediatrics, and director, Center for Chinese Herbal Therapy for Allergy and Asthma, Mount Sinai School of Medicine, New York City

David L. Katz, MD, MPH, director, Prevention Research Center, Yale University School of Medicine, New Haven, Connecticut.

The Journal of Allergy and Clinical Immunology, online.

A new herbal formula based in ancient Chinese medicine may be able to control allergic reactions to peanuts and other foods, researchers from New York City's Mount Sinai School of Medicine report.

"We can reverse the peanut allergic reaction," said lead researcher Xiu-Min Li, MD, director of the Center for Chinese Herbal Therapy for Allergy and Asthma at Mount Sinai.

BACKGROUND

Food allergies are potentially life-threatening for children and adults. Food allergies among children have increased 18% since 1997, and in 2007, some 3 million U.S. children had food allergies, according to the National Center for Health Statistics. Currently, there is no treatment for the allergies, so avoidance is the only protection.

Allergic reactions to food can range from mild hives to vomiting to difficulty breathing to anaphylaxis, the most severe reaction. Anaphylaxis causes muscles to contract, blood vessels to dilate and fluid to leak from the bloodstream into the tissues. This can result in narrowing of the upper or lower airways, low blood pressure, shock or a combination of these symptoms, and also can lead to a loss of consciousness and even death.

THE STUDY

For the study, Dr. Li's team tested their new herbal remedy, called Food Allergy Herbal Formula (FAHF-2), on mice allergic to peanuts. They found that the formula protected mice from allergic reactions to peanuts.

In fact, FAHF-2 protected the animals from anaphylaxis for more than 36 weeks after treatment was stopped. This is one-quarter of the mouse life span, Dr. Li noted.

Protection from less severe allergic reactions to peanuts persisted for almost nine months after treatment was stopped, Dr. Li said. "The herbal formula can stop peanut allergy and produce a prolonged protection," she said. "This formula may be effective for human peanut allergy."

The report was published in *The Journal of Allergy and Clinical Immunology*.

Dr. Li's team has also shown the formula protects mice against other food allergies including tree nut, fish and shellfish.

HUMAN TRIAL UNDER WAY

Based on these findings, FAHF-2 has been given investigational ncw drug approval by the U.S. Food and Drug Administration and an on-going Phase II human trial has begun.

The trial is testing the safety and effectiveness of the remedy for a variety of food allergies including peanut, tree nut, fish and shellfish, Dr. Li said. "The results of the trial have shown that FAHF-2 is safe and well-tolerated," she noted.

In addition to FAHF-2, Dr. Li's team has developed an herbal formula to treat asthma. That formula is also being tested in human trials, she said.

EXPERT REACTION

David L. Katz, MD, MPH, founding director of the Prevention Research Center at Yale University School of Medicine, said that no matter where it comes from, a cure for peanut allergy would be an important breakthrough.

"This paper suggests that traditional Chinese medicine may offer promising therapy for peanut allergy," Dr. Katz said.

For more information on food allergies, visit the National Library of Medicine's Web site, *www.nlm.nih.gov/medlineplus/foodallergy.html*.

Cleaning House May Be Risky for Women With Asthma

American College of Allergy, Asthma & Immunology, news release.

Housecleaning products may pose a threat to women with asthma, U.S. researchers say.

THE STUDY

During a 12-week study, researchers compared cleaning-related health effects in women who did and did not have asthma and found more lower-respiratory tract symptoms among the asthmatic women.

Jonathan A. Bernstein, MD, of the University of Cincinnati College of Medicine, and colleagues found that "women in both groups exhibited increased upper- and lower-respiratory tract symptoms in response to cleaning agents rated mild in toxicity, suggesting a subtle but potentially clinically relevant health effect of long-term, low-level chemical exposures."

The study was published in the *Annals of Allergy, Asthma & Immunology*.

IMPLICATIONS

The researchers recommended, "that women with asthma should be routinely interviewed as to whether they clean their home and cautioned about the potential respiratory health effects of these activities."

Asthma affects about 20 million people in the United States. Death rates from the disease are higher among women than men. In many homes, women are the primary cleaners.

Authors of the study concluded that "…longer, prospective studies of nonprofessional household cleaners are needed to determine whether there is an association between household cleaning agent exposure and the development of asthma."

For more information about asthma, visit the Web site of the National Heart, Lung and Blood Institute, *www.nhlbi.nih.gov* and search "What is asthma?"

Dance Your Way to Better Heart Health

Wayne Westcott, PhD, fitness research director and exercise physiologist, South Shore YMCA, Quincy, Massachusetts.

A weekly dance class can be fun, offer excellent aerobic exercise and provide a mental break from the hustle and bustle of life. Italian researchers have confirmed that waltzing is good for the heart as well. In fact, it is as good as—and in some respects may even be a little better than—conventional cycling and treadmill workouts.

Wayne Westcott, PhD, fitness research director and an exercise physiologist at the South Shore YMCA in Quincy, Massachusetts, believes in dancing's health benefits. He says that as long as exercise meets three important criteria—frequency (at least three days a week)…intensity (vigorous enough to raise the heart rate 60% to 80% of maximum, unless restricted by medication)…and duration (a minimum of 15- to 20-minute workouts)—it doesn't matter what type of activity you choose. If you find something you enjoy, you're more likely to stick with it. Warm up and cool down for five to 10 minutes with a lower-intensity exercise, such as walking or practicing dance steps, says Dr. Westcott.

In the study at the Lancisi Heart Institute in Ancona, Italy, researchers examined the impact of waltzing, cycling and treadmill workouts on people with chronic heart failure. In people with this long-term condition, the heart can no longer properly pump enough blood to other organs and tissues in the body. Consequently, the organs fail to receive sufficient oxygen and nutrients, which over time results in damage and loss of proper functioning. However, exercise may help improve functioning and quality of life.

The researchers divided heart failure patients into three groups. A group of 44 people exercised on a bicycle or treadmill three times a week for eight weeks…44 took waltzing classes for the same period…and 22 did not exercise at all. In those who waltzed or exercised, aerobic capacity improved. In people who did not work out, there was no change.

Specifically, researchers found that…

• **Oxygen uptake,** or the amount of oxygen reaching the tissues, rose 16% in exercisers and 18% in dancers.

• **The threshold of muscle fatigue,** or the time elapsed before muscles tire, increased 20% in exercisers and 21% in dancers.

• **While general fitness improvements in exercisers and dancers** were comparable, dancers showed greater improvements in quality of life—especially relating to emotions and mood.

These findings are in sync with earlier research showing that waltzing is beneficial in helping people recover the ability to function and improve quality of life following heart attacks.

PUT ON YOUR DANCING SHOES

Researchers speculate that the additional benefits of dancing stem from it's social nature and partnership. There's nothing magical about the waltz, of course. Dr. Westcott advises that you choose any type of dance—or other aerobic exercise—that you enjoy…but check with your doctor first. Then simply channel your inner Ginger Rogers or Fred Astaire and get moving.

Fast Fix for Unhealthy Hearts

Kathie Cole, RN, lead researcher of a study that evaluated the physical and psychological effects of introducing pet dogs to cardiac intensive care patients, and a cardiac care nurse at the University of California, Los Angeles (UCLA) Medical Center.

I t's been said before, and now confirmed again…spending time petting a dog can improve heart and lung function and relieve anxiety in heart patients—and it doesn't take long, according to a study presented at a meeting of the American Heart Association. A mere 12-minute visit with a dog resulted in measurable positive effects on patients' cardiac function and stress levels.

Seventy-six patients with heart failure at the University of California, Los Angeles (UCLA) Medical Center were randomly assigned to a 12-minute visit with either a dog and a human volunteer…a human volunteer only…or no visitors at all. In the dog and human volunteer group, specially trained dogs were placed on patients' beds so people could pet them during the observed study time.

The researchers showed significant results in three variables that characterize heart failure —changes in heart-lung pressures, stress hormone levels and anxiety.

HEART'S BEST FRIEND

In all three areas, those patients visited by a dog had superior results.

Cardiac-related improvements included a 5% drop in systolic pulmonary artery pressure during a dog visit and a 5% drop following the visit, as compared with rises in the other two groups. (Higher systolic pulmonary artery pressure— a measure of pressure in the lung—can make breathing more difficult in this group.)

Stress reduction occurred as levels of the stress hormone epinephrine dropped an average of 17% in those patients visited by a dog, as compared with a much lesser 2% drop in the human visitor only group and an average rise of 7% in those patients left alone.

And finally, those patients with a dog visitor had 24% less anxiety compared with a 10% drop in those visited by a human only and no drop in anxiety in those patients left alone.

Lead researcher Kathie Cole, RN, a cardiac care nurse at the UCLA Medical Center, says that the study shows that even short-term exposure to a dog can be extremely beneficial, both physiologically and psychologically. Perhaps more importantly, she says, studies like this one give animal-assisted therapy more credibility in the medical community. And, the positive effects from being around a dog are not limited to heart patients alone, but can be enjoyed by all people, in all conditions of health.

Is Your Attitude Hurting Your Heart?

Nalini Ranjit, PhD, research investigator, Center for Social Epidemiology and Population Health, University of Michigan, Ann Arbor.

A recent study is reminiscent of the "Type A" research of some years ago, that found that ambitious, achievement-oriented people with high levels of hostility were prone to heart disease. Now there's new affirmation that negativity affects our health from the University of Michigan in Ann Arbor, where researchers assessed 6,814 people, aged 45 to 84, to uncover potential health risks associated with three psychosocial factors— chronic stress, depression and cynical distrust. The researchers took blood samples from the participants and tested for three inflammation markers—C-reactive protein (CRP), fibrinogen and interleukin-6 (IL-6), all three of which are associated with increased heart disease risk. The results showed that chronic stress was linked with higher levels of IL-6 and CRP, while depression was linked only with higher levels of IL-6. Cynical distrust, however, took the highest toll, showing the strongest and most consistent positive association with all three of the markers.

Lead author Nalini Ranjit, PhD, research investigator at the university's Center for Social Epidemiology and Population Health, discussed the research. Her expectation was that depression would be the trait most highly associated with inflammation markers, so she was surprised to find the strong correlation between cynical distrust and inflammation markers. Dr. Ranjit describes "cynical distrust" as not only being cynical about life, but also having a deep-seated distrust and hostility toward other people. What was it about this attitude toward life that could change the body's chemistry? No one really knows conclusively how any of the three psychosocial factors connect physically to the raised measures of inflammation. Significantly, Dr. Ranjit says, the research team found a pattern of self-destructive behaviors, including smoking, alcohol use and a lack of physical activity in people with cynical distrust. A higher body mass index was also associated with cynical distrust (and may be indicative of another self-destructive behavior —overeating), but the connection seems to be deeper than that, since there are obese people and smokers in the depression and chronic stress categories as well. She also notes that it is important not to confuse this trait with cynicism, since cynical distrust includes hostility toward others.

While it is a big challenge to alter such deep-seated attitudes, Dr. Ranjit says that people who know themselves to be cynical and untrusting should be aware that they are potentially at risk for heart disease. They should do what they can to resolve their emotional pains, but also take extra care of their bodies with healthy diet and exercise.

Halt Climbing Blood Pressure Naturally

Louise Hawkley, PhD, senior research scientist, Center for Cognitive and Social Neuroscience at the University of Chicago.

C. Tissa Kappagoda, MD, PhD, director of the Coronary Heart Disease Reversal Program, University of California, Davis School of Medicine, Sacramento.

Because it clearly is a risk factor for heart attack and stroke, high blood pressure (HBP) is typically treated aggressively with medication, which also means there is the potential for drug side effects and other risks. But researchers continue to cast a wider net in search of more ways to treat HBP or, better yet, keep it from developing. Two recent studies identified surprising factors that appear to affect HBP.

THE LONELY HEARTS CLUB

Focusing on the many ways loneliness leads to HBP, one study, from the Center for Cognitive and Social Neuroscience and the department of psychology at the University of Chicago, found that people who feel chronically lonely (more detail on that later in the article) had as much as a 30-point increase in their systolic blood pressure number (the upper figure in blood pressure measurement). The data was based on 229 randomly chosen people aged 50 to 68 of varied ethnicity. Each participant completed surveys and interviews and had their blood pressure (and other cardiovascular measures) tested over the course of the day they spent in the laboratory. Participants responded to questions about their lives and attitudes, including ones that revealed loneliness. After adjusting for known HBP risks, such as body mass index and smoking, the study found that loneliness was associated with increased systolic blood pressure.

Why did researchers focus specifically on loneliness? Louise Hawkley, PhD, a senior researcher on the study fills in the details. She says that this study, funded in part by the National Institute of Aging, emerged from a previous one the team did that showed young people who were lonely had increased vascular resistance—that is, their blood vessels over-constricted when they experienced stress. Younger adults can compensate for this constriction by slowing the output of blood—thus keeping pressure normal—but over time, the extra work involved in peripheral (vessels anywhere but the heart) vascular resistance decreases elasticity, starting a cascade of physiological changes. Dr. Hawkley explains that researchers wondered about the long-term effect of loneliness, theorizing that inflammation, atherosclerosis and HBP may result—hence, the study.

Dr. Hawkley points out that she and her colleagues aren't prepared to say that loneliness can cause HBP, but they are beginning to believe that loneliness itself—apart from depression or other factors that might accompany it—has a relationship to HBP. Knowing as we do that acute stress raises blood pressure, Dr. Hawkley says it is reasonable to assume prolonged stress (such as that experienced by lonely people) does as well.

DEFINING "LONELY"

It's important to remember that the kind of loneliness looked at in this study has nothing to do with being alone, emphasizes Dr. Hawkley. Researchers looked at how perceived loneliness affected people, rather than at their actual social support. Even while socializing, lonely people still perceive themselves as unconnected. They often find it difficult to form good relationships, either expecting too much of them or avoiding them in general, and they respond to life's challenges with stressful despair. She adds that the study team is continuing to collect and analyze the data, and in a few more years should know even more about the specific mechanisms of how loneliness contributes to HBP. But in the meantime, it seems evident that lonely people can benefit from therapy to learn how to get past their passive coping strategies and develop effective social skills. Overcoming loneliness, she says, is an important step, probably for blood pressure and definitely for life.

STUDY 2: GREAT "GRAPE" NEWS

In the second study, researchers in the division of cardiovascular medicine at the University of California, Davis, evaluated how grape seed extract might impact blood pressure. This study is part of a continuing investigation into the health properties of this extract, an antioxidant flavonoid useful in removing a harmful excess of free radicals from cells. The findings were impressive.

The study examined 24 people diagnosed with metabolic syndrome (having a constellation of symptoms, including insulin resistance, abdominal obesity, elevated blood pressure and lipid abnormalities), and divided them into three groups. One group took 150 milligrams (mg) per day of the grape seed extract...another took double that dose (300 mg per day)...while the third group was given a placebo. Both groups taking grape seed extract had similar results—an average drop in systolic pressure of 12 points and in diastolic pressure of 8 points.

According to C. Tissa Kappagoda, MD, PhD, University of California, Davis director of the Coronary Heart Disease Reversal Program at the School of Medicine in Sacramento, and author of the study, laboratory experiments had previously established that grape seed extract relaxes blood vessels. Consequently, the study team is confident that this likely explains why it improves blood pressure in humans as well.

Note: The people studied belonged to a category of prehypertension (systolic blood pressure between 120 and 139 mmHg [a measure of pressure] and diastolic pressure between 80 and 89 mmHg). These people are not usually treated with medications. Instead, they are managed with lifestyle modifications (diet, exercise, stress management, etc.). Grape seed extract could be a part of such a regimen. It is not recommended for the treatment of hypertension. People with a diagnosis of hypertension should consult their physicians for appropriate treatment...and pregnant women and nursing mothers should consult their physicians for appropriate therapy.

Supplement That Lowers Hypertension Risk by 46%

Michael Hirt, MD, founding medical director, Center for Integrative Medicine, Encino-Tarzana Regional Medical Center, California and associate clinical professor, University of California, Los Angeles (UCLA). *www.drhirt.com.*

Folate, a B vitamin found in foods and also known as folic acid (the synthetic form used in supplements and fortified foods), has just earned another gold star. A study that evaluated the dietary habits of

150,000 women over an eight-year period showed that folic acid reduced their risk of developing high blood pressure.

The research, part of the ongoing Harvard Nurses' Health Study (Boston), evaluated women in two age groups—ages 43 to 70…and ages 23 to 44. Women in the younger group who consumed at least 1,000 micrograms (mcg) per day of folic acid in food and supplements had a 46% lower risk for hypertension (high blood pressure) compared with women whose daily intake was less than 200 mcg. In the older group, the risk was 18% lower. Women in both groups who consumed less than 200 mcg of folic acid in food per day but managed to increase the level to at least 800 mcg per day through supplements and foods showed a resulting decreased risk for high blood pressure of 45% in the younger group and 39% in the older group.

HOW FOLIC ACID WORKS

It's well-established that folic acid helps protect blood vessel health and that hypertension is most often a symptom of compromised vessel health. However, according to Michael Hirt, MD, medical director, Center for Integrative Medicine at Encino-Tarzana Regional Medical Center and associate clinical professor at the University of California, Los Angeles (UCLA) School of Medicine, folic acid's unique magic is in its ability to reduce dangerous *homocysteine levels.*

COPING WITH HIDDEN DANGERS

Nowhere do the study reports mention homocysteine, an amino acid in the bloodstream created by the liver. High levels of homocysteine may be related to genetic predisposition or to a deficiency in folic acid, B-12 or B-6. Homocysteine in elevated amounts damages blood vessel health and increases risk for stroke and heart attack. There are no symptoms that flag the presence of elevated homocysteine, and folic acid is the only thing that reduces homocysteine levels.

Consequently, to avoid the risks caused by elevated homocysteine levels and to lower your risk for high blood pressure, it is crucial to get plenty of folate on a regular basis. The good

news is that even if you don't want to take a supplement, folate is easily available in foods, says Dr. Hirt, especially in dark green, leafy vegetables such as spinach, kale, Swiss chard, romaine lettuce and others. It's also found in broccoli and cauliflower. Eat three or more servings a day of these. Many grain products are supplemented with folic acid, and virtually all multivitamins now contain 400 mcg of it.

Note: You should not take more than 1,000 mcg a day in supplements…however, you can eat any amount of it in foods without risk.

Men take note: Dr. Hirt says that men benefit equally from folic acid.

When you get your cholesterol checked, ask to have your homocysteine level tested as well. If you find that your level is high in spite of regular folate consumption, Dr. Hirt says this may reflect a problem with metabolizing it. Speak to a medical professional who is properly trained in nutritional supplementation about whether you need to supplement, and if so, by how much. High levels of folic acid supplementation have been linked to tumor growth, so you need proper guidance. Additionally, folic acid should be taken with B-12 and B-6 to be effective.

Prehypertension? What You Must Do Now

Adnan I. Qureshi, MD, executive director, Minnesota Stroke Initiative, University of Minnesota Medical Center, director, cerebrovascular program, Stroke Center, University of Medicine and Dentistry of New Jersey, Newark.

In May 2003, a new medical condition was born. That's when the Joint National Committee on Prevention, Detection, Evaluation, and Treatment of High Blood Pressure issued its statement that blood pressure previously considered "high normal"—falling between normal at 120/80 to the start of high at 139/89—was now an official medical condition named *prehypertension.* At the time, doctors were not certain of how much of a health risk prehypertension might be, but they knew that it was important to monitor.

DEALING WITH THE NEW NORMAL

Now a new study reveals that prehypertension dramatically increases the risk of heart attack and heart disease. An analysis of data taken over 50 years from the long-term ongoing Framingham Study (Massachusetts) showed that participants with the condition were three times more likely to have a heart attack and 1.7 times more likely to have heart disease than people with normal blood pressure. The study's lead author, Adnan I. Qureshi, MD, director of the cerebrovascular program in the Zeenat Qureshi Stroke Research Center, University of Medicine and Dentistry of New Jersey in Newark, says that this finding undoubtedly lies behind many so-called "inexplicable" heart attacks suffered by seemingly healthy people. And it focuses on the possible need for more aggressive treatment for prehypertension than the previously advised lifestyle changes alone.

PREHYPERTENSION MEETS METABOLIC SYNDROME

However, it gets more complicated. Dr. Qureshi explains that the increased risk in the study may have to do not only with just prehypertension, but with a coming together of other early risk factors as well. During the 50 years of data this study analyzed, doctors had not identified metabolic syndrome—defined as having at least three of the five known cardiovascular risk factors (obesity, elevated blood pressure, elevated triglycerides, elevated blood sugar and low high-density lipoprotein [HDL] levels). It is probable that a number of prehypertensive participants likely had other early risks included in metabolic syndrome and that the grouping of early risk factors caused the heart problems. This study suggests that all prehypertension patients discuss their particular risk profile with their doctor for an overall evaluation. Those with multiple risk factors may want to start a treatment program to normalize blood pressure as soon as possible.

Relaxation Tapes and Mozart Help to Lower Blood Pressure

Jean Tang, PhD, associate professor, College of Nursing at Seattle University, Seattle, Washington.
Robert Ostfeld, MD, cardiologist, associate professor of clinical medicine, Montefiore Medical Center, New York City.
American Heart Association's conference of the Council for High Blood Pressure Research, Atlanta.

Listening to relaxation tapes or classical music by Mozart reduces your blood pressure if you listen at least three times a week.

In a study of 41 seniors living in retirement communities, researchers found that regularly listening to relaxation tapes reduced average systolic (the top number) blood pressure readings by 9 points, while those who regularly listened to Mozart saw a 7-point reduction in their blood pressure.

"This is a simple program that's very easy to do, and blood pressure did decrease," said the study's lead author, Jean Tang, PhD, an associate professor at the College of Nursing at Seattle University in Washington. But, she added, "It won't replace medicine. It can only reduce blood pressure to a certain point—it's like making lifestyle changes."

Tang presented the findings at the American Heart Association's conference of the Council for High Blood Pressure Research, in Atlanta.

THE STUDY

Two groups of seniors were randomly assigned to listen to a 12-minute relaxation tape (which included the sound of ocean waves, instructions for breathing and relaxation exercises) or to a 12-minute Mozart sonata. Each group was asked to participate three times a week for four months.

Researchers took blood pressure readings before and after the intervention. At the end of the study, researchers asked participants to continue listening to the relaxation tape or to Mozart three times a week, if possible. Follow-up blood pressure readings were taken at one month and three months after the study.

The average blood pressure for the relaxation tape group fell from 141/73 before the beginning of the study to 132/70 four months later. For the Mozart group, the average blood pressure fell from 141/71 before the study to 134/69 after the study.

After the three-month post-study period, the researchers found that only about half of the seniors had continued listening to the relaxation tapes or to Mozart three times a week. Tang said the reduction in blood pressure only persisted for those who continued with the intervention program.

IMPLICATION

"High blood pressure is clearly a very significant and common problem. Approximately one in four people have hypertension, and about two-thirds of people with hypertension aren't adequately controlled," said cardiologist Robert Ostfeld, MD, of Montefiore Medical Center in New York City.

"This is a small, but very interesting study on a very safe and doable intervention," he added, but noted, "It's not clear if the reduction is sustained over time."

Dr. Tang said using a relaxation tape with instruction is likely a good supplementary treatment for lowering blood pressure. Eating right and exercising are also important, said both Dr. Tang and Dr. Ostfeld. "Exercise is the fountain of youth," added Dr. Ostfeld.

IMPORTANT

Both experts cautioned that relaxation exercises or listening to classical music are additional ways to help lower blood pressure, but they could not replace blood pressure medication.

Walk Away from High Blood Pressure

Janet P. Wallace, PhD, professor, department of kinesiology, Indiana University, Bloomington.

Surely everyone knows by now that regular exercise is vital in helping to prevent or control high blood pressure

(hypertension). How much and how often, though, are questions that have been the subject of speculation and more than a few studies. Now comes one from the department of kinesiology at Indiana University and Indiana University Medical Center, Bloomington, with results that surprised even the study authors.

Researchers wanted to find out which is better for reducing prehypertension—continuous physical activity, in this case walking, or walking that totaled the same amount of time but was performed in short spurts.

Prehypertension is blood pressure that runs from 120 to 139 millimeters of mercury (mmHg/systolic) over 80 to 89 millimeters of mercury (mmHg/diastolic), which are under the official level of hypertension. They discovered that 40 minutes of walking, whether in one continuous outing or in frequent spurts for shorter periods of time, reduced blood pressure by a similar amount compared with control subjects (a 5.4 to 5.6 drop in systolic pressure, and a 3.1 to 3.4 drop in diastolic pressure). However, when the group took shorter, more frequent walks (four times a day, in this study) the effect lingered for 11 hours, versus only seven hours when the group performed continuous walking.

THE 45-MINUTE RULE

The study's coauthor, Janet P. Wallace, PhD, says that both exercise groups did identical "work" (intensity)—whether it was continuous or broken up throughout the day. Participants walked at 50% of their capacity (or VO2 max, a measure of aerobic fitness), which is a moderate pace. "Brisk" walking is working at 70% of capacity, she says, but in treating blood pressure with exercise, the ideal is moderate intensity and longer duration—45 minutes is optimal and one hour is max, according to Dr. Wallace, since after an hour there is no further measured short-term benefit. (Anything over 60 minutes is affected by the law of diminishing returns...you do not get that much more out of working longer, she said).

Her advice, based on the study, is to do whatever fits best into your life—continuous or several briefer periods of activity in the day. And there's nothing magical about walking (other than how easily it can be done)...any kind of moderate intensity physical activity helps keep blood pressure down, she says. In a previous study her team discovered that even gardening and housework were helpful. The key is finding and doing activities that are easy for you to accomplish, and that you will do every day, be it 45 minutes on the treadmill at the gym or getting out of the house or the office every few hours for short walks outside.

When Your Blood Pressure Just Won't Go Down

David A. Calhoun, MD, professor of medicine in the Vascular Biology and Hypertension Program at the University of Alabama in Birmingham. He was chair of the committee that wrote *Resistant Hypertension: Diagnosis, Evaluation, and Treatment*, published in *Hypertension*.

High blood pressure (hypertension) is widely known as a "silent" disease because it increases the risk for health problems ranging from stroke and heart attack to erectile dysfunction—often without causing symptoms. For this reason, half of people with hypertension don't even seek treatment.

For most people, hypertension is defined as blood pressure of 140/90 mmHg or higher. Optimal blood pressure is lower than 120/80 mmHg. There are many who are trying to lower their blood pressure—but they are not successful. In fact, an estimated 20% to 30% of people being treated for high blood pressure are said to have resistant hypertension because their blood pressure remains high even though they are taking three or more medications simultaneously.

How to avoid—or overcome—this problem…

WHY TREATMENT MAY NOT WORK

Resistant hypertension is on the rise in the US, in part due to the dramatic increase in overweight individuals and those with diabetes and chronic kidney disease—all of which make high blood pressure harder to treat. When other health problems are diagnosed

and effectively treated, blood pressure usually drops.

Other conditions that can play a role in resistant hypertension…

•**Obstructive sleep apnea.** In one study, 83% of people with resistant hypertension suffered from sleep apnea (the airway relaxes and shuts during sleep, causing a temporary drop in oxygen).

Symptoms to watch for: Snoring, gasping for air during sleep and daytime drowsiness.

•**Aldosteronism.** This condition occurs when the adrenal glands secrete too much of the hormone aldosterone, leading to fluid retention, which raises blood pressure. Aldosteronism is much more common than previously thought—it affects about 20% of people with resistant hypertension. Potassium levels often drop as a result of aldosteronism.

Symptoms to watch for: Weakness, muscle spasms and temporary paralysis—all of which can occur with low potassium.

DRUGS THAT MAY INTERFERE

Drugs taken for other health problems can interfere with blood pressure treatment. *For example…*

•**Nonsteroidal anti-inflammatory drugs (NSAIDs)**—over-the-counter (OTC) painkillers such as *ibuprofen* (Motrin, Advil) and *naproxen* (Aleve)—often are overlooked as a factor in resistant hypertension. NSAIDs promote fluid retention. If you have trouble controlling your blood pressure, *acetaminophen* (Tylenol) often is a better choice for pain relief.

•**Decongestants and diet pills,** including OTC versions, can raise blood pressure by causing vasoconstriction (narrowing of blood vessels).

•**Stimulants and amphetamines may elevate blood pressure,** also through vasoconstriction. Such drugs—*methylphenidate* (Ritalin) and *dextroamphetamine* and *amphetamine* (Adderall), for example—are taken for attention deficit disorder.

•**Oral contraceptives may keep blood pressure high,** likely by promoting fluid retention.

LIFESTYLE CHANGES
THAT HELP

Some factors that often contribute to resistant hypertension…

•**Salt is a double threat.** A high-sodium diet not only increases blood pressure in many people, but also blunts the effectiveness of many antihypertensive drugs.

Not everyone with high blood pressure is sensitive to sodium, but nearly all people with resistant hypertension would benefit from cutting back to less than 2,300 milligrams (mg) daily.

•**Potassium in your bloodstream can become depleted if you take a diuretic (water pill).** If you develop symptoms of low potassium (described earlier), ask your doctor to check your potassium level with a blood test —and then take a potassium supplement if needed.

Otherwise, include potassium-rich foods (such as citrus fruits, bananas, dried apricots and avocados) in your diet.

Caution: Chronic kidney disease patients, who are at higher risk for hyperkalemia (abnormally high blood levels of potassium), should ask their nephrologist (kidney disease specialist) about an appropriate diet.

•**Physical activity has been shown to produce a small but significant drop in blood pressure**—4 mmHg in systolic (top number) pressure and 3 mmHg in diastolic (bottom number) pressure, on average. Exercise at least 30 minutes, most days of the week.

WHICH DRUGS ARE BEST?

Drugs work in different ways to lower blood pressure and should be tried in different combinations. For example, if an angiotensin converting enzyme (ACE) inhibitor doesn't do the job, a calcium channel blocker or diuretic, rather than another ACE inhibitor, should be added to the regimen. *Two kinds of medications that are particularly important for resistant hypertension…*

•*Thiazide* **diuretics lower blood pressure by ridding the body of excess water and salt** and also appear to increase the effectiveness of other types of blood pressure medications. If you take two or three blood pressure drugs, one should be a thiazide diuretic, such as *hydrochlorothiazide* or *chlorthalidone*.

•**Mineralocorticoid receptor antagonists,** such as *spironolactone* (Aldactone) and *eplerenone* (Inspra), have been shown to reduce blood pressure substantially when added to combinations of other drugs that haven't done the job.

Important: Even the most effective medications won't work if they stay in the bottle. If your blood pressure remains high despite treatment, make sure you take all the pills, all the time.

Smart idea: A pill-organizer box may help you adhere to your medication schedule.

DO YOU NEED A SPECIALIST?

If your blood pressure is still high after six months of treatment by your regular doctor, it may be time to see a hypertension expert. The American Society of Hypertension (ASH) maintains a directory of clinical hypertension specialists at *www.ash-us.org*. Or call the ASH at 212-696-9099. Your doctor also may know of a cardiologist or nephrologist with expertise in treating resistant hypertension.

Keep trying until you've found a treatment that works. All too often, resistant hypertension goes untreated, causing steady, silent damage for years.

New Research Reveals Inside Story on Salt

Glenn Rothfeld, MD, medical director, The Rothfeld Center for Integrative Medicine. *www.rothfeldcenter.com.*

There is no question that salt is essential to life. It regulates numerous bodily functions. However, for some people, even a little salt is sometimes too much and can damage their health. Who are these salt-sensitive people? Glenn Rothfeld, MD, medical director, The Rothfeld Center for Integrative Medicine, and a practitioner of integrative medicine who has long studied salt's role in health, provides details.

TWO TYPES OF HYPERTENSION

Salt sensitivity is when a person's blood pressure rises in response to salt intake. Although it's commonly assumed that anyone with high blood pressure (hypertension) is salt sensitive and so should greatly curtail salt intake, the data show this is not always the case. In fact, just over half of hypertensive people are salt sensitive. What about the others? Dr. Rothfeld explains that there are essentially two kinds of hypertension—one relates to volume, meaning an excess of fluid in the vessels, and the other to pressure, which reflects constriction of the blood vessels. For people who are volume sensitive, too much salt is a problem because salt can cause water retention and thus can increase the amount of fluid in the vessels. Those who have pressure-related hypertension are not as vulnerable to salt consumption problems.

OTHER PROBLEMS

But increased blood pressure alone is not the only indicator of salt sensitivity. About 26% of people with normal blood pressure are salt sensitive, making them vulnerable to possibly developing hypertension but also other health problems, as more research is showing. A National Institutes of Health (NIH) study revealed that salt sensitivity increases the risk of developing an enlargement of the heart's main pumping chamber, which compromises the chamber's proper functioning. Salt sensitivity also has been associated with kidney problems and now, says Dr. Rothfeld, it appears there is a relationship between salt sensitivity and insulin resistance as well. Our consulting medical editor Andrew L. Rubman, ND, says it is not surprising that researchers are finding a link between salt sensitivity and insulin resistance because both are regulated by hormones that are produced in the adrenal cortex.

It is important for anyone in the at-risk group to pay careful attention to salt sensitivity to protect his/her long-term health. *The following conditions, says Dr. Rothfeld, are indicators of being at risk...*

● **Having hypertension or a family history of it.**

● **Being obese.**

● **Having additional indicators of metabolic syndrome** (a cluster of findings that put people at elevated cardiovascular risk if they have three or more) such as high LDL cholesterol, an elevated C-reactive protein level, elevated triglycerides and insulin resistance.

● **Women with polycystic ovary disease** (ovarian cysts).

● **Being age 55 or older.**

● **Being African American.**

TESTING FOR SENSITIVITY

A definitive test for salt sensitivity, unfortunately, does not exist right now, although researchers at the University of Virginia are developing a genetic study for the condition that promises to have 94% accuracy. However, a simple blood test gives information about a person's *renin angiotensin-aldosterone system*, a hormone system that helps regulate blood pressure and blood volume, with results that suggest the type of hypertension the person has. The test is a good indicator of the presence of salt sensitivity as well, says Dr. Rothfeld.

It's also possible to do a two-week trial at home, although you will have to have a blood pressure measuring device. (Electronic ones are available at drugstores for about $70.) For two weeks, do not consume more than 2 grams (g) of salt a day (2,000 milligrams, or mg). Dr. Rothfeld says that some people notice a difference in just a few days because they lose puffiness, but the real measure is changes in blood pressure. If you have a five- to 10-point drop in the systolic reading (the higher one) at the end of the two-week period, it's highly likely you are salt sensitive.

SALT-REDUCTION STRATEGIES

Without question, our salt-saturated food culture leads people to consume far more salt than they need for health, even as much as 20,000 mg a day. If you are salt sensitive, restrict salt to 1,500 mg a day or less. This becomes much easier to accomplish by avoiding processed foods (including canned foods). Salt serves as a flavor enhancer and preservative in processed food, which in turn is the principal source of salt in the American diet. In fact, only about 10% of salt consumption comes from table salt.

Cheeses are often another culprit. Soft cheese in particular is high in sodium.

CALCIUM-MAGNESIUM-POTASSIUM BALANCERS

In addition to reducing salt, ensuring the adequate levels and balance of three minerals is crucial to addressing salt sensitivity, says Dr. Rothfeld. The three are potassium, calcium and magnesium. Imbalances in sodium can be caused by mineral deficiencies. Dr. Rothfeld recommends consuming 3,500 mg of potassium …800 mg to 1,000 mg of calcium—with 1,200 mg to 1,500 mg for post-menopausal women …and 500 mg to 800 mg of magnesium each day in addition to moderating salt intake.

Note: While it is safe to use supplements to ensure adequate levels of calcium and magnesium, it is not recommended to supplement potassium without a doctor's supervision. Excessive levels of potassium can be fatal. It is better to get your potassium through food. A list of potassium-rich foods can be found at *www.vaughns-1-pagers.com/food/potassium-foods.htm.*

Finding the Hidden Salt in Your Diet

Suzanne Havala Hobbs, DrPH, RD, author of *Get the Trans Fat Out* (Three Rivers). She is clinical associate professor and director, Doctoral Program in Health Leadership, Department of Health Policy and Management, School of Public Health, University of North Carolina at Chapel Hill.

The US Food and Drug Administration (FDA) has made it mandatory to include information about trans fat on food labels, and recently experts have taken aim at another dietary ingredient. The American Medical Association (AMA) has called for new label-

ing about the salt content in foods. However, while there's nothing good to say about trans fat, it's a different story with sodium. Simply put, it is essential to our health. It's just not healthy in the high quantities in which it appears in processed foods ranging from bread and cereal to canned soup, frozen snacks and prepared meals, and macaroni and cheese.

Suzanne Havala Hobbs, DrPH, RD—the author of *Get the Trans Fat Out* (Three Rivers), a doctor of public health and clinical associate professor at the School of Public Health at the University of North Carolina at Chapel Hill—provides insight. She says it's time to work on federal food policies that will support each American's efforts to cut down on sodium intake.

HIDDEN SODIUM IN PROCESSED FOODS

Reading labels is a good idea, especially for people who are salt-sensitive (individuals with high blood pressure that elevates or decreases with sodium intake or reduction) and must closely monitor their intake. Some people are more greatly affected by higher sodium intakes than others, but none of us need the extreme levels found in most processed foods, observes Dr. Havala Hobbs. However, reading all the labels in the world cannot protect your health if you continue to eat a diet high in processed foods and low in whole foods like fresh fruits and vegetables.

A BEHIND-THE-SCENES LOOK AT SALT REGULATION

Dr. Havala Hobbs shares some behind-the-scenes information about how salt is regulated. While the US government's Dietary Guidelines Advisory Committee discussed the Institute of Medicine's national sodium recommendation of 1,500 milligrams per day, the committee recommended a daily sodium level of less than 2,300 milligrams. Some experts speculate that it is because the food industry lobbied heavily against the lower level, arguing that salt is such an integral part of the food production system, used as a flavor enhancer, for texture, and as a preservative. The food industry also called the lower sodium level an unrealistic goal and suggested that the government not base its sodium recommendations on the 25% of population that is salt sensitive.

The government seemed to adopt the industry's position. The new salt guideline doesn't tell you what's really best for your health, says Dr. Havala Hobbs. Instead, it tells you what the government thinks is doable. Many people would likely benefit from reducing sodium intake considerably, and the sodium that naturally occurs in whole, unprocessed foods provides all the sodium we need, says Dr. Havala Hobbs.

GETTING THE SALT OUT

When it comes to sodium intake, the danger lies not so much in the salt shaker as in the hidden quantities of salt in processed foods. As a result, your best bet is to limit processed foods to the absolute minimum. For instance, sodium in canned beans, added as a preservative, can be easily rinsed away by placing beans in a colander and rinsing in running water, says Dr. Havala Hobbs. Unfortunately, there's often no practical way to remove excess sodium cooked into most processed food.

The take-home message is to spend the majority of your time in the outer aisles of supermarkets, where most whole foods, from fresh produce to meats and fish, are stocked.

The best recipe: Prepare more meals at home, using as many fresh ingredients as possible, and make foods in their natural state as large a part of your diet as you can, recommends Dr. Havala Hobbs. The greater the degree of processing and convenience of the prepared food, the lower the nutrient value and the greater the likelihood that the food is a health risk.

See Your Chiropractor for Lower Blood Pressure

George Bakris, MD, director, Hypertension Center, and professor of medicine, University of Chicago.

Lots of people consider a chiropractor vital to their good health, but few would consider seeing one for treatment to lower blood pressure. So it was a real surprise when a new study from the University of Chicago's Medical Center demonstrated that a specific type of chiropractic manipulation of the first vertebra (Atlas) of the neck can do exactly that. The pilot study included 50 people with stage 1 high blood pressure—25 of them had an adjustment to this vertebra…while the 25 controls had a sham adjustment.

Results: Compared with the control group, those with the Atlas adjustment had, on average, a drop of 14 points in systolic (the upper) pressure and eight in the diastolic (lower) reading. Study authors concluded that the results were similar to the effectiveness of treatment with two blood pressure medications in combination.

MORE EVIDENCE

Study author George Bakris, MD, director of the Hypertension Center at the University of Chicago, said he'd heard about this particular treatment from a doctor in family practice who told him about patients who'd had the manipulation and significantly lowered their blood pressure. The adjustment had been to correct a very slight misalignment in the Atlas vertebra, which sits at the top of the spine and relies on muscle and ligaments for alignment. Their misalignments typically were the result of a head or neck injury at some point in their life—including some from long ago—such as falling off a bike, a sports injury or car accident. Dr. Bakris speculates that the resulting misalignment had likely created a kink or kinks in blood vessels in the area of the lower brain stem, either impeding blood flow to the brain or abrupting up against a particular area of the brain stem, changing the autonomic nervous system in ways affecting blood pressure. At the end of six months, 88% were still corrected without follow-up treatment.

BEFORE YOU GO TO THE CHIROPRACTOR

Not everyone with high blood pressure is a candidate for an Atlas manipulation and not every chiropractor is qualified to do such manipulation. It may work for people with high blood pressure who have Atlas misalignment but that should be verified with imaging studies.

There is now a large-scale study to validate the evaluation of Atlas misalignment so that it will have broader use in clinical practice. It is important to note that at this time the observations regarding changes in blood pressure need to be confirmed and should not be used routinely for this purpose.

FIND THE RIGHT PRACTITIONER

Moreover, not only does the technique work only for a select population, but by no means are all (or even most) chiropractors able to perform this manipulation. Because it can be dangerous if improperly performed, it requires specific training and experience from a chiropractor associated with the National Upper Cervical Chiropractic Association (*www. nucca.org*).

Intriguing as this discovery is, Dr. Bakris says that for the moment, it is best to adopt a wait-and-see attitude. These single-center observations need to be confirmed with larger multicenter studies before a general recommendation for treatment can be made. To that end, two larger scale trials are being proposed to the National Institutes of Health, which is supportive of this work going forward.

Naturopaths—Today's Healing Experts

Jane Guiltinan, ND, past president of the American Association of Naturopathic Physicians. She is a clinical professor at the Bastyr Center for Natural Health, Seattle, Washington.

In North America, there are five naturopathic medicine programs currently accredited by the Council on Naturopathic Medical Education (CNME), and one naturopathic program that is a candidate for accreditation by the CNME. Candidates for admission to these programs must earn a baccalaureate degree (or equivalent) prior to admission, including standard premed training. The naturopathic doctor (ND) degree is a doctoral degree and typically takes four years to complete, just like an MD.

There are many similarities between the naturopathic and conventional medical school curriculum. The first two years of both curricula involve basic science courses—anatomy, pathology, physiology, biochemistry, and other Western medical sciences. In addition, naturopathic philosophy courses expose students to the concepts and principles and practices of natural medicine, says Jane Guiltinan, ND, past president of the American Association of Naturopathic Physicians. These include nutrition, homeopathy, botanical medicine, acupuncture and a variety of mind-body approaches.

During the third and fourth years, there's a mix of classroom courses such as gynecology, pediatrics and rheumatology, plus 1,200 hours or so of clinical training under the supervision of licensed naturopathic physicians. In this phase of training, naturopathy students observe and help manage patients in an outpatient setting.

THE NATUROPATH'S ROLE

Think of the ND as the equivalent of a family practice physician, says Dr. Guiltinan. Naturopaths provide excellent primary health care for individuals and families. Like the conventional general practitioner with an MD, an ND will assess your health and direct your treatment, either by treating you directly or by referral to mainstream or other natural care specialists such as chiropractors, acupuncturists, nutritionists or specialists in homeopathy, to name a few.

In Dr. Guiltinan's view, conventional physicians and naturopaths are most effective at different points in the spectrum of the healthcare system. "At one end of the spectrum is crisis medicine," she says "and it's here where I think conventional medicine is excellent. Emergency care intervention, trauma care, serious infections—this is where conventional medicine excels.

OUTSIDE THE BOX

"Where I think conventional medicine has not done its most effective work is in chronic disease management and in conditions that don't really fit into a clear medical box—chronic fatigue syndrome, for example, fibromyalgia or depression," says Dr. Guiltinan. With these types of conditions, the conventional, technological or pharmaceutical approach is not always effective as it focuses on symptom suppression, rather than finding the underlying causes and addressing these to support healing and the creation of health and wellness. This is where naturopathic physicians can play an important role."

THE ND OFFICE VISIT: WHAT TO EXPECT

What is different about a visit to an ND? At your initial visit you'll be asked about your health history and receive a physical exam that is similar to the physical at a conventional medical office. And like a conventional MD, an ND may order lab tests or diagnostic imaging tests. So, what's different?

"You'll find much more in-depth questioning about your current lifestyle," says Dr. Guiltinan. Naturopaths ask about your diet—at minimum they will ask you to describe it but more likely you'll be asked to complete a diet diary, detailing your food intake for a week or so. "We're also very interested in finding out if you exercise or not, and what your mental and emotional state is," she adds.

PHILOSOPHY AND TREATMENT

Dr. Guiltinan says that extensive questioning is necessary to get to the underlying issues around a health problem and address them, rather than just addressing the presenting symptoms of a problem.

Because naturopaths believe that the human body has an incredibly powerful ability to heal itself if given the chance, she says, one principle is to take a look at what the "obstacles to cure" are in an individual patients' life. What are obstacles to cure?

Sometimes it's genetics, which we can do little about, but some obstacles can be removed (for example, eating poorly, being too stressed out with work, exposure to environmental toxins, lack of exercise). If you can add support in the form of a good diet, proper exercise and stress reduction to promote the healing responses of the body, then you can further capitalize on the body's ability to heal.

WHAT TO EXPECT

In naturopathic medicine, most treatment plans, regardless of the condition, begin with diet modifications. In addition, supplements (vitamins and minerals) may be prescribed. In some cases, NDs will do the nutritional coun-

seling themselves. In others, patients may be referred on to a nutrition specialist.

Other common treatment modalities are homeopathy, botanical medicine, physical medicine and acupuncture and mind/body therapies. Again, depending on the patient's needs, the ND may provide treatment or refer the patient on to a specialist. Dr. Guiltinan says a big part of her naturopathic practice is preparing patients to make the little and big lifestyle changes that will impact their health.

HOW CAN I FIND A NATUROPATH IN MY AREA?

To find a qualified, licensed ND in your area, visit the American Association of Naturopathic Physicians Web site, *www.naturopathic.org* and click "Find a Doctor."

When "Good" Cholesterol Isn't So Good

Steven R. Jones, MD, an assistant professor of medicine and cardiology at Johns Hopkins University and director of inpatient cardiology at Johns Hopkins Hospital, both in Baltimore. He has presented several scientific papers on lipid research and is coauthor of a recent article in the *American Journal of Cardiology*.

For years, we've heard about two forms of cholesterol—the "bad" low-density lipoprotein (LDL) and the "good" high-density lipoprotein (HDL). Higher levels of HDL cholesterol—50 mg/dL or above—are considered desirable because this form of cholesterol has long been associated with the cleanup of lipids (blood fats) from the arteries.

New thinking: HDL cholesterol readings that appear on blood tests may not always be a good indicator of a person's heart disease risk after all. In fact, some people with lower HDL cholesterol actually can be at lower risk than those with very high HDL numbers.

Why is this so? Most people don't realize that unwanted cholesterol is removed from the arteries through a process known as reverse cholesterol transport.

Cutting-edge research: The HDL that is measured on standard cholesterol tests does not necessarily indicate the efficiency of the reverse transport mechanism, researchers now are discovering. This means that some people with very high HDL, for example, could have inefficient disposal of unwanted cholesterol.

Result: Excess lipids remaining in the arteries and an increased risk for heart disease.

Bottom line: High HDL generally confers protection—but only when it accompanies a robust transport mechanism.

IDENTIFYING HEART DISEASE RISK WITH GREATER ACCURACY

Routine cholesterol testing remains the mainstay of heart disease risk assessment, along with consideration of known cardiovascular risk factors, such as smoking, high blood pressure, family history and diet. Combined, these conventional risk factors identify most patients who are at risk for heart and vascular diseases.

Problem: About half of all heart attacks occur in people with so-called normal cholesterol levels.

Solution: There now are additional cholesterol tests that measure different types of LDL and HDL cholesterol, which may identify some people at risk for heart disease who are missed by conventional cholesterol testing and risk-factor assessment. These blood tests, which typically are covered by insurance, may give a more accurate assessment of your heart disease risk, when combined with standard measures.

You may want to ask your doctor about getting advanced tests, such as…

• **Lp(a).** Lipoprotein (a) is a small cholesterol particle that readily penetrates the artery wall, accelerating plaque formation. Lp(a) is associated with increased heart attack risk in most people.

• **Markers of abnormal LDL particle size,** density or number. Tests measuring these markers can help assess cardiovascular disease risk. For some patients, measurement of apolipoprotein B (another lipoprotein) levels may better represent the number of particles that cause atherosclerosis (fatty buildup in the arteries).

LOWERING YOUR RISK

Although it's important to know your cholesterol levels, lifestyle changes and other strategies are crucial for reducing heart disease risk. *They include…*

• **A Mediterranean-style diet,** which emphasizes fruits, vegetables, fish, whole grains and the use of olive oil as the main vegetable fat—and includes only small amounts of meat and saturated fats—is associated with very low cardiovascular disease risk.

• **Regular exercise** can increase HDL by up to 10%—and the weight loss that accompanies exercise can produce an additional 20% to 30% increase.

• **Omega-3 fatty acids,** taken either by prescription or as high-dose fish oil, can lower triglycerides (a type of blood fat) by about 40%. This treatment often is combined with other lipid-lowering drugs under the care of a physician.

• **Statin drugs,** such as *simvastatin* (Zocor), *lovastatin* (Mevacor) and *atorvastatin* (Lipitor), which work primarily by lowering LDL cholesterol as well as inflammation, are among the most effective ways to lower cardiovascular risk. In general, every 1% reduction in LDL reduces the risk for heart attack by 1%.

• **Niacin.** Nicotinic acid, a form of niacin, has long been known to raise HDL by up to 30%.

But the real benefit of niacin now is thought to be due to improvements in reverse transport and its additional ability to lower levels of triglycerides and LDL. Niacin also makes LDL particles less toxic to the arteries by favorably changing the chemical properties of LDL and HDL—and is used to lower Lp(a) levels.

Caution: Because improper use of niacin can cause serious liver damage, it should be taken only in prescription form under a doctor's supervision.

THE ROLE OF LDL

Even though lipids (blood fats) are generally perceived as harmful, they play an essential role in cellular functions.

Here's how: Cholesterol and triglycerides (a type of blood fat) are transported by lipoproteins (complex particles consisting of proteins and lipids) to the body's tissues, where they reinforce cell membranes and aid in the synthesis of hormones and other substances. However, once these useful lipids are stripped away from the transporting lipoproteins, the leftover portion is known as low-density lipoprotein (LDL)—and it can be harmful. LDL cholesterol can accumulate in artery walls and initiate changes that can lead to heart disease.*

*LDL cholesterol levels of 100–129 mg/dL are generally considered optimal for healthy adults…below 100 mg/dL is typically recommended for people at risk for heart disease (due to such factors as smoking and high blood pressure).

Improve Cholesterol With a High-Protein Plant-Based Diet

An Atkins-style plant-focused diet can improve cholesterol while helping people lose weight. The high-protein Atkins diet emphasizes meat, so it may not lower levels of LDL (bad) cholesterol.

But: A high-protein diet focusing on soy, gluten and nuts—as well as cereals, vegetables and fruits—led both to weight loss and to improvements in LDL cholesterol and blood pressure.

Study by researchers at various hospitals and universities in Canada and the US, published in *Archives of Internal Medicine*.

Three Ways to Control Cholesterol Naturally

Andrew L. Rubman, ND, consulting medical editor for *Bottom Line's Daily Health News* and director of the Southbury Clinic for Traditional Medicines in Southbury, Connecticut.

We spend an inordinate amount of time talking about how to raise good cholesterol and lower bad cholesterol. The body actually needs both kinds, and it's the balance between the two that is most important. Andrew L. Rubman, ND, recently

described how the media, along with all those "cholesterol lowering" drug manufacturers, are delivering the wrong message.

BALANCE THEORY OF CHOLESTEROL MANAGEMENT

"Cholesterol is necessary for life," says Dr. Rubman, "ergo it can't really be 'bad.'" It only causes trouble when it gets out of proportion, with too much low-density lipoprotein (LDL) and too little high-density lipoprotein (HDL) relative to each other. When it comes to the total cholesterol/HDL ratio, the American Heart Association recommends a ratio of less than 5:1, optimally, 3.5:1. Dr. Rubman says the ratio is more useful than a fixed target number that people are prone to strive for. "The real focus with cholesterol is—or ought to be—how to manage it better," he notes. In order to accomplish that, we need to understand what cholesterol is and what it does.

PROTEIN BUILDING BLOCKS

What we commonly call "cholesterol"—both the "bad" (low-density lipoprotein or LDL) and the "good" (high-density lipoprotein or HDL)—is actually a little container of protein and fat synthesized together by the liver. These help your body produce cell membranes, create estrogen, testosterone and other vital hormones.

Ideally, the body should naturally balance HDL and LDL when properly nourished. But that doesn't often happen in modern times on modern diets. Since the body works with whatever elements it has on hand to produce HDL and LDL, a first step to achieving balance is to eat and digest the right forms of protein.

What kind of protein should you eat? "High-quality, minimally processed food," says Dr. Rubman, suggesting you strive to include one "good high-value protein" at every meal. Dr. Rubman's favorite sources of protein include lean organic chicken or beef, and wild, deep-water fish, as well as beans and other legumes.

ABSORBING THE PROTEIN

Equally important (and less often understood) is that we need to make sure the protein is adequately digested and absorbed. "There's a huge digestive link to the whole issue of cholesterol," Dr. Rubman says. The digestion process starts in your mouth. When you chew, the action triggers the production of saliva, which contains enzymes that start to break down your food. So the more you chew your food, the more you help the digestion process. Proper chewing can actually influence how much cholesterol your body will absorb and then synthesize. Depending on what's on your fork, aim for 30 or more chews per bite to insure optimal digestion.

Similarly, having adequate amounts of stomach acid will help ensure complete digestion of your proteins. This means that older people and regular users of acid-suppressing medications—both over-the-counter (OTC) and prescription—may be inhibiting their body's ability to fully digest protein.

B VITAMINS, GARLIC AND FIBER

In order to manufacture cholesterol optimally, the liver also needs B vitamins, Dr. Rubman explains. For his patients, he prescribes a good, high-potency B complex vitamin to be taken at least twice daily, and often a separate vitamin B-12. Second, he advises regularly eating dark green, cruciferous foods (one serving daily is ideal) like Brussels sprouts, broccoli and kale.

Garlic can also be helpful in balancing cholesterol. Even in the mainstream medical community, garlic is understood to be an agent for lowering LDL cholesterol, while some research has shown it to actually raise HDL as well. Garlic supplements are usually unnecessary, says Dr. Rubman. "For most people, cooking regularly with garlic is adequate and helpful."

Finally Dr. Rubman recommends fiber: "Many types of soluble fiber can bind cholesterol and carry it out of the body with the bowel movement," he explains. This is how the body eliminates excess cholesterol. He often prescribes supplemental *glucomannan* (Konjac fiber), taken a half hour before the largest meal of the day with a large glass of water.

One last recommendation from Dr. Rubman on achieving cholesterol balance—exercise. It increases the metabolic use of lipids, enabling your liver to make more high-density lipoproteins (HDL).

Are Cholesterol Guidelines Too High?

Current cholesterol guidelines may be too high, reports Gregg C. Fonarow, MD. The current target for LDL (bad) cholesterol among people without cardiovascular disease or diabetes is 130 mg/dL.

However: In a recent study, 72% of patients admitted to hospitals because of coronary artery disease had LDL levels below 130 mg/dL.

Better: Research shows that LDL levels of 50 mg/dL to 60 mg/dL cut heart attack and stroke risk dramatically.

Gregg C. Fonarow, MD, director of the Ahmanson-UCLA Cardiomyopathy Center and associate chief, division of cardiology, David Geffen School of Medicine, University of California, Los Angeles. He is coleader of a study of 136,905 people, published in *American Heart Journal*.

Forget Statins—Here's The Best and Safest Cholesterol Reducer

Sonja Pettersen, NMD, naturopathic medical doctor, Scottsdale, Arizona. She is licensed to practice primary care medicine specializing in natural therapeutics.

Although it is important to keep cholesterol at a healthful ratio of total cholesterol to HDL (4 or under is ideal), all the focus on low-low cholesterol is not necessarily a good thing. You could keep cholesterol in check with the pop of a statin pill and consider the problem solved. Or, you could avoid the risk of side effects from statins, and instead go the natural route—red yeast rice… blueberries…or plant *sterols*. Plant sterols—and their cousins, plant *stanols*—are compounds that occur naturally in many fruits, vegetables, nuts, seeds, cereals, legumes, vegetable oils and other plant sources, and are both cheaper and safer than statins.

RESEARCH ABOUNDS

There's a considerable amount of research showing that plant sterols can lower cholesterol quite effectively. A study in the *European Journal of Clinical Nutrition* has shown that 2 grams (g) of plant sterols taken daily resulted in a 6.5% reduction in total cholesterol. In another study, 1.8 g taken daily, coupled with a fiber called *glucomannan* lowered total cholesterol. A third study in the *American Journal of Clinical Nutrition* got similar results. And an article in the *British Medical Journal* concluded that if 2 g a day of plant sterols (or stanols) were added to the diet, there would be a reduction in the risk of heart disease of about 25%, "larger than the effect that could be expected to be achieved by reducing…intake of saturated fat."

IT'S OFFICIAL

The cholesterol-lowering effects of plant sterols have been known for some time. The US Food and Drug Administration (FDA) has already authorized a coronary heart disease health claim for plant sterols and plant stanols. According to the "Talk Paper" released by the FDA to the press, this ruling was based on the FDA's conclusion that plant sterols "may reduce the risk of cardiovascular disease by lowering blood cholesterol levels."

GETTING YOUR STEROLS

Plant sterols can be incorporated into the diet by eating lots of plant foods. Vegetable oils including safflower, soybean and olive also are a good source, but be sure to buy cold-pressed—organic if possible—and balance your vegetable oil intake with nut oils and fish oil. Some margarines (such as Benecol) tout their cholesterol-lowering properties largely due to the addition of plant sterols. The best sources remain fruits and vegetables …however, supplements based on plant sterols also are becoming widely available (for example, CholestaPRO, CholestOff and Lipid-Shield).

Some top sources of sterols include…

- Rice bran oil
- Corn oil
- Sesame seeds
- Safflower oil
- Soybean oil
- Olive oil
- Peanuts
- Italian salad dressing
- Garbanzo beans
- Bananas
- Carrots
- Tomatoes

By keeping your cholesterol in check with plant sterols you will also reap additional benefits. According to Sonja Pettersen, NMD, based in Arizona, "Plant foods—and the compounds they contain—improve immune function, have anticancer properties and seem to be helpful in a wide variety of health conditions, from eczema to chronic fatigue."

Try Niacin to Curb Cardiovascular Disease

Niacin is an alternative to statins for fighting cardiovascular disease, reports Michael Traub, ND. Extended-release tablets of the B vitamin niacin are more effective than statin drugs for increasing HDL (good) cholesterol and decreasing harmful triglycerides (blood fats). Niacin also reduces LDL (bad) cholesterol—but less so than statins.

Recommended dosage: 1,500 mg to 3,000 mg daily. Consult your physician before use.

Caution: Like statins, niacin can affect liver function. People using it should have their liver enzymes monitored.

Michael Traub, ND, director of Lokahi Health Center, Kailua Kona, Hawaii, and past president of the American Association of Naturopathic Physicians. *www.michaeltraubnd.com.*

Beyond Cholesterol— Lowering Triglycerides For Better Health

Helene Glassberg, MD, assistant professor of cardio-vascular medicine, University of Pennsylvania Health System, Philadelphia.

Mark A. Stengler, NMD, naturopathic medical doctor in private practice, Encinitas, California…adjunct associate clinical professor at the National College of Natural Medicine, Portland, Oregon…author of *The Natural Physician's Healing Therapies* (Bottom Line Books).

The medical mantra for people age 50 or over is to "know your numbers," which is to say, your cholesterol, blood pressure and blood sugar levels as they relate to cardiac risk, so that you can take action to address potential problems. While many people pay attention to this advice, and because there is enduring truth to this medical sound bite, it is important to mention that there is one number that eludes even the savviest health consumers…it is tested right along with cholesterol and blood sugar and is becoming increasingly respected as a marker for cardiac risk—triglycerides.

A TRIGLYCERIDES PRIMER

Like cholesterol, triglycerides are a type of fat in the blood, but they are quite different from their more famous cousin. Triglycerides are produced by the body and ingested through food, as is cholesterol, but they serve a different purpose. If the body's energy needs are exceeded by food intake, the body converts the excess calories into triglycerides and stores them to provide extra energy when called for.

However, for a variety of reasons, triglycerides can rise to unhealthy levels in the blood, sometimes along with a rise in cholesterol, sometimes independently of that. Normal fasting levels of triglycerides are less than 150 milligrams per deciliter (mg/dL) and when triglycerides rise to a fasting level of 200 mg/dL or over it's considered high. Occasionally levels go to even 500 mg/dL or higher, though this is usually because of genetic disorders or an underlying disease.

A good deal of controversy exists about the exact role of high triglycerides and atherosclerosis, but there is definitely an association between high levels of them and heart disease. People who have triglycerides over 150 mg/dL and HDL cholesterol under 40 mg/dL, have a higher risk for heart disease. And high triglycerides are also associated with a number of other diseases as well.

HIGH LEVELS AND DISEASE

Helene Glassberg, MD, assistant professor of cardiovascular medicine at the University of Pennsylvania Health System in Philadelphia, says that high triglycerides are especially associated with insulin resistance—a prediabetic state—and diabetes, in particular when it is poorly controlled. In fact, high levels of triglycerides signal the need to check for the presence of diabetes. Other problems that are sometimes associated with high levels are hypothyroidism or kidney disease. Pancreatitis is also associated with high triglycerides, which Dr. Glassberg says can exacerbate or even cause this disease.

LOWERING YOUR TRIGLYCERIDES

The good news is that this is one problem that lifestyle changes can often turn around. *Dr. Glassberg recommends…*

• **Normalize your weight**—obesity is a risk factor for elevated levels, especially if you carry excess abdominal weight.

• **Reduce or eliminate alcohol**—excessive drinking has been directly associated with elevated triglycerides…in some people even modest amounts of alcohol can affect the level.

• **Eat a nutritious diet**—pay special attention to getting plenty of omega-3s and eliminate excess carbohydrates, saturated fat and all trans fat.

• **Exercise at least 30 minutes each day**—push away from the table before dessert and go for a walk instead.

• **Avoid smoking.**

When lifestyle changes are not enough to lower levels sufficiently, Dr. Glassberg says that there are excellent medications patients can take that address the problem in addition to lifestyle changes. Of course, pharmaceutical treatments often come with associated risks of their own.

THE NATURAL APPROACH

There are also supplements that can manage triglycerides. Mark Stengler, ND, naturopathic physician in private practice in Encinitas, California, advises all individuals with high triglycerides to talk with a trained professional first. His favorites include aged garlic extract (AGE)—the most commonly available brand is Kyolic—with the caveat that people on blood-thinning medications clear it with their doctor first. Those on the muscle-relaxant drug *chlorzoxazone* or the antiplatelet drug *ticlopidine* must not take garlic supplements. Pantethine has also been shown to lower triglycerides.

Dr. Stengler adds his advice to Dr. Glassberg's in emphasizing how important it is to treat insulin resistance and diabetes, since triglycerides tend to be high in these people. In addition to a careful diet and regular exercise, Dr. Stengler suggests taking chromium picolinate, which research has shown may lower triglyceride levels significantly. And to end on a tasty note, a recent study in Norway showed that eating two or three kiwi fruits each day lowered triglyceride levels by as much as 15%.

Lower Your Risk of Stroke 26%

J. David Spence, MD, director, Stroke Prevention and Atherosclerosis Research Centre, Robarts Research Institute in London, Ontario, Canada, and author of *How to Prevent Your Stroke* (Vanderbilt University).

Research is moving steadily forward on the challenge of rehabilitation after stroke—but it is much better to avoid a stroke altogether. Information on this has emerged from a report prepared at St. George's University in London. The report evaluated data from eight previous studies that tracked a total of 257,551 subjects for an average of 13 years.

The finding: People who ate three to five servings of fruits and vegetables each day had an 11% decreased risk for stroke. People who ate more than five servings each day had a 26% decreased risk.

J. David Spence, MD, director of the Stroke Prevention and Atherosclerosis Research Centre at the Robarts Research Institute in London, Ontario, notes that there are several important factors about fruits and vegetables as they relate to stroke prevention. First, eating a bounty of produce provides a high level of potassium—critical for regulating blood pressure as well as nerve and muscle activity—along with the numerous other important vitamins and minerals, especially calcium, magnesium and antioxidants. Dr. Spence reminds people to eat a variety of colored fruits and vegetables because the colors represent different antioxidants. As he says, Mother Nature is much better at combining antioxidants than any supplement could ever be. Various types of produce provide soluble fiber—part of what the body needs to properly manage cholesterol.

HEALTHFUL SUBSTITUTES

There is yet another consideration that Dr. Spence calls "the substitution issue." He points out that when you're eating five or more servings of fruits and vegetables each day, you are hopefully replacing fried and processed foods, trans fats and the like. Based on numerous studies, Dr. Spence recommends a Mediterranean diet, specifically from the Greek island of Crete. It includes olive oil, fish, beans and whole grains and, of course, lots of fresh fruits and vegetables. In fact, it's worth noting that in Crete people heap their plates with salad at lunch and dinner.

Treat Gums to Ease Arthritis

Patients with rheumatoid arthritis and gum disease had tartar beneath gums scraped away so that gums could heal. After six weeks, patients had significantly less joint pain, stiffness and swelling. Patients whose gums were not treated did not improve. Reducing oral bacteria may ease inflammation elsewhere. See your dentist if gums bleed—and especially if joints ache, too.

Nabil Bissada, DDS, chair, department of periodontics, Case Western Reserve University School of Dental Medicine, Cleveland, and leader of a study of 40 people.

Surprising Symptoms Caused by Too Much Bread

Andrew L. Rubman, ND, consulting medical editor for *Bottom Line's Daily Health News* and director of the Southbury Clinic for Traditional Medicines in Southbury, Connecticut.

National Digestive Diseases Information Clearinghouse, *http://digestive.niddk.nih.gov.*

I t's often hard to pin down just what's causing common gastrointestinal complaints such as gas, bloating, diarrhea or abdominal pain. Add to that some fatigue and a vague sense of not feeling quite right, and what do you have? Possibly gluten intolerance—an intolerance of a protein (gluten) in wheat, barley and rye, suggests Andrew L. Rubman, ND. A degree of gluten intolerance is common in the population and frequently under-diagnosed, he says.

GLUTEN SENSITIVITY RANGES FROM MILD TO SEVERE

Gluten intolerance is an autoimmune condition encompassing a variety of symptoms. In people with this condition, gluten causes some degree of change in the mucosal tissue lining the small intestine, says Dr. Rubman. When the severity of gluten intolerance progresses beyond a certain point of frequency, duration and intensity, it is called celiac disease.

Celiac disease affects one in 133 Americans, damaging their small intestine and causing lasting problems with nutrient absorption. Other reactions that may be associated with gluten intolerance include discomfort that is mild and fleeting, such as cramps or a feeling of uncomfortable fullness...sudden mid-meal bloat...chronic diarrhea. When people go to the doctor complaining of these problems—especially those on the milder end of the spectrum—it may be very difficult to diagnose the cause, since mild gluten sensitivities don't always show up on blood tests. Physicians may explain the symptoms away as a by-product of the passing years, anxiety or hereditary digestive difficulties. Typically medications are prescribed, including over-the-counter (OTC) remedies for gas or diarrhea—so the problem gets mistreated, and the cycle continues, usually getting worse.

INTESTINAL AND OTHER SYMPTOMS

Possible intestinal symptoms of gluten intolerance: Abdominal pain...bloating...gas ...diarrhea...constipation...changes in appetite ...nausea...vomiting...lactose intolerance... unexplained weight loss...and bloody, fatty or foul-smelling stools. As the problem persists, these symptoms may become chronic.

Possible nonintestinal symptoms include: Fatigue...depression...irritability...bone and joint pain...and behavioral changes. There may be skin problems, such as dermatitis herpetiformis, causing unattractive, uncomfortable rashes and water blister eruptions. Some hair loss is another possibility. Some suspect wheat proteins may be involved in degenerative diseases like MS, just as diet also plays a role in other autoimmune diseases such as diabetes. Many sufferers experience a sudden realization that the discomfort they've been living with is not necessarily "normal," leading them to look for the cause of their misery.

GOING AGAINST THE GRAIN

People diagnosed with celiac disease must maintain a gluten-free diet for the rest of their lives to allow the small intestine to heal and continue to function efficiently. For those with a mild form of gluten intolerance, total abstention isn't necessary, but moderating your intake is, says Dr. Rubman. People with mild gluten intolerance also suffer intestinal damage to a certain degree, and often times reducing gluten, rather than eliminating it, may be protective enough. However, this needs to be closely monitored by a physician.

Admittedly, this is easier said than done, since foods that contain gluten are all around us—in products such as bread, cereal, pasta, pizza, cookies, cakes and pies. Even more insidious is the fact that many processed foods—such as cold cuts, soy sauce, salad dressings, frozen yogurt and licorice—may also contain gluten. As yet, food labels are not required to identify gluten content, but the rules are being reconsidered. The US Food and Drug Administration (FDA) and the Codex Alimantarius, the international body responsible for setting food safety standards, are both proposing to standardize the definition of "gluten-free" for use on food labels. For now, a consumer's best bet may be to look for products that are specifically marked as "gluten-free." Gluten is also found in some medications (as an additive), so people should ask their pharmacist about any medications they are taking as well.

WHAT YOU CAN DO

If you frequently experience uncomfortable symptoms such as stomach upset, gas, irritability and fatigue, consider that the cause may be gluten intolerance. Stop eating all foods that contain wheat, barley, rye and oats for 10 days, advises Dr. Rubman. Instead, choose naturally gluten-free alternatives such as potatoes or rice, or grains such as amaranth, buckwheat and quinoa. Additionally, make it a point to consume more whole, fresh foods and fewer processed products.

If you don't have celiac disease, it's fine to slowly reincorporate two or three weekly servings of gluten back into the diet, enjoying foods such as pasta, cereal and sandwiches.

Note: People with severe symptoms that suggest celiac disease, including those with symptoms of irritable bowel syndrome (IBS), bloating, and appetite issues should consult their health-care providers before removing gluten from their diet. Otherwise, they may inadvertently cover up symptoms and further complicate later diagnosis by avoiding prompt medical care and diagnosis.

Living Well with Multiple Sclerosis

Patricia K. Coyle, MD, professor and acting chair of the department of neurology at Stony Brook University Medical Center, and director of the Stony Brook Multiple Sclerosis Comprehensive Care Center.

The term multiple sclerosis (MS) conjures up frightening images of life in a wheelchair—but thanks to recent advances, an MS diagnosis no longer means that disability is inevitable. This is especially good news for women, given that MS is two to three times more common in women than men.

It is now possible to detect MS earlier...begin effective treatment just about as soon as symptoms appear...and slow the disease's progression. Yet despite this encouraging news, MS often goes undiagnosed for months or years—narrowing the window of opportunity that early treatment provides.

What women must know in order to protect themselves...

MS EXPLAINED

With MS, the immune system's white blood cells mistakenly attack the myelin (nerve fibers' protective coating) and nerve fibers themselves in the brain, spinal cord and optic nerves. This impairs the nerves' ability to transmit messages.

Women's greater vulnerability to MS may be related to hormones. MS typically strikes young adults, but it can appear as late as in one's 70s. People of northern European descent are more genetically predisposed to MS. Parents, siblings and children of MS patients have a 2% to 5% chance of developing it, too. Genes alone don't bring on the disease, however. Something in the environment—such as exposure to the Epstein-Barr virus (which causes mononucleosis) or vitamin-D deficiency at a young age—seems to help trigger MS.

DIAGNOSIS DIFFICULTIES

MS diagnosis often is delayed because the first symptoms can be vague. Patients tend to attribute them to a minor problem, such as a pinched nerve...doctors may mistake MS for spinal disk disease, vitamin B-12 deficiency or anxiety.

Any of the symptoms below merit a call to the doctor. If MS is suspected, a neurologist or MS center can run tests.

Referrals to a specialist: National Multiple Sclerosis Society, 800-344-4867, *www.nation almssociety.org*...Consortium of MS Centers, 201-487-1050, *www.mscare.org*.

Initial symptoms...

- **Clumsiness, loss of balance**
- **Double vision, blurred vision**
- **Eye pain, facial pain**
- **Numb face, limbs or torso**
- **Shocklike sensations upon bending the neck**
- **Stiffness, muscle spasms**
- **Weakness, extreme fatigue.**

Later symptoms...

- **Bladder or bowel incontinence**
- **Difficulty becoming sexually aroused or climaxing**
- **Paralysis, typically in the legs**
- **Poor concentration and memory**
- **Speech or swallowing problems.**

Diagnosis is based on a patient's medical history, a neurological exam and magnetic resonance imaging (MRI) to check for damaged tissue in the brain and spinal cord. *There are four types of MS...*

- **Relapsing-remitting MS,** which affects about 85% of patients, is characterized by sudden flare-ups (relapses) of symptoms followed by periods of improvement, during which patients are stable.
- **Primary progressive MS accounts for about 10% of MS cases.** Symptoms worsen progressively from onset. No improvement is experienced.
- **Progressive-relapsing MS,** which affects about 5% of patients, involves steady worsening of symptoms from onset, in addition to later flare-ups.
- **Secondary progressive MS refers to relapsing-remitting MS that transitions to slow worsening.** Patients get increasingly disabled instead of stabilizing between flare-ups.

MS is rarely fatal. Except when vital brain stem functions (such as breathing and heart rate) are affected or the disease has led to severe disability, most patients have a near-normal life expectancy.

HOW NATURAL TREATMENTS CAN EASE SYMPTOMS

- **Dietary changes.** MS patients may benefit from eating less saturated fat and more vitamin B-12 (found in dairy foods, eggs, meat, poultry and shellfish)...vitamin D (found in dairy foods and fish)...omega-3 fatty acids (found in fatty fish, cod liver oil and flaxseed oil)...and omega-6 fatty acids (found in safflower seed oil and sunflower oil). If blood tests show a deficiency, supplements may be recommended.
- **Exercise.** Aerobics help reduce fatigue, stress and incontinence...stretching eases stiffness.

Recommended: Yoga, tai chi, aquatics.

- **Acupuncture.** For many patients, this eases pain, numbness, spasms and incontinence.
- **Massage.** This may reduce pain, stiffness and spasticity.

On the horizon: Though still a long way off, novel therapies—such as oral disease-modifying therapy drugs and a DNA vaccine to treat MS—hold some promise that, in the future, MS may become a thing of the past.

MS—Best Ways to Get And Stay Symptom-Free

Thomas A. Kruzel, ND, naturopathic physician in private practice in Scottsdale, Arizona, past president of the American Association of Naturopathic Physicians and former vice president of clinical affairs and chief medical officer at the Southwest College of Naturopathic Medicine in Phoenix. Dr. Kruzel is author of *Homeopathic Emergency Guide: A Quick Reference Handbook to Effective Homeopathic Care* (North Atlantic).

National Institute of Neurological Disorders and Stroke, *www.ninds.nih.gov*.

Swank MS Foundation, *www.swankmsdiet.org*.

Conventional medicine generally looks at multiple sclerosis (MS) as an incurable disease typically marked by sporadic flare-ups and remissions. In contrast, naturopathic physicians generally do not view MS as incurable, and some have had great success in treating this unpredictable disease of the central nervous system to keep symptoms at bay. According to Thomas A. Kruzel, ND, a naturopathic physician in private practice in Scottsdale, Arizona, and past president of The American Association of Naturopathic Physicians, people who closely follow dietary, homeopathic and other naturopathic recommendations have the best odds of becoming and remaining symptom-free.

MS—A PRIMER

MS is believed to be an autoimmune disease in which the immune system mistakenly attacks the nervous system. This results in inflammation and damage to healthy myelin sheath tissue that insulates nerve cells. *Inflammation and demyelination of nerve cells can disrupt the normal transmission of neural signals, which can lead to symptoms that include...*

- **Numbness**
- **A sensation of pins and needles**
- **Muscle weakness and spasms**
- **Tremors**
- **Impaired balance and coordination**
- **Paralysis**
- **Extreme fatigue**
- **Blurred or double vision**
- **Blindness**
- **Diminished bowel and/or bladder function**
- **Difficulties with memory and/or cognitive function**

Typically, the disease strikes adults between the ages of 20 and 40, with symptoms ranging from mild to debilitating. In people with a vulnerability toward MS, the disease can be precipitated by a physical or psychological trauma—for example, a death or divorce, a virus, or the body succumbing to some kind of long-term stress, illness, exposure to environmental toxins, poor diet, etc.

Conventional medications for MS, such as *beta-interferon* and steroids, are used to attempt to control recurrence and severity of the symptoms. They have serious side effects and varied success. In contrast, NDs use a mixture of less invasive modalities—from diet and nutrition to homeopathy to counseling and more—to address MS. *Here are some of the options that have been most successful for Dr. Kruzel's patients...*

THE SWANK LOW-FAT DIET

Most modern-day chronic, degenerative diseases are related to or worsened by a poor diet, and MS is no exception, observes Dr. Kruzel. He believes that it's no coincidence that the incidence of MS—along with the incidence of heart disease, obesity, diabetes and arthritis—rose as Americans increasingly adopted a pro-inflammatory diet high in saturated fat. There is also evidence suggesting that the more red meat a society consumes, the higher the incidence of MS.

Named for its creator, the late Roy Swank, MD, PhD, the Swank Low-Fat Diet is a strict, low-saturated fat program that has been demonstrated to ease the symptoms of MS, and possibly even cause the disease to go into remission.

While Dr. Swank recommended limiting the saturated fat in your diet, he also advised a teaspoon of fish oil daily. You are encouraged to eat more white fish and a specific amount of fatty fish such as wild salmon, tuna, and sardines, which count toward your daily allowance of oil. Fatty fish are also a good source of healthful essential fatty acids. Flaxseed oil is also rich in EFAs.

People who follow the Swank Low-Fat Diet can expect to start feeling better within four to six weeks, says Dr. Kruzel. The longer they follow it and the more strictly they adhere to it, the more they will improve. *The basic elements of the Swank Low-Fat Diet are...*

- **No red meat for the first year,** and only 3 ounces per week after that.
- **No more than 15 grams of saturated fat daily.**
- **No more than 50 grams of unsaturated fat per day.**
- **No processed foods that contain saturated fat.**
- **Any dairy product must have 1% or less butterfat.**

• **Take 1 teaspoon (or equivalent in capsule form) of cod liver oil daily.** A daily multivitamin and mineral supplement is also required.

HOMEOPATHY

Dr. Kruzel views homeopathy—treatments that are known to stimulate the body's healing responses—as a cornerstone of his MS treatment approach. He points out that certain personality types tend to develop MS—most often serious or sensitive people who hold in their emotions and are reluctant to express them, possibly increasing stress. This makes homeopathy an especially appropriate treatment, since these remedies are intended to fit not only a person's symptoms, but also his/her personality, temperament and lifestyle. An ND is apt to prescribe homeopathic remedies such as *Natrum muriaticum, phosphorus* or *sepia*. It is important to work with a professional trained in homeopathy to ensure that you use the best remedy for your symptoms and persona.

BEE VENOM THERAPY

It may sound unorthodox, but Dr. Kruzel has seen many MS patients benefit from diluted bee venom injections, or apitherapy. Bee venom contains a variety of compounds—such as anti-inflammatory *mellitin* plus anti-inflammatory and pain-blocking *adolapin*—that work together to invoke the body's own natural immune reaction. Dr. Kruzel generally administers 20 sessions of bee venom therapy, one week apart. Unfortunately, the injections are painful, and some people cannot tolerate them. If they can, however, there is usually an improvement in symptoms.

Caution: Because a small percentage of the population is allergic to bee venom, this therapy should be closely supervised by your ND. There should be a bee sting kit available to treat any allergic reactions.

COUNSELING

Dr. Kruzel says he sees a huge mental and emotional component to MS. In his first lengthy consultation with each MS patient, he discusses not only physical symptoms but also core psychological issues and memories that may be an underlying cause of stress, thus aggravating the disease. Dr. Kruzel has found that once a person deals with these important emotional issues they begin to feel better. Once the emotional issues are dealt with, symptoms may abate. If the mental/emotional symptoms are not dealt with, or return, the MS may come back. That is why counseling in addition to homeopathic treatment is essential.

STRESS MANAGEMENT

Stress—whether due to a sudden shock such as an illness or loss, or a long-term battle with an unhappy marriage or legal troubles—is suspected to be a major contributing factor to worsening MS symptoms. To cope effectively with stress, Dr. Kruzel recommends modalities such as meditation, yoga and deep breathing.

EXERCISE

Exercise and physical therapy can keep neurological pathways functioning properly, says Dr. Kruzel. He adds that many people with MS unwisely give up on exercise. This is a big mistake which can lead to further muscle weakness and loss of muscle mass. When you work out, just be careful about heat, which can aggravate symptoms. Although there are people with MS who run marathons, most prefer less intense (and less heat-producing) forms of exercise such as swimming or yoga.

Reason: Becoming overheated aggravates symptoms of MS, so exercises that generate lower amounts of body heat are tolerated better.

NATURAL WAYS TO TREAT MS

While no two people with MS are alike and different individuals have different needs, certain supplements can benefit most people with this disease…

• **Essential fatty acids.** People with MS may be typically short on essential fatty acids, which are necessary for brain and nervous system health. Cod liver oil and other fish oils are good sources of essential fatty acids.

• **Antioxidants.** People with MS are apt to have higher levels of molecules called free radicals, which contribute to inflammation and demyelination. To control them, Dr. Kruzel recommends antioxidants such as alpha lipoic acid and vitamins C and E.

Other possible supplements: B vitamins (to support brain and nervous system function), vitamin D (to give the immune system a boost) and magnesium (to relieve stiffness and cramping).

HYDROTHERAPY

The alternate use of brief hot and longer cold applications—a short, hot bath followed by a long cool shower, alternating hot and cold compresses, etc.—is beneficial in a number of ways. According to Dr. Kruzel, this type of hydrotherapy increases circulation…delivers more oxygen to the blood…increases the white blood cell count…and promotes tissue rebuilding. Hydrotherapy treatments need to be directly supervised by a caregiver and the benefits and risks should be reviewed by a physician in each individual case.

POSITIVE ATTITUDE AND COMMITMENT ARE ESSENTIAL

Dr. Kruzel finds that the people who are most successful in getting their symptoms under control have a commitment to getting well, follow naturopathic recommendations closely, live a "squeaky clean" life (no alcohol or smoking, little saturated fat or processed foods, regular exercise, etc.) and maintain a positive attitude.

To locate a naturopathic physician in your area, visit the Web site of the American Association of Naturopathic Physicians at *www.naturopathic.org*. To learn more about MS, visit Web sites such as the National Institute of Neurological Disorders and Stroke (*www.ninds.nih.gov*), the Multiple Sclerosis Foundation (*www.msfocus.org*), the National Multiple Sclerosis Society (*www.nationalmssociety.org*) and the Swank MS Foundation (*www.swankmsdiet.org*).

The Baffling Bladder Condition Antibiotics Can't Cure

Kristene E. Whitmore, MD, professor and chair of urology and female pelvic medicine and reconstructive surgery at Drexel University College of Medicine, and medical director of the Pelvic and Sexual Health Institute, both in Philadelphia. She is coauthor of *Overcoming Bladder Disorders* (Harper Perennial). *www.pelvicandsexualhealthinstitute.org*.

Perplexing, painful and inconvenient, the chronic condition interstitial cystitis/painful bladder syndrome (IC/PBS) affects women more than nine times as often as men. Its symptoms, including bladder pain and frequent urination, often are mistaken for those of a bladder infection—yet tests reveal no bacteria, and antibiotics bring no relief.

Though IC/PBS affects up to 6% of American women, its cause is a mystery.

What is known: The bladder wall becomes inflamed and super-sensitive…pinpoints of bleeding and ulcers often appear…stiffness and scarring may develop.

Many women suffer for years without a proper diagnosis, taking antibiotics for infections that they do not actually have. This delay causes needless pain…raises the odds of becoming resistant to antibiotics…and increases the risk that an IC/PBS–triggered inflammatory reaction will spread to other organs. In severe cases, surgery may be needed to remove part or all of the bladder. IC/PBS cannot be cured—but treatment can relieve symptoms and reduce complications.

GETTING DIAGNOSED

If you have symptoms that suggest IC/PBS, visit your doctor. If no infection is found or symptoms persist despite treatment, consult a urologist or urogynecologist.

IC/PBS symptoms…

• **Bladder pain or pressure**

• **Frequent urination (more than eight times in 24 hours)**

• **Urgent need to urinate**

• **Discomfort, pain or pressure in the lower pelvis or vulva**

• **Pain during or after sex**

• **Flare-ups during menstruation.**

There is no definitive test for IC/PBS. Diagnosis involves excluding other conditions, such as a bladder infection, overactive bladder or bladder cancer. Testing may include blood and urine tests, bladder biopsy and cystoscopy (exam of the bladder using a viewing instrument).

Good news: For about 70% of patients, natural remedies ease symptoms with few or no side effects.

SOOTHING DIETARY STRATEGIES

Your diet affects how your bladder feels. *Helpful…*

•**Identify foods that spark symptoms.** A chief culprit is cranberry juice. Yes, this juice combats bladder infections—but with IC/PBS, you aren't fighting an infection. And cranberry juice is acidic, so it irritates a sensitive bladder.

Other top troublemakers: Alcohol... artificial sweeteners...caffeine (coffee, soda, tea)...carbonated drinks...citrus fruits, citrus juices...spicy foods...and tomato products.

For a comprehensive list of problematic foods, visit the Web site of the Interstitial Cystitis Association (*www.ichelp.org*, click on "Living with IC"). To identify your personal triggers, for one month do not eat anything on the ICA list. Then, reintroduce one food from the list every three to five days. If symptoms flare up, swear off that food.

•**Drink more, not less.** You may think that limiting fluids reduces your need to urinate—but skimping on water makes urine more concentrated and thus more irritating. Drink six to eight cups of water daily—and sip, don't gulp.

•**Take supplements.** *With your doctor's okay, try the following...*

•Prelief (sold at drugstores) contains *calcium glycerophosphate*, which makes food less acidic.

•CystoProtek (sold at *www.cysto-protek.com*) has antioxidants and anti-inflammatories (glucosamine, quercetin, rutin) that help repair the bladder lining.

Note: If you take a multivitamin or other supplement that contains vitamin C, choose one with ascorbate, not ascorbic acid.

MIND OVER BLADDER

Try any or all of the following mind-body therapies...

•**Bladder retraining.** Urinating temporarily relieves pain, so patients use the toilet often—in some cases, up to 60 times a day—but this habit further reduces the bladder's capacity to comfortably hold urine.

Best: Try to increase your typical time between bathroom trips by 15 minutes. After two weeks, increase by another 15 minutes. Continue until you can wait at least two hours.

•**Stress reduction.** Practice relaxation techniques daily, such as deep breathing, meditation and yoga. Also consider craniosacral therapy (gentle head and spine massage).

Practitioner referrals: Upledger Institute, 800-233-5880, *www.upledger.com*.

•**Acupuncture.** This reduces IC/PBS pain for some patients.

Referrals: American Association of Acupuncture and Oriental Medicine, 866-455-7999, *www.aaaomonline.org*.

LIFESTYLE CHANGES

To make day-to-day life with IC/PBS more comfortable, try...

•**Modified exercise routines.** When symptoms flare up, reduce the intensity and duration of workouts—for instance, by walking instead of running. Rinse off after swimming to remove irritating chlorine.

•**Bathing.** Soak in bathwater mixed with colloidal oatmeal (sold at drugstores). Avoid bubble baths and bath oils—these tend to be irritating.

•**A personal lubricant for sex.** This makes intercourse more comfortable.

Try: The organic Good Clean Love line (541-344-4483, *www.goodcleanlove.com*).

Constantly Cold? Here Are Some "Hot" New Healers

Erika T. Schwartz, MD, a New York City physician who specializes in women's hormones and author of *The 30-Day Natural Hormone Plan* and *The Hormone Solution* (both from Grand Central).

M ost midlife women are proactive about seeking relief from hot flashes, yet they seem resigned to accept chronic coldness as an inevitable part of getting older. However, constantly wearing extra layers to get warm isn't normal. A woman who's always chilled may have a hormone problem.

WHAT'S A WOMAN TO DO?

We spoke with Erika T. Schwartz, MD, a New York City physician who specializes in women's hormones, and author of *The 30-Day Natural Hormone Plan* and *The Hormone Solution* (both from Grand Central). *She explains that feeling cold all over, or chilled to the bone, can signal a number of conditions...*

- **An oncoming cold or flu.**
- **Depression** (which is often accompanied by hormonal problems).
- **Extremely low body fat** (such as in women who have eating disorders).
- **Premenstrual dips in estrogen and progesterone,** which can trigger sensitivity to cold.

A THYROID CHECK

"If sensitivity to cold is ongoing, it's usually an indicator of thyroid issues," Dr. Schwartz warns. The problem is, it's not unusual for women's thyroid tests to come back "normal," so many cases of subclinical hypothyroidism are missed and women often don't receive the treatment they need. According to Dr. Schwartz, many conventional doctors rely on an "antiquated" range of normal that was determined 50 years ago. Seeing an endocrinologist or a physician who is sensitive to hormone issues and treats a woman's symptoms, not her test results, can help.

WHY YOUR TEMPERATURE BAROMETER IS DROPPING

By midlife, the hormone levels begin to shift. As women approach menopause, estrogen and progesterone begin to diminish. Additionally, since all these hormones are integrated in a complex chain of events, the effect of thyroid hormone goes down too, Dr. Schwartz explains.

Taking cholesterol-lowering medications and/or following a restrictive cholesterol-lowering diet may add to the problem.

In addition to feeling cold, those with low thyroid levels may experience significant fatigue,

weakness, mental sluggishness, low-back pain, muscle cramps, mood swings, weight gain or difficulty losing weight, and dry skin and nails. Dr. Schwartz points out that "there is a great deal of crossover, which is why it is important to work closely with a skilled physician to evaluate and diagnose."

To give your body the support it needs to continue making hormones, Dr. Schwartz recommends taking these steps...

- **Eat "hormone-friendly foods."** Skip coffee, alcohol, dairy foods, processed foods and foods with hormones in them, such as nonorganic meats.
- **Exercise regularly.**
- **Manage your stress as much as possible.** Every stressful event or period of stress affects your hormone balance. A stressful event can cause your thyroid levels to nosedive.
- **Use the right supplements.** Dr. Schwartz recommends women in midlife take L-carnitine, CoQ10, omega-3 fish oil, vitamin C, folic acid, all the B vitamins, calcium, magnesium, zinc, boron and alpha-lipoic acid. These nutrients boost the immune system, decrease inflammation, increase energy and support hormone balance. It is best to work directly with a trained physician who can prescribe the proper dosing and supplements specific to your needs.

If, despite living a hormone-friendly lifestyle, you still have the symptoms of low thyroid—the most significant symptom being exhaustion or severe fatigue—talk to your doctor. According to Dr. Schwartz, no over-the-counter supplement or herb will support your thyroid like thyroid medication. Untreated hypothyroidism can cause memory problems, lower your resistance to illness and lead to arthritis, high cholesterol, circulatory problems and arteriosclerosis.

4

Detox and Rejuvenate

The One-Week Detox Diet

Every minute of your life, your body is detoxifying—breaking down hundreds of hazardous chemicals that you breathe in or ingest. To do this, your body relies on specific nutrients. Yet even if your everyday diet is reasonably healthful, your body faces an enormous toxic load.

Problem: The world is filled with synthetic toxins—industrial pollutants and car exhaust...fumes from copy machines and dry cleaning...foods grown with pesticides or processed with potentially harmful additives. Chemicals in tobacco and alcohol increase the liver's burden.

Theory: Toxins in the body may lead to cell damage, increasing the risk for disease.

Solution: A one-week detoxification diet, followed four times a year, can give your body a break from the toxic onslaught...replenish healthful nutrients...alleviate cell-damaging

inflammation...combat disease...even slow the aging process.

Get your doctor's approval before beginning the one-week detox diet. This regimen may not be appropriate for people with certain chronic health conditions, such as heart disease, a kidney disorder, cancer or anemia. Do not follow the detox diet if you are pregnant or breast-feeding or if you have diabetes or hypoglycemia.

WHAT TO EAT

The majority of the body's self-cleansing takes place in the liver, which uses enzymes to break down hazardous toxins. The dual goal of a one-week detox is to boost intake of nutrients that these enzymes may need...and to lighten the liver's workload by limiting ingestion of additional toxins.

Shari Lieberman, PhD, CNS, FACN, a nutrition scientist in Hillsboro Beach, Florida, in private practice for more than 25 years, *www.drshari.net*. She is a board member of the Certification Board for Nutrition Specialists, fellow of the American College of Nutrition and coauthor of *User's Guide to Detoxification* (Basic Health).

Choose a week when you don't expect to be under stress or eating out a lot. Plan on three meals a day plus two snacks. Eat until satisfied —there's no need to go hungry.

Important: The main components of the detox diet are vegetables and fruits. Buy organic to avoid pesticides that make the liver work harder.

• **Eat a variety of vegetables.** These are loaded with antioxidants and may fuel liver enzymes. Choose any veggies you like—carrots, cucumbers, eggplant, mushrooms, peppers, salad greens, spinach, sprouts, tomatoes. Add in sulfur-rich vegetables—asparagus, broccoli, brussels sprouts, cabbage, cauliflower, garlic, onions—which are especially supportive of detoxification enzymes.

Fresh is best, but frozen or canned vegetables are all right if they have nothing added. Eat vegetables raw, steamed or sautéed in a bit of olive oil. Try a salad or crudité platter for lunch…and a medley of cooked vegetables for dinner.

• **Focus on fruit.** Most fruits are rich in antioxidants. Try something new—boysenberries, guavas, kumquats, passion fruit—plus familiar favorites, such as apples, blueberries, cherries and raspberries. Mix up a fruit salad for breakfast…have a pear or an orange as a snack… drink juice with lunch or dinner. Choose fresh or frozen fruits and juices with no added sugar or syrup.

• **Enhance flavor.** Many ready-made salad dressings, dips and sauces contain unhealthful oils and too much sugar and salt.

Better: Make your own dressing using monounsaturated oil, herbs and other healthful ingredients.

For salads: Toss greens with one teaspoon each of olive oil and balsamic vinegar plus a pinch of oregano…or one teaspoon of olive oil plus a splash of lemon juice.

For dipping: Try hummus, made from chickpeas and tahini (ground sesame seeds)… and baba ghanoush, made from eggplant and tahini.

For cooked vegetables: Sprinkle with ground cloves, turmeric or other spices.

• **Add a little protein for energy.** Many people feel energized during a detox week, but others feel tired because they are eating less protein than usual. Nuts and seeds are excellent sources of protein. Choose unsalted varieties to avoid bloating. If energy remains low after the first three days, once or twice a day have a poached or hard-boiled organic egg… four ounces of fish, such as wild Alaskan salmon (try it poached with dill)…or four ounces of baked or broiled free-range chicken.

• **Have eight glasses of filtered water daily.** Staying hydrated helps your body excrete toxins.

• **Drink tea.** Green and white teas are rich in antioxidants. Drink tea hot or over ice. Add a wedge of lemon or lime—this improves absorption of antioxidants.

• **Try "green drinks."** Typically these are made from powdered dehydrated wheatgrass, green barley, vegetables and herbs. Some include the naturally sweet and calorie-free herb stevia. Once a day, stir the label-recommended amount of green drink mix into one cup of water or unsweetened diluted juice.

WHAT NOT TO EAT

Throughout your detox week, avoid foods with a high glycemic index (GI). The GI is a ranking system that indicates a food's potential to cause rapid spikes in blood sugar and insulin levels, which in turn promote cell-damaging inflammation and hinder detoxification.

Helpful: To find the GI of various foods, see *www.glycemicindex.com.*

Sugar has a very high GI—so avoid foods such as cakes, cookies, donuts, honey, soda and syrup. Other potentially high-GI foods include those made with white flour (bread, crackers) and all types of rice.

Even some vegetables and fruits have a high GI. Avoid or limit consumption of beets, parsnips, potatoes and pumpkin…as well as watermelon, raisins and dates.

Also stay away from dairy foods. Milk contains sugars and proteins that can be difficult to digest.

Many people do not realize that they are sensitive to gluten, a protein found in wheat, rye, barley and many other grains. During detox week, stick to gluten-free grains that have a relatively low GI, such as quinoa and buckwheat.

Avoid alcohol, preservatives and artificial colorings and sweeteners. These can tax the liver.

DETOX SUPPLEMENTS

Throughout your weeklong detox, continue taking whatever supplements you normally take. *Also take the three supplements below to enhance detoxification activity (continuing even after the detox week, if desired)...*

•**Alpha-lipoic acid.** This antioxidant may help maintain normal liver function and improve glucose metabolism.

Dosage: 100 milligrams (mg) daily. Avoid if you have thyroid problems.

•**Milk thistle extract.** Studies show that this herb protects the liver from toxins...and can lower blood sugar levels.

Dosage: 100 mg to 200 mg daily.

•**N-acetylcysteine (NAC).** This antioxidant is so effective at protecting the liver that hospitals use it to treat overdoses of acetaminophen (Tylenol), which can cause liver failure.

New finding: NAC may help the body excrete mercury, often found in fish.

Dosage: 500 mg daily.

When detox week is over, gradually reintroduce whole grains, lean beef and other healthful foods into your diet, while continuing to eat lots of organic fruits and vegetables. Your liver will benefit—and your whole body will, too.

Are Drugs Stealing The Life Out of You?

Mark A. Stengler, NMD, naturopathic medical doctor in private practice, Encinitas, California...adjunct associate clinical professor at the National College of Natural Medicine, Portland, Oregon...author of *The Natural Physician's Healing Therapies* (Bottom Line Books).

Suzy Cohen, RPh, pharmacist, syndicated health journalist and author of *The 24-Hour Pharmacist* (HarperCollins) and *Drug Muggers* (DPI). *www.DearPharmacist.com.*

What does a pharmacist see from his/ her side of the counter, especially a pharmacist like Suzy Cohen, RPh, who is passionate about natural healing? Ms. Cohen was a pharmacist for nine years before becoming a syndicated columnist who writes about health and natural healing. She has raised awareness of the dangerous effects of pharmaceutical drugs and how the use of natural substances can decrease and even prevent damaging side effects from these drugs.

We spoke with her about her experiences on the other side of the counter...

What exactly do you mean by the term "drug mugger"?

It's a term I use for all medications that deplete vital nutrients from the body. In so doing, these drugs slowly steal the life out of patients. Sadly, drug mugging takes place on several levels. You can take a drug for months or even years without seeming to have a problem with it—but that really might not be the case. It's just that medical problems develop very slowly. When they finally erupt, people don't think to associate them with the medications they have been taking.

I often saw this problem in women who were taking lots of estrogen-containing hormones, such as birth control pills, which deplete B vitamins, magnesium and zinc. Women who are deprived of these key nutrients during childbearing years are at increased risk for heart attack, stroke, depression and fatigue after menopause, but their doctors seldom make that connection.

On the other hand, some medications cause almost instant side effects and symptoms. Antibiotics, for example, destroy friendly intestinal bacteria after only a few days of use. Many patients develop cramps, diarrhea and vaginal yeast infections while taking antibiotics. Antibiotics might help with their infections, but they often would call me in a panic about their digestive discomfort and I would steer them to a good probiotic.

I wrote *Drug Muggers* to heighten the public's awareness of this problem and to help people protect themselves. If you know in advance the nutrients that will be depleted when you take a particular drug, you can prepare to immediately replenish the vitamins, minerals and other substances that you will need.

These substances generally are inexpensive and readily available in health-food stores and will make all the difference in your health and quality of life. (See the end of this article for a list of common drugs and what they deplete.)

What do you think about patients taking both pharmaceutical drugs and natural remedies?

Pharmaceutical drug use is soaring, as a recent study in *The Journal of the American Medical Association* pointed out. One-third of Americans over age 57 take at least five prescription drugs. At the same time, interest in natural remedies is flourishing. As a result, I see many people combining natural substances with various medications without investigating the possibly dangerous interactions.

What drugs do people most often take with natural substances that can be dangerous?

Blood-thinning medications, such as *warfarin* (Coumadin), generally given to people who are at risk of developing blood clots, fall into this category. Aspirin also is a blood thinner. When you take one of these medications and then you add on other natural blood-thinning substances, such as high-dose fish oil, vitamin E, ginkgo biloba or the enzyme *nattokinase*, you risk an overload. This dangerous combination puts people at risk for hemorrhage because they are reducing the body's ability to form a blood clot, which is needed to stop internal and external bleeding.

What do you tell people about the interaction between the medications they take and the foods they eat?

Many people don't know that the foods they eat can affect their medications. Foods can keep drugs from being fully absorbed. They can slow or blunt the effect of a drug or exaggerate its effect. All of these potential problems can be serious.

Grapefruit's effect on medication may be the food-drug interaction that people have heard most about, but there are many others. For instance, people who take diabetes medication, including *glucophage* (Metformin), need to be extremely careful about foods that raise blood sugar and affect the pancreas. The worst offenders include artificial sweeteners, high fructose corn syrup and alcohol. They also need to supplement with coenzyme Q10 and

folic acid, both of which will help them avoid muscle weakness, fatigue, memory loss and heartbeat irregularity.

Thyroid drugs also interact with certain foods and supplements. Dairy products and calcium supplements can interfere with the absorption of thyroid medications. Oatmeal and other high-fiber foods and supplements can bind to thyroid medications so that they are not absorbed as well. It is important to have these foods and supplements no sooner than several hours after you take your thyroid medication.

What stands out as the one thing that people are least aware of when it comes to nutrients?

I would have to say trace minerals. People seem to be familiar with some of the minerals that are essential to the human body. We hear a lot about the essential minerals that we need in large amounts, including magnesium, sodium, potassium and calcium. But many people don't know much about their need for trace minerals—very small amounts of minerals that help the body function well. These include chromium, selenium, manganese, zinc, iodine, cobalt and copper. Most of us can get the trace minerals we need by eating steamed vegetables or drinking raw vegetable and fruit juices. But our supply of trace minerals is jeopardized by our exposure to dangerous heavy metals, such as mercury, cadmium and lead, that disrupt our mineral balance. One natural way to remove heavy metals is with PectaSol Chelation Complex (800-308-5518, *www. econugenics.com*). Made from citrus peel and a seaweed extract, this supplement removes harmful metal toxins from the body without disturbing essential trace minerals.

You have written about how lifestyle habits can also deplete nutrients. Can you give an example of this?

Certain ordinary habits can be comforting, but these too can rob the body of nutrients. For example, regular coffee and tea consumption depletes minerals. Alcohol, even one drink, depletes the body of B complex vitamins, vitamin C and trace minerals. Stress plays a role as well. Long-term stress especially causes problems. I find that vitamin B complex and antioxidant-rich foods and supplements help people combat the effects of stress. The anti-oxidant astaxanthin, a red pigment found in salmon, shrimp and red plants and vegetables, is a powerful way to replenish the body.

If there were only one thing you could tell patients, what would it be?

I would urge everyone to tell their conventional medical doctors about all the supplements and natural remedies they are using. Studies have shown that the majority of people do not share this information with their doctors. It is critical for your doctor to know everything about your medical condition, including every medication and supplement you are taking. That way, the doctor has the full picture and really can evaluate your health.

In fact, patients who are being helped by natural substances actually could educate their doctors about them. But doctors won't know that natural remedies played a role unless patients tell them. Telling conventional doctors what really happened could open up their minds to natural healing—and give these doctors the opportunity to help other patients in the future.

THE DRUG MUGGERS

Here are several common drugs and what they take from us. Talk to your doctor about whether you need to supplement.

Common Drug	What Is Depleted
Acetaminophen	Glutathione
Acid-blocking medications, including proton-pump inhibitors and H2 blockers	Vitamin B-12 (When supplementing, look for the type known as *methylco-balamin,* which is better utilized by the body than others.)
Antibiotics	B vitamins and healthy gut flora (which can be replaced by probiotics)
Diabetes medication	Coenzyme Q10 and folic acid
Diuretics (both regular and potassium-sparing) for high blood pressure	Vitamin B complex and trace minerals
Estrogen	B vitamins, calcium, magnesium, zinc
Ibuprofen	Folic acid
Laxatives	Calcium, zinc, iron, magnesium
Sleep medications	Melatonin, the hormone that maintains a normal circadian cycle, including sleep
Statin drugs (cholesterol-lowering medications)	Coenzyme Q10
Steroids (prednisone)	Calcium, vitamin D, vitamin C, potassium

More from Mark A. Stengler, NMD...

Medical Mystery Cured With Detox

The word "detox" often bears negative connotations, either because it's associated with drug addictions, or because practitioners who practice "detox" are often thought of as "wacky" by those who are not familiar with the practice. But detox does have its place. Mark Stengler, NMD, makes this clear when he shares the details of a recent case, in which one patient's "mystery symptoms" were resolved with detoxification.

A 41-year-old airline pilot had the unpredictable schedule that is typical of airline crews. He was suffering from acne rosacea...on-again, off-again outbreaks of another type of rash... trouble getting to sleep and staying there...and even tinnitus, a nearly constant ringing in his ears. So those where the symptoms...what was the diagnosis?

TRACKING THE CLUES

Dr. Stengler says he suspected there were a number of reasons the pilot had developed a constellation of toxic challenges and needed to detox. The fact that his skin rashes came and went and that the pilot ate most of his meals in fast-food places and hotel coffee shops indicated this need...and the fact that his patient's bowel movements were irregular and sluggish confirmed the working diagnosis for Dr. Stengler. He chose to supervise his patient on a diet that featured much more healthful, natural and nutritious foods and give him special supplements that would cleanse his liver and kidneys.

The regimen was as follows…

• **Large amounts of produce—with a produce ratio of 80% vegetables and 20% fruits.** Although this man had a difficult schedule, he was easily able to greatly increase the number of fruits and vegetables he ate daily, in part by taking them with him and snacking on them as he worked and traveled.

• **Organic eggs and poultry, brown rice and small amounts of whole grains.**

• **No alcohol, sugar or coffee.**

• **A greens supplement (six capsules daily of one called Deeper Greens, which is manufactured by Ortho Molecular Products, Inc.** and available only through health-care professionals) that contains wheatgrass, chlorella, spirulina, barley grass and other greens. This helps the liver and kidneys to detox.

• **A second detoxification powder,** containing vitamins and minerals that support liver detoxification including vitamins E and C, carotenoids, selenium, magnesium, potassium, molybdenum, calcium, chromium, B vitamins and glutathione.

• **A combination liver support supplement of milk thistle, dandelion root and burdock.**

• **Saunas (preferably a dry sauna) every other day.** Fortunately, the patient belonged to a gym with a sauna and the hotels he stayed in on layovers generally had them. Sweating in saunas is an excellent way to pull toxins out of fat tissue.

• **Exercise.** A moderately intense cardio workout—at least 25 minutes a day—that made the patient break a sweat.

NATURE OF THE FAST

The cleansing regimen used for this patient lasted a few weeks. It is not unusual for people to feel somewhat worse before they feel better, primarily due to the increased movement of wastes out of the liver and into the intestinal tract. During the first two days, it is common for people to experience headaches and fatigue, and sometimes have skin breakouts, especially if their previous diet was particularly poor.

For most, though, the unpleasant side effects don't last longer than that. Within a reasonably short time, in fact, most people find they feel more energetic and they think more clearly. Their bowels move regularly, their skin begins to look better, and their mood improves.

The pilot noticed these kinds of changes, too. In fact, even his tinnitus improved, something that Dr. Stengler says is plausible but not common.

CLOGGED UP SYSTEMS

People who feel sluggish and have low energy or frequent low-grade depression often have poor eating habits (as did this patient), which challenges the body's functioning. Many times people turn to pharmaceutical or recreational drugs, alcohol or excessive amounts of sugar in attempts to pick themselves up. Unfortunately, those actions never help. In fact, they often make the situation much worse. A proper medically supervised detoxification protocol can help nearly all of these symptoms as well as chronic fatigue, allergies, headaches and digestive problems, including stomachaches and constipation. Dr. Stengler advises many of his patients to consider a detox of this nature every fall and spring to help them counteract the effect of the rich and fatty foods so common in our culture.

It is important not to try this detoxification on one's own, as blood pressure, blood sugar levels, heart and kidney function can be stressed from a radical detox.

Also from Mark A. Stengler, NMD…

Detoxifying Footbaths and Pads

We are constantly bombarded by reports about environmental toxins that permeate the air we breathe, the food we eat and the water we drink. So the promise of detoxifying your body by simply soaking your feet in a warm footbath or wearing foot pads overnight sounds enticing. The manufacturers of these footbaths and pads claim that they can eliminate toxins from the body, improve kidney and liver function, increase energy, alleviate pain, strengthen the immune system and much more. But can they?

• **Detoxifying footbaths.** You immerse your feet in a small tub of warm water with mineral salts added. Two electrodes in the tub generate a mild current in the water. The color of the water changes as you soak—from milky white to green to dark brown. Manufacturers claim that the color of the water indicates the area of the body that has been detoxified—for example, orange when toxins are removed from the joints…brown or black when the liver is detoxified…and green when it's the kidneys.

The manufacturers' claims are absurd. Toxins can be drawn out of the skin but not as rapidly as the makers of these footbaths would have you believe—and the color of the water does not represent different organs. The water changes color because of the amount of salts added and the corrosion of the metal electrodes in the tub that create the current.

Nevertheless, these detoxifying footbaths have become serious business, both in terms of time and money. It's generally recommended that patients have 30-minute treatments several times a week, at a spa or in a holistic practitioner's office, for between $30 and $75 per treatment. The machines also can be purchased for home use for $1,000 to $3,000.

•**Detox foot pads.** The companies that sell these foot pads also claim that they drain toxins, such as heavy metals, metabolic wastes, parasites and more, out of the feet when the pads are worn to bed for one week. Advertisements even show the "after" pad stained brown in the morning—but this staining actually is caused by foot perspiration and some of the ingredients in the pads, including vinegar and plant extracts, which are known to darken when they are exposed to air.

I have heard of informal studies in which researchers sent worn pads to a lab to be analyzed—and no toxins were found.

Bottom line: I am amazed by how many holistic practitioners have been misled by these treatments and recommend them to their patients. The claims seem implausible—and there is no scientific evidence to back them up.

My advice? Save your money.

Instead, to keep your body healthy and reduce toxins, consume fresh vegetable juices (that you make yourself or purchase at a juice bar), take saunas and use detoxifying substances, such as milk thistle (250 milligrams, or mg, three times daily with meals)…green tea (two to three cups daily)…and N-acetylcysteine

(NAC), an amino acid derivative that supports detoxification. I recommend taking 500 mg to 600 mg of NAC daily throughout the year.

Regular bowel movements are one of the body's natural ways of detoxification—as is working up a sweat during exercise.

The UltraSimple Way To a Healthier Life

Mark Hyman, MD, author of *UltraMetabolism* (Scribner) and *The UltraSimple Diet* (Pocket). Dr. Hyman is the founder and medical director of The UltraWellness Center in Lenox, Massachusetts, and the editor-in-chief of *Alternative Therapies in Health and Medicine.*

W hether you are trying to lose weight for health reasons or appearance, it's often easier said than done. Many people think that eating less and exercising more are the keys to weight loss—however, the body's inflammatory response to stress and toxins (physiologically and psychologically) is increasingly recognized as an important contributor. Mark Hyman, MD, the former co-medical director at Canyon Ranch in Lenox, Massachusetts, has spent years studying the role of inflammation and its impact on body weight. In his latest book, *The UltraSimple Diet* (Pocket), he outlines a detailed, step-by-step, seven-day program to help people structure their eating habits and lifestyle to keep inflammation and its destructive role at bay. This isn't a "diet" in the traditional sense, Dr. Hyman notes, but an eating program for optimal wellness that he believes everyone, whatever his/her weight, can benefit from.

Here's the logic behind it: Being overweight often is a symptom of underlying health problems. The same "bad-for-you" foods (think super-sized burgers and sodas) that make you fat can also cause inflammation and make you sick. Getting rid of these inflammatory influences, while learning to replace them with healthful alternatives (i.e., whole foods that the body is naturally designed to eat) will help you not only lose weight, but also will simultaneously make you feel more energized, sleep better, have clearer skin, enjoy a more positive mood and develop a greater resistance to disease.

Dr. Hyman shared more thoughts on the factors that lie behind obesity and chronic medical conditions, and described his program to overcome them.

THE TWO KEY CULPRITS: TOXICITY AND INFLAMMATION

We are always surrounded with potentially "toxic" influences, and are bombarded daily by fast, fried and other junk foods, poisonous pollutants, negative thoughts and destructive behavior.

Normally, inflammation is the body's short-term healing response to such insults and injuries. But under continuous attack like this, your immune system shifts into high gear to protect you. The hormones and other chemical messengers it fires out are meant to defend the body, but instead (because they are over-utilized) often cause chronic inflammation.

Experts believe this chronic inflammation is what lies at the root of a multitude of diseases, including obesity, heart disease, cancer and Alzheimer's disease.

Although the body's natural state is healthy and slim, many of us have developed a "protective coating" (excess weight) as a by-product of our constant state of self-defense. In order to return to the optimal state, we can normalize the environment by ridding our bodies of inflammatory influences.

Once you eliminate the sources of inflammation by replacing bad foods with good ones, limiting your exposure to pollutants and controlling stress, you will not only safely and effectively begin to lose weight, but also reduce the symptoms of many chronic illnesses.

STRATEGIES TO REDUCE TOXICITY AND COOL INFLAMMATION

Dr. Hyman acknowledges that while the steps to reduce inflammation are not complicated per se, they do require commitment since they are a departure from current bad habits.

Here are several key aspects of the UltraSimple program...

• **Eat an anti-inflammatory diet.** Focus on eating whole foods in the form nature intended. This means getting rid of highly processed foods that stimulate inflammation. Convenient foods with long ingredient lists should be avoided completely.

Beware: This long list includes white flour and sugar products, high-fructose corn syrup, trans fats, additives, preservatives, pesticides, hormones, alcohol, caffeine, fast and fried foods—and, for the first week at least, red meat, too. Because they are potential allergens, Dr. Hyman also has patients eliminate dairy, gluten, eggs, corn, yeast and peanuts the first seven days. While you may not be sensitive to all these foods, the only way to find out is to avoid them for a week and see if you feel better. This first step can be very difficult for some people. However, Dr. Hyman finds that once you try it and realize how much better you feel, the dietary limitations get easier.

UltraSimple tip: Try to make healthful substitutions. For example, replace your morning cup of coffee with antioxidant-packed, anti-inflammatory green tea. In place of sugary soft drinks, treat your body to cool, clean, filtered water or sparkling water with a twist of lemon or lime.

Whenever possible, forego foods grown with hormones, antibiotics and petrochemical pesticides and eat those that have been organically grown. The idea is to make healthier choices, not deprive yourself. That's why Dr. Hyman says you won't be hungry on his program. You'll be satisfied longer with real nutrition.

• **Add good foods.** Next, feed your body the way nature intended by eating more nutrient-packed whole foods. A sample day's meal plan on The UltraSimple Diet might include a cup of green tea, hot water with lemon, and a protein shake for breakfast (see sample recipe on the following page)...2 cups of steamed or lightly sautéed veggies, one-half cup of brown rice and an (optional) protein shake for lunch...1 cup of vegetable broth, 2 cups of vegetables, one-half cup of brown rice, and 4 to 6 ounces of fish or chicken for dinner.

ULTRASHAKE RECIPE

To make a tasty, healthful protein shake, in a blender, combine...

½ cup of plain, unsweetened, gluten-free almond or hazel nut milk

1 to 2 tablespoons of nut butter (almond, macadamia, pecan) or ¼ cup of nuts (soaked overnight in water) such as almonds, walnuts, pecans or any combination of these

1 tablespoon organic combination flax and borage oil

2 tablespoons ground flaxseeds

½ cup fresh or frozen noncitrus organic fruit, such as cherries, blueberries, raspberries, strawberries, peaches, pears or frozen bananas

Ice (made from filtered water if desired)

2 to 4 ounces of filtered water to desired consistency.

Note: Use flaxseeds in up to two shakes a day, no more.

Dr. Hyman's tip: To reduce food cravings, eat protein for breakfast every day, and have a healthy snack (for example, a handful of walnuts, almonds or pumpkin seeds) when hungry. These strategies help keep your blood sugar—and thus your energy level—on an even keel.

Note: Those with digestion challenges due to stomach acid levels may find it better to stick with three solid meals a day in order to make optimal use of your stomach's acid.

• **Detoxify.** Dr. Hyman finds it helpful to kick-start the process of fighting inflammation with a cup of homemade detoxifying vegetable broth. This keeps hunger at bay while cleansing the system.

Broth recipe: To make a detox vegetable broth, combine 10 cups filtered water...6 cups chopped mixed organic veggies...and fresh or dried herbs and spices, such as bay leaf, oregano, lemongrass, fennel and ginger. Use a variety of vegetables that include at least four of the following—shiitake mushrooms, burdock root, sweet potatoes, carrots, onions, celery, sea vegetables, dark leafy greens, daikon and daikon leaf, and root vegetables such as turnips and parsnips. (In the case of less widely available vegetables such as burdock root and daikon, it may be necessary to visit a specialty grocery store such as Whole Foods Market or any other health food store near you.) Add the herbs to the veggies and water, and bring to a boil in a large stockpot. Simmer on a low boil for approximately 60 minutes. Strain and drink warm, at least 3 to 4 cups a day. The broth lasts for two days, so you may want to freeze a portion for future use.

Note: You may feel a bit foggy or fatigued the first day or two, as your body adjusts to your healthful new eating program. However, this should clear up quickly.

WHAT'S NEXT

Of course, given the intense focus on eating only those foods that are healthy for you and avoiding foods that are toxic and cause inflammation, almost everyone loses weight and feels better at the end of the week.

Some people choose to gradually re-incorporate some eliminated foods back into their diets—but since the goal is to feel and function better, it is critical to be careful about what foods are re-introduced.

Better to consider these the "first" seven days in your new lifestyle of healthful eating and living. Also be sure to check with your doctor before starting this or any other diet program.

Dr. Hyman's UltraSimple program is simple to remember—but there's no doubt that it takes commitment to complete. If you make even some of the changes he recommends, he says it will greatly improve your health and well-being. With new energy and the pride of achievement, you can continue down the path of a healthier life.

Get Fit in Just a Few Minutes

Joan Price, a certified fitness instructor and motivational speaker based in Sebastopol, California, and author of six books, including *The Anytime, Anywhere Exercise Book* (iUniverse). She credits her commitment to exercise for her success in twice regaining the ability to walk and dance after two head-on car crashes. *www.joanprice.com.*

Lack of time is a primary reason people give for failing to get the recommended 30 to 60 minutes of moderate-intensity exercise most days of the week. Admittedly, it can be tough to find such a big chunk of time in your busy schedule.

What helps: Instead of feeling compelled to cram an entire day's worth of exercise into a single block of time, commit to fitting in little bursts of physical activity—two minutes, five minutes, 10 minutes—throughout the day. The more these "fitness minutes" add up, the more you reap the benefits of exercise, including improved health, better weight control, increased energy and a sense of well-being.

IN THE MORNING...

•**When your alarm clock rings**—instead of pressing the snooze button, get up and use those extra minutes to do some gentle yoga poses.

•**While brushing your teeth**—do calf raises. Standing, slowly rise onto the balls of your feet...hold for several seconds...return to the starting position. Repeat, continuing for two minutes.

•**In the shower**—give your upper back muscles a workout. Squeeze your shoulder blades together...hold for five to 10 seconds...rest for a moment. Repeat 10 to 15 times.

•**While you style your hair**—squeeze your buttocks muscles as hard as you can for 10 seconds...rest for several seconds...repeat five to 10 times.

•**When going down stairs**—turn around at the bottom of the stairs and go back up, making one or more extra up-and-down trips.

•**As the coffee is brewing**—hop on your right foot 10 times...then hop on the left foot. Repeat twice.

•**When letting the dog out**—go with him for a short walk.

OUT AND ABOUT...

•**At the gas station**—walk inside to pay rather than swiping a credit card at the pump. Instead of sitting in your car as the gas flows, clean all your windows, alternating the hand that holds the squeegee.

•**At every red light**—do shoulder shrugs and roll your shoulders...repeatedly tighten and release your thigh muscles...rotate one wrist, then the other wrist.

•**When parking**—instead of finding a spot close to your destination, get one a few blocks away.

•**Upon entering a store**—if all the items you need will fit in a shopping basket, choose a basket instead of a cart.

•**As you shop**—if you need a cart, do 10 bicep curls with weightier items—soup cans, juice jugs—before placing them in your cart. (If you feel silly doing this in public, do your bicep curls at home as you put the items in the pantry.)

•**While waiting in line**—work your abdominal muscles. Suck in your belly and tighten your abs...hold for 10 seconds...relax. Repeat five to 10 times.

•**On a long car trip**—stop every 50 miles or so, and take a walk around a rest stop or scenic area.

•**When traveling by bus, plane or train**—walk up and down the aisle for at least five minutes every hour.

AT YOUR DESK...

•**While on the phone**—march in place or pace around your office.

•**As you read e-mail**—lift your right foot several inches off the floor...rotate your ankle clockwise several times, then counterclockwise...lower the foot. Repeat on the left side.

•**If you need to talk with a coworker**—walk over to her office instead of phoning. When you get back to your own desk, before sitting down, hold your arms out to the side and circle them forward 15 times, then circle them backward.

●**Each time you finish a task**—do "chair dips." With feet flat on the floor, place your hands on the armrests and push your body up (so your rear end hovers above the seat)…hold for several seconds…lower yourself back into the chair. Repeat 10 times. (Skip this if your chair has wheels.)

●**During your lunch break**—take a walk through the office complex.

●**In the restroom**—stand and reach for the sky for 30 seconds…then do 10 jumping jacks.

●**If you drop a pencil (or at least once a day)**—do a variation on toe touches. Stand up, bend down, pick up the pencil, straighten up …drop the pencil again. Repeat 10 times.

IN THE EVENING…

●**Before starting dinner**—take a quick ride around the neighborhood on your bicycle.

●**At the dinner table**—do leg lifts. Sit with feet flat on the floor. Straighten your right leg to hold your right foot out in front of you…lift your right thigh a few inches off the chair and hold for several seconds…lower the foot. Repeat 10 times, then switch to the left leg.

●**Doing laundry**—when you grab a basket of clothes, tighten abdominal muscles and, with your back straight, lift the basket from hip height to chest height five times.

●**Listening to the radio or a CD**—dance around the room for one entire song. Repeat several times.

●**While watching TV**—pop an exercise video or DVD in your player. Every time the TV show cuts to a commercial break, turn on the player and follow along with the workout for several minutes.

●**Climbing the stairs**—take the steps two at a time. (Do not do this if you have balance problems.)

●**After washing your face**—tilt your head slowly from side to side, feeling a good stretch along your neck…try to touch your chin to your chest to stretch the back of your neck.

●**Before climbing into bed**—raise your arms overhead…tilt gently to the right, feeling the stretch along the left side of your torso… then tilt to the left. Repeat five times.

●**When you lie down**—do knee hugs. Lie on your back with your knees bent, feet flat on the mattress. Raise one leg, place your hands behind the thigh and draw the leg toward your chest. Hold for 30 seconds…return to starting position. Repeat with the other leg.

●**Closing your eyes**—breathe in and out deeply 10 times, feeling grateful for all that your body was capable of doing during the day.

Natural Ways to Boost Energy—and Feel 10 Years Younger

Woodson Merrell, MD, chairman of the department of integrative medicine at Beth Israel Medical Center and assistant clinical professor of medicine at Columbia University College of Physicians and Surgeons, both in New York City. He is author, with Kathleen Merrell, of *The Source: Unleash Your Natural Energy, Power Up Your Health, and Feel 10 Years Younge*r (Free Press). Dr. Merrell's Web site is *www.woodsonmerrell.com*.

Exhaustion is an underrecognized epidemic in the US. Up to 75 million Americans report feeling "extreme" fatigue at work. Fatigue is among the top five complaints that people discuss with their doctors—even though it's estimated that two-thirds of people with chronic exhaustion never mention it to their doctors.

Every physical activity, from the beating of the heart to running to catch a train, depends on *adenosine triphosphate* (ATP), chemical energy produced inside cells. Nearly everyone can significantly increase daily energy by increasing the cellular production of ATP and reducing unnecessary consumption of ATP. *Most people know that exercise boosts energy—but you also can boost your ATP in other ways…*

STRESS REDUCTION

Stress activates the sympathetic nervous system, which triggers thousands of chemical reactions that consume tremendous amounts of energy—energy that is then unavailable to the body. People who experience chronic stress may have insufficient energy even for normal body repairs. It is estimated that up to 80% of all illnesses are due in part to stress. *What to do…*

● **Keep a stress log.** Every day, write down the events or situations that put you over the edge. These might include rush-hour traffic or dealing with a difficult boss. Once you recognize your flash points, try to eliminate them—by taking a different route to work, for example, or avoiding unnecessary encounters with difficult people.

● **Create the perception of control.** People who feel helpless experience more stress than those who take a proactive approach—even when they're exposed to similar stressful events.

Example: Maybe your job involves daily, high-pressure meetings. The source of stress won't go away, but you can blunt the impact by deciding to do something about it—by taking a brisk walk before each meeting, perhaps, or simply telling yourself to stay calm.

● **Take frequent breath breaks.** Harvard mind-body researcher Herbert Benson, MD, found that the body's energy expenditure dropped by as much as 17% during meditation. A less formal approach, when you notice signs of stress, is to take a "breath break."

How to do it: Inhale slowly to the count of four, pause for one second, then exhale slowly and completely to the count of six. Pause for one second, then repeat four more times.

People who take a breath break every one to two hours usually notice that they have more energy throughout the day. They also have a slower pulse, lower blood pressure and lower levels of cortisol (the primary stress hormone).

HIGH-ENERGY FOODS

A Harvard study found that the majority of American adults are deficient in vitamins and minerals. These deficiencies usually aren't severe enough to cause diseases, but they can impair the body's ability to manufacture usable forms of energy. *Helpful…*

● **Choose a "rainbow diet"**—including blueberries, broccoli, carrots, spinach, tomatoes and even dark chocolate. A variety of colors is important because different plant pigments, such as carotenes and flavonoids, help prevent metabolic by-products from damaging the mitochondria (energy-producing machinery) within cells.

● **Eat fish two to three times a week.** The omega-3 fatty acids in cold-water fish reduce inflammation—saving the energy that is normally needed to fight it. To avoid the risk of excessive mercury, eat small fish, such as sardines, anchovies or trout. Large, predatory fish, such as tuna and sea bass, tend to have the most mercury.

● **Avoid refined carbs.** White bread, sweets and other refined carbohydrates are rapidly converted to blood sugar. This causes an energy surge that is followed by a longer-lasting energy decline. Spikes in blood sugar also cause glycation, a process that prevents cells from working efficiently.

Better: Whole grains, lentils, beans and other foods high in complex carbohydrates. These are digested more slowly and provide the materials for longer-lasting energy.

● **Drink water**—at least six glasses a day. The majority of my patients are dehydrated. Water supports the body's ability to eliminate free radicals (cell-damaging molecules) and other toxins that impair energy production.

THE JUICE CLEANSE

Juice fasts allow the digestive tract to rest while promoting detoxification, reducing inflammation and dramatically increasing energy. One study even found that people who fasted once a month were 39% more likely to have healthy hearts than nonfasters.

Once a month, consume nothing but juice for an entire day. Use a juicer to combine a variety of organic vegetables, such as spinach, carrots and broccoli. Add a small amount of apples, cherries or other fruits as a natural sweetener.

It's normal to feel a little worse during the day of the fast. That's when the body is shedding the most toxins. Most people feel much more energized and clear-headed on the day after the fast.

Caution: If you have a severe chronic disease, diabetes or are pregnant, consult your physician before fasting.

SUPPLEMENTS CAN HELP

I recommend supplements only to patients who don't notice significant energy improvements within a few weeks of eating a healthier diet or making other lifestyle changes. *If this is the case for you, try...*

• **Ashwagandha.** It's an "energy-balancing" herb that improves the body's ability to metabolize sugars as well as cortisol.

Standard dose: 250 milligrams (mg) twice daily.

• **Probiotics that include acidophilus and bifidophilus.** People who take probiotic supplements have improvements in immunity and digestive function.

Standard dose: One to two daily supplements containing at least 10 billion organisms per dose.

• **Multivitamin that includes at least 400 international units (IU) of vitamin D.** People who have been diagnosed with low vitamin D need 1,000 IU to 2,000 IU daily. Vitamin D is very important for immune strength and cardiovascular health—and is crucial for maintaining healthy circulation and energy.

10 Quick Energy Boosters

Jon Gordon, best-selling author of *The Energy Bus: 10 Rules to Fuel Your Life, Work, and Team with Positive Energy* (Wiley) and *The 10-Minute Energy Solution* (Putnam). His performance-energy consulting firm is based in Ponte Vedra Beach, Florida. Clients have included the PGA Tour, the Jacksonville Jaguars football team, General Electric, State Farm Insurance and Wachovia Bank. *www.jongordon.com.*

Three-quarters of the people I meet complain of tiredness during the day. This epidemic of exhaustion is brought about by mental and physical stress, including too much caffeine and sugar as well as too little sleep and exercise.

Here are easy ways to feel more alert and energetic...

• **Stop hitting the snooze button on your alarm clock in the morning.** Your brain goes through periods of light and heavy sleep. Falling back to sleep for just five more minutes can cut short a new sleep cycle, leaving you groggier when you do arise.

Better: Set your clock for when you really have to get up. Open your shades right away, and get as much light as possible—bright light wakes you up and invigorates you. Raise your heartbeat for at least five minutes in the morning by running in place or doing sit-ups, push-ups or jumping jacks.

• **Eat a power breakfast.** It will energize you as you start the day.

My favorite power breakfast: Mix low-fat plain yogurt and one-half cup of old-fashioned raw oatmeal when you first get up. The yogurt will soften the oats while you shower and dress. Add a few chopped walnuts or some fruit. Try one-half cup of pineapple or one-quarter cup of blueberries.

• **Sit up straight.** Bad posture can decrease your oxygen intake, and slouching exhausts your neck, shoulders and upper-back muscles.

Correct posture for sitting: Your back should be aligned against the back of the chair, so that you can work without leaning forward. Your knees should be a bit higher than your hips. Keep both feet flat on the floor and your arms flexed at a 75- to 90-degree angle

• **Replace coffee with green tea.** The rich taste of coffee and the mental alertness it imparts make coffee drinking a tough habit to break. But coffee raises stress hormones, and just a few cups a day creates an energy roller coaster that increases overall fatigue. I have found that people who have the most success giving up coffee switch to green tea. It contains one-third the amount of caffeine (20 mg to 25 mg per six-ounce cup), so you get an energy boost without feeling irritable or experiencing a slump later on.

Bonus: Green tea is loaded with disease-fighting antioxidants.

If you have no intention of giving up your daily coffee, at least try cutting back to half regular/half decaf.

• **Consume protein with meals.** It helps your body absorb sugar at a slower rate, so your energy levels don't fluctuate so much during the day.

Examples: Fish, eggs, hummus, skinless poultry breast, lean red meat.

• **Go for a 10-minute walk after lunch.** It raises your metabolism and prevents you from falling into the familiar, post-meal "coma."

If it's inconvenient to go outside, try chair squats.

How to do that: With a chair behind you, stand with your feet positioned shoulder-width apart. Keep your back straight and your chin up. Squat down, and push out your rear as if you were going to sit in the chair behind you. Just as your rear touches the chair, return to your starting position. Repeat five to 30 times—or until you feel your muscles have had enough.

• **Take a short nap, no more than 25 minutes.** Longer than that and you move into a deeper phase of sleep, which, if interrupted, can leave you groggier than before your nap. The optimal time to take a nap is eight hours after you wake up.

• **Eat an energy snack, such as a banana or a handful of walnuts or almonds.** Avoid commercial energy drinks and energy bars—they often work by introducing caffeine and/or sugar into your system.

Helpful: I do recommend a caffeine-free, multivitamin energy powder that I use myself each day—Fatigued to Fantastic! from Enzymatic Therapy, available at health-food stores.

Cost: About $30 for a month's supply.

• **Try peppermint.** It boosts mood and motivation. Have a cup of peppermint tea, or dab peppermint oil (available at health-food stores) on your wrists.

• **Breathe.** We tend to hold our breath when we work intensely or are under stress—and this contributes to fatigue.

To practice energy-boosting breathing: Stand up straight with your arms at your sides. Inhale for two seconds as you raise your arms slowly over your head with your palms open. Continue lifting your arms until they are directly over your head with fingertips touching. Exhale for three seconds as you bring your arms down. Repeat 10 times.

Dr. Kenneth H. Cooper— 12 Powerful Ways to Boost Your Energy

Kenneth H. Cooper, MD, MPH, a pioneer in the fields of preventive medicine and physical fitness. He is chairman of Cooper Aerobics Center, Dallas, and author of 18 books, including *Regaining the Power of Youth at Any Age* (Nelson). His books have sold more than 30 million copies worldwide. *www.cooperaerobics.com.*

As we get older, we often complain that we're "running on empty." I call this age-related loss of energy *youth drain*—but we don't have to be victims of it. At 81 years of age, I work 60 hours a week, travel widely and still feel energetic.

Youth drain can be caused by a variety of factors, including obesity…chronic medical problems, such as anemia, diabetes, emphysema or an under-active thyroid gland…depression…cancer…use of sedatives and sleeping pills…menopause…poor diet…inadequate sleep and stress. These factors batter us over the years and drain our vitality—unless we learn how to respond to them and counter their effects.

Here, 12 revitalizing strategies for us all…

1. Eat less but more frequently. Consuming large meals (more than 1,000 calories per sitting) makes you feel sluggish, as your body's resources are directed toward digesting all that food.

Instead, graze on small meals and snacks that contain a mix of carbohydrates and protein (but little fat) to provide a steady stream of fuel.

Examples: Yogurt smoothie (one cup light nonfat yogurt, one-half cup fat-free milk, one-half peach, blended)…peanut butter and banana sandwich (one slice wholewheat bread, one-half tablespoon peanut butter, one-half banana, sliced)…fruity cottage cheese (one-half cup 1% low-fat cottage cheese, one-half cup pine-apple chunks in juice, drained).

2. Exercise. The health benefits of exercise are well-known, but many people tell me they continue to exercise year after year because it makes them feel good and gives them more energy. I recommend at least 30 minutes of sustained activity five times a week. The best activities for most people tend to be brisk walking, jogging, swimming, cycling and aerobic dance.

3. Take a multivitamin. In a clinical trial, people who took multivitamins daily not only had improved immunity against infectious diseases but also had more energy. In general, it is best to get vitamins from food, but many people don't get the necessary amounts, so I suggest taking a multivitamin/mineral supplement daily.

4. Prevent dehydration. Consuming an inadequate amount of fluids, particularly if it's hot outside or you're exercising, can deplete energy and lead to weakness, dizziness and headaches. Drink at least six to eight eight-ounce glasses of water daily. On days that you exert yourself to the point of perspiring, increase that to up to 13 glasses.

5. Watch what you drink. Drink no more than one caffeinated beverage a day. Coffee, tea, cola and other caffeinated beverages provide a temporary energy boost, but energy levels plunge rapidly when the stimulant's effects wear off.

Caffeinated drinks also have a diuretic effect, which may cause you to lose fluids because you urinate more frequently.

Also, limit alcohol consumption to no more than one drink a day—any more can lead to fatigue.

6. Practice the "relaxation response." This technique, developed by Herbert Benson, MD, of Harvard University, has been shown to reduce blood pressure and heart rate. For me, doing this for just five minutes in the middle of the day is rejuvenating.

How to do it: Sit in a chair in a quiet room. Close your eyes. Starting with your feet, begin to relax your muscles, progressively moving up the body to the top of the head. While you do this, breathe in slowly and naturally through your nose and out through your mouth. As you exhale, silently repeat a focus word or phrase that has meaning for you, such as "peace." Push away distracting thoughts by focusing on your breathing and the word you have chosen to repeat.

For more information, read *The Relaxation Response* by Herbert Benson, MD (Harper-Torch).

7. Take naps. Surveys show that most Americans don't get as much sleep as they need (most of us require seven to eight hours a night). Daily naps of 15 to 20 minutes are energizing—and longer naps can help you catch up if you are sleep-deprived. I sleep only five to six hours a night, so I often take a two-hour nap on Saturdays.

8. Don't immerse yourself in bad news. The glut of negative information coming our way from TV, radio, newspapers, the Internet, etc. can hurt the psyche, causing stress and fatigue. Reduce the amount of time you spend watching, listening to or reading the news, and focus on things that bring you joy.

9. Be social. Studies show that isolation can lead to depression and early death. We gain energy by being with others (both humans and animals). Make time for family, friends and pets.

10. Explore your creativity. Boredom leads to a lack of motivation and energy. Finding a creative outlet that absorbs you is invigorating. Developing your creativity also teaches you new skills…challenges your brain…and leads to the release of endorphins, feel-good brain chemicals. Take up a new hobby…learn a musical instrument…take on an unusual project at work.

Added benefit: Mentally stimulating activities can lower your risk of Alzheimer's disease.

11. Laugh. Laughter appears to release endorphins just as creative pursuits do. By improving your outlook, you'll feel more energetic and ready to tackle life.

Helpful: Watch funny movies…read cartoons…share humorous stories and jokes with friends.

12. Think young. To a large extent, your mindset dictates how much energy you have as you age. If you expect the worst, you're likely to feel tired and unwell. If you expect to stay vital, you'll fight off disease that can sap energy and well-being—and you'll add years to your life.

Can Fasting Improve Energy Level?

Mark A. Stengler, NMD, naturopathic medical doctor in private practice, Encinitas, California…adjunct associate clinical professor at the National College of Natural Medicine, Portland, Oregon…author of *The Natural Physician's Healing Therapies* (Bottom Line Books).

Fasting can be an effective way to detoxify the body and subsequently improve energy levels. It works by giving the organs and cells of the body a rest from some of the metabolic functions they perform every second of the day. This rest allows the body to expel toxins and cleanse the tissues.

During the first day of a fast, the body burns stored sugar, known as glycogen. The cells also begin to burn fat for fuel, while the brain continues to burn glucose (blood sugar). During the second day of a fast, muscle tissue may be broken down into amino acids, which then are converted by the liver into glucose to feed the brain. On the third day, the fasting body goes into ketosis. During this state, the liver converts stored fat into chemicals called ketones, which can be used by the brain and muscles, including the heart, to sustain energy levels.

Around the third day of the fast, most people lose their hunger pains and notice increased energy and a heightened sense of awareness and clarity of mind. People may lose up to two pounds per day during this stage.

There are many different types of fasts. A water-only fast (80 ounces of water daily for one to three days) is the most aggressive type and should be used only by those in good health.

Juice fasts (80 to 100 ounces of juice daily for two to five days) also are common and are especially useful for boosting energy. These fasts often include the fresh juice of carrots, lemons, apples, beets and celery. Wheatgrass juice, which helps detoxify the liver and kidneys, and other greens also can be added.

For a modified type of fast, you can eat homemade broths and soups (three to four bowls a day containing carrots, celery, chicken broth, potatoes and spices)…or drink 30 to 40 ounces daily of detoxification meal-replacement drinks (containing rice or pea-protein, added vitamins and minerals, and detoxifying herbs, such as milk thistle and green tea extract), plus 32 ounces of water. Meal-replacement drinks are commonly available through natural health-care practitioners and at health-food stores.

People with diabetes should avoid fasts. If you have a chronic health condition, you should fast only under the supervision of a medical professional. People who do not react well to fasts often do better on the modified versions, such as the use of meal-replacement drinks. If you have little experience with fasting, work with a nutrition-oriented doctor for guidance.

5

Drug-Free Remedies For Good Digestion

IBS Breakthroughs

If you're among the estimated one in six American adults who suffers from chronic abdominal pain or discomfort due to irritable bowel syndrome (IBS), you know that effective, long-lasting treatment remains elusive.

Good news: The American College of Gastroenterology recently published a review of the most effective treatments, including dietary approaches, nondrug therapies and medications, that should finally give relief to people with IBS.

WHAT IS IBS?

A disorder of the digestive tract, irritable bowel syndrome (IBS) affects about 35 million Americans. Symptoms include bloating, abdominal pain and changes in bowel function (constipation and/or diarrhea). The cause of the condition is unknown, but genetics may play a role. IBS symptoms can be triggered or worsened by such factors as diet and emotional upset.

DO YOU HAVE IBS?

With IBS, the nerves that control the gastrointestinal tract are hypersensitive—that is, sensations that other people wouldn't notice, including those produced by the ordinary process of digestion, are amplified and often painful.

Research has shown that many times IBS begins after a severe bout of digestive upset caused by a bacterial or viral infection, such as "stomach flu" or "traveler's diarrhea"—perhaps because such infections temporarily or permanently affect nerves in the gastrointestinal tract.

What most people don't know: Researchers have found that people with a history of abuse (physical, emotional or sexual) are at heightened risk for IBS—probably due to stress on the intestinal nervous system.

Brian E. Lacy, MD, PhD, associate professor of medicine at Dartmouth Medical School in Hanover, New Hampshire, and director of the gastrointestinal motility laboratory at Dartmouth–Hitchcock Medical Center in Lebanon, New Hampshire. He is the author of *Making Sense of IBS* (Johns Hopkins).

Diagnosis of IBS can be tricky because symptoms, including abdominal pain, bloating and troublesome bowel patterns (frequent or persistent bouts of diarrhea, constipation or both, generally occurring at least three days a month), often wax and wane in severity. So-called "flares" (episodes of severe symptoms) may occur weeks, months—or even years—apart.

IBS symptoms that may be missed: Mucus in the stool or straining during, or a feeling of incomplete evacuation after, a bowel movement.

•***If you think you may have IBS:*** See your primary care doctor. IBS almost always can be identified with a standard history and physical exam.

WHEN FOOD IS THE TRIGGER

Lactose intolerance (the inability to digest dairy sugar) can lead to misdiagnosis because its classic symptoms—bloating and diarrhea—mimic those caused by IBS.

My advice: If your digestive problems seem to worsen when you consume dairy products, follow an *elimination diet*.

What to do: Go without all dairy products for seven to 10 days—and slowly reintroduce each type of dairy product, such as yogurt or cheese, to see how much you can tolerate before symptoms return.

IBS food triggers that often are overlooked—try the elimination diet (as described above) with each…

•**Soft drinks and other high-fructose drinks and foods.** Fructose—a sugar commonly added to carbonated soft drinks and sports drinks and naturally occurring in fruit juices and high-sugar fruits (such as dried fruits)—can cause bloating, gas and diarrhea in people with IBS.

•**Caffeine.** It stimulates the digestive tract and may cause cramps and more frequent bowel movements in people with IBS.

THE FIBER FACTOR

For many people with IBS—especially those with recurrent constipation—adequate fiber intake (25 mg to 30 mg per day) helps relieve symptoms. If you are not consuming this much fiber, increase your intake of fruits and whole grains or take a fiber supplement containing psyllium (such as Metamucil or Konsyl).

Fiber-rich foods I recommend most often: Raspberries, artichokes, green peas, almonds, oatmeal, oat bran and whole-grain bread.

Important: IBS patients who have recurrent diarrhea should *limit* fiber intake to about 10 g daily and avoid leafy greens and cruciferous vegetables (such as cauliflower) because high-fiber foods can worsen symptoms in these patients.

BEST ALTERNATIVE APPROACHES

If dietary changes (described above) do not relieve IBS symptoms, there is credible scientific evidence to support the use of two natural remedies for IBS…

•**Peppermint oil.** In enteric-coated capsule form, peppermint oil appears to relax smooth muscle in the gastrointestinal tract and therefore reduce IBS abdominal pain caused by muscle spasms. For dosage, follow label instructions.

•**Probiotics.** Probiotics augment the "friendly" bacteria in the large intestine. Probiotic dietary supplements containing the *Bifidobacterium* species are worth trying when bloating and diarrhea are prominent. Look for probiotic supplements providing at least 100 million colony-forming units per dose. Be patient—it may take up to three months to produce substantial benefits.

Using Your Mind to Ease Irritable Bowel Syndrome

Olafur S. Palsson, PsyD, associate professor, medicine, Center for Functional GI & Motility Disorders, University of North Carolina at Chapel Hill.

Jeffrey M. Lackner, PsyD, associate professor, medicine, University at Buffalo School of Medicine & Biomedical Sciences, Buffalo, New York.

International Foundation for Functional Gastrointestinal Disorders, Milwaukee.

When standard lifestyle adjustments such as dietary changes and drug therapy don't provide relief from the pain, bloating and other unpleasant gastrointestinal symptoms of irritable bowel syndrome, patients may want to try a different approach.

Recent studies show that using one's own thoughts, as taught in cognitive behavioral therapy, may help ease symptoms. Likewise, using hypnosis to visualize the pain and imagine it seeping away can be a powerful treatment strategy, too.

"Research indicates that the probability of achieving benefits is excellent with either approach, even for patients who haven't improved from the standard medical care," said Olafur S. Palsson, PsyD, a clinical psychologist and associate professor of medicine at the University of North Carolina at Chapel Hill's Center for Functional GI & Motility Disorders.

BACKGROUND

As many as 45 million Americans may have irritable bowel syndrome, or IBS, the International Foundation for Functional Gastrointestinal Disorders reports. Sixty to 65% of IBS sufferers are women.

In addition to pain and discomfort, people with IBS experience chronic or recurrent constipation or diarrhea—or bouts of both. While the exact cause of the condition isn't known, symptoms seem to result from a disturbance in the interaction of the gut, brain and nervous system, according to the Foundation.

Doctors generally advise patients to avoid certain foods that may exacerbate symptoms. Several different medications may be recommended for relieving abdominal pain, diarrhea and constipation. But these approaches don't always provide adequate relief.

"For some people, medications and dietary changes are the perfect match, but most of our patients—the great, great majority of patients—have not responded to medications and dietary changes," said Jeffrey M. Lackner, PsyD, associate professor of medicine at the University at Buffalo School of Medicine & Biomedical Sciences, and a behavioral medicine specialist whose research focuses on gastrointestinal disorders, particularly IBS.

For many patients, cognitive behavioral therapy, which uses the power of the mind to replace unhealthy beliefs and behaviors with healthy, positive ones, may be the answer. But, Dr. Lackner observed, very few facilities around the country specialize in this type of treatment. Recognizing this, he and his colleagues set out to devise and test a treatment program that IBS patients could administer themselves.

THE COGNITIVE BEHAVIORAL STUDY

Seventy-five women and men were divided into three groups. One group was placed on a "wait list" for 10 weeks while they monitored their symptoms. Another group received the standard treatment of 10 cognitive behavioral therapy sessions over weekly. The third group had once-a-month therapy sessions over four months and practiced relaxation and problem-solving exercises at home.

Not surprisingly, people on the wait list did not do well at all, while those in the weekly and monthly sessions showed significant improvement. "They said at the end of treatment they had achieved adequate relief from pain and adequate relief from bowel problems, and a significant proportion of patients said they improved their symptoms," Dr. Lackner explained.

While more studies are needed, the findings suggest that traditional and self-administered cognitive behavioral therapy both provide adequate relief and improve symptoms, said Dr. Lackner, who first reported the findings at a large meeting of GI professionals.

THE HYPNOSIS STUDY

Hypnosis may be another option. A pair of Swedish studies presented at that same meeting found that patients who received "gut-directed hypnotherapy" had significant improvement in symptoms compared with those who did not receive this intervention.

Hypnosis treatment has been reported to improve symptoms of the majority of treated IBS patients in all published studies, noted Dr. Palsson.

RECOMMENDATIONS

For patients who have tried the diet-and-drug regimen to no avail, Dr. Palsson said he would recommend either of these two psychological treatments.

"If a patient's main goal is substantial relief of bowel symptoms, hypnosis is probably the better choice," he said, for the research literature strongly suggests that it improves the gastrointestinal symptoms far more reliably.

On the other hand, he added, if a patient wants to cope better with the illness or improve mental well-being, then cognitive behavioral therapy is equally good or perhaps even the better treatment option.

For more information on treating IBS, visit the Web site of the International Foundation for Functional Gastrointestinal Disorders, *www.iffgd.org*.

The Covered-Up Cause of IBS

Nancy Kraft, RD, clinical dietitian, University of Iowa, Iowa City.

Theodore M. Bayless, MD, professor of medicine, Johns Hopkins University, Baltimore.

American College of Gastroenterology annual meeting, Baltimore.

Cutting back on sugar and fat makes sense for people trying to control their weight, but there may be another health benefit. Two studies suggest that fat and fructose, the sugar in fruits and honey (and also a component of high fructose corn syrup, or HFCS, that is used to sweeten many soft drinks and packaged foods), also can contribute to gastrointestinal discomfort.

Irritable bowel syndrome (IBS) is a common disorder of the intestines that leads to pain, gassiness, bloating and changes in bowel habits, according to the American Gastroenterological Association. The disorder can lead to constipation in some and diarrhea in others. Some people experience both.

In the first report, Nancy Kraft, a clinical dietitian from the University of Iowa, and her colleagues say some patients who have IBS are fructose-intolerant, and restricting that type of sugar can improve their symptoms.

Kraft says fructose intolerance often is an overlooked component of IBS.

Her colleague Dr. Young Choi says that, "A fructose-restricted diet significantly improved symptoms in some IBS patients. Fructose intolerance is yet another piece of the IBS puzzle."

THE STUDY

In the study, the 14 patients with IBS who followed a fructose-free diet for one year experienced a significant reduction in abdominal pain, bloating and diarrhea.

However, IBS symptoms remained the same for the 12 patients who did not stick with the diet, the researchers report.

Kraft believes these results are encouraging, because "people who limit their intake of fructose see their symptoms improve or disappear," but that further study is needed.

SECOND STUDY

Researchers from the Mayo Clinic in Rochester, Minnesota, led by Yuri Saito, MD, collected data on the diets of 221 adults, aged 20 to 50 years. Of these patients, 102 had gastrointestinal disorders and 119 were healthy.

The research team found that patients with IBS or dyspepsia (indigestion) reported eating more monounsaturated fats compared with healthy patients. These patients also ate fewer carbohydrates than their healthy counterparts.

The Mayo investigators concluded that "future studies are needed to determine whether fat intake causes gastrointestinal symptoms."

Theodore M. Bayless, MD, a professor of medicine at Johns Hopkins University, is not surprised that fat and fructose are linked with IBS and dyspepsia.

He notes that both fat and fructose are hard to digest and can aggravate both conditions. But Dr. Bayless does not believe that restricting fructose cures IBS...it may only relieve symptoms.

He advises patients to avoid fatty foods and foods that contain high levels of fructose, such as grapes, dates, honey and apple and pear juice. He also advises patients to check food labels for HFCS to limit intake of the sweetener and to increase fiber intake.

Simple Key to Better Digestion

Lita Lee, PhD, chemist and enzyme therapist, and author of *The Enzyme Cure* (Ten Speed).

You may have read a lot on the subject of vitamins and botanicals. But *enzymes* are critical to body function, and they are just starting to make headlines. Digestive enzymes are becoming more prominent as the dangers of long-term antacid use come to the attention of consumers and medical personnel. But, there are many other enzymes that make the body function. What do you need to know about them?

WHAT ARE ENZYMES?

Described as the "sparks of life" by Edward Howell, MD, an early and prominent enzyme researcher, enzymes are mostly protein molecules that act as catalysts for every single biochemical process in the body, from digestion to tissue regeneration. Without enzymes there would be no life...and when a person's supply of certain enzymes is inadequate, health problems follow. Because each bodily function needs a specific enzyme for activation—somewhat akin to the key that starts a car's engine—the body makes hundreds of thousands of them. *However, there are just three main categories...*

- **Metabolic enzymes**—manufactured by cells to carry out various functions.
- **Digestive enzymes**—primarily manufactured by the pancreas to digest foods and absorb nutrients.
- **Food enzymes**—exogenous (from outside the body) enzymes found in plants and animals, also necessary for aiding and accelerating digestion.

PANCREATIC IMPORTANCE

Chemist and enzyme therapist Lita Lee, PhD, explains why we hear so little about many enzymes. There is no reason to worry about metabolic enzymes, she says, if digestion is functioning well. So the focus is on enzymes needed for digestion—those created by the pancreas and food enzymes. *Enzymes produced by the pancreas also fall into three distinct categories...*

- **Amylase**—digests carbohydrates (a whole industry has grown up around the amylase enzyme lactase, a deficiency of which causes lactose intolerance).
- **Lipase**—splits fats and oils into fatty acids.
- **Protease**—breaks down protein into component amino acids.

ABOUT PLANT ENZYMES

Food enzymes are primarily plant enzymes (more about that later in the article), and include cellulase, another category of enzyme that is found only in plants and which digests soluble fiber.

To get the picture of what enzymes are about and why they are so important requires a brief review of digestion. Most digestion takes place in the small intestine, but the process of predigestion actually starts in the mouth. Saliva moistens the food, chewing releases enzymes from our food, and the stomach continues the enzyme release. The enzymes that do the work of predigestion are salivary amylase and plant enzymes and these, says Dr. Lee, are the key to a healthy digestive system. Pancreatic enzymes do not take over the job until food reaches the small intestine, and having adequate and appropriate plant enzymes for predigestion not only enhances digestion in general, it also greatly decreases the load that's put on the pancreas, a hardworking organ in the best of times. In fact, she says that enzymes in the mouth and stomach can predigest up to 60% of carbohydrates, 30% of protein and 10% of fat.

The catch: Few people have robust digestion—and so by definition few have adequate and effective plant enzymes. Many people point to age as the culprit here, with the belief that aging compromises enzyme function, but Dr. Lee disagrees because children often have poor digestion as well. In addition, few people also eat adequate levels of plant enzymes at each meal, which contributes to digestive problems over time. Ideally, every meal should include fruits and fruit juices, she says.

REASONS FOR POOR ENZYME DIGESTION

Enzymes become less effective when heated above 140°F. Hence, much of the enzyme benefit is lost in highly cooked foods. The second factor for enzyme function has to do with pH balances in the digestive system. To be activated, an enzyme needs a highly specific and particular pH range. The popular antacid medications, both over-the-counter (OTC) and prescriptive, directly affect pH balance. A common misconception is that stomach acid is there to directly digest food. Rather, when a person eats, acid comes in to lower the pH balance of the stomach so that it will be the proper environment to activate the digestive enzyme pepsin. If there is too little stomach acid, the pH balance is incorrect and the digestive process is dramatically compromised.

BUILDING YOUR ENZYME PERFORMANCE

Virtually everyone benefits from improved plant enzyme ingestion. According to Dr. Lee, the place to start is with food. Dr. Lee advises eating all foods whole and usually organic—in other words, no processed foods (processing to create shelf life destroys enzymes), no "low-fat" items, no reconstituted and certainly, no fake foods such as artificial sweeteners. She staunchly advocates eating meat and fish because protein contributes to a healthy thyroid, and that contributes to healthy enzyme activity. She is strongly against estrogenic foods such as soy because she believes they affect thyroid function and may be carcinogenic.

MORE FOOD SPECIFICS

Look for grass-fed meats and poultry, and wild fish. Raw milk and cheeses, especially from goats or sheep, if you can find them, are full of healthy enzymes. Pasteurizing, however, destroys these enzymes—especially ultra-pasteurizing, the process used to make organic milk. Eat raw carrots and salads, of course, but avoid commercial salad dressings. Do not eat raw cruciferous vegetables such as cauliflower, broccoli, cabbage, kale and brussels sprouts, because they contain thyroid-inhibiting factors. Cooking these foods destroys the risk to the thyroid. It is best to steam them until brightly colored on the outside. This will preserve some enzyme activity while removing the *isothiocyanates* responsible for the antithyroid effect.

SUPPLEMENTING MAKES IT SIMPLE

Since most people don't eat a lot of raw food, Dr. Lee suggests taking plant enzyme supplements before each meal. The ones she recommends are those from leading enzyme practitioner Edward F. Loomis, Jr., DC (*www. naturalenzymes.com* or call 800-614-4400).

Note: If you have digestive problems, work with a health-care professional who has been trained in enzyme therapy. This person can evaluate individual situations and prescribe a balanced formula of enzymes that will address your needs.

It's All About the Gut

Mark A. Stengler, NMD, naturopathic medical doctor in private practice, Encinitas, California...adjunct associate clinical professor at the National College of Natural Medicine, Portland, Oregon...author of *The Natural Physician's Healing Therapies* (Bottom Line Books).

We *really* are what we eat—but more important, we are the foods we absorb. That's what I think about when patients come to see me feeling cranky and complaining of fatigue, poor memory, aching joints and/or moodiness. They want me to treat their symptoms, but to heal them, I have to go deeper and focus on their digestive health.

The reason: A root cause of many chronic problems often turns out to be poor digestion and inadequate absorption of nutrients. In fact, I find that nearly every patient with a chronic condition needs to address digestion issues... and even most healthy people would feel much better if they improved their digestion.

I have developed a successful protocol that heals the lining of the gut. I recommend this protocol for people with chronic digestive problems and systemic conditions related to poor digestion. It also helps healthy patients who want to improve their digestion.

GOOD DIGESTION...
AND BAD

To understand what goes wrong with digestion, it is important to understand how it works. As food mixed with saliva enters the stomach, it is broken down into small particles by stomach acid, then by enzymes produced by the pancreas and bile produced by the liver. "Good" bacteria (flora) in the small intestine complete the job of breaking down nutrients so that they can be absorbed. Undigestable parts of food, such as fiber, and other waste products are pushed into the colon where they remain until eliminated.

The small intestine plays the important role of gatekeeper, allowing nutrients—thoroughly digested particles of fats, proteins and starches, as well as vitamins and minerals—to pass through its wall into the bloodstream for distribution around the body. It also serves as a barrier to prevent undigested food, large molecules and foreign substances, such as harmful bacteria and yeast, from getting through. When the lining of the small intestine becomes irritated and inflamed, it is unable to do its job properly. As a result, bacteria and undigested food "leak" into the bloodstream. Officially this is called increased intestinal permeability, but more often the problem is called leaky gut syndrome.

THE DIGESTION–CHRONIC
ILLNESS LINK

Leaky gut syndrome wreaks havoc on immune function and nutritional status. When the gut "leaks," the immune system believes that it has been invaded by foreign bodies and goes on attack. It produces antibodies, which can inflame the gut and further damage the intestinal lining. This inflammatory response can result in the worsening of systemic symptoms, such as fatigue, arthritis and headache, among others.

In addition, leaky gut syndrome decreases nutritional absorption. When your gut doesn't efficiently absorb food, you can develop serious nutritional deficiencies that worsen systemic problems. The only way to stop the cycle is to heal your digestion.

CAUSES OF LEAKY GUT

There are many reasons people develop leaky gut syndrome. *Some causes are unique to our modern society, while others are age-old...*

• **Poor diet.** Fast foods are hard to digest, in part because their low fiber content slows their progress through the gastrointestinal (GI) tract. Foods high in sugar, artificial sweeteners, colorings, preservatives and omega-6 fatty acids (from vegetable oils) may cause inflammation in the gut.

• **Chronic stress.** The body responds to stress by going into "emergency" mode. As a result, digestion slows.

• **Chronic illnesses.** Cancer, depression and autoimmune diseases, such as rheumatoid arthritis and multiple sclerosis, often are associated with poor digestion.

• **Existing digestive problems.** Conditions such as colitis, Crohn's disease and irritable bowel syndrome can cause—and worsen—leaky gut syndrome.

• **Common pain relievers.** With regular use, aspirin, ibuprofen and other anti-inflammatory drugs damage the lining of the small intestine.

• **Acid-blocking medications.** Proton pump inhibitors (PPIs), such as *esomeprazole* (Nexium) and *omeprazole* (Prilosec), reduce stomach acid. Long-term use of these drugs intrudes on the GI system's ability to properly break down food, particularly proteins.

• **Other pharmaceutical drugs.** Certain anticancer drugs and oral steroids destroy the gut's "good" flora.

• **Bacterial imbalance.** Dysbiosis is an imbalance between good and bad bacteria. A deficiency of good bacteria in the gut often occurs as a result of excessive use of antibiotics or an overgrowth of harmful bacteria.

• **Environmental toxins.** Toxic metals in the environment, such as mercury (from seafood) and chlorine (from tap water), kill good flora.

• **Excessive alcohol intake.** Depending on the individual, two or more alcoholic beverages daily can damage the intestinal tract and reduce absorption abilities.

HEALTHY GUT PROTOCOL

In addition to clearing up all kinds of digestion problems, the new protocol I have developed gives the immune system a boost. My patients tell me that they have improved energy, less gas and bloating, better concentration, less arthritis pain and fewer colds and infections.

Another benefit: This protocol helps people with chronic conditions cope with food sensitivities—adverse reactions to foods containing sugar, dairy, wheat, corn or eggs that irritate and inflame the lining of the small intestine. Many holistic practitioners advise patients to identify these sensitivities with an elimination diet, in which one food at a time is avoided to determine if it is an offender. These diets can involve eliminating between 12 and 24 common foods—which can be time-consuming and stressful and deprive the body of valuable nutrients. My protocol enables my patients to eat many of the foods they want and get the nutrients they need.

I recommend taking all of the following supplements because each will have a different effect on digestion. Unless otherwise noted, they are safe for everyone, but discuss your intention to start this protocol with your doctor. Also, be sure to eat a healthful diet, avoiding alcohol, sugar, caffeine and hydrogenated fats (trans fatty acids found in packaged foods).

•**High-potency digestive enzymes.** These plant enzymes assist in the breakdown of all types of food. Because intolerance to dairy products and gluten (a protein in wheat and some other grains) is so common, I prefer enzymes that contain dipeptidyl peptidase (DPP-IV), which help break down gluten and the milk protein casein. Try Integrative Therapeutics Similase GFCF (gluten-free/casein-free) (800-931-1709, *www.integrativeinc.com*). Take two capsules with or at the end of each meal.

Caution: These enzymes do not allow people with celiac disease to eat gluten, although they can help digest hidden gluten in foods. Avoid these enzymes if you have active gastritis or ulcers.

•**N-acetyl d-glucosamine (NAG).** This amino sugar helps to form the mucous coating on the intestine, which protects it from contact with digestive enzymes and acids and helps discriminate between normal and unhealthy particles. NAG seems to directly reduce food-sensitivity reactions. It also may promote a healthy balance of good flora throughout the intestines. I often recommend NAG made by Allergy Research Group, which is available only through a health-care professional (800-545-9960, *www.allergyresearchgroup.com*). Take 500 mg twice daily before meals.

•**Glutamine.** This amino acid has been shown in several clinical studies to restore intestinal barrier function. It helps promote intestinal cell turnover, guards against intestinal infection and helps soothe inflammation of the digestive tract. My patients tell me that they have less cramping and abdominal pain. Take 1,000 mg three times daily before meals.

•**Deglycyrrhizinated licorice (DGL).** This type of licorice root extract stimulates intestinal mucus production and has an anti-inflammatory and soothing effect on the lining of the digestive tract. Chew one 400-mg tablet three times daily before meals. One widely available, high-quality DGL is made by Natural Factors (800-322-8704, *www.naturalfactors.com*).

•**Probiotics.** These healthful bacteria help prevent overgrowth of yeast and other potentially harmful organisms in the intestines. They also help break down food and normalize gut immune reactions, reducing food sensitivities. Try probiotics made by Jarrow (800-726-0886, *www.jarrow.com*)...Bio-K+ (800-593-2465, *www.biokplus.com*)...or DDS Multiflora (800-422-3371, *www.uaslabs.com*). Follow instructions on the label.

What to do: Take these supplements for two months, and then evaluate how you feel. Most of my patients notice a marked improvement in their digestion, energy level and chronic conditions. If you continue to have digestion problems, see a holistic practitioner. If you're doing well, stay on the protocol for three months or more and assess how you feel. If you have a chronic condition and this protocol helps, you can stay on it indefinitely.

Leaky gut syndrome is associated with many medical conditions, including...

•**Acne**

- **Arthritis (all types)**
- **Asthma**
- **Attention-deficit hyperactivity disorder (ADHD) in adults**
- **Chronic fatigue**
- **Depression**
- **Eczema**
- **Headache (migraine)**
- **Inflammatory bowel diseases**
- **Indigestion**
- **Irritable bowel syndrome**
- **Lupus**
- **Memory problems**
- **Multiple sclerosis**
- **Osteoporosis**
- **Psoriasis**
- **Weight loss and weight gain**
- **Yeast infections**

Making Bacteria Work for You

Andrew L. Rubman, ND, director, Southbury Clinic for Traditional Medicines, Southbury, Connecticut.

Americans tend to be bacteria-phobic. We've been taught that germs are the enemy, and to keep ourselves and our families healthy, we should kill as many of them as possible. So we obediently scrub our bathrooms and kitchens with potent antibacterial cleaners and wash our hands with antibacterial soaps. However, as I've pointed out before, this obsession with cleanliness has a downside for wellness and immune function, for there are "friendly" as well as "unfriendly" bacteria.

To indiscriminately wipe them all out is not what's best for our health. In fact, studies have shown weakened immune function as a result of all this excessive cleanliness. Living in this clean bubble, surrounded by bacteria-fighting antibiotics, ironically seems to have left our immune systems more vulnerable to illness.

ENTER PROBIOTICS

Probiotics are live micro-organisms similar or nearly identical to many of the beneficial micro-organisms (usually bacteria) that naturally populate the human gut. Available as dietary supplements and in foods (more on these later), probiotics can help maintain and support the digestive system's natural balance of good and bad micro-organisms or healthy flora. Adding probiotics to your diet contributes to more efficient digestion and absorption of food and nutrients, helps suppress disease-causing "germs," and helps optimize immune system function, explains digestion expert Andrew L. Rubman, ND. The key is having enough good bacteria, in the right balance, living throughout your digestive tract, from your stomach to your colon.

BACTERIA AND THE LARGE INTESTINE

You may be surprised to learn that about four pounds of bacteria reside in the intestinal tract of a normal adult, with most of it in the large intestine. Our wellness and resistance to disease depends on the proper balance of these bacteria. According to Dr. Rubman, these friendly bacteria help keep the intestinal walls healthy and intact and inflammation-free. This prevents unfriendly bacteria in food we eat from leaking out into other areas of the body, where it may trigger problems such as arthritis, eczema, migraines and asthma or allergies. Dysfunction in the gastrointestinal tract may also contribute to irritable bowel syndrome, vaginal candidiasis (yeast infections), skin rashes and other problems, including immunological disorders, kidney disease and hormone imbalances, according to Dr. Rubman.

The problem is that our intestinal flora is delicately balanced, easily upset by such factors as illness, inflammation, infection, stress and certain conventional medicines. In particular, certain antibiotics cause problems, injuring or killing off both helpful and harmful bacteria, Dr. Rubman points out. That's why many people experience diarrhea, gas and cramping when they take these medications. Reducing the population of friendly bacteria in the large intestine results in a weakened ability to fight disease-causing micro-organisms.

PROBIOTIC SUPPLEMENTS HELP OPTIMIZE YOUR HEALTH

One way to support healthy flora in the large intestine is by taking probiotic supplements, which Dr. Rubman believes are more effective than foods. He compares beneficial bacteria to state troopers stationed along the highway—if you pass one every five miles or so, they're likely to keep you honest. Likewise, in the intestine, it's the job of these friendly micro-organisms to keep the unfriendly ones at bay. Their role is to provide reinforcement to ensure an adequate level of good bacteria to keep the "bad guys" at bay. (Though generally mild, some people experience gas or bloating for a while when they begin taking probiotic products, caused by the dying off of bad bacteria as the helpful ones move in.)

Probiotic supplementation is not something you should try on your own, cautions Dr. Rubman, especially if you already suffer from a chronic illness. And, he adds, if that is the case, the sicker you are, the more issues you have that may directly or indirectly involve the large intestine. If you try to resolve a floral imbalance yourself, you may inadvertently trigger an even greater imbalance, and encounter more serious health challenges. The best way to determine the state of flora in your large intestine is to have a comprehensive laboratory digestive and stool analysis, ordered by a physician knowledgeable about gastrointestinal issues beyond diagnosing disease and parasites. Since a proper balance is key, this test will tell your doctor where you stand, and help him/her determine the type and dosage of probiotic that best fits your individual needs.

QUESTIONABLE BENEFITS WITH PROBIOTIC FOODS

What about just eating yogurt? It's not so simple. More questions arise when it comes to probiotic foods (these include most yogurts, miso, tempeh and certain milks, juices and soy beverages).

As awareness and popularity of probiotics grows, marketers are positioning yogurt, in particular, as a functional food promoting digestive health. The problem is that 90% of probiotic foods don't work as advertised, explains

Dr. Rubman, because they have far too little culture and too many unhealthy ingredients, such as sugar and pasteurized milk. And the "active" bacteria in the yogurts, in particular, come from bovine strains of bacteria that the human body will not easily accept as native. Similarly, the cultures present in non-dairy probiotic-containing products vary widely, but are also not particularly compatible with our human digestive system, says Dr. Rubman.

GET A NATUROPATHIC PHYSICIAN ON BOARD

Many conventional practitioners of medicine now believe probiotics can be helpful and effective in optimizing health, but haven't received much training or acquired much experience in working with them. Therefore, if you think you might benefit from probiotic supplementation, perhaps because of frequent gastric upset or autoimmune ailments, consider adding a naturopathic physician to your health care team. Naturopathic physicians are specially trained in and attuned to how gastrointestinal issues affect the body as a whole, and will be helpful in advising you on the right probiotic supplementation program to address your health issues. To locate an ND in your area, visit the Web site of the American Association of Naturopathic Physicians (AANP) at *www.naturopathic.org*.

Difficult-to-Treat GERD

Mark A. Stengler, NMD, naturopathic medical doctor in private practice, Encinitas, California...adjunct associate clinical professor at the National College of Natural Medicine, Portland, Oregon...author of *The Natural Physician's Healing Therapies* (Bottom Line Books).

I have tried every therapy you can think of," said my new patient Esther, who had suffered from heartburn and bad breath since high school. "I hope you have something that can help me!" This 59-year-old financial adviser had tried pharmaceutical medications and natural remedies—but nothing seemed to stop the constant burning in her chest.

In high school, Esther had been diagnosed with both gastroesophageal reflux disease (GERD), a condition in which stomach acids back up into the esophagus, and irritable bowel syndrome (IBS), a condition that causes diarrhea, constipation and digestive discomfort. Over the next 40 years, she had taken various acid-blocking medications, such as *esomeprazole* (Nexium) and *omeprazole* (Prilosec). While these medications helped the reflux symptoms (the burning or pressure in her chest), they worsened her IBS symptoms, including diarrhea and abdominal pain.

Esther was especially concerned about the potential long-term side effects of these medications. Her concerns had inspired her to try alternative medicine remedies.

She had already taken many of the classic dietary supplement remedies for GERD that I always first recommend to patients with the condition. These included calcium (which neutralizes stomach acid), deglycyrrhizinated licorice root (DGL), probiotics, aloe vera juice and digestive enzymes. Esther was not overweight (which can be a risk factor for GERD) and found that what she ate did not have much impact on her reflux.

For Esther's difficult-to-treat GERD, I suggested a new, less commonly known supplement that has been shown to be effective—orange peel extract. I am using it with more and more patients, and it may become a first-line treatment. Heartburn Free (800-783-2286, *www. enzymatictherapy.com*) contains orange peel extract that is standardized to contain a high concentration of *d-limonene*, a phytochemical found in citrus. The supplement is believed to help the lower esophageal sphincter close more efficiently so that acid doesn't rise up as easily from the stomach. Heartburn Free has no reported side effects. It is safe for all adults except those with gastric ulcers and women who are pregnant or nursing (for whom it has not yet been tested).

I had Esther take one capsule every other day for 10 days. When she followed up with me a month later, she reported that her GERD was 80% better overall and that she had not taken a citrus peel extract capsule in two weeks. Her bad breath, a symptom of GERD,

had subsided, as had her IBS, which is not uncommon, because these conditions frequently overlap. This was the best result that she had ever gotten from any treatment. If she experienced any increase in her symptoms, she could start taking the capsules again.

More from Mark Stengler, NMD...

Beneficial Prebiotics

Everyone has heard of antibiotics, and some people are familiar with probiotics—but how many are in-the-know about prebiotics?

First, a primer on probiotics: Beneficial bacteria, such as *Lactobacillus acidophilus* and *Bifidobacterium*, are found in yogurt, miso, kefir and other cultured foods (and in supplements, too). These good bacteria populate the digestive tract, as well as the respiratory and urinary tracts. Probiotics play an important role in digestion, detoxification, synthesis of various nutrients (such as B vitamins and vitamin K) and a healthy immune system.

Also vital to good health are prebiotics. These nondigestible components of foods contain unique sugar chains that stimulate the growth and activity of certain probiotics (particularly Bifidobacterium) in the colon. One important group of prebiotics is known as inulins, which are found in wheat, all types of onions, leeks, bananas, garlic, Jerusalem artichokes and chicory root (available as a coffee substitute). Another group of prebiotics, called *soy oligosaccharides*—found in soy, peas and most other members of the legume family— also stimulate the growth of Bifidobacterium.

Studies have shown that prebiotics are helpful in treating constipation and inflammatory bowel disease. Some data suggest that they also fight cancer, especially of the colon...protect against digestive-tract infections...lower cholesterol and triglycerides...and improve calcium absorption, which helps reduce bone loss.

My advice: Include at least three half-cup servings of prebiotic foods in your diet every week.

Natural Remedy For Bloating

Boil two tablespoons of fennel seeds in two cups of water for at least three minutes. Strain the seeds, add honey to taste and drink. Bloating should be relieved in one to two hours. Fennel promotes gastrointestinal motility and acts as an antispasmodic. Fennel seeds are available at health-food stores.

Birgit Rakel, MD, integrative physician, Jefferson-Myrna Brind Center for Integrative Medicine, Thomas Jefferson University Hospital, Philadelphia.

Fabulous Flaxseeds

Mark A. Stengler, NMD, naturopathic medical doctor in private practice, Encinitas, California...adjunct associate clinical professor at the National College of Natural Medicine, Portland, Oregon...author of *The Natural Physician's Healing Therapies* (Bottom Line Books).

Flaxseeds can be an effective natural remedy for constipation, along with maintaining overall health. *They provide...*

• **Fiber,** which prevents and treats constipation and reduces blood glucose and cholesterol levels.

• **Lignans,** compounds that convert during digestion into hormonelike substances that may protect against breast and prostate cancers by preventing the cancer-promoting effects of estrogen.

• **Omega-3s,** fatty acids that reduce inflammation and promote heart, brain, joint and skin health.

• **Flaxseeds** also provide copper to protect connective tissues...folate for normal cell division...magnesium to help the heart contract...manganese for joint health...phosphorous to strengthen bones...and vitamin B-6 to aid in liver detoxification. Flaxseed oil offers some but not all of the benefits of the seeds.

How to eat flaxseeds: To be digested properly, flaxseeds must be ground before being eaten. Grind seeds in a coffee grinder until flaky—about five seconds for the recommended daily serving of one to two tablespoons—or buy preground flaxseeds called flax meal. To prevent cramps and constipation, always drink eight to 10 ounces of water when eating flaxseeds. (If you have the digestive disorder diverticulitis, ask your doctor before eating seeds.)

Choose a product in a vacuum-packed, re-sealable bag to prevent spoilage. Once opened, keep the bag in the refrigerator. Ground flaxseeds are delicious when added to cereals, salads and shakes. When cooking, substitute three tablespoons of ground flaxseeds for one tablespoon of butter...or replace each egg with one tablespoon of ground flaxseeds soaked in three tablespoons of water. Recipes for chicken, rice, baked goods and more can be found at *www.ameriflax.com.*

For a light, nutritious snack, try Golden Flax Crackers from Foods Alive (*www.foodsalive. com*), sold at health-food stores. They come in eight flavors, including onion/garlic and Mexican harvest.

My favorite: Maple and cinnamon.

Quick Recovery When Food Poisoning Strikes

Sonja Pettersen, NMD, a naturopathic medical doctor. She is licensed to practice primary care medicine specializing in natural therapeutics, in Scottsdale, Arizona.

Although headlines sometimes describe food poisoning as the killer that lurks in your dinner, the problem rarely causes death. But food poisoning does create extreme discomfort in as many as 76 million Americans every year with vomiting, diarrhea and abdominal pain that can last from a few hours to more than a week. Sometimes food poisoning is also accompanied by fever, severe dehydration and even shock—which can be life-threatening, so it's very important to take symptoms seriously. Though there are ways to decrease the incidence of food poisoning, it's nearly impossible to avoid ever facing it—so it is important to know how to handle the problem.

According to Sonja Pettersen, ND, food poisoning in North America mostly comes from assorted naturally occurring bacteria, including *Salmonella*, *E. coli* and *Campylobacter*. *Listeria* is not common, but approximately 20% of patients die from it…and *botulinum*, which causes botulism, is also rare. (Another kind called *Shigella* is found in tropical climates, especially where poor hygiene is present.) Botulism is far and away the most serious of these. It usually results from poor canning techniques, and fortunately occurs much less often than it once did. Nevertheless, when the live botulism organism is ingested, it can kill quickly, so it is crucial to act immediately. In the case of food poisoning, botulism is a toxin that paralyzes nerves—so it can affect many bodily functions, including breathing, balance, speech and swallowing, notes Dr. Pettersen. The onset is rapid (incubation is six hours to 10 days) and unmistakable, characterized by paralysis in any or all of those functions. Effective anti-toxin treatment is now available, and any sign of botulism requires a 9-1-1 call and a rush trip to the ER.

Fortunately, most other cases of food poisoning can be handled at home. The goal is to eliminate the bad bacteria promptly—if it is allowed to linger, toxins develop that can cause much more serious problems. The violent elimination through vomiting and diarrhea is your body's natural defense against the organisms and their associated toxins. Therefore, you shouldn't take medications, such as Imodium, to slow or stop the diarrhea. "Better out than in," says Dr. Pettersen. Also, don't take an antacid to quell the upset. Stomach acid is crucial as the first line of defense to diminish the toxins and keep the live bacteria from spreading through the rest of the GI tract.

AT HOME

Even as your digestive system is turning inside out, there are ways to make yourself more comfortable. Dr. Pettersen advises taking a probiotic in the form of a high-quality acidophilus powder in capsules or mixed in a liquid per instructions on the container, and as prescribed by your physician. Often you'll be instructed to take a dose every half hour or so even when vomiting—it can't hurt you and will get more good bacteria into your system when it stays down. Other natural remedies include anti-microbial essential oils, herbs and/or supplements such as cilantro, ginger, tarragon, oregano, garlic, thyme or peppermint. Activated charcoal caps neutralize toxins to help stop symptoms quickly. (It is usually the bacterial toxins and not the bacteria itself that create the symptoms.) A homeopathic remedy often prescribed is *Arsenicum album*.

POST-ATTACK CARE

Within a few days, the attack begins to ebb and you will start to feel better. But understand that your digestive system has been under siege, and isn't ready for a normal diet. Instead, *Dr. Pettersen advises the following…*

• **Drink Pedialyte,** an electrolyte-replacement drink. (Avoid Gatorade, though, because it will make you feel worse, according to Dr. Pettersen. The high fructose corn syrup (anything sweet) can easily induce an osmotic diarrhea on top of gut troubles.)

• **Eat simple foods**—remember the acronym BRAT (bananas, rice, apple sauce, dry toast). Do not challenge your system.

• **Avoid sugar completely**—and this includes the 7-Up and ginger ale your mother probably gave you as a child after a bout (disruptive gut organisms tend to thrive on such sugary treats).

EMERGENCY MEASURES

Bleeding from the nose or mouth, or blood in your urine, feces or vomit are signs of an emergency. If this happens, go to an ER right away. Any neurological symptoms such as balance or visual problems, muscle weakening and the like also mean you need to get immediately to the hospital. Barring these symptoms, you'll need to stay in touch with your doctor if the debilitation from food poisoning is prolonged. Your physician will decide if IV fluid replacement is necessary and, in the case of *Salmonella*, if you need an antibiotic.

Note: Dr. Pettersen says that with many cases of food poisoning, the general prescription of antibiotics without a specific target can make the situation worse because they kill the friendly bacteria in the gut that would otherwise be warriors in the battle.

6

Eat Well to Stay Healthy

Eggs, Butter and More Secret Superfoods

Conventional wisdom on nutrition often shifts gears. Remember butter? And how about eggs? First they're evil, now they're our best friends. It is a good idea to periodically revisit some of those cherished beliefs about foods and health. Nutritionist and weight-loss coach Jonny Bowden, whose book, *The 150 Healthiest Foods on Earth* (Fair Winds) weighs in with some surprising entries—and some surprising omissions.

FAT CAN BE YOUR FRIEND

"Many foods suffered from bad reputations in the past because of the deeply held belief that all saturated fat is bad for you," Mr. Bowden says. "Saturated fat is the general name for a collection of fatty acids—and some of these fatty acids are really good for you." For example, he says, "two of the healthiest foods on earth are whole eggs and coconut. Yet to this day people eat Egg Beaters and shun coconut oil because of the saturated fat."

EGGS—GREAT PROTEIN SOURCE

Mr. Bowden believes whole eggs are among the finest sources of protein on the planet. "On three of the four methods used by scientists for rating protein quality, eggs score better than milk, beef, whey and soy," he tells us. "Whole eggs contain all nine essential amino acids, plus they're loaded with vitamins and nutrients that are excellent for your eyes, brain and heart." Mr. Bowden explains that the fear of saturated fat causes people to shun one of the healthiest parts of the egg—the yolk. "The yolk contains *lutein* and *zeaxanthin*, two members of the carotenoid family that are emerging as superstars of eye nutrition. And the yolk is also one of the best sources of *choline*.

Jonny Bowden, CNS, a board-certified nutritionist, the "Nutritionist–Life Coach" on iVillage.com and author of the best-selling *Living the Low Carb Life* (Sterling) as well as *The 150 Healthiest Foods on Earth* (Fair Winds). Find out more at *www.jonnybowden.com*.

"Choline creates *betaine*, which helps lower homocysteine, a risk factor for heart disease. It's part of a compound called *phosphatidylcholine* that helps prevent the accumulation of fat and cholesterol in the liver. It's also needed to make *acetylcholine*, which is critical for memory and thought," Mr. Bowden explains. Incidentally, he doesn't perceive the amount of cholesterol in whole eggs as a problem. "Virtually every study has shown absolutely no link between eating eggs and heart disease," he notes.

NUTS FOR COCONUTS

"In my view, coconut and coconut oil are superfoods," Dr. Bowden says. A half cup of shredded coconut has almost 4 grams (g) of fiber, 142 milligrams (mg) of potassium and almost no sugar. As for the saturated fat, he explains that in coconut, 50% of it comes from a fatty acid called *lauric acid*, which is antiviral and antimicrobial, and enhances the immune system. As for those saturated tropical fats that give coconuts a bad reputation...the saturated fat in coconut oil comes mostly from a family called MCTs or *medium-chain triglycerides*, making it particularly easy to metabolize. "The body likes to use it up as a source of energy, rather than turn it into a source of padding," says Mr. Bowden. "Long-term studies of people from the Pacific Islands who eat coconut and coconut oil regularly show that they have extremely low levels of heart disease."

BUTTER BARGAIN

Mr. Bowden has kind words to say about butter, too. "It's a rich source of vitamin A, needed both for maintaining good vision and the optimal functioning of the immune system. Butter also contains other fat-soluble vitamins, like vitamin K and vitamin D. And when it is made from the milk of healthy, grass-fed cows, butter contains CLA (*conjugated linolenic acid*), a kind of fat that has proven anti-cancer properties."

HEALTHY BREWS

Coffee's reputation has also been resurrected, says Mr. Bowden. Coffee is actually a major source of antioxidants in the American diet. "Caffeine is good for the brain," he explains, "and new studies show that it may be protective against type 2 diabetes and Parkinson's too. As long as you're not sensitive to the caffeine and you don't overdo it, coffee is fine for you." He also points out that black tea is nearly as good for you as green tea, because it, too, is loaded with *flavonoids* and *catechins* and antioxidants. But adding milk to your tea disables the antioxidants, so it's best to take it straight, with lemon or with your favorite sweetener.

NATURAL DISEASE FIGHTERS

Then there are the foods that are the unrecognized multitaskers in the health tool chest—like pumpkin. It has more potassium than a medium banana, is loaded with vitamin A, and has two carotenoids that are beneficial for the eyes—lutein and zeaxanthin. "Plus, pumpkin has less than 50 calories per cup, and you can season it with all kinds of great spices like cinnamon and nutmeg," adds Mr. Bowden. Another of his favorites is guava. "Guava has a whopping 9 g of fiber per cup. It's another potassium heavyweight, and it contains the cancer-fighting compound called lycopene," he said.

Cherries are another unappreciated fruit. These are loaded with *quercetin* and *ellagic acid*, two cancer-fighters. In addition, cherries have lots of natural anti-inflammatories, which is why they've traditionally been used to fight the pain of gout. And frozen cherries contain the same nutritional value as fresh, ripe fruit.

Supercharged Food Combinations

Lisa R. Young, PhD, RD, adjunct professor of nutrition at New York University and a dietitian in private practice, both in New York City. She is author of *The Portion Teller Plan: The No Diet Reality Guide to Eating, Cheating and Losing Weight Permanently* (Broadway), *www.portion teller.com*.

Good nutrition depends not only on what you eat, but also on how well your body absorbs or uses vitamins and minerals in your food. Some nutrients are best absorbed or utilized when consumed with certain other nutrients. Here are easy dishes that combine complementary foods for a synergistic nutritional bonanza—and taste great.

BOOST BETA-CAROTENE TO...

• **Provide antioxidants that protect cells from harmful free radicals.**

• **Enhance immune function.**

Eat with polyunsaturated fat to...

• **Support cognitive function.**

• **Fight inflammation.**

Easy steps for beta-carotene and polyunsaturated fat...

• **Steam sliced butternut squash or carrots** just until soft...for polyunsaturated fat, serve the vegetables with tuna or herring.

• **Bake a sweet potato or half an acorn squash...**for polyunsaturated fat, drizzle with flaxseed oil.

BOOST CALCIUM TO...

• **Build bones.**

• **Help control blood pressure.**

Eat with vitamin D to...

• **Strengthen bones and teeth.**

• **Protect against various cancers.**

Easy steps for calcium...

• **Toss together chopped fresh collard greens and shredded Swiss cheese.**

• **Broil salmon or perch and serve on a bed of spinach or dandelion greens.**

For vitamin D...

• **Top with mushrooms.**

• **Stir into beaten eggs to make an omelet or a quiche.**

BOOST FOLATE TO...

• **Reduce risk for Alzheimer's disease.**

• **Protect against birth defects.**

Eat with vitamin C to...

• **Neutralize the toxic by-products of fat metabolism.**

• **Improve absorption of iron, needed for red blood cells.**

Easy steps for folate...

• **Make a spinach and asparagus salad.**

• **Cook great northern beans or black-eyed peas.**

For vitamin C...

• **Toss with orange slices, strawberries and lemon vinaigrette.**

• **Stir in chopped tomatoes and red or orange bell peppers.**

BOOST LUTEIN TO...

• **Protect eyesight.**

• **Combat skin cell damage.**

Eat with monounsaturated fat to...

• **Lower cholesterol and blood pressure.**

• **Combat cancer-causing cell damage.**

Easy steps for lutein...

• **Make a salad of romaine lettuce, green peas and hard-boiled egg.**

• **Mix up a fruit medley of sliced peaches, papaya and oranges.**

For monounsaturated fat...

• **Add avocado slices, shredded low-fat mozzarella and olive oil.**

• **Stir in chopped hazelnuts, slivered almonds and pumpkin seeds.**

BOOST POTASSIUM TO...

• **Promote function of nerve and muscle cells.**

• **Maintain normal blood pressure and heart function.**

Eat with magnesium to...

• **Regulate heartbeat and muscle contractions.**

• **Strengthen bones.**

Easy steps for potassium...

• **Combine lentils and lima beans.**

• **Toss together dried apricots and dried banana chips**

Easy steps for magnesium...

• **Stir the legumes into quinoa or bulgur.**

• **Add bran cereal, pumpkin seeds and Brazil nuts to make trail mix.**

BOOST ZINC TO...

• **Strengthen the immune system.**

• **Speed wound healing.**

Eat with protein to...

• **Help build and repair body tissues.**

• **Make hormones and body chemicals.**

Easy steps for zinc...
- **Stir-fry diced chicken with chickpeas.**
- **Mix wheat germ into enriched break-fast cereal.**

For protein...
- **Sprinkle with chopped cashews.**
- **Top with low-fat yogurt.**

The No-Hassle Guide to Eating Right

Suzanne Havala Hobbs, DrPH, RD, clinical associate professor in the department of health policy and management at University of North Carolina at Chapel Hill. She is the author of 10 books, including *Get the Trans Fat Out: 601 Simple Ways to Cut the Trans Fat Out of Any Diet* (Three Rivers). *www.onthetable.net.*

How many times have you vowed to change the way you eat—to fill your plate with nutritious foods that can give you more energy and improve your health? Yet time and again, you may have been put off by complicated, bite-by-bite, by-the-book nutrition plans...or foiled by having no plan at all.

Good news: Whether your goal is to lose weight, gain energy or just feel better, you can give your diet a healthful makeover by taking these seven steps.

1. Get real. To make changes, you first must recognize how you really eat now—including those little bad habits that are so easy to overlook. You've heard it before, but it truly does work best—keep a daily food diary for a week or longer.

Easy option: Use the online service *www.myfooddiary.com* ($9/month) to record what you eat, automatically track calories and get a personal nutritional analysis...or simply keep a list in a notebook.

Record in detail everything you eat or drink—your three mugs of coffee with cream and sugar, the type of bread and condiments used on your sandwich, the french fries nibbled off your husband's plate—and estimate all portion sizes. Note this information within a few minutes of each meal or snack rather than trying to remember it all at the end of the day. This brings a heightened awareness of your diet that can lead to immediate improvement.

2. Get smart. Recent research findings have made today's nutrition guidelines clearer and more consistent—but this means that many people need to update their nutrition knowledge. I recommend the books *Eat, Drink and Be Healthy* by Walter Willett, MD (Free Press) and *What to Eat* by Marion Nestle, PhD (North Point)...as well as the monthly newsletter *Nutrition Action Health Letter* from the Center for Science in the Public Interest (10 issues, $20/yr., 202-332-9110, *www.cspinet.org*). Also consider consulting a nutritionist.

Referrals: Academy of Nutrition and Dietetics, 800-877-1600, *www.eatright.org.*

3. Shop right. In most supermarkets, outer aisles hold the most healthful foods—fresh fruits, vegetables, nonfat dairy products and fish. The center aisles have packaged and processed foods. Fill your cart primarily with items from the outer aisles, particularly produce, and minimize what you buy from the center aisles. Always shop from a list to avoid unwise impulse purchases.

Exception: Each time you shop, buy one unfamiliar healthful food to try.

4. Don't be fooled. Food labels are intended to help consumers shop wisely, but sneaky marketing tricks can thwart that goal. *What to watch for...*

- **Percent daily values (DV).** These figures (derived from USDA guidelines) are based on a daily diet of 2,000 calories, which is typical for men. Yet for many women, a more appropriate target is 1,500 calories per day—though this is not reflected in the percentages on the label.

  Example: A label may say that a food contains total fat equal to 50% of the DV for fat—yet for a woman on a 1,500-calorie diet, the food actually contains significantly more than half of her day's recommended maximum of fat.

- **Designated serving size.** Suppose you check the calorie count on a muffin, see that it has 150 calories per serving, and figure it's a good choice—but did you notice that this single muffin is supposedly three servings? Do the math based on how much you'll really eat, not on the manufacturers' gimmicks.

●**First word on the ingredients list.** Ingredients are listed in order of predominance, so the first one is what the food contains most of. For instance, if the front label boasts "made with real fruit juice," but the ingredients list begins with high fructose corn syrup (which has been linked to rising rates of obesity and diabetes), skip that beverage in favor of one that is 100% juice.

5. Spice it up. As you cook, experiment with high-flavor ingredients, such as onions and garlic, as well as herbs and spices—these provide a variety of nutrients and antioxidants yet add few or no calories.

Bonus: Research suggests that boosting the flavor of foods may help you feel fuller faster and decrease the amount you eat.

Flavorful: Bay leaves, cardamom, cinnamon, cloves, cumin, oregano, pesto, salsa.

Easy recipe: Sauté onions, bell peppers, garlic and olive oil, and add to vegetables, rice or pasta.

6. Trim portions. For an on-line slide show from the National Institutes of Health that demonstrates how drastically portion sizes have ballooned in the last 20 years, check out *www.nhlbi.nih.gov/health/public/heart/obesity/wecan/portion/index.htm. To practice portion control...*

●**Japanese approach.** Eat until you feel about 80% full—then stop.

●**Use smaller plates so portions seem larger.** Remove serving platters from the table—research shows that people unintentionally eat more when offered larger portions or when serving themselves from larger containers.

●**Take a piece of fruit with you when you're running errands or working in the afternoon.** Far from "spoiling your dinner," it will take the edge off your hunger so that you don't overeat later.

●**If you can't banish tempting but unhealthful foods from your house,** at least keep them out of sight. Put ice cream in the

back of the freezer...store cookies and chips on a high shelf. Place healthful foods in front and at eye level.

7. Go ethnic. Indian, Mediterranean and Middle Eastern restaurants generally serve abundant vegetables and a variety of whole grains... Japanese and Korean establishments offer plentiful fish and other healthful fare. Be open-minded about trying unfamiliar dishes—you'll discover some healthful new favorites.

Smarter Nighttime Noshing

Stephen P. Gullo, PhD, president and founder of the Center for Health and Weight Management in New York City. Dr. Gullo is author of *Thin Tastes Better* (Dell).

Many people enjoy an evening snack, and that's fine—as long as you stick mostly to healthful foods and reasonable portions. Yet it is all too easy to overindulge if your willpower weakens as the evening wears on or if you're too distracted to notice how much you're nibbling.

This is "night eating syndrome." As I have learned in treating nearly 15,000 patients, it's quite common, especially among people who stay up late (past 10 pm). Fortunately, changing this pattern does not require depriving yourself of an evening snack. *Here's how...*

●**Don't mistake sleepiness for hunger.** A few hours after dinner, hormonal shifts indicate that there is no more need for food as you prepare for sleep. If instead of going to bed, you stay up to read or to pay bills, you may feel an increased urge to eat. This is not true hunger, because you've probably already eaten enough for the day—but, nonetheless, it can spark a snack attack.

●**Identify snacking patterns.** Evening activities lend themselves to mindless or mood-triggered eating. You may munch as you watch TV or balance your checkbook, scarcely noticing as the food disappears. Or perhaps you are bored or anxious about the day's events, so you eat to fill the void or forget your troubles.

115

Reality check: For a week, keep a journal of what and how much you eat at night…and what you're doing and how you're feeling as you snack. Thereafter, to overcome bad habits, plan your snack schedule in advance, listing healthful foods and what time you will eat them.

• **Make a "no-shopping" list.** Do you go out at night to buy the foods you crave? Probably not. Most people keep their kitchens stocked with favorite snacks, yet this creates constant temptation. It's easier to resist just once—when you're at the grocery store.

How: On your shopping list, include a separate section for foods you won't buy.

• **Eat dinner—again.** Sometimes a small treat stimulates rather than satisfies the appetite, so a morsel only leads to frustration. Instead of a calorie-dense smidgen of fudge or a sliver of cheese, have a satisfying mini-meal.

Consider: An egg-white omelet with fat-free cheese (try Borden Fat-Free American Singles, 30 calories)…two low-fat hot dogs (such as Hebrew National 97% Fat Free Beef Franks, 45 calories each) on a bed of sauerkraut (skip the buns)…or shrimp cocktail with a green salad.

• **Indulge yourself—100 calories' worth.** Go ahead and have a sweet nighttime treat or favorite salty snack—but control the portion. Products that come in 100-calorie single-serving sizes include pudding (Jell-O Fat-Free Chocolate Vanilla Swirl), frozen treats (Breyers Pure Fruit strawberry bar), popcorn (Pop Secret, Orville Redenbacher) and crackers (Goldfish, Wheat Thins). Sure, you get more food for your buck when you buy in bulk—but if single-serving packages help you slim down and safeguard your health, the extra money is well spent.

Know Your Produce

It's okay to buy nonorganic produce, as long as you know which fruits and vegtables have the least contaminants.

MOST CONTAMINATED PRODUCE
(best to buy organic)

•Apples	•Peaches
•Bell peppers	•Pears
•Celery	•Potatoes
•Cherries	•Red raspberries
•Imported grapes	•Spinach
•Nectarines	•Strawberries

LEAST CONTAMINATED PRODUCE
(buy nonorganic, if desired, but wash vigorously)

•Asparagus	•Eggplant
•Avocados	•Kiwi
•Bananas	•Mangoes
•Broccoli	•Onions
•Cabbage	•Papaya
•Cauliflower	•Peas (sweet)
•Corn (sweet)	•Pineapples

Environmental Working Group, *www.ewg.org.*

What to Eat So You Can Fall Asleep Fast

Chin Moi Chow, PhD, researcher, Delta Sleep Research Unit, and senior lecturer, discipline of exercise and sport science, the University of Sydney in Australia. Co-researchers included Ahmad Afaghi and Helen O'Connor (PhD).

Researchers at the University of Sydney in Australia wanted to see if the glycemic index of a meal eaten before bed would have any effect on sleep. The glycemic index is a measure of how much your blood sugar goes up (and how quickly) after eating a particular food. Previous research has suggested that high-carb foods raise tryptophan, which then converts to serotonin and makes you sleepy.

"We hypothesized that a high glycemic index meal was going to be effective in inducing sleep," Chin Moi Chow, PhD, said. "We believed it would directly impact the increase of tryptophan." She and her colleagues gave 12 healthy men three meals on three separate occasions. One meal was a high glycemic meal one hour before bed...one was a high glycemic meal four hours before bed...and the third was a low glycemic meal four hours before bedtime.

Researchers found that the men who ate the high glycemic meal four hours before bedtime fell asleep the fastest, in only nine minutes on average. The low-glycemic diners who ate at the same time took almost twice as long to fall asleep, while the men who had the high glycemic meal one hour before bed fell asleep a little sooner than the low carb diners (about 15 minutes). Though the research leaves some questions unanswered, and therefore should not be considered "conclusive," Dr. Chow did sum up the findings, suggesting that "a high GI carb meal may help people with insomnia, both occasional and chronic."

But is that really a smart way to eat? When asked about the wisdom of recommending high-carb meals at night, which increase insulin and may increase the amount of calories converted to fat, Dr. Chow acknowledged the concern. She said "we caution that it may not be appropriate for people who are obese or who have diabetes to use a high GI meal or snack to promote sleep, since these individuals are often advised to adopt a low glycemic eating plan."

Dr. Chow was also quick to point out that the men in the study were good sleepers, and the effect might be different with chronic insomniacs. "We are currently planning a study of that."

"Getting a good night's sleep is about having good sleep habits," Dr. Chow said. "That means regular bedtime and wake-up time, and avoiding caffeine and alcohol before bedtime. If you struggle to fall asleep even after paying attention to those things, you can discuss with your doctor if a high GI evening meal might help you." For the record, the high GI meal Dr. Chow and her colleagues gave to subjects was a very low-fat dinner of jasmine rice with just a little protein from vegetables.

Eat Just One a Day...and Fight Colds, Flu and More

Carol Johnston, PhD, RD, director, Nutrition Program, College of Nursing & Health Innovation, Arizona State University in Mesa, Arizona. She has published more than 75 research papers and book chapters on nutrition subjects and received the 2008 Mark Bieber Professional Award from the American College of Nutrition in recognition of her research.

Wouldn't it be nice if you could add one simple item to your diet each day to help your body fight colds, flu, fatigue and other ailments related to a weakened immune system?

You can, according to recent research conducted at the University of California at Los Angeles. The six-year study of 17,688 men and women, published in the *Journal of the American Dietetic Association*, found that people who eat at least a one-cup portion of salad, including raw vegetables and salad dressing, every day have high blood levels of vitamins C and E as well as folic acid, all of which help promote a healthy immune system.

But some salads provide more disease-fighting nutrients than others. *Here's how to make sure your salad is as healthful as possible...*

1. Use salad dressing. In an effort to reduce fat and calories, many people sprinkle salad greens with just lemon juice or vinegar. That's a mistake.

A small amount of fat actually helps promote the absorption of fat-soluble vitamins, such as vitamins A, E, D and K. In addition to the health benefits these vitamins themselves provide, they also aid in the absorption of certain other nutrients—for example, vitamin D helps facilitate the absorption of calcium. Aim to include about two tablespoons daily of olive oil or another healthy oil, such as canola, in your salad dressing.

Smart idea: To ensure that your salad dressing is healthful, make your own.

An easy recipe: Combine one-half cup of balsamic vinegar, one-quarter cup of olive oil, two tablespoons each of finely grated Parmesan cheese and sugar, one teaspoon of oregano and one-half teaspoon of garlic salt.

117

Calories: About 80 per two-tablespoon serving.

Sodium: 60 milligrams (mg).

Fat: 7.5 grams.

If you want the convenience of a bottled salad dressing, shop carefully. Many brands contain as much as 700 mg of sodium per serving (the recommended daily allowance is 1,500 mg for people age 50 and older) as well as partially hydrogenated or hydrogenated oils —code words for trans fat, which has been shown to raise blood cholesterol and heart disease risk—and 100 calories per tablespoon. If your salad contains healthful fat from avocado or nuts, consider using a low-fat dressing.

2. Don't overdo the fat content. Even though a certain amount of healthful fat is good for you, people who try to make a meal of their salad often end up adding too much fat by piling on processed meats, fried chicken, creamy salad mixtures, such as egg salad, tuna salad or macaroni salad, and high-fat cheeses.

Smart idea: Use low- or nonfat cheeses, cubed tofu, poultry (except fried or breaded versions) or fish (salmon and tuna are good choices because of their omega-3 fats).

3. Choose lettuce that is dark green or reddish. The majority of Americans make their salads with iceberg lettuce. However, this is the least nutritious type of lettuce because it contains mostly water.

Smart idea: Select romaine lettuce for your salad, then for variety, add any combination of dandelion greens, arugula, endive, chicory, butterhead lettuce or spinach, all of which are rich in folic acid, a vitamin that is important to cardiovascular health.

In general, the darker the color of the lettuce leaf, the more vitamins and minerals the lettuce contains.

4. Choose a variety of richly colored vegetables. Americans tend to pile their salads with celery and cucumbers. Even though these vegetables make good snacks—they are very low in calories—they are also relatively low in nutrients, compared with some other vegetables.

Smart idea: Add tomatoes, broccoli, snow peas and bell peppers to your salad. They are excellent sources of vitamin C and other key nutrients.

Rule of thumb: The brighter the vegetable's color, the more vitamins and minerals it contains.

5. Get your phytochemicals. These chemicals are antioxidants or enzyme inhibitors that protect our bodies from disease-causing free radicals and help slow down the aging process.

Smart idea: Add white, yellow or red onions, garlic (crushed or chopped) and mushrooms (such as shiitake or maitake)—all are loaded with healthful phytochemicals.

6. Add nuts. Many people like to top their salads with croutons or bacon bits to add flavor, but croutons often are high in calories and most bacon-bit products contain nitrates—which have been linked to cancers of the digestive tract and the pancreas—as well as harmful fats and sodium.

Smart idea: Add a tablespoon or two of unsalted nuts, such as almonds, pistachios, cashews, walnuts, hazelnuts or peanuts. All of them contain healthful fats and are excellent sources of vitamin E. As an alternative, add unsalted sunflower seeds, which are high in fiber, potassium, phosphorus and other nutrients.

Five Foods Proven to Prevent Heart Attacks

Bonnie T. Jortberg, RD, CDE, assistant professor, department of family medicine at University of Colorado at Denver and Health Sciences Center. She was program director of Colorado Weigh, a weight-loss and healthy-living program offered throughout the Denver metropolitan area. She is coauthor of *The Step Diet Book* (Workman).

Cardiovascular disease is still the number-one killer in America. It accounts for about 37% of all deaths, according to the American Heart Association.

Most of us know that a diet rich in fruits, vegetables and whole grains and low in saturated animal fats lowers the risk of heart disease. But certain foods have been shown to be particularly beneficial. *Of course, no food is a magic bullet—you still need to exercise daily and maintain a healthy weight—but eating the recommended amounts of the following can go a long way toward preventing heart disease...*

SPINACH

Like most fruits and vegetables, spinach is rich in vitamins and minerals. What makes spinach stand out for keeping the heart healthy is folate, one of the B vitamins. According to several studies, including an extensive report from the Harvard School of Public Health, folate helps prevent the buildup of homocysteine, an amino acid in the blood that is a major risk factor for heart disease and stroke.

How much: Two cups of raw spinach (about two ounces) has 30% of the daily value (DV) for folate...one-half cup of cooked spinach provides 25%. Frozen and fresh spinach are both good, but beware of canned spinach—it may have excessive amounts of salt. Too much salt increases blood pressure, and high blood pressure is another major risk factor for cardiovascular disease.

Alternatives: Asparagus. Four spears have 20% of the DV of folate. Also, many breakfast cereals are fortified with folate—check the labels.

SALMON

Salmon is rich in omega-3 fatty acids. Omega-3s reduce inflammation and make your blood less "sticky," which prevents plaque—fatty deposits—from clogging your arteries. Having unclogged arteries reduces the risk of heart attack and stroke.

How much: The American Heart Association recommends two to three three-ounce servings of salmon a week. Fresh or frozen, farmed or wild, is fine, but go easy on canned salmon, which may be high in salt.

Alternatives: Other cold-water fish high in omega-3 fatty acids include mackerel, lake trout, sardines, herring and albacore tuna. If you don't like fish, have one teaspoon of ground flaxseeds daily—sprinkle on cereal, yogurt or salads, and drink plenty of water to avoid constipation.

TOMATOES

Tomatoes are loaded with lycopene, a carotenoid that gives them their color. Lycopene reduces cholesterol in the body. Too much cholesterol can lead to atherosclerosis (hardening of the arteries), which decreases blood flow to the heart—and that can lead to heart attack and stroke.

Cooked and processed tomato products, such as spaghetti sauce and tomato juice, provide the greatest benefits. Researchers at Cornell University found that cooking or processing tomatoes boosts lycopene levels and makes lycopene easier for the body to absorb. Look for low-sodium or no-salt-added products.

If you like ketchup, another source of lycopene, buy an organic brand, made with pure cane sugar, not processed high-fructose corn syrup. Organic ketchup can contain up to three times as much lycopene as nonorganic brands, according to a study published by the United States Department of Agriculture. Other organic tomato products weren't studied, so it is not yet known if they're also higher in lycopene.

How much: One cup of tomato juice (about 23 milligrams, or mg, of lycopene) or one-half cup of tomato sauce (20 mg) daily. A medium raw tomato has 4.5 mg.

Alternative: Watermelon (one and a half cups of cut-up watermelon contain 9 mg to 13 mg of lycopene).

OATMEAL

Oatmeal is one of the best and most studied sources of soluble fiber. Soluble fiber absorbs water and turns to gel during digestion. It then acts like a sponge to absorb excess cholesterol from your body. That's good for your heart. Studies show that five grams (g) to 10 g of soluble fiber a day can reduce LDL "bad" cholesterol by about 5%.

Soluble fiber also helps remove saturated fat in your digestive tract before your body can absorb it. That's also good for your heart.

How much: One and a half cups of cooked oatmeal daily. This provides 4.5 g of fiber, enough to lower cholesterol. Rolled oats and steel-cut oatmeal work equally well to help lower cholesterol, but beware of flavored instant oatmeal—it is likely to have sugar added. Too much sugar in your diet increases the chance of inflammation, a risk factor for atherosclerosis. Sugar also can lead to weight

119

gain, which is another risk factor for cardio-vascular disease.

Alternatives: Kidney beans and brussels sprouts each have three grams of soluble fiber per one-half cup cooked.

POMEGRANATES

Pomegranates are loaded with polyphenols, antioxidants that neutralize free radicals, which can damage the body's cells. Polyphenols help maintain cardiovascular health by scooping up free radicals before they damage arteries. They also are believed to reduce LDL "bad" cholesterol. Red wine and purple grape juice are great sources of polyphenols, but pomegranates have the highest amount.

How much: 1.5 ounces of concentrated pomegranate juice daily. This is the amount used in most studies. Look for products that are labeled 100% juice, or concentrated, with no added sugar.

Caution: Pomegranate juice may affect the metabolism of prescription drugs and may cause blood pressure to decrease too much when combined with certain blood pressure medications. Check with your doctor.

Alternatives: Red wine (no more than two five-ounce glasses a day for men and one for women) and purple grape juice (four to six ounces a day).

A "Berry Good" Fruit May Stop Cancer

Stephen T. Talcott, PhD, associate professor of food chemistry, Texas A&M University, Department of Nutrition and Food Science, College Station.

A Brazilian berry known as acai (pronounced AH-sci-EE) has become the exotic fruit juice of choice in health food stores. On the Internet, articles suggest that it can be used to fight cancer and boost cardiovascular health. Is there good science to back up these claims?

So far, the fact is that most of these healthful properties have yet to be tested scientifically.

However, Stephen T. Talcott, PhD, associate professor of food chemistry at Texas A&M University, has been studying acai berries and believes there is some basis for those claims. Acai berries are a rich source of disease-fighting antioxidants as well as health-promoting essential fatty acids, fiber and amino acids. Those attributes certainly make them a better-than-neutral choice, while we await the findings of research currently underway.

CANCER-FIGHTING POTENTIAL?

In his former post at the University of Florida, Dr. Talcott and his colleagues investigated the cancer-fighting potential of acai berries in the lab setting. They found that four out of six chemical extracts prepared from acai fruit pulp killed a significant number of leukemia cells in vitro. This was a lab study involving cells, not human beings, but the results are still encouraging. The next step at Texas A&M is to explore the impact acai has on healthy human subjects.

ALL BERRIES GOOD

Dr. Talcott said that products made with the processed berries have only been available here for a short time. The dark-purple acai berries, which are the size of blueberries, have a thin layer of fruit surrounding a large seed. Dr. Talcott and other sources say they taste like a mix of red wine and chocolate. The berries grow on acai palms, which are abundant around the Amazon River. One reason the berries are relatively new to us here in the US is that they're highly perishable.

TRY SOME ACAI

An assortment of products made from acai is now available to consumers. If you want to try some acai, go right ahead—just don't forget to balance it with a variety of other health-promoting fruits and vegetables. For optimal health, make it a habit to enjoy fresh produce—familiar as well as exotic—nine times a day, every day.

Delicious Fruit with 10 Times More Antioxidant Power than Broccoli

Jules Beekwilder, PhD, bioscience researcher, Plant Research International, Wageningen, The Netherlands.

For all you lovers of raspberries, there is more good news on the health front. According to recent research from The Netherlands, red raspberries rank just about at the top of antioxidant-loaded foods. In fact, the antioxidant activity in raspberries may be up to 10 times higher than that of tomatoes or broccoli and on a par with the "superloaded" blueberry. (Antioxidants, of course, are the soldiers that fight off damaging free radicals roaming the body and looking to cause trouble.)

A RASPBERRY BONUS

And there is yet another antioxidant bonus in red raspberries—*ellagitannins*, an important type of antioxidant found in a short list of foods, make up about 50% of the antioxidant effect of raspberries. While ellagitannins belong to the tannin family (which are ubiquitous in fruits, notably in grapes, and thus red wine), this particular compound is found largely in a few fruits and nuts. Other food sources include strawberries, blackberries and walnuts. Seldom talked about due to their rarity, ellagitannins provide powerful protection in assorted ways.

THE POWER OF ELLAGITANNINS

Jules Beekwilder, PhD, led this research at Plant Research International in Wageningen, The Netherlands. We contacted him for more information about his findings. Dr. Beekwilder says that while raspberries have many other nutrients—vitamin C, folate, vitamins B-2 and B-3, magnesium and others and, of course, fiber—it is the ellagitannins that make the raspberry unique. In addition to being powerful antioxidants, these tannins are also antimicrobial and so inhibit the growth of bacteria such as *Salmonella*. Furthermore, the tannins, which are similar to those in red wine, act as relaxants for the blood circulatory system, a long-held tenet of traditional medicine that has held up in test tube studies. Indeed, people with circulation problems are often advised to drink raspberry-leaf tea, says Dr. Beekwilder. That said, people with diabetes and others with circulation problems should always check with a trained professional about their individual needs.

FRAGILE FEEDING

Unlike other power-packed foods such as broccoli, raspberries are among the most fragile of fruits. Purchase them fresh in season, during the summer, and refrigerate the berries—unwashed—immediately after purchase. Remove any that might be moldy or otherwise spoiled so that they do not damage the remaining healthy berries. Plan to enjoy the fruit within a day or so of purchase and wash just prior to serving. Dr. Beekwilder says, though, that you should make raspberries part of your diet year-round and thanks to flash freezing you can. While this process does destroy up to half of the vitamin C, it does not hurt the other antioxidants. Bags of flash-frozen berries are found in all supermarkets today.

Food Superstar— Pomegranate

Kelly Morrow, MS, RD, registered dietitian and assistant professor, Bastyr Center for Natural Health and Bastyr University, Kenmore, Washington.

Like other fruits and vegetables with vibrant, intense colors, pomegranates are antioxidant-packed superfoods. In fact, studies indicate that the juice contains even more disease-fighting antioxidants than green tea, blueberries or red wine. In addition to vitamins A, C and E—and potassium and iron—pomegranate juice is brimming with healthful components, including *polyphenols, anthocyanins* and *tannins*.

Too many people make dull brown and white foods the centerpiece of their diets, observes Kelly Morrow, MS, RD, an assistant professor at Bastyr University in Kenmore, Washington. In her opinion, we would all be better off if we filled our plates with fewer empty carbohydrates and more richly pigmented produce

121

such as pomegranates, blueberries, kiwis, spinach and sweet potatoes.

HEART PROTECTION AND MORE

The pomegranate's abundant antioxidant and anti-inflammatory properties confer a wealth of health benefits. *Morrow describes some of the more well researched of these...*

- **Better cardiovascular health.** At the Technion-Israel Institute of Technology in Israel, researchers have found that drinking a glass of pomegranate juice a day slows cholesterol oxidation by nearly half, leading to less plaque in the arteries. In diabetic patients, who are at increased risk of cardiovascular disease, pomegranate juice successfully lowered blood lipids (fats) without affecting blood sugar. Morrow adds that preliminary evidence suggests that pomegranate may also modestly reduce blood pressure.

- **Potent cancer fighter.** Pomegranate also shows promise as a cancer fighter. At the University of Wisconsin in Madison, researchers demonstrated that pomegranate juice can stop the growth of prostate cancer in mice. In Israel, scientists discovered that pomegranate seed oil triggers apoptosis—a self-destruct mechanism—in breast cancer cells. They also found that the juice is toxic to estrogen-dependent breast cancer cells, while leaving normal breast cells intact.

- **Good news for expectant mothers.** Pregnant women at risk of giving birth prematurely may benefit from drinking pomegranate juice, according to an animal study at Washington University School of Medicine in St. Louis. Decreased oxygen and blood flow to a premature baby's brain can result in what is known as hypoxic ischemic brain injury. Researchers found that newborn mice whose mothers were given pomegranate juice were 60% less likely to experience this problem.

- **Skin support.** Pomegranate seed oil, readily available in health food stores or via the Internet, acts as a soothing moisturizer that protects the skin from ultraviolet radiation. While pomegranate seed oil can't replace conventional sunscreen, you can increase the effectiveness by applying the oil beneath the sunscreen. According to Morrow, vitamin C and polyphenols in pomegranate work together to support healthy collagen (the protein that makes up connective tissue) and prevent breakdown of the structural components of the skin. Naturally anti-inflammatory, the oil also can be used to relieve cracked, dry skin or a mild sunburn. In mouse studies, pomegranate resulted in a reduced incidence of skin cancer.

A POMEGRANATE A DAY

Most studies of pomegranate have focused on the juice, probably because the fruit is a bit messy and hard to get at.

Next time you're in the grocery store, think about giving pomegranate a try. Whether you sip a glass of juice, add it to your fruit smoothie or munch on the juicy red seeds, adding pomegranate to your diet is one simple yet positive step you can take toward good health.

Cloudy Juice—The Clear Choice for Extra Nutrients

Sonja Pettersen, NMD, naturopathic medical doctor. She is licensed to practice primary care medicine specializing in natural therapeutics in Arizona and is based in Scottsdale.
Journal of the Science of Food and Agriculture.

Many moms give their toddlers and young children apple juice boxes thinking it's a healthy choice. Truth be told, research indicates that the health risks of sugar-rich juice products can outweigh their benefits—especially in the quantities many children consume them in, and particularly in light of the national crisis of childhood obesity. Now some more research shows how processing in even the "all-natural" products affects the health value of apple juice.

THE CLOUDY AND THE CLEAR

To test the nutritive quality, Polish researchers made four batches of juice from two different varieties of apples (Champion and Ida Red). From each type, they produced one cloudy (like in apple cider) juice and one clear juice. Then they tested all four for antioxidants (those important compounds that can help fight cell damage). Regardless of which variety of apple was used, the cloudy version was better—in fact, antioxidant content of the cloudy juice was almost double that of the clear kind from the same variety of apple.

"The nutrient content of any juice depends on how it is processed and what's removed," explains Sonja Pettersen, NMD, an Arizona-based naturopathic physician. In their attempt to make clear juice, researchers in this study used an enzyme pectinase. The clear juice was then pasteurized in the same way as cloudy juice. The resulting clear, amber-colored juice looks appealing, and, not unimportantly, also has a longer shelf life—but a lot of what's good for you is lost in the processing, with the clarified product containing as little as one-quarter of the polyphenol content—and antioxidant power—of the unfiltered, unprocessed kind.

JUICE DRINKS vs. JUICE

And, notes Dr. Pettersen, this particular finding probably underestimates the variance between the juices, since many of the products available in supermarkets are even more processed than those the researchers produced for the study. "Many 'juices' given to children are actually 'fruit juice drinks,' which are primarily fruit-flavored sugar water," she says. Fruit juice drinks often contain as little as 10% juice, so consumers should look for labels that say 100% juice. "Even if it's clear, a juice can be nutritious, depending on the fruit—it all depends on what they leave in, and what they take out." These researchers removed the pectin (an important fiber with cardiovascular benefits) and the pulp, the source of so many powerful plant compounds that make apples healthy.

MAKE YOUR OWN

Are any juices really good for you? Healthiest of all are those made at home. Two good juicer machine choices are Vitamix (*www.vitamix.com*) or the Acme Juicerator (*www.healthnutalternatives.com*). These juicers range from approximately $160 to $700. At the supermarket, look for juices that are unfiltered and "cold-pressed" (meaning they are processed at very low heat if at all, preventing most of the enzymes from being killed).

But best of all, says Dr. Pettersen: "Eat an apple."

Amazing Way to Double the Nutrients In Watermelon

Penelope Perkins-Veazie, PhD, plant physiologist, US Department of Agriculture (USDA) Agricultural Research Service in Lane, Oklahoma.

Watermelon, like many fruits today, is in our supermarkets nearly year round, but it's still a hot summer afternoon that makes an ice-cold slice a real taste treat. Beyond being yummy, watermelon is full of healthful benefits—high in the antioxidant *lycopene*, a carotenoid pigment that produces the deep red color, and is fairly rich in vitamins C, B-6 and B-1 (thiamine), and beta-carotene. It also has magnesium and potassium—all for just 46 calories a cup. But now researchers at the USDA Agricultural Research Service in Lane, Oklahoma, have discovered a way to improve the melon's health benefits even more.

It's this simple: Just leave the melon out of the fridge for seven to 10 days if fresh-picked and a few days if store-bought before you open it. A watermelon kept at room temperature has double the level of beta-carotene and some 11% to 40% more lypocene.

MAXIMUM RIPENESS

Penelope Perkins-Veazie, PhD, was a lead researcher on this study. She says that allowing melons to be at room temperature for several days before eating gives them the chance to reach maximum ripeness. As the melon sits, the color of the red flesh inside becomes more intense and the rind thins, reflecting the fact that the fruit is continuing to ripen. For this study, watermelons were stored at 41° F, 55.4° F and 69.8° F, with 69.8° F representative of room temperature. If your room is warmer, keep in mind that increased heat will accelerate the process, she says. When you are preparing to serve the melon, it is fine to chill it first, though this will slow any further increase in nutrients. How do you know when a melon is ripe? Completely ripened melon will sound almost hollow when tapped sharply.

EAT WHEN AT PEAK

Dr. Perkins-Veazie also cautions to refrigerate melon once cut or damaged because yeast organisms, bacteria and mold can easily invade it. But when you do open the fruit, you'll know that you have let the melon ripen too long if the rind is soft, pitted or has dark spots…or if the melon flesh has an orange tint and a pumpkin-type odor (which is not a surprise, since watermelons are in fact related to pumpkins).

While the study was performed on watermelons, tomatoes—another lycopene-rich food—as well as other fruits and vegetables are best eaten at their peak ripeness, and best bought when they have been harvested close to that peak ripeness to maximize their nutritional benefits.

Our Five Favorite Fruits

Susan M. Kleiner, PhD, RD, CNS. Dr. Kleiner is owner of High Performance Nutrition, a consulting firm on Mercer Island, Washington, and author of several books, including *The Good Mood Diet: Feel Great While You Lose Weight* (Springboard), *Power Eating, 3rd Edition* (Human Kinetics) and *The Powerfood Nutrition Plan* (Rodale). Dr. Kleiner is cofounder of the International Society of Sports Nutrition.

Nutrition expert Susan M. Kleiner, PhD, author of *Power Eating* (Human Kinetics), from Mercer Island, Washington, shares her favorite healthful fruit choices, based on everything from antioxidant content to taste, accessibility and portability.

Dr. Kleiner generally recommends that her nutrition clients eat three pieces of fruit a day, including some type of berry (for the *anthocyanins* and vitamin C) and an orange-flesh fruit such as a peach, nectarine, cantaloupe, papaya or mango (for beta-carotene). Add frozen fruit to smoothies when fresh isn't available. You may be comforted to know that frozen is almost as good as fresh as long as it is completely ripe when frozen—which is generally the case.

See if any of Dr. Kleiner's top five fruits makes *your* list…

1. Dried plums (also known as prunes). Rich in fiber, especially pectin, a soluble fiber that may help decrease cholesterol. Packed with phenols that neutralize free radicals in the body and a good source of potassium and iron, too. "And because they're so portable, dried plums are on top of my list," says Dr. Kleiner.

2. Blueberries. These are full of super nutrients, including anthocyanins, *pterostilbene* and *ellagic acid*. They protect you from an assortment of health problems, including cancer, cardiovascular disease, vision loss and cognitive decline. And don't forget strawberries, blackberries or raspberries, says Dr. Kleiner, which are also rich in fiber and other health-protective nutrients.

3. Mangoes. Exotic and sweet, mangoes are rich in vitamin A, vitamin C and beta-carotene, plus potassium and fiber. The mango also has other nutrients that promote cardiovascular health and protect against colon cancer. Choose other beta-carotene-rich fruits, too, such as cantaloupes, peaches, nectarines and papaya.

4. Apples. Apples are antioxidant-rich and full of phytonutrients that may reduce your risk of cancer, heart disease, asthma and type 2 diabetes. Make sure you also eat the peel, which is rich in soluble and insoluble fiber (pectin)—great for gut health—plus compounds like *quercetin* and *proanthocyanidins*.

5. Bananas. Bananas are high in potassium, which may protect against high blood pressure, heart disease, stomach ulcers and bone loss. They are also surprisingly full of antioxidants.

EAT FRUITS IN SEASON

So should you eat brain-protective blueberries every day if dementia is in your family history? Dr. Kleiner thinks that's a miscalculation.

Better: Enjoy the wonderful fresh fruits of the season, which will give you a variety of delicious nutrients that help your body in assorted ways. You'll feel better and enjoy your food more.

Explained! How Food Keeps You Healthy

Boxin Ou, PhD, director, Dover Sciences, Boston, Massachusetts. Dr. Ou is a scientist who studies phytochemicals in plant foods, and his research has been widely published in peer-reviewed journals. He regularly collaborates with leading food companies and university research programs.

If you are going to give thoughtful consideration to the healthful properties of the fruits and vegetables you eat, it's a good idea to get familiar with the appropriate terminology. One of those terms—ORAC—requires a little explaining.

ORAC BASICS

The letters ORAC stand for *oxygen radical absorbance capacity*, a reflection of the *antioxidant* ability of just about anything, including foods, to subdue the *peroxyl radical* (one of the harmful free radicals) in the test tube. Free radicals are highly reactive substances that can occur naturally in the body as a result of oxidation. When not being pressed into service by the immune system to attack pathogens, these free radicals might be considered the body's bad boys, having been shown to trigger much of the aging process and also to be involved in degenerative diseases. Antioxidants neutralize free radicals.

WHAT'S MAGICAL ABOUT ANTIOXIDANTS?

Studies at the Jean Mayer US Department of Agriculture (USDA) Human Nutrition Research Center on Aging at Tufts University in Boston suggest that consuming fruits and vegetables with a high ORAC value may help slow the aging process in both body and brain. Other research has shown that in middle-aged rats, foods with a high ORAC value can reduce loss of long-term memory and learning ability, maintain the ability of brain cells to respond to stimuli (thought to decrease with age) and protect blood vessels against oxygen damage. The assumption is that these high ORAC foods benefit people in much the same way. Most recently, Ronald Prior, PhD, and colleagues at the USDA reported on several small human clinical studies on high ORAC foods consumption with positive results.

WHICH FOOD IS BEST?

There isn't a simple way to measure antioxidant capacity or activity because different antioxidants respond to different pro-oxidants or radicals, much like different antibiotics kill different strains of bacteria. In fact, there are at least six kinds of potentially destructive free radicals…and when the original ORAC test was developed, it simply measured the ability of a food to fight one of these species specifically, the peroxyl radical, the one most abundant in the human body, says Boxin Ou, PhD, former vice president of Brunswick Laboratories in Norton, Massachusetts, a leader in ORAC testing. Though the ORAC measure only relates to that, he explains that our bodies also have to defend against the other five. So Dr. Ou's team developed several other tests (with different designations, such as HORAC, NORAC, SORAC and SOAC) to describe how a food defends against the other types of potentially dangerous free radicals.

Carotenoids, primarily found in yellow and orange foods such as carrots, for example, score poorly on the standard ORAC test, Dr. Ou told us. Carotenoids do not defend well against the peroxyl radicals that are the basis of the ORAC test. But carotenoids defend brilliantly against a *different* type of free radical called *singlet oxygen*, measured by the SOAC assay. The antioxidant power rank assigned to them would depend on which test was used—but the only score you'd hear about would be the brilliant one.

MEANINGFUL OR NOT?

So should you pay attention to those claims about a product's ORAC value? The answer is, yes…but while it is true that a higher ORAC rating is better than a lower one, and any high rating is potentially good, just be sure that you realize the rating reported may be for an isolated and less prominent antioxidant action than the combined environmental assault you may be facing.

What are some high ORAC foods?

ORAC values of common fruits and vegetables (per 100 grams—approximately 3½ ounces):

Spinach	1,515
Prunes	6,552
Raisins	3,037
Blueberries	6,552
Blackberries	5,347
Alfalfa sprouts	1,510
Broccoli	1,362
Beets	1,767
Red bell pepper	791
Strawberries	3,577
Onion	1,034
Raspberries	4,882

Source: United States Department of Agriculture, *www.usda.gov.*

"Grape" Way to Lower Cholesterol

Leo Galland, MD, director of the Foundation for Integrative Medicine in New York City. He is author of *The Fat Resistance Diet* (Broadway). *www.fatresistancediet.com/trial/.* Dr. Galland is a recipient of the Linus Pauling award.

Plant foods offer a cornucopia of health benefits, and mounting evidence continues to reveal new plant chemicals that promote health. A recent darling is red grape juice. New studies are showing that compounds in the juice actually lower cholesterol and other cardiovascular risk factors.

GRAPE JUICE AND CHOLESTEROL

In one recent study in Spain, researchers took a group of 15 healthy subjects and 26 subjects who were receiving dialysis and gave all of them a total of 100 milliliters (ml) of red grape juice concentrate daily (100 ml is a little more than half a six-ounce can of the concentrate). Dialysis patients were chosen for the study because they're at a higher risk for developing cardiovascular disease.

After only two weeks of drinking the juice concentrate, all subjects had reductions in low-density lipoprotein (LDL) cholesterol (the "bad" kind), oxidized LDL cholesterol (the *really* bad kind) and total cholesterol. As a bonus, their high-density lipoprotein (HDL, or good) cholesterol went up. In addition, an important marker of inflammation, MCP-1, went down by half after three weeks.

WHAT MAKES GRAPE JUICE GO?

Red grape juice is a rich source of *polyphenols*, potent antioxidants that "mop up" harmful free radicals, which are a big part of the aging process and are associated with degenerative diseases. The polyphenols (also known as *polyphenolics*) include all sorts of plant compounds such as catechins and anthocyanins that have been shown to be protective against various cancers and heart disease. "This is yet another piece of evidence for the importance of consuming fruits and vegetables that are rich in the polyphenolics," says Leo Galland, MD, an expert in nutritional and integrative medicine.

Dr. Galland explains that cholesterol metabolism in the body is influenced by a process known as oxidative stress—the damage that occurs when free radicals attack your cells and DNA, much the way oxygen attacks apple slices left out on your kitchen table and turns them brown. The phenolic compounds in red grape juice—and in other plant foods—work to disarm the free radicals. By preventing the oxidation of LDL cholesterol (which increases the risk for LDL to generate cardiovascular disease), the compounds have strong benefits on heart health.

GOOD RED FRUIT JUICES

The good news is that the phenolic compounds that lowered oxidation of LDL cholesterol, prevented oxidation and also lowered inflammation in the study are not specific to red grape juice. "You should be able to achieve similar results with other kinds of red fruit juice, like pomegranate, for example," Dr. Galland said.

Bottom line: Red grape juice contains antioxidant and anti-inflammatory compounds that rank high among the established benefits of other well-known antioxidants such as vitamin E, lycopene and vitamin C. And one of the benefits seems to be a significant improvement in cholesterol. Not only that…it tastes good, too.

Dig Into These Five Power Veggies

Susan M. Kleiner, PhD, RD, CNS. Dr. Kleiner is owner of High Performance Nutrition, a consulting firm on Mercer Island, Washington, and author of several books, including *The Good Mood Diet: Feel Great While You Lose Weight* (Springboard), *Power Eating, 3rd Edition* (Human Kinetics) and *The Powerfood Nutrition Plan* (Rodale). Dr. Kleiner is cofounder of the International Society of Sports Nutrition.

Carrots are an excellent source of nutrition. Of course, as healthful as carrots are, other veggies also pack a lot of disease-fighting power. What are the best? Nutrition authority Susan M. Kleiner, PhD, RD—from Mercer Island, Washington, and author of *Power Eating*—provides details on the five vegetables she considers the most healthful. The choices can be difficult, since Dr. Kleiner says *variety* and what *looks good* to you as you shop should be your top priorities. There probably are thousands of health-promoting nutrients whose value is still unknown, so don't pass up the green beans you love because you think you should be eating broccoli every day, says Dr. Kleiner.

That said, here are Dr. Kleiner's top five vegetables...

●**Broccoli.** No surprise here, since *indoles* and *sulforaphanes* contained in broccoli are top cancer-fighters. Eat broccoli raw or lightly cooked. Or select other members of the crucifer family *Brassica* genus, such as kale, cauliflower, Brussels sprouts, kohlrabi and cabbage.

●**Garlic.** Along with onions and leeks, garlic is a member of the *Allium* group of vegetables, known for their cancer-fighting and immune-strengthening properties. While the more pungent varieties of onions and garlic are richer in health-protective compounds, enjoy them all, including mild elephant garlic and sweet onions. No need to chew raw garlic cloves, says Dr. Kleiner. She uses lightly sautéed garlic liberally in her cooking.

●**Red chard.** This is a leafy green, like collard greens and mustard greens, but less bitter and simpler to prepare. Red chard is chock-full of vitamins and minerals, including high amounts of vitamin K, beta-carotene and potassium, plus cancer-fighting *anthocyanins* and fiber. Dr. Kleiner loves red chard stir fried with a bit of sweetened rice vinegar and soy sauce.

●**Carrots.** It's hard to beat carrots for their appealing taste, portability and nutrition. Carrots are rich in beta-carotene and vitamin K, plus carotenoids that protect against cancer, heart disease and vision loss. Also try other carotenoid-rich deep orange produce, such as sweet potatoes, apricots or cantaloupe.

●**Red peppers.** These are rich in beta-carotene and vitamin K, cardioprotective vitamin B-6 and folic acid, plus an excellent choice for *lycopene*, a carotenoid that can reduce your risk for certain cancers. Other good sources of lycopene are tomatoes, watermelon and pink grapefruit.

Select the freshest vegetables you can find, or buy quality frozen vegetables since they retain nutrients longer than veggies stored for a week at the bottom of your fridge, says Dr. Kleiner. Although cooking vegetables involves some degree of nutrient loss, don't be afraid to sauté them lightly, steam them or boil them briefly in water. Season vegetables with a little salt, pepper and grated lemon zest or healthful sauces —whatever it takes for you and your family to enjoy them regularly, says Dr. Kleiner.

Go Nuts for Almonds!

Andrew L. Rubman, ND, medical director, Southbury Clinic for Traditional Medicines, Southbury, Connecticut.

Nuts have gained popularity in recent years as an excellent source of protein and "good fats." One of the best nuts? Almonds. According to our consulting medical editor Andrew L. Rubman, ND, almonds are one of the most nutrient-dense, good-for-you foods there is.

ALMONDS BENEFITS

Although Dr. Rubman encourages eating a variety of nuts, just as you do fruits and vegetables, he particularly likes almonds because of their fatty acid content (almonds are high in monounsaturated fats). Furthermore, almonds have many health-promoting minerals, especially magnesium, but also potassium, which means the nuts help other dietary and supplemental sources protect cardiovascular health. Eating almonds with their skins provides significant amounts of vitamin E and flavonoids. Studies have shown that these two work synergistically to help boost low-density lipoprotein (LDL, or bad) cholesterol's resistance to oxidation by more than 50%, important because LDL cholesterol is not dangerous in and of itself. It is oxidation that makes LDL plaque-building and dangerous.

PROTEIN PROVIDER

Dr. Rubman adds that almonds are also a good source of protein (6 grams per ounce) nearly as much as one egg (6.3 grams of protein/egg) …and they have fiber and assorted vitamins and minerals.

DON'T ADD CALORIES

Still, some are concerned about the high calorie content of almonds and other nuts. Dr. Rubman has counseled many dieters about how to receive the health benefits of almonds without adding extra calories to their diet.

The solution: If you want to lose weight do not eat more than an ounce a day of unsalted almonds. That ounce would come to 23 nuts, he says, and the unsalted type is simpler because it is easier to stop at your limit with unsalted nuts than the salted, tastier form. Another good way to enjoy the health properties of almonds without toting up too many calories is to add them to other foods rather than eating them plain. Nuts toasted in a dry skillet are even more flavorful. Try chopping some into salads, sprinkling them over string beans or white fish. You can also coat fish or chicken with almond flour—make your own by grinding the nuts in a blender, food processor or even coffee grinder.

Eat Nuts to Prevent Heart Disease

Among women who have type 2 diabetes (which puts them at high risk for heart disease), those who ate five or more servings a week of nuts or peanut butter had a 44% lower risk for heart disease than those who rarely or never ate these foods.

Theory: Monounsaturated fat in nuts reduces cholesterol and inflammation.

Best: At least five times weekly, have one ounce of nuts or one tablespoon of peanut butter.

Frank Hu, MD, PhD, professor of nutrition and epidemiology, Harvard School of Public Health, Boston, and lead author of a 22-year study of 6,309 women.

Latest News on Garlic

Matthew Budoff, MD, professor of medicine at the David Geffen School of Medicine at UCLA and director of Cardiac CT Imaging at Harbor-UCLA Medical Center in Torrance, California. He has published more than 100 articles.

If there's ever been a spice or a food that just about everyone agrees is healthy, it's garlic. In his book, *The 150 Healthiest Foods on Earth* (Fair Winds), author Jonny Bowden calls garlic "a global remedy" and "one of the oldest medicinal foods on earth." More than 1,200 studies have been done on garlic, and even many conventional medical doctors agree that garlic helps lower cholesterol. In a meta-analysis published in the *Journal of the Royal College of Physicians*, garlic supplements lowered total serum cholesterol levels by 12% after only four weeks of treatment. Now a new study in the *Archives of Internal Medicine* throws some doubt on that, though there may be cause to be skeptical of the results. *Let's take a look…*

FAULTY RESEARCH

Researchers tested three forms of garlic (raw garlic, powdered garlic supplement and aged garlic extract supplement) on a population with elevated low-density lipoprotein (LDL) cholesterol and found disappointing results. They concluded that none of the garlic treatments had clinically or statistically significant effects. What gives? We went to Matthew Budoff, MD, a renowned researcher on the healing powers of garlic, to find out.

Acknowledging that the study was "a bit disappointing," Dr. Budoff stresses that it was not only "inconsistent with other studies," but that it also had more than a few problems in its design and methodology, including requiring participants to show up every day to receive both a sandwich (with garlic condiments or placebo condiments) and a pill (supplement containing garlic or a placebo) and then not checking to be sure they ate it.

Dr. Budoff also points out that this single study is hardly reason to question the many health benefits of garlic that have been documented in countless other studies. Put it in an overall context, he urges. The benefits of garlic are multifactorial, and not just about cholesterol. Garlic also lowers blood pressure and helps "regress" plaque—meaning the size of the blockage diminishes. Additionally, he notes that garlic decreases homocysteine, a dangerous inflammatory compound in the blood that has been linked to greater risk of heart disease and stroke.

WHAT'S IN A CLOVE

We also asked Dr. Budoff about another study, published in the *Journal of Agricultural and Food Chemistry*, reporting that crushing or chopping garlic before moderate cooking releases an enzyme that allows its active ingredients to work. (Dr. Bowden adds that chewing whole cloves may also be effective, though perhaps off-putting to friends and family.) "There are definitely challenges with studying garlic, and isolating its most active ingredients," he said. "When you take fresh garlic and process it differently, the benefits may be different. I think that's why there have been inconsistencies in the findings."

KEEP THE FAITH

In spite of this study, Dr. Budoff believes there's every reason to retain faith in the health properties of this food. "There is long-standing and consistent evidence that garlic consump-tion does improve your cardiovascular health," he says, adding that aged garlic extract (such as the widely available Kyolic brand) delivers similar benefits as well. It's just not quite so good in spaghetti sauce and soup.

Spice Up Your Health With Everyday Seasonings

Jonny Bowden, CNS, a board-certified nutritionist, the "Nutritionist–Life Coach" on iVillage.com and author of the best-selling *Living the Low Carb Life* (Sterling) as well as *The 150 Healthiest Foods on Earth* (Fair Winds). Find out more at *www.jonnybowden.com*.

It's exciting to see the increasing focus of research on the health benefits of everyday spices like chilies for prostate cancer …turmeric to reduce inflammation…ginger for nausea, to name just a few. Herbs and spices, derived from various plants, have a long history of medicinal use in Chinese medicine, Ayurveda and other traditional medical systems. What else is there in the spice rack that we can use to "healthify" our meals in a delicious way?

"Everyday spices are an amazing source of phytochemicals, which are plant compounds with extraordinary healing properties," explains nutritionist and weight-loss coach Jonny Bowden, author of *The 150 Healthiest Foods on Earth* (Fair Winds). "Many of these spices have been used in traditional medicine for hundreds of years, and Western medicine is just beginning to realize their potential." *Here are a few of Mr. Bowden's top picks for powering up your foods…*

CINNAMON

"There are anti-inflammatory compounds in cinnamon that can be helpful in alleviating pain, stiffness and even menstrual discomfort," says Mr. Bowden. "Additionally, compounds in cinnamon increase the ability of the cells to take in sugar, which is how it effectively lowers blood sugar and reduces the need for higher levels of insulin." A study published in *Diabetes Care* showed that cinnamon lowered not only blood sugar, but also triglycerides, total cholesterol and low-density lipoprotein (LDL), the "bad" cholesterol, in people with type 2 diabetes. Though it's not always the case with our other plant-based remedies, the inexpensive supermarket variety of cinnamon is basically as good as any of the pricier oils and extracts sold in specialty stores.

GINGER

Ginger, known as the "universal medicine" in Ayurvedic medicine, is often used to soothe an upset stomach and quell nausea. In fact, in one study on ginger root, it was shown to be as effective as Dramamine in holding seasickness at bay. Ginger also packs plenty of powerful antioxidants, Mr. Bowden says. "And animal studies show that ginger has antimicrobial effects and helps boost the immune system as well."

TURMERIC

Turmeric—the spice Mr. Bowden waxes most enthusiastic about—is a member of the ginger family, and also a heavy hitter in health benefits. "It's as close to a magical substance as you're likely to find in the kitchen cupboard," he points out. He attributes this spice's anti-inflammatory properties to *curcumin*, the substance responsible for making some Indian food and curry dishes yellow. In India, turmeric is used to treat arthritis precisely because of its ability to lower inflammation, Mr. Bowden says, noting that research indicates that curcumin also may have an anti-tumor effect. If you're not an Indian food eater, you can try it in rice dishes or even on eggs. Do not use medicinal amounts of turmeric during pregnancy, though, because it stimulates contraction of the uterus.

OREGANO

Another spice touted for its health properties is oregano, which Mr. Bowden tells us "has been shown by research to have 42 times more antioxidant activity than apples and 12 times more than oranges." Oregano contains a powerful cancer-fighting compound called *rosmarinic acid* as well, and its anti-inflammatory properties make it useful in supporting joint function. Oregano is also a source of calcium, magnesium, zinc, iron and potassium.

GARLIC

Of course garlic is not always used as a spice, but it does have a well-deserved reputation for

adding flavor and boosting health. One of the oldest medicinal foods we know of, it is recognized even by mainstream medical professionals as being helpful in reducing cholesterol. Dr. Bowden cites a study that found garlic reduces triglycerides by up to 17%. It has a small but notably positive effect on blood pressure. "In places where the consumption of garlic is high, there's a decreased risk of stomach and colon cancer," Mr. Bowden adds.

Some other spices that have health-promoting properties include...

• **Cardamom.** Another member of the ginger family, cardamom is found in spiced chai tea, used to flavor Turkish coffee, and is added to baked goods in Scandinavia. It stimulates digestion and flow of bile.

• **Mustard seeds.** These are a source of magnesium and selenium, and can be taken orally to stimulate appetite and circulation, and to help neutralize inflammatory materials in the GI tract.

• **Parsley.** A good source of vitamin K and potassium, parsley is also helpful for detoxification.

• **Rosemary.** Contains lots of antioxidants and anti-inflammatory compounds, plus substances that help prevent the premature breakdown of acetylcholine, a neurotransmitter that's vital for memory and healthy brain function.

• **Sage.** Contains rosmarinic acid (like oregano), which is both an antioxidant and an anti-inflammatory, along with *thujone*, which can be protective against *Salmonella* and *Candida*.

• **Thyme.** Helps relieve chest and respiratory problems, including coughs and bronchitis.

MORE THAN A PINCH?

How much of each seasoning is needed to make a difference? Mr. Bowden says it's usually more than is typically required for cooking to achieve a notable benefit—though it seems logical that adding a variety of spices, more often and in plentiful amounts, would have a cumulative positive effect. Though some of the dried spices retain their healthful properties, fresh herbs are usually nutritionally superior—not to mention delicious, and fun and easy to grow.

Uh-Oh! Milk Zaps the Healing Power of Tea

Verena Stangl, MD, professor, department of internal medicine, cardiology and angiology, Charité Hospital, University of Berlin, Germany.

Enjoying a cup of tea feels positively virtuous these days, given all we hear about the health-promoting antioxidants and flavonoids that researchers have discovered are in the brew. There's a surprising catch, however, for those who enjoy milk in their tea. According to a new study, tea with milk may do much less for your health.

TAKE TEA, THEN SEE

The study, from the Charité Hospital, University of Berlin, Germany, included 16 healthy postmenopausal women who, over the course of three clinical visits, drank half a liter of freshly brewed black tea alone...another time tea with 10% skim milk...another time just boiled water. Researchers measured the function of the endothelium (the cell lining) of the brachial artery before and for two hours after consumption of the beverage. The brachial artery was used since it is easy to access and measure and reacts quickly to inflammatory stimuli. Black tea alone, they found, improved the artery's ability to relax and expand, but adding milk to the tea inhibited this biological effect.

Further tests on rats measured the effect of both tea and tea with milk on the rodents' aortic tissue and endothelial cells produced similar results. This could explain why in some tea-drinking cultures, such as in Asia, the incidence of heart disease is lower than elsewhere, whereas in England, with its heavy consumption of tea with milk, it is not.

MORE RESEARCH COMING

Verena Stangl, MD, professor of cardiology and angiology at Charité, was the senior author of the study. She says that when combined with tea, the proteins in milk, called *caseins*, decrease the concentration of healthful flavonoids (*catechins*). Although only women were measured in this study, Dr. Stangl feels confident that the effect on men's endothelial function would be the same. She notes that

other small studies have similarly shown that the antioxidant effects of tea are diminished when milk is added, but this hasn't been firmly established. Could a similar effect be noted in drinkers of coffee with milk? Does milk also diminish coffee's antioxidant effect? Dr. Stangl believes that theoretically this would be true, but says it hasn't been confirmed through research. She is now at work on another study to determine if there is any difference between the health benefits of green and black teas. Stay tuned for the results.

Health Food Phonies You Should Leave On the Shelf

Jonny Bowden, CNS, a board-certified nutritionist, the "Nutritionist–Life Coach" on iVillage.com and author of the best-selling *Living the Low Carb Life* (Sterling) as well as *The 150 Healthiest Foods on Earth* (Fair Winds). Find out more at *www.jonnybowden.com*.

Grocery-store aisles abound with foods purported to be healthy. In fact, they are junk disguised in wholesome packaging.

A prime example of this is margarine. It was originally introduced as a healthy alternative to butter, but many margarines, loaded with trans fat, may be far worse for you than the butter it replaced. (It's possible that an exception is the plant sterol-enriched margarines recently brought to market, but we don't know enough about them yet, so the jury is still out on their health value.) And what about some of the other staples of the health-food industry? Are they really as "good" for us as we've been led to believe?

Board certified nutritionist and weight-loss coach Jonny Bowden, CNS, provides valuable perspective on that topic. *Here's what he had to say...*

BREAKFAST CEREALS AND MEAL-REPLACEMENT BARS

The claim that many cereals are "whole grain" is wholly misleading. "The fact that something started as whole grain doesn't mean

131

much if all the nutrition has been processed out of it," says Mr. Bowden. "Many cereal labels today say 'made from whole grains.' These 'whole grain' cereals have been processed to the point where they have around 2 grams (g) or less of fiber per serving, which is minimal." In Mr. Bowden's opinion, whole grain cereals with less than 5 g of fiber per serving are no better than the cereals they replaced.

"Additionally, many cereal- and grain-based breakfast products are loaded with sugar, some have trans fat, and most also have additives," says Mr. Bowden. He advises reading the labels carefully. Strive to find brands with about 10 g of protein (or close to that), no hydrogenated oils and no more than a couple of grams of sugar per serving. This doesn't mean you have to give up this convenient food category altogether. For example, the Atkins Advantage bars meet that criteria, as do a few—very few—others. "There are also good bars that have more sugar than three grams," he added, "but those are specialty whole-foods bars, such as Omega Smart…Bumble Bars…and Lara-Bars, made from nothing but real fruit, spices and nuts." All of these are healthy. Most other energy and meal replacement bars have very high sugar and belong in the candy aisle.

OY! SOY, TOO

Soy has been a health darling of recent years. It has become the primary source of protein in many protein-enriched products. Now, however, the bloom is off that rose. "I don't think soy is the worst thing in the world for you," Mr. Bowden says, "but I think it's been way oversold as a health food." The healthy kind of soy is that which is traditionally fermented, like miso and tempeh, or minimally processed, like edamame. Other soy products (such as those in some meal-replacement bars) should be enjoyed in moderation, according to Mr. Bowden.

CANOLA OIL: NO CAN DO

Neither is Mr. Bowden a fan of canola oil. "The presence of canola oil in the marketplace is a triumph of marketing over science," he says. "Canola oil is a highly processed oil that needs to be deodorized at high temperatures, which frequently creates trans fat," he notes. "In addition, the omega-3s in it are easily damaged by heating." If you want to use canola oil,

stick to cold-pressed organic canola oil and use it for dressings, but not for cooking.

YOGURT

Yogurt—a major health craze a couple of decades ago—is not all that healthy in the drinkable and squeezable and high-sugar forms that are available today. What about frozen yogurt? "Its only resemblance to real yogurt is that they're both white," Mr. Bowden laughs. "Seriously, it can be a delicious dessert, but don't fool yourself that frozen yogurt is healthier than ice cream. In fact, the nonfat kind is often filled with aspartame, which can be a problem for many people," he says. Why not go ahead and eat the ice cream, and get the highest quality you can find? "Just eat it less often," he suggests.

FRUIT DRINKS

Another great pretender? Commercial fruit beverages, especially many of the kinds marketed and conveniently packaged for kids' lunches, are nothing but sugar water. "You are far better off drinking water and flavoring it with lemon or cherry or berry juice concentrate, which are high in antioxidants. Or, if you really want the juice, dilute it with water in a 1:4, solution so you take in less sugar," Mr. Bowden says. Healthy exceptions to the "no juice" rule are 100% juices made from cranberry and pomegranate, which do, in fact, contain plenty of important and desirable nutrients.

It's easy to be fooled by the advertising claims made for many products. Be skeptical, smart and look for foods that are minimally processed.

More from Jonny Bowden, CNS…

Start Your Day with A Super Breakfast

There's an old saying that goes 'Eat breakfast like a king, lunch like a prince and dinner like a pauper,'" says nutritionist and weight-loss coach Jonny Bowden, CNS. "But most of us do the opposite." According to Mr. Bowden, this is exactly the wrong way to eat if we're trying to lose weight. It also works against us if we're trying to keep our energy up during the day and our performance level high. "Remember, you've just completed eight hours without food," he says. "You're literally breaking a fast. Your body is craving nourishment, and your brain needs glucose to function at its best. Skipping breakfast is one of the worst possible things you can do. You set yourself up for disaster in a number of different ways later in the day. People who skip breakfast are more than four times as likely to be obese than people who eat something in the morning."

EARLY EATER ADVANTAGES

Then there's performance. "Numerous studies over the years have shown that skipping breakfast impacts the behavior and mental performance of school kids," Mr. Bowden says. "Kids who eat breakfast have better memory, and higher math and reading scores. And kids who are hungry have a large number of behavior problems, including fighting, stealing, having difficulty with teachers and not acknowledging rules."

Additionally, people who eat breakfast are far more likely to get a healthy intake of vitamins and minerals than those who don't. In one study published in the *Journal of the American College of Nutrition*, researchers found that people who ate a hearty breakfast containing more than one-quarter of their daily calories had a higher intake of essential vitamins and minerals and lower serum cholesterol levels to boot.

THE BEST BREAKFAST

So what constitutes a good breakfast? "Higher protein breakfasts translate into a more sustained level of energy throughout the morning and possibly the day," Mr. Bowden says. "Protein fills you up longer, and you're less likely to have midmorning cravings. You're also less likely to overeat at lunch." And more protein at breakfast may increase metabolism, helping you to maintain a healthy weight. "In one study, a high-protein breakfast increased the metabolism of healthy young women by a shocking 100%," Mr. Bowden tells us.

"There are definite advantages to higher protein intakes in the morning," Mr. Bowden continues, "but that doesn't mean 10,000 calories of bacon." He recommends that at least one-third of your breakfast come from a lean

protein source and the rest from healthy fats and fibrous carbs. "If you eat eggs, for goodness' sake, don't throw out the yolks," he urges. They're loaded with good nutrition, and may even lower your cholesterol levels, he adds.

INSIDE THE BENTO BOX

"Moreover, don't be afraid to think outside the box," Mr. Bowden advises. He points out that in Asia, the traditional Japanese breakfast consists of a small piece of fish (like salmon), some light vegetables and a tiny portion of rice, accompanied by a small bowl of miso soup. "The health benefits of fish and vegetables in the morning are huge," Mr. Bowden reports. "And the omega-3s in salmon are terrific for your skin, plus they help regulate mood."

If salmon's a stretch for you, Mr. Bowden has his own list of favorite protein-packed breakfasts for more Western palates…

● **Eggs.** "I think eggs are one of nature's perfect food sources," he opines. "They are loaded with protein and other nutrients such as *phosphatidylcholine* for the brain and heart."

A Bowden breakfast favorite: Scramble some eggs with spinach and sliced apples in some coconut oil, and season with turmeric and lemon pepper. "It's loaded with protein and nutrients for the eyes, like *lutein* and *zeaxanthin*," he explains. "Plus it includes turmeric, one of nature's great anti-inflammatories." (*Note:* Mr. Bowden strongly recommends free-range eggs—from hens that had access to the outdoors where they could run around and eat more natural food, which changes the fat and nutrition profile of their meat and eggs.)

● **Yogurt that contains active cultures.** "One of my favorite quick breakfasts is yogurt with nuts and red or purple grapes," Mr. Bowden says. "I always use goat's or sheep's milk yogurt because it's less likely to have added hormones in it and has a better nutrient balance. Then I sprinkle on some walnuts or almonds or pecans."

● **Peanut butter and banana sandwich.** "If you're someone who can tolerate grains," says Mr. Bowden, "buy a good whole-grain bread, preferably sprouted grain, take one slice and make a half sandwich using natural, unsweetened peanut or almond butter, a banana and, if you like, a dollop of yogurt on top."

• **Whey protein shake.** "Whey is my favorite protein powder," Mr. Bowden explains, because it raises *glutathione*, the most important antioxidant in the body, and has shown in one study to lower blood pressure by about 5 millimeters of mercury (mmHg; a unit of pressure). "You can make a nutritious shake using water, whey protein and frozen berries, with a little cranberry or pomegranate juice or almond or rice milk. Throw in a handful of raw oats for texture—it tastes much better than it sounds. Adding a splash of olive oil to the shake will reduce the glycemic index and help the smoothie 'stick' with you a little longer. Experiment. Peanut butter is another great add-in."

• **Homemade muesli or granola.** According to Mr. Bowden, "Raw foods have a lot to offer. They contain enzymes, they haven't been processed, they tend to have fiber and they're loaded with nutrients."

Mr. Bowden's favorite: "Take some raw oats…soak in a little pomegranate juice…add nuts, berries or sliced apples, and flaked coconut. You can sweeten with *xylitol* if you need to (though it has been found to cause diarrhea in some), but it's delicious without it. You can also use raw cold-pressed honey or blackstrap molasses if you like."

Moove Over, Milk: Better Sources for Calcium

Mark A. Stengler, NMD, naturopathic medical doctor in private practice, Encinitas, California…adjunct associate clinical professor at the National College of Natural Medicine, Portland, Oregon…author of *The Natural Physician's Healing Therapies* (Bottom Line Books).

In spite of the US Department of Agriculture's (USDA's) latest dietary guidelines recommending milk as part of a balanced diet, evidence continues to mount that cow's milk is best left to the calves.

INTOLERANCE AND ABSORPTION ISSUES

Many Americans are lactose intolerant, meaning that they find it difficult to digest the milk sugar lactose, reacting with symptoms such as nausea, bloating, gas, cramps and diarrhea. Others have a milk allergy and cannot tolerate casein or whey proteins in milk. When they drink a glass, the uncomfortable consequences may include digestive disturbances, skin rash, vomiting, wheezing, immune system reactions and mucus build-up in the sinuses. Even Lactaid—a lactose-free milk made for lactose intolerant people—still contains casein. Organic milk poses other challenges of its own.

Not only is milk difficult to digest, it may also not be among the best forms of calcium for absorption, says Mark Stengler, NMD. He suggests that people who drink milk limit themselves to 24 ounces a week and bulk up on calcium-rich foods. This holds truer for children, due to the sensitivity of developing immune systems to milk's allergy-inducing properties, says Dr. Stengler. He notes that there is a possible association between cow's milk and recurring ear infections in children.

In other studies, cow's milk has been associated with cardiovascular disease and cancer. In the Harvard Nurses' Health Study (Boston), women with an increased intake of calcium from dairy products actually had a higher risk of bone fractures.

BETTER OPTIONS?

What *should* you put on your cereal and in your coffee?

Dr. Stengler points out that some people with an intolerance to milk seem to do better on goat's milk. However, those with allergies should use goat's milk with caution—it also contains casein-like proteins. Like cow's milk, goat's milk is packed with calcium. A cup of goat's milk supplies 327 milligrams (mg) of calcium along with 271 mg of phosphorus. In comparison, a cup of cow's milk provides 276 mg of calcium and 222 mg of phosphorus. Goat's—and sheep's—milk aren't adequate for babies under one year, since they don't contain the right amount of nutrients.

Other alternative sources of calcium include goat's and sheep's milk cheeses, as well as calcium-enriched plant-based milks such as almond, oat, hazelnut, rice and soy. Plant-based milks are good substitutes for people with milk allergies. While plant-based milks are not naturally rich in calcium, manufacturers fortify them. Dr. Stengler says that any of these enriched plant-based milks generally have just as much calcium per glass as cow's milk or more.

A WORD ABOUT SOY

Lately, there has been some controversy concerning soy products. Women with a history of, or existing, breast cancer should not consume soy milk, as it has an estrogenic effect on the body. In Dr. Stengler's opinion, children can have soy milk in moderation, but it is best to rotate with other plant milks.

Of course, if your goal is to find alternative sources of calcium rather than another kind of milk to drink, there are plenty of other food sources of calcium…

Food	Calcium (mg)
Broccoli, raw, ½ cup	21
Cereal, fortified, 1 cup	100 to 1,000
Chinese cabbage, raw, 1 cup	74
Kale, cooked, 1 cup	94
Orange juice, fortified, 6 oz.	200 to 260
Salmon, canned with bones, 3 oz.	181
Sardines, canned with bones, 3 oz.	324
Spinach, cooked, ½ cup	120
Turnip greens, cooked, ½ cup	99

Source: National Institutes of Health, Office of Dietary Supplements.

TOO MUCH OF A GOOD THING

Does Dr. Stengler agree with the standard government recommendations for calcium intake (1,000 mg/day for those age 19 to 50, and 1,200 mg/day for people age 51 and over)? Because there are questions about a possible link between calcium and prostate cancer, until this issue is resolved, he recommends 500 mg daily for men.

A study published in the *Journal of the National Cancer Institute* reviewing 12 studies on this association concluded, "High intake of dairy products and calcium may be associated with an increased risk of prostate cancer, although the increase appears to be small." Another study found that calcium intake exceeding 1,500 mg a day might be associated with a higher risk of advanced and fatal prostate cancers.

Calcium is a vital nutrient for building and maintaining bone, but it is best to get it from a variety of sources, being especially careful to limit consumption from cow's milk and soy.

The Latest Buzz on Honey

Rosa Ana Perez, PhD, researcher in the Department of Food Science and Technology in Madrid, Spain.

Honeydew" honey (no relation to the melon of the same name) is superior to other honey, according to Spanish researchers, because it has a higher antioxidant capacity.

ABOUT HONEYDEW HONEY

Honey is actually a complex natural product produced (by honeybees, naturally) from one of two sources. The one most commonly available, produced by bees that feast on the nectar of flowers, is called, unsurprisingly, nectar honey. It comes in a variety of forms, some raw and some processed to the point where it could practically be called "liquid sugar."

In contrast, honeydew honey is an antioxidant-packed sweetener, with a rich, earthy, malty taste, made by bees that have relied on a different food source. These bees eat a kind of sap-like excretion (called honeydew) produced on trees and plants that have been attacked by insects.

A HONEY OF A STUDY

We contacted Rosa Ana Perez, PhD, a researcher in the Department of Food Science and Technology in Madrid to learn more about her study of honey. Her research group performed chemical analyses of 36 different Spanish honeys from a variety of origins. They found that the antioxidant properties of honeydew honeys were more potent and powerful than the conventional nectar honeys. The total *polyphenol* content is also higher in honeydew honeys, and their anti-browning properties (which, for example, can prevent apples from turning brown) further demonstrate antioxidant-capacity. It's

135

possible that not everyone will like the different flavor of the honeydew honey, which has a darker, caramel color, a spicy, woody fresh odor and is not as sweet as traditional honey. However, it is quite common in other countries and is used the same way nectar honey is used. Given its health benefits, it may be worth a try.

Onions Reduce Cancer Risk Up to 88%

Carlotta Galeone, PhD, Istituto di Ricerche Farmacologiche "Mario Negri," Laboratorio di Epidemiologia Generale, Milan, Italy.

If you're a fan of TV chef Emeril, you know that he heaps on the onions and garlic when he cooks. Bam! The good news is that onions and garlic not only taste great, they are also very healthful. In a recent analysis of European studies, Italian and Swiss researchers discovered that the more onions and garlic people ate, the less likely they were to develop common cancers such as oral, colorectal and ovarian cancer.

Lead author Carlotta Galeone, PhD, of the Istituto di Ricerche Farmacologiche "Mario Negri" in Milan, provided more information about the analysis. According to Dr. Galeone, past research focused primarily on the protective role that onion and garlic played in the diet of Chinese, who have distinctive dietary habits. This study confirms that benefits also extend to Western populations, who consume considerably less garlic.

FLAVORFUL CANCER-FIGHTING COMPOUNDS

Onions and garlic are packed with natural cancer-fighting chemical compounds, notes Dr. Galeone. In particular, onions are rich in *flavonoids* (e.g., *quercetin*), disease-fighting antioxidants that prevent oxidative damage to body cells that can eventually lead to cancer. Garlic is packed with *organosulfur* compounds that inhibit tumor growth.

ONIONS, GARLIC AND CANCER

In the study, Dr. Galeone and her colleagues discovered that people who ate approximately one medium-sized onion a week reduced their colorectal cancer risk by 14%, in comparison with those who ate no onions. The protective benefits became more evident with higher intake. Eating at least two medium-sized onions per week reduced cancer risk at several other sites—larynx (56%), ovary (43%) and kidney (25%). Dr. Galeone found the results at even higher intakes even more interesting. People who consumed about one medium-sized onion a day reaped more protection in nearly all cancer sites studied (with the exceptions of prostate and breast cancer). The reduction in cancer risk for frequent consumers (seven or more medium-sized onions) varied from 56% for colorectal cancer to 88% for oral cancer. High intake of garlic was protective against all cancer in all sites studied (with the exception of breast cancer) in comparison with low intake. The reduction in risk ranged from 19% for prostate cancer to 57% for esophageal cancer.

AN OVERALL HEALTHFUL DIET

It is possible that combining onions and garlic with other healthful foods may have contributed to their protective effect, says Dr. Galeone. The researchers speculate that people who eat lots of onions and garlic are likely to follow a healthier, plant-based diet overall, which is known to be protective against cancer. In the Italian diet, for example, they are often eaten with tomatoes and olive oil in salads and pastas.

To help protect yourself and your loved ones, consider spicing up your dishes with plenty of garlic and onions. Simply toss into salads and stir-fries. And for even greater protection, don't forget to add a variety of other fresh, cancer-fighting veggies.

Note: Garlic also has blood-thinning properties. If you take blood-thinning drugs such as *warfarin* (Coumadin), or if you are about to undergo surgery, consult your physician before increasing your garlic intake.

Tomatoes' Latest Health Coup

Steven G. Pratt, MD, board-certified ophthalmologist. Dr. Pratt lectures nationally and internationally on the benefits of a diet based on whole foods and adopting healthy lifestyle choices to prevent diseases. He is author of *The New York Times* best-seller *SuperFoods Rx: Fourteen Foods That Will Change Your Life* (Harper), and *SuperFoods HealthStyle: Proven Strategies for Lifelong Health* (William Morrow). Dr. Pratt has appeared on various national TV shows, including *Today*, *Oprah* and *The View*.

Not long ago the news media was abuzz with a new report about the connection between pizza and lower rates of prostate cancer. Everyone made a mad dash for the local pizzeria. The truth was a bit more nuanced—it turned out that men eating more than 10 servings per week of tomato-based products (including pizza) had lower rates of prostate cancer. The lowly tomato became reborn as a superstar of the produce section.

Now tomatoes are back in the news. A recent report found that a tomato extract product actually lowered blood pressure in patients with stage 1 hypertension. The product—Lyc-O-Mato—is an extract of red, ripe tomatoes, including carotenoids (especially lycopene), polyphenols and vitamin E, all known to have significant health benefits. Steven G. Pratt, MD, author of a number of books on "superfoods" provides some perspective on this food. As it turns out, he is a big fan of tomatoes.

"Tomatoes themselves have many bioactive compounds that are good for cardiovascular health," Dr. Pratt says. "In particular are polyphenols that can decrease blood pressure by causing vasodilation, or widening of the blood vessels," Dr. Pratt explains. "Ninety percent of Americans are at risk for being diagnosed with high blood pressure at some point in their lives and reducing blood pressure by as little as a single digit produces a reduction in cardio risk factors."

THE GOOD TOMATO

Dr. Pratt explains that the benefits of tomatoes —and tomato extracts or tomato food products like tomato paste—go beyond just blood pressure and prostate cancer. "Two separate studies in the *American Journal of Clinical Nutrition* recently showed that tomato extracts have antiplatelet function, which means they help prevent your blood from clotting, reducing risk for stroke and heart attacks." This is precisely the benefit that many doctors want patients to get from taking aspirin. "The tomato extract does the same thing as aspirin and doesn't have any side effects except for those folks who are sensitive to nightshade alkaloids or allergic to tomatoes or other vegetables in the nightshade family, such as eggplant," says Dr. Pratt.

The tomato extract product, Lyc-O-Mato, is available in stores such as GNC and the Vitamin Shoppe. Dr. Pratt also sings the praises of other tomato products such as tomato paste. "I personally drink a daily tomato-based veggie cocktail, R.W. Knudsen Very Veggie Cocktail (Low Sodium). It has only 50 calories and 22 mg of lycopene per 8 ounces," he notes.

Take a Bite Out of Health Problems— Load Up on Sauerkraut

Thomas A. Kruzel, ND, naturopathic physician in private practice in Scottsdale, Arizona, past president of the American Association of Naturopathic Physicians and former vice president of clinical affairs and chief medical officer at the Southwest College of Naturopathic Medicine in Phoenix. Dr. Kruzel is author of *Homeopathic Emergency Guide: A Quick Reference Handbook to Effective Homeopathic Care* (North Atlantic).

Not only does sauerkraut (fermented cabbage) taste good—tart, tangy, sweet and sour all at the same time— it's also an extremely healthful food, good for the digestion and a potential weapon against a host of disease-causing microbes.

A JUICY GERM FIGHTER AND MORE

The digestive benefits of sauerkraut have been known for a long time, but recent interest in Korean fermented cabbage, kimchi, and its protective benefits in the fight against flu, indicate that it might be time to take an even closer look at this ballpark favorite. Thomas A. Kruzel, ND, a naturopathic physician in private practice in Scottsdale, Arizona, and past president of the American Association of Naturopathic Physicians, was recently asked for his assessment of the food's value.

Dr. Kruzel said there are indeed a wealth of benefits in eating sauerkraut, because it's…

• **A germ fighter.** Dr. Kruzel says that sauerkraut contains lactic acid, a natural by-product of the fermentation process that discourages invasive microorganisms such as disease-causing yeast, bacteria and viruses. This even includes the bird flu virus, according to Korean researchers at Seoul National University. (*Note:* The same benefits apply with kimchi and other fermented vegetable products, including pickles.)

• **A digestive aid.** In addition to fighting infectious germs, sauerkraut generates beneficial bacteria and healthy flora throughout the digestive tract. This helps support digestion, soothe stomach irritation, ward off food poisoning and boost immune function.

• **A weapon against cancer.** The fermentation of cabbage also produces isothiocyanates, a group of compounds that may help prevent breast, colon, liver and lung cancer. In addition, Dr. Kruzel points out that cabbage is a cruciferous vegetable, like brussels sprouts and cauliflower. According to the US Department of Health and Human Services, eating several servings weekly of cruciferous vegetables can reduce colon cancer risk.

• **A source of valuable nutrients.** Sauerkraut is rich in vitamins C and K, and also contains B-6, iron, folate, calcium, potassium and fiber. A one-cup serving has only 32 calories and no fat or cholesterol.

BUY FRESH OR MAKE YOUR OWN

Unfortunately, as with many foods, there's sauerkraut and there's sauerkraut. The stuff you buy in a can at your local supermarket does not provide the health benefits—not to mention the zippy flavor—of the fresh sauerkraut made at health food stores and old-fashioned delicatessens. The problem is that commercially processed sauerkraut no longer contains the live cultures that combat germs, as pasteurization kills off friendly, as well as unfriendly, bacteria. To get quality sauerkraut, Dr. Kruzel

recommends that you buy the fresh variety, or if you're really ambitious, make your own.

NOT FOR HOT DOGS ALONE

We're all familiar with sauerkraut as a topping for hot dogs, and after all, what's a summer afternoon at the ballpark without a dog with the works? But sauerkraut is not for hot dogs alone. At juice bars, sauerkraut juice is increasingly popular. Sauerkraut is likewise a tasty accompaniment to meat dishes, a zesty addition to salads and soups, and an ingredient in ethnic favorites such as pierogies, knishes and strudels.

To learn more tasty ways to incorporate sauerkraut into your diet, visit one of the many Web sites that feature recipes (such as *www. sauerkrautrecipes.com*). Try hot potato salad with sauerkraut or Bloody Mary mix combined with sauerkraut juice instead of vodka.

Note: If you have high blood pressure or heart disease, watch out for the high salt content of some sauerkraut.

Unhealthy Elements in Your Healthy Produce

Devon Zagory, PhD, former senior vice president, Food Safety and Postharvest Programs, Davis Fresh Technologies, LLC, Davis, California.

Americans may be gaining weight and exercising less, but they are at least taking their nutrition a bit more seriously these days. Consumption of fruits and vegetables is up, but produce-borne illness is also on the rise. In fact, produce has now surpassed meats, poultry and eggs as the cause of large-scale outbreaks of food-borne illnesses. Our editors called Devon Zagory, PhD, former senior vice president, Food Safety and Postharvest Programs, at the consulting firm Davis Fresh Technologies, LLC, in Davis, California, for his advice.

Dr. Zagory says that fruits and vegetables are always going to carry some degree of risk despite careful monitoring by the industry. Produce grows in nature where it could be exposed to bird and animal feces and sometimes polluted water. Furthermore, much of the produce today undergoes additional steps on its journey from the field to the table. Heads of lettuce are wrapped, many are shredded and bagged, some are put out as part of a salad bar. Fruits get peeled, chunked and tucked into plastic containers. And, unfortunately, the more food is handled, the more opportunities there are for contamination from nature or from human hands. *However, there are several key steps you can take as a consumer that will go far to ensure that the produce in your home is safe to eat…*

WORST OFFENDERS

Interestingly, cantaloupes and tomatoes have been particularly problematic. Pathogens can get inside produce, including tomatoes and cantaloupes, through cracks and fissures in the skin or even along the base of the stem. Dr. Zagory says to check produce carefully before you buy it and avoid any that is cracked. Wash all produce before you eat it by rinsing thoroughly under running water—this includes melons and bagged greens even if the label says they are prewashed.

SAY NO TO SOAKING

Some people prefer to soak produce, in particular leaves, but Dr. Zagory says soaking only makes the problem worse.

The reason: If a pathogen is on one leaf or spot on the produce, the water frees the pathogen and enables it to spread throughout the basin and onto the rest of the food. Should you have produce such as sandy spinach leaves that beg for a soak, you can eliminate any pathogens by adding a capful of *sodium hypochlorite bleach* (Clorox, or other household bleach, but be sure to check the label to be sure it is sodium hypochlorite) to a full basin of water.

CROSS OFF CROSS-CONTAMINATION

Cross-contamination is a major culprit in food safety, says Dr. Zagory, and careful hygiene is a must to avoid it. Wash hands carefully before and after handling produce. When slicing or peeling produce, always use a freshly washed knife and be sure the surface on which you are cutting is spotless. Cut out soft spots on fruits because that indicates the

area has started to decay. Once produce is cut, refrigerate it—pathogens cannot thrive and multiply rapidly in cold temperatures. When sliced fruit or vegetables are allowed to sit out for any length of time, room temperature will liberate even a tiny speck of a pathogen that might have been on it and it will multiply. The same holds true of cooked produce. Refrigerate leftovers promptly.

But keep eating those fruits and vegetables. The benefits to health are countless.

Seven Cheers for the Health Benefits of Beer!

Margo A. Denke, MD, former associate professor of internal medicine, University of Texas Southwestern Medical Center, Dallas.

Meir J. Stampfer, MD, DrPH, chair, department of epidemiology, Harvard School of Public Health…professor of medicine, Harvard Medical School…physician, Brigham and Women's Hospital, Boston.

Good news, beer drinkers! The health benefits we know to be found in wine are also found in alcoholic drinks like beer. The key word, of course, is "moderation"—most experts advise no more than two alcoholic beverages a day for men and no more than one for women.

HERE'S TO YOUR HEALTH

An increasing body of serious research backs up beer's benefits…

• **Bone protection.** According to a medical team at Tufts University in Boston, beer may help prevent bone-thinning osteoporosis. Dietary silicon in grain products such as beer appears to reduce bone loss and promote bone formation. Beer contains silicate, a highly absorbable form of silicon that works by facilitating the deposit of calcium and other minerals in bone tissue. Margo A. Denke, MD, former clinical professor of medicine at the University of Texas Southwestern Medical Center in Dallas, cautions that excessive alcohol intake is a risk factor for bad bones, perhaps because calories from nutrient sources are replaced with calories from alcohol.

•**Lower risk for cardiovascular disease.** Like wine, beer has well-documented heart benefits. Regular moderate drinking has a protective effect in both men and women against cardiovascular disease, confirms Meir J. Stampfer, MD, DrPH, chair of the department of epidemiology at the Harvard School of Public Health. He told us that moderate alcohol consumption in any form has an equivalent benefit—"Wine is not better than beer, red wine is not better than white and spirits (in moderation) are also associated with lower risk."

•**Better heart attack survival.** A study at Beth Israel Deaconess Medical Center in Boston concluded that moderate drinkers (who consumed more than seven alcoholic beverages a week) had a 32% lower risk of dying from a heart attack than those who drank no alcohol. Light drinkers (less than seven drinks weekly) had a 21% lower risk. Like other alcohol, beer acts as a blood thinner to help prevent clogged arteries. Other research links moderate alcohol consumption with improved blood circulation in the brain and lower risk for stroke.

•**Improved cholesterol levels.** In her research, Dr. Denke discovered that people who consumed one to three drinks daily had higher levels of high-density lipoprotein (HDL), the "good" cholesterol. She also found that regular moderate intake of alcohol resulted in lower blood insulin levels. In a related US Department of Agriculture (USDA) study, women who drank one alcoholic beverage daily lowered their low-density lipoprotein (LDL—"bad") cholesterol and levels of harmful blood lipids known as triglycerides.

•**Sharper brains.** In the long-term Nurses' Health Study (Harvard Medical School in Boston), Dr. Stampfer and his colleagues found that moderate consumption of alcohol seemed to preserve the mental abilities of older women. From 1995 to 1999, more than 9,000 women between ages 70 and 79 were interviewed regarding their alcohol use, and seven different tests of mental function were administered. Moderate drinkers scored better on five of seven tests, and on total overall scores.

•**Healthier kidneys.** Researchers found that men who consumed seven or more drinks a week experienced a 29% lower risk of developing kidney problems.

•**Antioxidant effect.** Japanese scientists have found that antioxidants such as polyphenols in beer may offer protection against cancer-causing chemicals. This repeats earlier research conducted in Portugal, which suggested that antioxidants slow the proliferation of breast cancer cells. According to Dr. Denke, isoflavonoids in beer are phytoestrogens that mimic the activity of the natural human hormone estrogen. In laboratory experiments, isoflavonoids have also been shown to inhibit the growth of cancers of the breast, prostate and colon.

PROCEED WITH CAUTION

Promising as all this research appears, talking about alcohol always requires special caution. It's all too easy to slip over the line from healthful consumption to overconsumption and physical damage, warns Dr. Denke. Yes, regular moderate consumption can benefit the heart, kidneys, bones and more. But drinking too much alcohol can seriously harm vital organs and processes in the body. As always, moderation in all things is the best path to follow.

Cracking the Myths on Coconut Oil

Udo Erasmus, PhD, author of *Fats that Heal, Fats that Kill* (Alive). Learn more about Dr. Erasmus's work at his Web site, *www.udoerasmus.com*.

Is it a dangerous saturated fat or a tropical wonder that we should use in place of olive oil? Confusion and debate surround coconut oil. Mainstream organizations such as the American Heart Association and the National Cancer Institute recommend avoiding it because coconut oil is a saturated fat that, they say, raises blood cholesterol and cardiovascular risk. However, an increasing number of alternative voices are popping up on the Internet claiming that it was unfair to lump coconut oil in with unhealthful fats during the fanatical no-fat era, and this tropical oil is really a magic elixir, a virtual fountain of youth.

To learn more, we consulted Udo Erasmus, PhD, author of *Fats that Heal, Fats that Kill* (Alive). He says that it is difficult to determine where science ends and marketing begins, and both camps are misleading in their one-sided approaches. As usual, the truth lies somewhere in-between, he says. Coconut oil is neither as bad as traditionalists would have you believe, nor is it the miraculous cure-all hawked by aggressive Internet entrepreneurs.

NOT AS BAD AS TRADITIONAL CLAIMS

First, let's take a look at coconut oil as a saturated fat. Coconut oil and its tropical cousin palm oil are composed of medium-chain fatty acids that are relatively easy to digest, absorb and metabolize. In contrast, longer-chain fatty acids in beef and dairy fats (other than butter fats, which are short-chain) place a greater burden on the liver.

In other words, while it's not exactly a health food, coconut oil has nowhere near the artery-clogging impact of the saturated fats in hamburgers and milk shakes. Coconut oil is not an essential fat like the omega-3 fatty acids that we require for good health. However, Dr. Erasmus believes that it is a neutral fat that is safe to use in moderation, as long as you also make sure that you consume the right balance of essential fatty acids.

NOT AS GOOD AS INTERNET CLAIMS

And now for the health claims—you'll lose weight, have more energy, feel younger, and it will cure thyroid problems and banish wrinkles. *Dr. Erasmus responds…*

• **If you replace carbohydrates in your diet with fats such as coconut oil,** you will cut back on food cravings and turn on fat burning. True, and while essential fatty acids such as omega-3s are a better all-around choice in this regard, coconut oil will also help get the job done.

• **Coconut oil boosts metabolism and energy.** False. In fact, it appears to slow the metabolic rate. There is no evidence supporting coconut oil as a cure for thyroid disease.

• **Coconut contains good antioxidants,** and by thwarting free radical development

you can, to some extent, counter the effects of aging. True, but you also can accomplish this by eating lots of fruits, veggies and cold-water fish.

• **Coconut oil can be a useful addition to skincare regimens.** True. For more youthful and supple skin, use moisturizing lotions, bath oils and cosmetics enriched with coconut oil.

MODERATION IN ALL THINGS

As always, there's some truth in marketing, but you have to take it with a grain (and sometimes a pillar) of salt. In the case of coconut oil's popularity, Dr. Erasmus believes that it is a fad riding on the coattails of essential fatty acid research. He points out that essential fatty acids are essential to good health and that coconut oil is not. That said, coconut is fine to use in moderation, and many people love its aroma. Always buy it in glass bottles (not plastic), and feel free to add a tasty tablespoon to smoothies or salad dressings.

How Foods Affect Our Moods

Elizabeth Somer, MA, RD, author of *Food & Mood: The Complete Guide to Eating Well and Feeling Your Best* (Henry Holt).

Robert E. Thayer, PhD, professor of psychology, California State University, Long Beach, and author of *Calm Energy: How People Regulate Mood with Food and Exercise* and *The Origin of Everyday Moods* (both from Oxford University).

We often call it comfort food, but for millions of Americans, it is not comforting at all. Many people fail to make the connection, but how and what we eat has a direct effect on our moods. Not only is our consumption affecting us from moment to moment throughout the day, but bad eating habits can contribute to long-term mood troubles of all kinds, including depression.

Elizabeth Somer, MA, registered dietitian (RD), and author of the book *Food & Mood: The Complete Guide to Eating Well and Feeling Your Best* (Henry Holt), says that it is not only what we eat but also our style of eating that contribute to our state of mind. The most important thing Somer recommends is that you actually eat. "Many people skip breakfast," she says, "and then wonder why they lack energy midmorning." Food is energy, and if we do not give our body fuel, it is going to run out of gas. Although we've all heard the advice about the importance of eating breakfast, it's astonishing how many people still start their day with a body that may not have eaten for more than 12 hours.

THE COMFORT OF CARBS

Somer also cautions against the "low-carb" craze and recommends that we stop fighting our carb cravings. Our bodies, and specifically our brains, need carbohydrates. Carbohydrates raise our levels of *tryptophan*, which increases our *serotonin* levels. This actually calms us, increases our pain tolerance, improves our sleeping habits and reduces our cravings for more carbohydrates.

Somer's definition of carbs is not a double fudge sundae or chocolate chip cookies, however. She is talking about all-natural, low-glycemic index complex carbohydrates such as whole grains, fruits, vegetables, seeds, beans and nuts. Foods that are high in carbs, but also rich in nutrients, are the real comfort foods, with long-lasting effects.

CUT BACK ON SUGAR SHOCK

Somer recommends cutting back or eliminating refined and processed sugars and caffeine. For those people who are very sensitive to sugar, a sweet such as a single cookie can begin a vicious cycle of feeling bad, eating more sugar, crashing again and so on. If this sounds like you, eliminate all processed sugar from your diet. Look for the hidden sugars in condiments such as ketchup and salsa, canned fruits, juice drinks and other processed and prepared foods. If you are not as sensitive, Somer still recommends cutting back on concentrated sugars such as candy and pastries.

CAFFEINE CAN SLOW YOU DOWN

Although caffeine may seem like a pick-me-up, studies show that it actually might add to depression. When tested on rats, researchers concluded that caffeine decreases the conversion of tryptophan to serotonin. For people who suffer from depression, caffeine can actually aggravate their symptoms.

BETTER PICK-ME-UPS

Robert E. Thayer, PhD, psychologist and author of *Calm Energy: How People Regulate Mood with Food and Exercise* (Oxford University), says that most people make poor eating choices because they experience what he calls "tense tiredness." A lack of energy or increase in tension causes people to seek foods that will quickly raise their blood sugar. They often go for a sugar snack, which will temporarily "fix" the problem. Unfortunately, a snack high in refined, processed sugar will only relieve symptoms of tense tiredness for a short period of time, which is usually followed by a sugar crash.

A far better solution for tense tiredness is to release tension and/or increase energy. For people practiced in meditation or muscle relaxation techniques, taking a few minutes to relax will usually do the trick. For nonmeditators, Dr. Thayer recommends exercise. In most cases, a brisk, 10-minute walk increases energy for up to two hours, based on research findings.

Getting enough sleep and eating small meals throughout the day are also healthier ways to regulate your mood. If you have more energy, you are less vulnerable to tension, and you will be less likely to start the sugar binge cycle in the first place.

EVERYONE IS DIFFERENT

While Dr. Thayer has studied eating habits and their effect on mood, he is also a proponent of knowing your own body and habits. In his book *The Origin of Everyday Moods* (Oxford University), he suggests systematic self-observation. *Try this experiment…*

Notice the association between your feelings, thoughts and behavior before having a sugar snack. Rate your energy on a number scale. Are you a peppy 5? An exhausted 1? Then do the same after you eat your sugar snack. Note how long the energy lasts. Do this several times. Keep your findings in a notebook. Make a chart or a graph. Notice what the snack is doing to you. Then, try the same experiment before and after taking a walk or using relaxation techniques.

Knowing why you make food choices is the first step to lasting dietary changes and a healthier, happier state of mind.

7

Key Vitamins and Minerals for Women

Antioxidant Vitamin Supplements: The New Findings

The disappointing results of a nine-year clinical trial on supplements of antioxidant vitamins (nutrients that neutralize harmful molecules called free radicals) show once again that achieving good health is not as simple as popping a pill. The Women's Antioxidant Cardiovascular Study involved 8,171 women, average age 61, who had a history of cardiovascular disease or multiple risk factors, such as high cholesterol, high blood pressure, diabetes, smoking and/or obesity. Some participants took placebos, and the rest took supplements of 500 mg of vitamin C daily… 600 international units (IU) of vitamin E every other day…and/or 50 mg of beta-carotene every other day. These dosages are several times greater than the recommended daily allowances (RDAs) and are similar to dosages used by members of the general public.

Results: Antioxidant supplements, taken singly or in combination, did not prevent heart attacks, strokes or other cardiovascular events among high-risk women.

Possible exception: Vitamin E supplementation was associated with marginally fewer cardiovascular events among participants who had a prior heart attack or stroke and those who took their pills faithfully. These results, though intriguing, are not conclusive and may have been due to chance, given the large number of subgroups studied. Most other trials have been similarly discouraging, providing no convincing evidence that antioxidant supplements prevent cardiovascular events in people who are healthy or in those with cardiovascular disease.

JoAnn E. Manson, MD, DrPH, professor of medicine and women's health at Harvard Medical School and chief of the division of preventive medicine at Brigham and Women's Hospital, both in Boston. A lead investigator for two highly influential studies on women's health. Dr. Manson is coauthor of *Hot Flashes, Hormones & Your Health* (McGraw-Hill).

Antioxidant-rich foods—fruits, vegetables, whole grains, nuts, vegetable oils—are another story. Studies show that an antioxidant-rich diet reduces cardiovascular disease risk, perhaps in part because these foods contain hundreds of additional nutrients that supplements cannot duplicate.

If you think that antioxidant pills might help and can't hurt, consider...

•**Antioxidant supplements** may reduce the effects of some drugs, such as cholesterol-lowering statin drugs.

•**Taking more than 400 IU of vitamin E daily** may increase heart failure risk.

•**Megadoses of antioxidants may hinder** the absorption and function of other nutrients.

Example: High doses of beta-carotene may hamper other beneficial carotenoids.

•**Smokers who take high doses of beta-carotene** are more likely to get lung cancer.

•**High doses of vitamin C** may increase risk for kidney stones.

Best: Get your antioxidants from foods rather than supplements. It's fine to take a multivitamin that contains 100% of the RDAs, plus a calcium/vitamin D pill to protect bones. But don't let an overly optimistic faith in supplements make you complacent about the proven ways to protect your heart—with diet, exercise and, if necessary, drugs to control blood pressure, cholesterol and diabetes.

Best Supplements for Healthy Aging

Jamison Starbuck, ND, naturopathic physician in family practice and a lecturer at the University of Montana, both in Missoula. She is past president of the American Association of Naturopathic Physicians and a contributing editor to *The Alternative Advisor: The Complete Guide to Natural Therapies and Alternative Treatments* (Time-Life).

Of all the changes that occur with aging, one of the most under-recognized is the body's reduced ability to absorb nutrients. As we grow older, our bodies become less efficient at secreting the digestive enzymes that are necessary for the absorption of essential vitamins. Because of this absorption problem, I advise my older patients to follow the nutritious and heart-healthy Mediterranean diet—rich in fresh greens (such as chard, kale and spinach), fresh fruit, whole grains, nuts, seeds, beans, healthful oils (olive, for example) and lean protein, such as turkey and fish. For more on the Mediterranean diet, visit the Web site of the American Heart Association, *www.heart.org*.

But it's not always easy to stick to a nutritious eating plan. What's more, many older adults suffer conditions that interfere with appetite—for example, dry mouth, nausea or constipation caused by common medications, such as pain relievers and hypertension drugs. Dentures and waning senses of smell and taste also can interfere with the consumption of healthful meals. In my opinion, all people over age 50 should consider taking certain supplements—in addition to a daily multivitamin—to compensate for nutrients that might be lacking in their diets. *My favorite "healthy aging" supplements (all available at health-food stores)...*

•**Vitamin B-12**—800 micrograms (mcg) to 1,000 mcg daily, in sublingual (dissolved under the tongue) form. It helps with poor memory, a lack of energy, depression and neuralgia (nerve pain).

•**Vitamin A**—10,000 international units (IU) daily. It helps promote health of the eyes and skin and general immunity. If you also take a multivitamin containing vitamin A, do not exceed 10,000 IU daily unless recommended by your doctor.

•**Vitamin E**—400 IU daily. It protects nerve and muscle cells, reduces leg cramps and helps prevent heart disease.*

•**Vitamin D**—1,000 IU daily. Recent research shows that many older adults are deficient in vitamin D, a nutrient that is essential for calcium absorption and osteoporosis prevention and may protect against certain malignancies, including cancers of the breast and colon.

*If you take a blood-thinning drug, such as *warfarin* (Coumadin), check with your doctor before taking vitamin E supplements.

• **Essential fatty acids,** in the form of fish oil, containing 1,800 milligrams daily of combined *eicosapentaenoic acid* (EPA) and *docosahexaenoic acid* (DHA). Fish oil acts as a natural antidepressant for patients of all ages and improves brain function.

• **Digestive enzymes.** Typically derived from papaya or pineapple, digestive enzyme supplements promote digestion—and, in turn, the absorption of nutrients from foods and other supplements. Follow the manufacturer's directions for dosages. If you have a gastrointestinal disease, such as an ulcer or diverticulitis, consult your physician before taking plant enzymes, which can irritate an inflamed gastrointestinal tract.

Nutrients that Cure What Ails You

L. Kathleen Mahan, RD, CDE, clinical associate at University of Washington School of Medicine in Seattle. She is a certified diabetes educator and coauthor of *Krause's Food & Nutrition Therapy* (Saunders).

Various physical symptoms can be triggered by nutritional deficiencies. Fortunately, the fix often is as easy as taking a certain supplement and adding specific foods to your diet.

The supplements below are available at health-food stores and/or on-line and, unless otherwise noted, generally are safe to take indefinitely. If you are pregnant or breastfeeding, get your doctor's okay before taking supplements. Follow the guidelines below until symptoms are gone. If your condition is severe or does not improve within six weeks, see your doctor.

BLEEDING GUMS

Supplement with: Vitamin C at 100 milligrams (mg) to 200 mg daily.

Choose a supplement labeled "esterified" for easier absorption. (It's also important to floss!)

And eat more: Citrus fruit (clementines, grapefruit, kumquats, oranges, pummelos, tangelos), guava, kiwifruit, peppers, strawberries.

BRITTLE NAILS

Supplement with: Calcium at 1,000 mg daily.

Avoid supplements derived from unrefined oyster shells or dolomite—they may contain toxins, such as mercury or lead.

And eat more: Canned fish (salmon, sardines), dairy, green vegetables (collards, spinach, turnip greens), calcium-fortified soy milk and tofu.

DERMATITIS (ITCHY, INFLAMED SKIN)

Supplement with: Vitamin B-6 (pyridoxine) at 1.3 mg daily.

Get your doctor's okay before taking B-6— excess amounts can cause pain and numbness in the legs and feet.

And eat more: Bananas, chicken breast, garbanzo beans, pork loin, potatoes with skin, sunflower seeds.

HAIR LOSS

Supplement with: Zinc at 8 mg to 15 mg daily.

Look for the words "zinc chelate" in the ingredients list for easier absorption.

And eat more: Beef, lamb, nuts, oysters, peas, sesame seeds, shrimp, venison, whole grains, yogurt.

LEG OR FOOT CRAMPS

Supplement with: Potassium at 4.7 grams daily.

Get your doctor's okay before taking potassium if you use heart medication.

And eat more: Bananas, beets, oranges, prunes, sweet potatoes, white beans.

Helpful: Drink more water.

NUMBNESS IN FINGERS OR TOES

Supplement with: Vitamin B-12 at 2.4 micrograms (mcg) daily.

Since B-12 is found primarily in animal foods, supplementation also is recommended for most vegetarians.

And eat more: Clams, eggs, fish (halibut, salmon, snapper, trout), liver, milk, scallops, venison, yogurt.

POOR APPETITE

Supplement with: Folic acid (folate) at 400 mcg daily.

Smokers and celiac disease patients are especially prone to folic acid deficiency.

And eat more: Asparagus, avocado, beef liver, broccoli, papaya, peanuts, spinach, wheat germ.

PSORIASIS

Supplement with: Vitamin D at 1,000 international units (IU) daily.

Choose the most active form, called vitamin D-3 or cholecalciferol.

And eat more: Cod-liver oil, fish (salmon, mackerel, tuna), eggs, fortified milk.

VISION PROBLEMS AT NIGHT

Supplement with: Vitamin A at 4,000 IU daily.

Do not exceed the recommended dosage—excess vitamin A is toxic. Do not use if you take oral medication containing retinol, such as Accutane.

And eat more: Apricots, cantaloupe, carrots, dairy, eggs, kale, organ meats, pumpkin, spinach, sweet potatoes with skin, winter squash.

The Most Common Vitamin Deficiencies— A Few Key Vitamins Can Make a Big Difference

Andrew L. Rubman, ND, director, Southbury Clinic for Traditional Medicines, Southbury, Connecticut.

Office of Dietary Supplements, National Institutes of Health, *http://ods.od.nih.gov.*

According to Andrew L. Rubman, ND, key vitamin and mineral deficiencies can hit people with the most healthful of diets, because diet alone is often insufficient to provide enough of these vitamins and minerals to meet a person's needs. In these cases supplements come into play, but often at levels significantly different than the government-recommended Daily Value (DV) or Recommended Dietary Allowance (RDA), which are not necessarily the levels for optimal health, according to Dr. Rubman. Of particular concern are vitamin B-12, calcium, magnesium and iron.

VITAMIN B-12: ESSENTIAL TO PROPER LIVER FUNCTION

One of the most common deficiencies of all is B-12, which the liver requires for optimal function in a myriad of roles, including nutrient synthesis and transportation, and waste management and selective recycling, says Dr. Rubman. He notes that older people, in particular, are very often functionally deficient in B-12. The truth is that normal government-recommended values are based on vulnerability to pernicious anemia (a type of anemia caused by extreme B-12 deficiency) rather than reflective of individual needs. While most people don't develop this severe type of anemia, a significant percentage of the population has a functional deficiency such that they are unable to operate at an optimal level. Given how essential B-12 is to brain and nervous system function, a functional deficiency can lead to neurological issues. Problems such as impaired memory, confusion and decreased cognition may seem subtle at first, but if the deficiency is not addressed, over time these problems may grow more pronounced. In older people, a B-12 deficiency is one contributing factor to dementia. This is why they must seek professional oversight.

What you can do: Dr. Rubman encourages people to get a serum blood test to assess their level of B-12. If there is a functional deficiency, he recommends sublingual B-12 pills, either *hydroxocobalamin* or *methylcobalamin*, which are equally as effective as and less expensive than B-12 shots. (Avoid *cyanocobalamin*, which is poorly absorbed.) B-12 should be taken under a doctor's supervision. Because B-12 requires other B vitamins to function properly in the body, take a multi-B supplement twice daily, as they do not last 24 hours in circulation.

Note: Take B-12 and a multi-B supplement under the supervision of your physician. A good way to know if you're taking in sufficient

B is to look at the color of your urine. Ideally, it should remain yellow through the day.

CALCIUM AND MAGNESIUM: FOR BONE HEALTH AND MORE

Calcium is the most abundant mineral in the body, required for bone formation and for maintaining strong bones throughout life as well as for assisting in sleep and blood clotting. Insufficient calcium can lead to the bone-thinning disorders osteoporosis and osteopenia. While dairy products are the most popular sources of calcium, cow's milk is difficult to digest and may not be the best form of calcium for absorption. Other sources you may want to try are calcium-enriched plant milks (e.g., almond, oat, hazelnut, rice and soy) and leafy green vegetables such as spinach and kale.

Magnesium, the fourth most abundant mineral in the body, is required to ensure calcium absorption as well as proper muscle and nerve function, bone strength and to keep heart rhythm steady. Many people do not take in enough magnesium (through foods such as legumes, nuts, whole grains and vegetables), which is believed to offer protection against cardiovascular disease and immune dysfunction. Gastrointestinal disorders such as insufficient stomach acid or Crohn's disease may impair the absorption of magnesium.

What you can do: Dr. Rubman often prescribes calcium and magnesium in the combination supplement Butyrex, made by T.E. Neesby. These capsules contain calcium/magnesium as butyrates, a form which makes them much easier for the body to absorb than that found in other commonly available supplements. Butyrex has a number of gastrointestinal benefits. It supports the lining of the gastrointestinal tract, allowing for optimal absorption of nutrients, and helps maintain a balanced microbial population in the gut. While the standard RDA for calcium is adults: 1,000-1,300 milligrams/day along with magnesium in a 2:1 proportion, Butyrex's formulation is so well absorbed that the dosing is often lower. According to Dr. Rubman, patients often start feeling better within just a few days of taking Butyrex.

IRON: FOR OXYGEN TRANSPORT AND ENERGY

Iron is a tricky nutrient. According to the World Health Organization, iron deficiency is the most common nutritional deficiency in the world, with as many as 80% of the global population suffering from iron deficiency or iron deficiency anemia. On the other hand, too much iron can also cause problems, warns Dr. Rubman.

If you don't take in enough iron, oxygen is not transported efficiently to the body's cells. As a result, you're apt to feel tired and weak, and be more susceptible to infection. Women with heavy menstrual periods are at risk for iron deficiency, as are pregnant women, children and teens, all of whom have a high need for iron. Gastrointestinal disorders such as Crohn's disease, celiac disease, ulcers and other GI disorders, as well as the chronic use of antacids and acid suppressing medications, may impair the absorption of iron.

What you can do: Dietary sources of iron include animal proteins such as red meat, turkey, chicken and fish. Other sources include lentils, soybeans, kidney beans, spinach and enriched breads and cereals. If needed, it is fine to take iron as part of a multivitamin supplement, says Dr. Rubman. Otherwise, he recommends taking the superior iron supplement Proferrin, only under medical supervision.

While you can pick up some of these supplements yourself at the local health food store, you should see a licensed naturopathic physician. Remember that treating deficiencies is always a medical issue, no matter how readily available the pharmacy may be. When you provide your body the right fuels to work with, in no time at all you're likely to feel more healthy, fit and energetic.

Magnesium Makes You Stronger

In a recent study of 1,138 men and women, participants with the highest blood levels of magnesium were stronger (based on tests for handgrip strength and power in leg muscles) than those with the lowest levels.

Theory: Magnesium is essential to the body's cellular energy production, thereby promoting optimal muscle performance.

Self-defense: To get the recommended intake of magnesium (420 milligrams [mg] daily for men age 31 or older…320 mg daily for women age 31 or older), eat such foods as green, leafy vegetables, navy beans and pumpkin seeds.

Ligia J. Dominguez, MD, researcher, geriatric unit, University of Palermo, Palermo, Italy.

Magnesium Improves Absorption of Calcium

Leon Root, MD, attending orthopedic surgeon, Hospital for Special Surgery, New York City.

Magnesium helps transport calcium into and out of bones. In most instances, magnesium is so plentiful in one's diet—in foods, such as brown rice, spinach and almonds—that supplements are not necessary. If your diet lacks these foods and you want to take a magnesium supplement, the amount of magnesium you take should be half that of the calcium. For example, if you are taking 1,500 mg of calcium daily, the magnesium dose should be 750 mg. Your body cannot absorb more than 500 mg of supplemental calcium at one time, so it's best to take calcium supplements in divided doses. Make sure that you get enough vitamin D, which is even more essential for calcium absorption than magnesium is. The current recommended daily intake for vitamin D is 600 international units (IU) for adults age 70 or younger…and 800 IU for those age 71 or older.

Caution: Vitamin D and calcium supplements can affect the potency of high blood pressure medications known as calcium channel blockers, such as *nifedipine* (Adalat) and *amlodipine* (Norvasc). If you use these medications, check with your physician before taking the supplements described above.

Magnesium Miracle

In a recent study, women with normal blood pressure who got a daily average of 434 mg of magnesium through their diets lowered their risk for high blood pressure by 7%.

Best: Consume foods that are rich in magnesium, such as whole grains, nuts, legumes, leafy green vegetables, fish and yogurt.

Yiqing Song, MD, associate epidemiologist, division of preventive medicine, Brigham and Women's Hospital, and instructor in medicine, Harvard Medical School, both in Boston, and leader of a study of 28,349 women, published in *The American Journal of Cardiology.*

Calcium for Weight Loss

Calcium can help weight loss. Some research says that when the body is deficient in calcium, it secretes more calcitrol—a substance that fights weight loss. In some studies, taking calcium has reduced this effect.

There is no harm in trying calcium for 90 days to see if it helps. For maximum absorption, take 600 milligrams of calcium with 300 international units (IU) of vitamin D twice daily. If you do not like tablets, you may find that capsules or softgels are easier to swallow. Schiff (800-526-6251, *www.schiffvitamins.com*) makes calcium softgels. Also get as much calcium as possible through diet—from low-fat yogurt, cheese and skim milk.

Stephen Gullo, PhD, president, Institute for Health and Weight Sciences Center for Healthful Living, New York City, and author of *Thin Tastes Better* (Random House) and, most recently, *The Thin Commandments Diet* (Rodale).

Choose Food Over Supplements

Calcium from food is better for bones than calcium supplements.

New finding: Women who got most of their daily calcium from food, such as low-fat dairy products, had higher bone density than women who got most of their calcium from vitamin supplements.

Best: Get three cups or the equivalent of milk products daily.

Reina Armamento-Villareal, MD, former associate professor of medicine, department of endocrinology, metabolism and lipid research, Washington University's School of Medicine, St. Louis, and leader of a study of 168 women, published in *American Journal of Clinical Nutrition*.

Calcium and Vitamin D Guard Against Breast Cancer

Mark A. Stengler, NMD, naturopathic medical doctor in private practice, Encinitas, California…adjunct associate clinical professor at the National College of Natural Medicine, Portland, Oregon…author of *The Natural Physician's Healing Therapies* (Bottom Line Books).

Researchers from Harvard and the National Institutes of Health analyzed 10 years of data from 10,578 premenopausal women and 20,909 postmenopausal women.

Findings: Premenopausal women with a high daily intake of calcium (about 1,350 milligrams, or mg) and vitamin D (about 550 international units, or IU) had a 30% lower risk of breast cancer. Also, aggressive breast tumors were less likely to occur in premenopausal women (but not postmenopausal women) with high calcium and vitamin D intake.

My view: Many postmenopausal women take calcium and vitamin D to prevent osteoporosis (brittle bones). This study underscores the value of taking these nutrients before menopause, as well. Though the link between calcium and breast cancer prevention is not well-understood, research increasingly shows that vitamin D boosts immunity.

Recommended: Women should take 1,000 mg to 1,200 mg of calcium plus 1,000 IU of

vitamin D daily before menopause, to reduce breast cancer risk—and after menopause, to strengthen bones.

Are You Getting Enough Vitamin D?

JoAnn E. Manson, MD, DrPH, professor of medicine and women's health at Harvard Medical School and chief of the division of preventive medicine at Brigham and Women's Hospital, both in Boston. A lead investigator for two important studies on women's health, Dr. Manson is coauthor of *Hot Flashes, Hormones & Your Health* (McGraw-Hill).

Up to half of American women don't get enough vitamin D, even though this nutrient has significant health benefits. Some experts now recommend a particular form of vitamin D, in amounts significantly higher than current governmental guidelines.

You may have a deficiency of vitamin D if you don't get much sunshine, because ultraviolet B (UVB) rays trigger vitamin D synthesis in the skin…if you have dark skin, which is less efficient at converting UVB to vitamin D…or if you have liver or kidney disease or a digestive disorder that impairs vitamin D absorption. *Among its benefits, vitamin D may…*

•**Lower death rates.** Researchers analyzed 18 studies in which 57,000 adults took vitamin D pills or a placebo for about six years.

Result: Vitamin D cut risk for death by about 7%.

•**Protect against breast, ovarian, colon and other cancers.** In a trial involving 1,179 postmenopausal women, participants who took daily vitamin D at 1,100 international units (IU) plus calcium were 60% less likely to develop cancer than those who took a placebo or calcium alone.

Reasons: Vitamin D strengthens the immune system and may inhibit out-of-control cancerous cell growth by reducing blood supply to tumors.

• **Strengthen bones** by promoting absorption of calcium and phosphorous from the intestines.

• **Help prevent diabetes** by improving sugar metabolism.

• **Protect against autoimmune disorders,** such as multiple sclerosis and rheumatoid arthritis, by fighting inflammation.

• **Lower risk for heart disease and stroke** by inhibiting accumulation of artery-clogging plaque.

Current guidelines call for intakes of 200 IU daily until age 50...400 IU between ages 51 and 70...and 600 IU after age 70.

More recent: Adults should get at least 800 IU to 1,000 IU of vitamin D daily from foods and/or supplements in addition to whatever they get from sunlight. *How...*

• **Food sources of vitamin D** include cod liver oil (1,360 IU per tablespoon)...fatty fish, such as salmon, mackerel and tuna (200 IU to 300 IU per three ounces)...fortified milk (100 IU per cup)...and some cereals (about 40 IU per cup).

• **Choose supplements that provide the more active form**—vitamin D-3 (*cholecalciferol*), the type produced by our bodies—rather than the less active D-2 (*ergocalciferol*) from plants.

• **Don't go overboard.** Excessive vitamin D can cause high blood calcium levels, which in turn can contribute to gastrointestinal problems, cognitive impairment, heart rhythm abnormalities and kidney stones. Multivitamins, calcium pills and osteoporosis drugs often include vitamin D—so check all labels to tally your daily total, making sure not to exceed 2,000 IU per day.

Vitamin D May Lower Diabetes Risk Among Children

A recent study finds that infants who get large amounts of vitamin D from food,

supplements and exposure to sun are 29% less likely to develop type 1 (juvenile) diabetes, an autoimmune disease, later in childhood.

More evidence: Rates of type 1 diabetes are lower in sunny equatorial countries, where children are subject to significant amounts of vitamin D–producing sunlight...and higher in northern countries that have less sunlight.

Cedric F. Garland, DrPH, researcher, Moores Cancer Center, University of California, San Diego, and leader of a study published in the online issue of *Diabetologia*.

The Vitamin D–Breast Cancer Connection

Carlo Palmieri, PhD, Cancer Research UK Laboratories and Imperial College, London.

Vitamin D, the "sunshine vitamin," has been the focus of intense study in recent years as researchers have found evidence it may help lower the risk of developing several types of cancers, among them colon, prostate, pancreatic and breast cancer. Now, a new British study suggests that low vitamin D levels may play a role in the progression of breast cancer in women who already have it. The study involved 279 women...204 of them had early-stage breast cancer, while the rest were in advanced stage cancer. While measuring the blood levels of vitamin D in all these women, the researchers discovered that those with early-stage cancer had significantly higher levels of D than the ones with advanced cancer.

Carlo Palmieri, PhD, of Cancer Research UK Laboratories and Imperial College in London, was the lead author of the study. When I contacted him for more information on this finding, I asked whether he believes that vitamin D hinders the progression of breast cancer, or if the vitamin is depleted as a result of the disease. That's the big question, he acknowledged, and the answer is not yet evident. "What we do know is that lab tests have shown vitamin D inhibits the proliferation of breast cancer cell lines, somehow inducing them to die. We also know that in countries at higher latitudes, where there is less sunshine and people are more likely to be D deficient, there is a higher incidence of breast cancer." Yet more evidence—a case control study showed that women with no cancer had higher levels of vitamin D than women with breast cancer. (Results were only in Caucasian women.) We also know that vitamin D treatment boosts the activity of the p21 gene—important, says Dr. Palmieri, because the gene ensures that cells divide appropriately. "So, problems with adequate p21 activity could potentially lead to abnormal cell growth, and therefore, cancer."

This is not a reason to rush out to get vitamin D supplements, however. According to Dr. Palmieri, his study adds to mounting evidence about the importance of vitamin D, but more research is needed to establish the case conclusively. For now, the best advice is to be sure you are getting a balanced diet full of all nutrients, and that you get regular, safe levels of sun exposure. And remember that vitamin D supplementation should only be done under the guidance of a knowledgeable professional, as too much can cause a medical emergency.

Better Vitamin D Source

Boston researchers recently measured the vitamin D content in local seafood.

Result: Farm-raised salmon contained about 25% of the vitamin D content found in wild-caught salmon. In earlier research, however, farmed salmon contained, on average, higher levels of beneficial omega-3 fatty acids than wild salmon.

Bottom line: If you're trying to maximize your vitamin D intake, look to wild salmon over farm-raised salmon.

Michael F. Holick, MD, PhD, professor of medicine, physiology and biophysics, Boston University School of Medicine.

Vitamin D and PAD

Vitamin D may protect against peripheral artery disease (PAD), in which fatty deposits reduce blood flow to the legs. PAD causes pain and numbness and makes it hard for people to walk.

Recent finding: People with the lowest levels of vitamin D in their blood were 80% more likely to have PAD than people with the highest levels. Further study is necessary to confirm the findings.

Michal Melamed, MD, associate professor of medicine (nephrology) and epidemiology and population health, Albert Einstein College of Medicine of Yeshiva University, New York City, and leader of an analysis of a US government health survey of more than 4,800 adults, published in *Arteriosclerosis, Thrombosis and Vascular Biology.*

Take Vitamin D for Lung Support

Vitamin D may help lung tissue to rejuvenate, a process that occurs throughout life but declines with age. The most important source of vitamin D is sun exposure, which leads to synthesis of vitamin D in the skin. Good food sources of vitamin D include fortified milk and seafood, such as herring, salmon and mackerel. To ensure that you're getting enough vitamin D, take a supplement daily. To aid lung function, most people need about 20 micrograms (mcg) of vitamin D a day…people over age 50 need double that amount—about 40 mcg.

The late Peter Black, MD, clinical associate professor, department of pharmacology and clinical pharmacology, University of Auckland, New Zealand, and lead author of a study of 14,000 people, published in *Chest.*

Sun Shield for Skin Cancer

Marianne Berwick, PhD, division chief and head of cancer epidemiology and prevention program at the University of New Mexico School of Medicine.

Eugene Butcher, MD, professor, department of pathology, Stanford University Medical Center.

Having had the skin cancer–causing dangers of sunlight drilled into us, we Americans have become sun-phobic. We smear on sunscreen every time we venture outside. But as more and more research shows, the truth is that some un-protected sun exposure is not only okay but beneficial. The latest news comes from a lab study at Stanford University that builds upon research from 2005 findings from the University of New Mexico regarding, believe it or not, survival rates in melanoma patients.

ABOUT THE STUDIES

Back in 2005, skin cancer researcher Marianne Berwick, PhD, division chief and head of cancer epidemiology and prevention program at the University of New Mexico School of Medicine published research showing that melanoma patients who had greater amounts of sun exposure had better rates of survival than those who had some sun exposure, but not enough to significantly effect the deep layers of the skin. According to Dr. Berwick, sun exposure was measured by recreational sun exposure (the number of times per year individuals engaged in outdoor recreation as well as vacations)…the number of sunburns (any versus none)…and solar elastosis (a measure of collagen damage around the area of the melanoma as assessed by a pathologist). She says that they are following up on individuals to find out whether they died from melanoma or another cause. "At the time the paper was published, we found that those who did have solar elastosis lived twice as long as those who did not," said Dr. Berwick.

The most useful form of vitamin D is produced when the skin is exposed to ultraviolet radiation, though it may also be absorbed from food sources. Dr. Berwick explained that the operational hypothesis with regard to the cancer survival rates is that when activated by sunlight, vitamin D in the bloodstream will also stimulate apoptosis, or cell death, to fast-growing cancer cells.

And now a new study from Stanford University provides further illumination on the subject, confirming the hypothesis from the 2005 study regarding the impact of sunlight on the activation of Vitamin D-3.

Having triggered this process in the lab, the Stanford scientists found that the "activated" vitamin D signals T-cells to localize to the epidermis, the surface layers of the skin, more than when they were not stimulated by the vitamin D, says Stanford University study coauthor, Eugene Butcher, MD.

He adds that these T-cells may help protect against cancer and may target cancer cells to reduce their survival.

Based on these studies, Drs. Berwick and Butcher say we should add the ability of sunlight to improve local vitamin D activity in the skin to the list of its many healthful benefits, since they may help target anti-cancer T-cells as well as help protect against proliferation of cancer cells.

So don't be afraid of the sun. Most experts say that how much sun you need depends on where you live and the color of your skin (dark skin is more protected and needs a bit more).

For most people, 15 minutes a few times a week in the morning or late afternoon should do it. "We don't want people spending the day at the beach with no protection," Dr. Berwick said, "but neither do we want them to be completely afraid to get a little sun. In fact, we believe it may be good to do so."

Vitamin K—the Forgotten Vitamin

Sarah Booth, PhD, director of the Vitamin K Laboratory at the Jean Mayer USDA Human Nutrition and Research Center on Aging and a professor at the Gerald J. and Dorothy R. Friedman School of Nutrition Science and Policy, both at Tufts University in Boston. Dr. Booth has led or participated in more than 50 scientific studies on vitamin K.

Vitamin K is the first nutritional supplement that most Americans ever receive. That's because newborns routinely get a shot of the nutrient—which is crucial for coagulation (blood clotting)—to help prevent a severe and sometimes fatal bleeding disorder.

Discovered by a Danish scientist in 1934, the vitamin was dubbed "K" for "Koagulation" (the Danish spelling). But it wasn't until years later that scientists figured out how it works—by helping the liver manufacture several proteins that control blood clotting.

Latest development: Researchers are now discovering that vitamin K provides a wide variety of health benefits that extend well beyond blood clotting.

VITAMIN K FOR BETTER HEALTH

Vitamins C and E tend to get the most media attention, but recent findings on vitamin K's ability to help curb the development and/or progression of certain common medical ailments are worth noting.

Examples...

•**Arthritis.** Research shows that low dietary intake of vitamin K may play a role in the development of osteoarthritis.

Scientific evidence: In a study published in the journal *Arthritis & Rheumatism,* higher blood levels of dietary vitamin K were associated with a lower risk for osteoarthritis of the hand and knee.

•**Heart disease.** Vitamin K aids the function of the biochemical matrix Gla-protein, which helps prevent calcium buildup in plaque-filled arteries.

Scientific evidence: Researchers in the Netherlands studied more than 4,800 people over age 55. Compared with those with the lowest intake of vitamin K, those with the highest intake were 52% less likely to have severe calcification of the aorta, the major artery leading from the heart. The participants were 57% less likely to die of heart disease.

•**Liver cancer.** Cirrhosis of the liver, which occurs when alcoholism or infection with the hepatitis B or C virus results in scarred, abnormal liver tissue, can lead to liver cancer.

Scientific evidence: Studies of animal and human cells show that vitamin K may help control the progression of liver cancer. For example, in a study published in the *Journal of the American Medical Association,* Japanese researchers divided 40 women with viral cirrhosis of the liver into two groups. One group received vitamin K daily...the other did not. Two of the women in the vitamin K group developed liver cancer, compared with nine in the non-vitamin K group. Statistically, vitamin K lowered the risk for liver cancer by 80%.

•**Osteoporosis.** Vitamin K aids in the formation of osteocalcin (a protein that helps calcium bind to bone). This bone-strengthening process may help prevent and/or treat osteoporosis, the brittle-bone disease that afflicts more than 10 million older Americans—80% of them women.

Scientific evidence: Scientists at Harvard Medical School analyzed data on vitamin K intake and bone health in more than 70,000 women. Those with the highest dietary intake of vitamin K had a 30% decreased risk for hip fracture compared with those who had the lowest intake. Other studies show similar results for men.

In England, researchers analyzed data from 13 Japanese clinical trials that used large, pharmacological doses of vitamin K to treat osteoporosis. Overall, the vitamin reduced the rate of spinal fractures by 40% and hip fractures by 13%.

Latest development: Scientists at the University of Toronto, Tufts University and the University of Wisconsin have completed three clinical trials to determine whether nutritional doses of vitamin K can prevent bone loss in postmenopausal women.*

*To stay abreast of this research, go to the National Institutes of Health Web site, *www.clinicaltrials.gov.*

ARE YOU GETTING ENOUGH?

The US government's recommended daily intake for vitamin K is 90 micrograms (mcg) for adult women...and 120 mcg for adult men. That level is high enough to prevent vitamin K deficiency, a rare condition that can lead to impaired blood clotting.

But is it high enough to keep your blood, bones and heart healthy? That's a question nutritional scientists are asking—but haven't yet answered.

However, scientists do know an easy, natural way to maximize your intake of vitamin K. It comes down to the classic parental advice—eat your vegetables.

Green vegetables—leafy and otherwise—are among the best dietary sources of vitamin K. (For amounts, see table to the right.)

Don't have a taste for kale or spinach? Don't worry. One-half cup of broccoli sautéed in olive oil gives you plenty of vitamin K. And don't worry about cooking—it doesn't destroy the vitamin. Or try a lettuce salad (using any type except iceberg) with a teaspoon of salad dressing that contains vegetable oil (some fat is needed for absorption of vitamin K).

Among vegetable oils, the richest sources of vitamin K (per two-tablespoon serving) are soybean oil (50 mcg) and olive oil (13 mcg).

Another good source: Mayonnaise (23 mcg).

Should you take a vitamin K supplement? Scientists don't have enough data at this point to recommend a dietary supplement of this nutrient for healthy adults.

IF YOU TAKE WARFARIN

Warfarin (Coumadin and Jantoven) is a widely used blood-thinning medication given to people who have had or are likely to develop an artery-blocking blood clot. Warfarin is often prescribed following a heart attack, stroke, blood clot in the leg (deep vein thrombosis) or a clot that has traveled to the lung (pulmonary embolism). The drug is also used in people who have an irregular heart rhythm (atrial fibrillation) or an artificial heart valve.

Warfarin works by decreasing the activity of vitamin K.

If you take warfarin: Don't eat dark, leafy green vegetables. The amount of vitamin K in these foods can vary threefold, depending on where they're grown. For example, a serving of spinach could contain 200 mcg of vitamin K ...or 600 mcg. That's a significant difference in vitamin K intake for someone taking warfarin, who should not have large fluctuations in intake of this vitamin.

Instead, eat three daily servings of vitamin K–rich foods with lower but predictable amounts of the nutrient. That could include one-half cup of broccoli, one-half cup of green peas or six ounces of tomato juice. Other good choices of foods that contain relatively low amounts of vitamin K include asparagus and green beans.

To help determine the dose of warfarin that prevents blood cots from forming, doctors test the coagulation time—a measurement known as the International Normalized Ratio and Pro-thrombin Time (INR/PT). INR/PT is checked monthly, and the patient is instructed to maintain a consistent dietary intake of vitamin K to avoid altering the effectiveness of warfarin.

VITAMIN K IN VEGETABLES

(estimated micrograms, per one-half cup, cooked)

	mcg
Kale	530
Collard greens	500
Spinach	440
Beet greens	350
Swiss chard	290
Turnip greens	260
Brussels sprouts	190
Dandelion greens	100
Broccoli	75
Asparagus	45
Cabbage	36
Green peas	20
Green beans	10

Source: US Department of Agriculture.

B Vitamins Score A+ Results for MS

Shinjiro Kaneko, MD, PhD, research fellow at Children's Hospital, Boston.

Allen C. Bowling, MD, PhD, consulting advisor at the Rocky Mountain Multiple Sclerosis Center, Englewood, Colorado.

There are 400,000 Americans with multiple sclerosis (MS). MS generally strikes people between the ages of 20 and 50, and two-thirds of them are women. Most MS patients are Caucasian of northern European descent, and having a sibling with MS makes the risk of developing it several times greater.

There isn't much conventional doctors can offer for treatment to ease symptoms and stall the disease, and what drugs are available come with difficult side effects, such as fever, chills, muscle aches and fatigue. But new hope—in the form of an everyday vitamin—may be in the offing for the many who have MS.

WHAT IS MS?

The complexity of MS has puzzled scientists for decades. Given that mostly women are affected, do hormones play a role? There is surely a genetic connection, but what? Scientists concur that MS is an inflammatory disease of the central nervous system (brain and spinal cord). It causes lesions to develop, apparently at random, on various spots on the nerve fibers (called axons). These lesions degenerate the myelin—material that coats and insulates nerves—damaging the ability of the axons to do their job, which is to transmit communication signals to and from the brain to nerves in the spinal column and elsewhere.

MANY SYMPTOMS

Because lesions can develop on axons anywhere in the central nervous system, they can affect a variety of signals...consequently MS has a wide and lengthy list of possible symptoms. These include fatigue, visual impairment, difficulty walking, spasticity, emotional and cognitive changes, pain and digestive problems. For most patients with MS, disease progression is slow, and their symptoms come and go, but about one-third of patients eventually need a wheelchair.

THE PROBLEM WITH DRUGS

Until the early 1990s there was no treatment for MS, but now there are several drugs that help reduce inflammation or preserve myelin in the early phase of the disease. However, these come with serious side effects and none have been successful in stopping the degeneration of axons that occurs in the later disease phase, which causes the greatest disability. Adding to everyone's frustration—especially people who have MS—there have been several promising medications that ultimately failed to deliver. All this makes a recent study on a common and inexpensive substance (that's unlikely to cause side effects) particularly exciting. Scientists at Children's Hospital Boston, affiliated with Harvard Medical School, have been working with a form of vitamin B-3 (commonly known as niacin) that seems to not only fight inflammation and stop myelin loss, but also appears to halt axon degeneration.

B-3 LOOKS GOOD BUT THERE'S MORE TO LEARN

To explain the study, it's useful to have a brief background about a coenzyme named *nicotinamide adenine dinucleotide* (NAD). Coenzymes are organic chemicals that help enzymes do their jobs, and this coenzyme in particular is present in every cell. It is used by the body to produce energy. The precursor of NAD is nicotinamide, which is a form of vitamin B-3 closely related to niacin.

For these studies, the scientists bred mice to have an MS-like disease. When the researchers administered nicotinamide to the mice, it increased NAD levels in their nervous systems, and the increased NAD delayed the onset of neurological disability. The more NAD the mice had when symptoms developed, the less neurological damage they suffered...conversely, the mice with the least NAD had the most neurological damage. Furthermore, the scientists found strong evidence that administering nicotinamide protected against damage to the axons in the later chronic disease stage as well.

FURTHER STUDIES NEEDED

Shinjiro Kaneko, MD, PhD, a research fellow at Children's Hospital, Boston, was the lead author of the study. He says that the mouse studies were an extension of some they had done in the lab in vitro with the same results. Although B-3 (niacin) is often used by people who are trying to reduce high cholesterol levels, Dr. Kaneko says that this is the first study that researches how B-3 might be used in treating MS. The obvious question is whether B-3 should now be taken by all MS patients, but Dr. Kaneko says that it is too early to make that suggestion. He explains that the doses they administered to the mice in their studies were substantially higher than people normally take, and until clinical trials have been done to investigate further, he is concerned about safety issues.

Allen C. Bowling, MD, PhD, is former medical director at the Rocky Mountain Multiple Sclerosis Center in Englewood, Colorado, and author of *Complementary and Alternative Medicine and Multiple Sclerosis* (Demos Medical Publishing). Dr. Bowling agrees with Dr. Kaneko that, based on these studies, it is too early to recommend B-3 to MS patients. He adds that other substances have seemed promising in studies, and then turned out to disappoint. We need to wait and see about B-3.

Research Shows Vitamin D–MS Connections

Kassandra Munger, MSc, research associate, department of nutrition, at the Harvard School of Public Health, Boston.

Michael F. Holick, MD, PhD, professor of medicine, physiology and biophysics, Boston University School of Medicine.

Get out in the sun! This advice comes after a study involving data from Army and Navy personnel that revealed that those with the highest blood levels of vitamin D, the "sunshine vitamin," were 62% less likely to develop multiple sclerosis (MS). The results may help to shed light on why MS is more common in people living far from the equator, where exposure to year-round sunlight is less intense.

STUDY FINDINGS

Working with a military database, study researchers sorted through more than seven million Army and Navy personnel records and identified 257 cases of MS. Each MS case eligible for the study was assigned two matching controls (same age, gender, ethnicity and dates of blood collection). Vitamin D levels were obtained by blood samples taken before the onset of MS symptoms.

Decreased MS risk was very strong in people younger than 20 years old, suggesting that vitamin D exposure before adulthood could be particularly important. Interestingly, these findings were true for white study participants, but not for black or Hispanic ones, for whom no significant association between vitamin D and MS was found. According to Kassandra Munger, MSc, researcher at the Harvard School of Public Health in Boston, and lead author of this study, people with darker skin have lower vitamin D levels overall, because their pigmentation "blocks" UV light.

WHAT IT MEANS TO YOU

According to Michael Holick, MD, PhD, author of several papers on vitamin D, and program director of the General Clinical Research Center at Boston University School of Medicine, the findings do not change advice on tanning. During the summer months, 10 to 15 minutes a day (20 minutes or more for dark-skinned individuals), two to three days a week without sunscreen during the peak hours of 10 am to 3 pm, is plenty of exposure for a light-skinned person to produce adequate vitamin D levels.

SUN SUBSTITUTES

During winter in the northern latitudes, the strength of the sun's rays reaching the Earth are inadequate to produce beneficial amounts of vitamin D.

Dr. Holick says sunlamps that transmit UVB radiation can help the body produce amounts of vitamin D. However, he recommends that users limit "sunbathing" to 50% of the manufacturers' product guidelines in order to prevent skin damage that could increase cancer risk.

HOW ABOUT PILLS?

Should we now be taking vitamin D supplements to prevent MS? Munger is quick to point out that the study does not prove that increasing vitamin D levels will prevent MS, or that a lack of vitamin D causes MS. Future research is necessary to further illuminate the relationship. However, she reminds us that there is a growing body of evidence supporting vitamin D in overall health maintenance, including bone health. For this reason, individuals should ensure that their vitamin D levels are adequate—at 1,000 IU (international units)/day (and if you take the supplement form, look for the "natural" D-3, derived mostly from fish oil). People with chronic *granulomatous* diseases such as *sarcoidosis* should avoid high levels of vitamin D supplementation.

Omega-3s—Good for Your Heart and Bones!

Bruce A. Watkins, PhD, professor of nutrition and director of the Diet and Health Initiative at University of Connecticut, Storrs, and former professor at Purdue University.

It is well known that omega-3 essential fatty acids are crucial for cardiovascular health, but now scientists have discovered that they also slow osteoporosis—the thinning of bones in older people, women in particular. Researchers at Purdue University's Center for Enhancing Foods to Protect Health conducted a rat study in which they removed the ovaries in two groups of rats, making them instantly estrogen deprived and therefore vulnerable to osteoporosis. They then fed one group a diet high in omega-6s (a ratio of 10:1) and the other a diet high in omega-3s (a ratio of 5:1). At the end of three months, the researchers evaluated the rats' bones and discovered that the 5:1 group preserved significantly more bone mineral than the other group.

TIME TO REMODEL

Bruce A. Watkins, PhD, professor of nutrition at UConn and the study's coauthor, shares some details about the importance of the omega-3s to bone health. He explains that bone building takes place throughout life in a cycle called remodeling. Certain cells break down bone and remove the particles and other cells come in to rebuild. (Exercise enhances remodeling because, he says, the muscles surrounding the bones being used message these cells to build more "here.") Dr. Watkins says that estrogen deprivation seems to elevate the activity of bone removal relative to the rate of bone formation, and the omega-3s—with their anti-inflammatory properties—slow that escalation down again. Omega-3s might also help bones by setting the stage for proper mineralization and use of calcium, another nutrient needed to build bone mass.

HOW TO GET YOUR 3s

Because of the way food is processed today, few people are getting the health benefits of omega-3s. Omega-6s, found primarily in vegetable oils, have deluged 3s in the modern diet. The ratio of 6s to 3s is now 10:1 or higher, the optimal ratio is 5:1 or lower. Because omega-6s are ubiquitous—in the corn-based vegetable oils that fill processed baked and fried foods as well as in animal feed and thus in meats—it's crucial to increase omega-3s in the diet to establish a good ratio.

COLD-WATER FISH x THREE

The American Heart Association recommends three meals a week featuring cold-water fish such as salmon, herring, mackerel, sardines or tuna (packed in water, *not* soy oil, which is filled with omega-6s, Dr. Watkins says). Omega-3s are also found in leafy green vegetables, walnuts and flaxseed and its oil. The drawback of flaxseed, however, is that the only omega-3 it contains is *alpha-linolenic acid* (ALA), which the body must convert to the two most important omega-3s, *eicosapentaenoic acid* (EPA) and *docosahexaenoic acid* (DHA). To be sure you are getting enough EPA and DHA, many experts advise taking 1,000 milligrams (mg) a day of a combination of both.

Best sources: Good-tasting fish oil products from Pharmax and Nordic Naturals.

Supplement Conquers the Food–Depression Cycle

John P. Docherty, MD, adjunct professor of psychiatry, Weill Cornell Medical College, Cornell University, New York City.

All too often, depression can feed on itself. Such is the case for the approximately eight million Americans who suffer from *atypical depression*, a variety of depression in which sufferers have an increased appetite leading to weight gain, sleeping too much, excessive lethargy and hypersensitivity to interpersonal rejection. Although atypical depression symptoms are quite apparent and they account for about 42% of the 19 million Americans who suffer from clinical depression, the problem frequently goes undiagnosed.

RECENT RESEARCH CAN HELP

The good news for these people is that a recent study looked at the role of chromium salts in helping to control blood sugar, and in turn, cravings. John P. Docherty, MD, adjunct professor of psychiatry at Weill Cornell Medical College, Cornell University in New York City, says that the carbohydrates that patients overindulge in the most are not surprising—baked goods and pasta, both ranking high as comfort foods. The result is weight gain, which adds to patients' depression. Unfortunately, a common side effect of selective serotonin reuptake inhibitors (SSRIs)—antidepressant medications, such as *fluoxetine* (Prozac) and *sertraline* (Zoloft)—is weight gain, as well.

CHROMIUM PICOLINATE

The 113 participants in the eight-week study, all people with atypical depression and a mean body mass index (BMI) that was borderline obese, were randomized into a group taking up to 600 microgram (mcg) of *chromium picolinate* a day or a placebo. The findings showed that the chromium picolinate group had a significant improvement—65% versus 33% in the placebo group—in terms of decreased appetite and lowered carbohydrate craving.

Dr. Docherty says we don't know exactly why chromium picolinate works to decrease carb cravings, but it probably has to do with the fact that it seems to enhance insulin regulation. (Many people with type 2 diabetes take it for this reason.) The picolinate form of chromium was used in the study not because it's the most effective form to use, but because it is the most widely available form. Chromium is abundantly available in whole grains, seafood, green beans and broccoli, among other foods, though it can be safely supplemented with physician oversight. People with diabetes especially should never start chromium supplements without medical supervision.

WEIGHT GAIN AND LETHARGY

Dr. Docherty stresses that it is important for all family members, friends and doctors to pay close attention when an individual starts to gain weight and seems unusually lethargic. These may well be signs that the person is suffering from depression or another physical illness such as sleep apnea disorder and should be evaluated.

8

Lift Your Spirits, Relieve Your Stress Naturally

Drug-Free Ways to Overcome Depression

Everyone feels blue occasionally, but for the one in eight American women who are depressed, feelings of sadness and hopelessness persist for months or years.

Conventional treatment for depression includes medication, most often with a selective serotonin reuptake inhibitor (SSRI), such as *fluoxetine* (Prozac), or a selective serotonin/norepinephrine reuptake inhibitor (SSNRI), such as *venlafaxine* (Effexor). The mechanism is unclear, but these drugs may work by blocking reabsorption of the brain chemicals *serotonin* and/or *norepinephrine*, leaving more of these mood-lifting neurotransmitters in the brain.

Problem: Antidepressants' side effects can include lowered libido, weight gain, headache, fatigue, anxiety, zombie-like moods and even suicidal tendencies.

New finding: An analysis of numerous clinical studies concluded that SSRIs were not significantly more effective than a placebo against mild-to-moderate depression. Other studies are more favorable for antidepressants, and medication is a vital part of treatment for some patients—but given the concerns about antidepressants, many experts believe that these drugs are overprescribed.

Better: A natural approach that treats depression with minimal side effects. *How it works…*

GETTING STARTED

Research demonstrates the mood-elevating effects of regular exercise, proper diet, sufficient sleep and moderate sunshine—yet depression can erode motivation to pursue healthful habits.

Hyla Cass, MD, board-certified psychiatrist with expertise in integrative medicine based in Pacific Palisades, California. She is author or coauthor of 10 books, including *Natural Highs: Supplements, Nutrition, and Mind/Body Techniques to Help You Feel Good All the Time* (Penguin) and a board member of the American College for Advancement in Medicine. *www.cassmd.com.*

159

What helps: Certain dietary supplements are natural mood enhancers, combating depression by correcting biochemical imbalances and increasing motivation to make healthful lifestyle changes.

Important: Before using supplements, check with a doctor knowledgeable about natural medicine, especially if you take medication, have a medical condition or are pregnant or breast-feeding. *Best...*

•**If you are not depressed,** take the nutrients listed below under "Mood Boosters for Everyone" to maintain healthful neurotransmitter levels.

•**If you are depressed but are not taking an antidepressant,** try natural remedies before considering drugs.

•**If you take an antidepressant but see no improvement in mood and/or suffer from side effects,** ask your doctor about weaning off the drug and starting natural therapies. Do not discontinue drugs on your own!

•**If an antidepressant is helping you and side effects are minimal,** continue your medication and ask your doctor about also taking supplements.

Supplements below are available in health-food stores and online.

Guideline: Begin at the low end of each recommended dosage range. If symptoms do not improve within a week, gradually increase the dosage.

MOOD BOOSTERS FOR EVERYONE

The following supplements are appropriate for most adults. Take all of them indefinitely to prevent or treat depression. They are safe to take while on antidepressants.

•**Omega-3 fatty acids.** These are essential for production of neurotransmitters that affect mood and thinking. Most effective are *eicosapentaenoic acid* (EPA) and *docosahexaenoic acid* (DHA), found in fish oil. Take 1,000 milligrams (mg) to 2,000 mg of combined EPA/DHA daily.

Caution: Fish oil may increase bleeding risk in people taking a blood thinner, such as *warfarin* (Coumadin).

•**B vitamins and magnesium.** The B vitamins help carry oxygen to the brain and produce neurotransmitters. They work best together and are absorbed best when taken with magnesium. Take a daily multivitamin or a vitamin-B complex that includes the following—25 mg each of vitamins B-1 and B-2...20 mg each of vitamins B-3 and B-6...50 mg each of B-5 and magnesium...and 100 micrograms (mcg) each of B-12 and folic acid.

Caution: Avoid supplements of B-3 if you have diabetes, gout or liver problems...avoid B-6 if you take *L-dopa* for Parkinson's disease.

•**Vitamins C, D and E.** These aid neurotransmitter production and/or protect brain cells. Take a daily multivitamin that includes 500 mg to 1,000 mg of vitamin C...2,000 international units (IU) of vitamin D...and 400 IU of vitamin E.

FOR EXTRA HELP

If you still are depressed after taking the nutrients above for seven to 10 days, also take either of the following supplements. If symptoms do not improve within two weeks, switch to the other supplement. If you still see no improvement, take both.

Important: Though many patients are successfully treated with a combination of these supplements and antidepressants, this requires close medical supervision. Theoretically, the combination could lead to the rare but potentially fatal *serotonin syndrome*, caused by excess serotonin. Symptoms include headache, increased body temperature, fast heart rate, blood pressure changes, hallucinations and/or kidney damage.

Once you find an effective regimen, continue for several months. Then reduce your dose by one-quarter for one week. If symptoms return, resume the former dose. Otherwise, continue reducing until you find an effective maintenance dose or can stop completely.

•**St. John's wort.** This herb raises serotonin and possibly the neurotransmitter *dopamine*, and may calm nerves. With breakfast, take 300 mg to 900 mg daily of a standardized extract of 0.3% *hypericin* (the active constituent).

Caution: Side effects may include digestive distress and a sun-sensitivity rash. St. John's wort may interact with some drugs, including *warfarin*, the heart drug *digoxin* (Digitalis) and birth control pills.

●**5-HTP (5-hydroxytryptophan) or L-tryptophan.** These are forms of the amino acid *tryptophan*, which converts to serotonin. With fruit juice, take either 50 mg to 100 mg of 5-HTP or 500 mg to 1,000 mg of L-tryptophan once or twice daily.

Caution: Occasional side effects include nausea and agitation.

TO REV UP...

If your symptoms include low energy and sleepiness, add either of the following to your regimen for as long as necessary. They may be taken with an antidepressant under close medical supervision.

●**Tyrosine.** This amino acid aids production of energizing adrenaline, dopamine and thyroid hormone. Take 500 mg to 1,000 mg before breakfast and in mid-afternoon.

Caution: Tyrosine may raise blood pressure —talk to your doctor. Do not use tyrosine if you have melanoma—it may worsen this concern.

●**SAMe (s-adenosylmethionine).** This compound boosts neurotransmitters and energy. Take on an empty stomach no less than 20 minutes before or after eating or taking any other supplement.

Dosage: Take 200 mg to 400 mg once or twice daily.

Caution: It may cause irritability and insomnia. Do not take SAMe if you have bipolar disorder—it could trigger a manic phase.

TO WIND DOWN...

If depression symptoms include anxiety and/ or insomnia, try...

●**Valerian.** This herb enhances activity of *gamma-aminobutyric acid* (GABA), a calming neurotransmitter. Take 150 mg to 300 mg one-half to one hour before bed. After one to two months, stop for a week. If insomnia returns, resume use. It is safe to take with an antidepressant.

Caution: Don't take valerian while using sedatives, such as muscle relaxants, antihistamines or alcohol.

Meditation for Women Who Hate to Sit Still

Judith Boice, ND, LAc, naturopathic physician and acupuncturist in private practice in Montrose, Colorado. She conducts wellness seminars nationwide and is author of eight books, including *Menopause with Science and Soul: A Guidebook for Navigating the Journey* (Celestial Arts). *www.drjudithboice.com.*

Meditation is good for us—it can relieve tension by shifting brain activity away from the stress-prone right frontal cortex and into the calmer left frontal cortex. But some people have trouble finding time to meditate—or just can't seem to sit still.

Solution: Combine exercise and meditation through rhythmic, repetitive motions, such as walking, swimming or rowing, so you simultaneously strengthen the body and soothe the mind.

Bonus: "Meditation in motion" makes exercise easier, because while you do it, you won't be thinking about tired muscles or tasks that await after your workout. *Begin with walking meditation...*

●**Pick a spot.** Find a secluded outdoor area where you won't feel self-conscious...or an empty hallway where you won't bump into furniture.

●**Begin walking.** Start slowly, focusing on the rhythm of your heels striking the ground and your toes pushing off. Keep your eyes open for safety, but don't get distracted by the sights around you.

●**Recite a mantra.** Choose or invent a rhythmic chant, such as "I am one with the world, I am filled with peace." Repeat it over and over, out loud or in your mind, melding its rhythm with the movement of your feet. I recommend not listening to music—it may distract you from your mantra.

●**Try to stay focused.** At first you may succeed for only a few minutes before thoughts of daily life intrude. Work your way up to a 30-minute session daily.

●**Meditate at the gym.** Once you've mastered walking meditation, try the technique while using a treadmill or elliptical machine or while swimming laps.

On-the-Spot Antidote to Stress

Ask yourself these four questions whenever you suspect you're taking on another person's stress.

1. Is this situation *important* to me?

2. Is my level of anxiety *appropriate*, given the facts?

3. Is the situation *modifiable*?

4. Considering the effort involved, is taking action *worth it*?

If your answer to any one of these is no, you are needlessly "catching" someone else's stress—and can justly put the problem out of your mind.

Bottom Line/Women's Health.

Ashwagandha—Ancient Remedy for Stress

Mark A. Stengler, NMD, naturopathic medical doctor in private practice, Encinitas, California...adjunct associate clinical professor at the National College of Natural Medicine, Portland, Oregon...author of *The Natural Physician's Healing Therapies* (Bottom Line Books).

In the ancient tradition of Ayurvedic medicine—as practiced in India for thousands of years—the herb ashwagandha (*Withania somnifera*) has been used to treat conditions such as fatigue, chronic disease, impotence and waning memory. Now, in the twenty-first-century United States, this well-respected herb has a new and even brighter reputation as a much-needed stress reliever.

Sometimes referred to as "Indian Ginseng," "Winter Cherry" or "Withania," ashwagandha herb has many similarities to Chinese ginseng. In Ayurvedic medicine, it may be used to treat a number of other diseases besides those already mentioned—including asthma, bronchitis, psoriasis, arthritis and infertility. Ayurvedic doctors prescribe it in very specific ways that are suited to certain constitutional types. It's often given with the so-called "warming herbs," such as ginger, to increase its tonic effect.

Ashwagandha root differs from Chinese ginseng in having a mild sedative action. This makes it well suited for the Type A person—that is, someone who's always "on the go" at such a high rate that he or she may be headed for burnout.

MULTITONIC

Research shows that this herb is an excellent adaptogen that helps the body cope with physical and mental stress. Studies show that ashwagandha can help people who have exhaustion from chronic stress, weakened immunity (for instance, if they have cancer) and as a tonic for chronic diseases, especially inflammatory disorders.

This herb also has overall benefits for many body systems. Ashwagandha is unique in acting as a tonic to the nervous system, but also has sedative and antiepileptic effects. It mobilizes different components of the immune system to fight invading microbes and has a modulating or balancing effect if you have inflammation.

A number of animal and laboratory studies have shown this herb has antitumor activity. Ashwagandha has also been shown to have antioxidant activity, so it's helpful in protecting brain cells (which could explain why it helps to prevent memory loss). It also stimulates red blood cell production. Ashwagandha is also said to be a rich source of iron, so it's a potential choice for the treatment of iron-deficiency anemia.

Animal studies have shown that it increases thyroid hormone levels.

Over 35 chemical constituents have been identified, extracted and isolated in this plant. These include some groups of chemicals such as alkaloids, steroidal lactones, saponins and withanolides.

Ashwagandha has been used in only a few human studies—far outweighed by the number of animal or test-tube studies that have been done. However, it has remained popular and highly valued through thousands of years of use in Ayurvedic medicine. This is a classic case of an herb that has often been used for successful treatments yet never "proven" by modern scientific research. In my opinion, ashwagandha should be used when indicated. I am sure there will be continued scientific research that will eventually shed light on the reasons why this wonderful plant has proven so helpful to so many people.

Dosage: The standard adult dosage is 1,000 to 3,000 milligrams (mg) daily of the root.

What are the side effects?: No side effects or toxicity have been reported with ashwagandha.

Recommendations for...

•**Aging.** For one full year, 3,000 mg of purified ashwagandha powder or placebo was given to 101 normal healthy male volunteers, all between the ages of 50 and 59. The herb had some physical effects that slowed the effects of aging for all the men in the study. All men showed significantly increased hemoglobin and red blood cell count. Improvements in nail calcium and cholesterol were also noted. In addition, nearly 72 percent of the men reported improvement in sexual performance.

•**Anemia and slow growth.** Ashwagandha has been shown in two human studies and several animal studies to increase hemoglobin, red blood cell count and serum iron levels. In a scientific trial that continued for 60 days, 58 healthy children between the ages of 8 and 12 were given milk that was treated with fortified ashwagandha (2,000 mg a day). The herb improved the health factors that contribute to growth—leading to a significant increase in hemoglobin and albumin. Researchers concluded that ashwagandha can be a growth promoter in children—and they also noted that these children were less likely to have anemia.

•**Arthritis.** Ashwagandha is used in Ayurvedic herbal formulas for the treatment of arthritis and conditions involving inflammation. In a double-blind, placebo-controlled study, 42 people with osteoarthritis were given a formula containing ashwagandha (along with the herbs boswellia, turmeric and zinc) for three months. Their health was compared with a control group that received a placebo.

The herbal formula significantly reduced the severity of pain and the degree of disability. There were no significant changes in the control of inflammation, however. For this rea-son, ashwagandha is mainly used in formulas where inflammation-controlling substances are also part of the mix.

•**Fatigue.** Ashwagandha has been historically used for the treatment of chronic fatigue, especially a patient who shows signs of nervous exhaustion.

•**Memory problems.** Some holistic practitioners recommend ashwagandha for its benefit to the brain. It helps improve the ability to reason and solve problems as well as improve memory. Practitioners of Ayurvedic medicine, who are familiar with these outcomes, often recommend it for patients who are starting to experience memory loss. Studies on rats have shown that it improves cognitive function.

•**Stress.** Ashwagandha appears to help the body cope with the effects of stress more effectively. I am sure that ashwagandha will become as popular as the ginsengs in helping to deal with this all-too-common problem.

Deep Breathing Techniques to Reduce Stress

Start with a big sigh of relief to relax the diaphragm. Then do circle breathing. Close your eyes and inhale through the nose, imagining a warm stream of peaceful energy flowing into a spot a few inches below your navel. Continue inhaling, picturing the stream moving to the base of your spine...up your back...and into your head. Then exhale through the nose, envisioning your breath traveling back down the front of your body to the starting point below your navel. Repeat 10 times, continuing to visualize your breath making this circle.

Joan Borysenko, PhD, psychologist and director of Mind-Body Health Sciences, LLC, in Boulder, Colorado. She is the former director of the mind-body programs at two Harvard teaching hospitals and author of many books, including *Minding the Body, Mending the Mind* (Bantam). *www.joanborysenko.com.*

Surprising Stress Relievers

Tamara Eberlein, editor, *HealthyWoman from Bottom Line* E-letter. Boardroom Inc., 281 Tresser Blvd., Stamford, Connecticut 06901.

Deep breathing does work, I know—but there are other effective ways to de-stress. *Unique techniques from experts…*

• **Create a personal stress-relief kit that holds five favorite objects, one for each of the senses**—for example, a smooth stone to touch, a sachet to smell, flavorful gum to taste, a beloved photo to look at, a mantra to read aloud. When stress overwhelms, focus on one or more of these objects to help you feel centered, suggests psychotherapist Leila Keen, LCSW, of Durham, North Carolina.

• **Stretch your arms upward and shout "north!"**…lower arms, bend down and yell "south!"…stand and sweep arms to the right ("east!")…swing to the left ("west!"). This "Four Directions" exercise is from executive coach Millie Grenough of New Haven, Connecticut, author of *Oasis in the Overwhelm* (Beaver Hill). It sounds kooky—but I tried it, and it worked.

Suggestions from my colleagues…

• **Keep a bottle of bubbles handy**—blowing bubbles blows off steam (and helps you breathe deeply, too).

• **Bake something that calls for repetitive movements to promote a meditative state of mind**—kneading dough, slicing apples to make pie.

• **Color with crayons, recalling carefree childhood days.**

• **Sing loudly when stuck in traffic.**

• **Laugh.** Even if you fake it at first, you'll feel calmer…and you may end up giggling for real.

• **Reread the final chapter of a favorite novel** in which good triumphs and everything works out.

Fall Asleep Faster… Without Drugs

John Hibbs, ND, senior clinical faculty member at Bastyr University in Kenmore, Washington, and family practitioner at Bastyr Center for Natural Health, in Seattle.

If you often toss and turn for 30 to 60 minutes or more before finally falling asleep, you may be tempted to use prescription sleeping pills.

Problem: These make it even harder to reconnect with your normal sleep cycle, robbing you of the most restorative type of sleep.

Better: Try natural strategies that support normal sleep patterns…

• **Go to bed earlier.** This may seem counterintuitive, as if you would only lie awake even longer than you already do. But for many people, the body's biochemically preprogrammed bedtime falls between 9:00 pm and 10:00 pm. If you stay up until midnight, your body may secrete stress hormones to cope with the demands of being awake when it wants to be asleep—and this interferes with your body clock.

Best: Move up your bedtime by an hour… give yourself several weeks to adjust…then advance your bedtime again until you're regularly hitting the hay before 10:00 pm.

• **Exercise at the right time.** Don't try to exhaust yourself with strenuous workouts, especially in the evening—this raises adrenaline levels and makes sleep more elusive.

Instead: Exercise for at least 30 minutes every *morning*. This reduces the stress hormone *cortisol*, helping to reset your biochemical clock.

• **Get wet.** Hydrotherapy—especially close to bedtime—calms the nervous system by acting on sensory receptors in the skin. Typically it is most effective to take a half-hour bath in water that's the same temperature as the skin. However, some people respond better to a hot bath…others feel more relaxed after a "contrast shower," first using hot water, then cold.

• **Adopt a pro-sleep diet.** Eliminate all stimulant foods (caffeine, sweets, *monosodium* *glutamate*) from your diet. Magnesium calms the nervous system, so eat more magnesium-rich foods (black beans, pumpkin seeds, salmon, spinach)…and/or take 200 milligrams (mg) to 300 mg of supplemental magnesium twice daily. Do not skip meals—when hungry, the body secretes stress hormones that can interfere with sleep. Avoid eating too close to bedtime —a full stomach distracts the body from normal sleep physiology.

●**Try nutraceuticals.** Certain supplements help balance brain chemicals.

Recommended: At bedtime, take 500 mg to 1,000 mg of *gamma-aminobutyric acid* (GABA), a calming brain chemical. Another option is to take a bedtime dose of 50 mg to 100 mg of *5-hydroxytryptophan* (5-HTP), a natural compound that relaxes by balancing levels of the brain chemical *serotonin*. GABA and 5-HTP can be used separately or together for as long as needed. Both are sold in health-food stores and rarely have side effects at these doses.

Feng Shui in the Bedroom

The practice of arranging objects to achieve harmony with your environment, feng shui balances energy and helps you relax. Place the head of your bed against a wall for stability —but leave space on both sides so that energy can circle freely. To feel secure, position the bed so that you can see the bedroom door and window, but not directly across from either.

Ellen Whitehurst, feng shui consultant, Virginia Beach, Virginia, and author of *Make This Your Lucky Day* (Ballantine).

To Live Longer, Volunteer

Seniors were asked if they had spent any time in the past 12 months doing volunteer work for religious, educational or other charitable organizations. Even after researchers

adjusted for factors such as chronic health conditions, physical limitations and socioeconomic status—as earlier studies had not— volunteers were *less than half as likely to die* during the four-year study as nonvolunteers.

Theory: Volunteering encourages social networking, physical and mental activity, and self-esteem—all of which contribute to good health.

Sei J. Lee, MD, assistant professor of geriatrics, University of California, San Francisco, and leader of a study of 6,360 people over age 65.

How I Calm Down

Joy Browne, PhD, clinical psychologist in New York City. Her internationally syndicated call-in radio show, *The Dr. Joy Browne Show*, is the longest-running of its kind (*www.drjoy.com*). She is the author of many books, including *Getting Unstuck: 8 Simple Steps to Solving Any Problem* (Hay House).

In prehistoric times, if you failed to feel enough anxiety to trigger a fight-or-flight response, you got eaten by a saber-toothed tiger. Even today, the body's instant reaction to danger includes a surge of the stress hormone *adrenaline*—causing rapid breathing, pounding heart, tingling hands and nausea. This floods large muscles with energy-giving oxygen by increasing breathing and heart rate and by diverting blood from the extremities and digestive tract.

Problem is, this also occurs in situations that aren't physically dangerous—such as being caught in traffic on your way to an appointment. It's tough to focus on the task at hand during an anxiety attack. Worse, repeated adrenaline surges and other anxiety responses can contribute to hypertension, digestive disorders, weakened immunity and depression.

To ease anxiety: A technique called *square breathing* helps me regain control over my body and mind by reestablishing the proper ratio of oxygen to carbon dioxide in my system. I inhale deeply for a count of four…hold for four…exhale slowly for four…hold for four…and repeat until anxiety subsides. It's like giving my body a mini-vacation. You can use it any time—when preparing to make a toast, waiting for test results—because it is inconspicuous.

Seven Easy Steps to Guided Imagery

Michael Samuels, MD, an instructor at San Francisco State Institute of Holistic Medicine. He has a private practice specializing in guided imagery in Bolinas, California, and is the author of 20 alternative healing books, including *Shaman Wisdom* (Wiley).

For best results, practice this guided-imagery program for 15 to 30 minutes twice a day.

1. Find a comfortable place where you will not be disturbed. Sit or lie down with legs uncrossed, arms at your sides or resting on your abdomen. Close your eyes. Inhale slowly and deeply. Let your stomach rise on the inhale and fall on the exhale.

2. Shift your consciousness to your feet and allow them to relax. Concentrate on feelings of tingling, warmth and lightness. Next, relax your ankles. Let the feeling continue to the back of your legs and thighs. Let your mind float free. Feel the air moving through your nostrils, and concentrate on the body part you are relaxing.

3. Relax your pelvic area, abdomen and chest.

4. Relax your shoulders. Spread the feeling to your upper arms, lower arms and hands.

5. Let your neck relax. Loosen the big muscles that support the head. Now focus on your head. Relax your scalp, drop your jaw. Soften the muscles around your eyes and forehead.

6. Picture a place you love, such as the ocean or the mountains. Hear, smell and feel this place—the waves crashing, the smell of the fresh air, the mist touching your face. If you have an illness, such as cancer, picture white blood cells eating cancer cells.

7. Stay in this state for the remainder of your session. When you're finished, gently move your feet and count one...two...three.

The Amazing Power of Affirmations

Louise L. Hay, one of the founders of the self-help movement. She is author of numerous books, including *You Can Heal Your Life* (Hay House), which has sold more than 35 million copies. *www.louisehay.com*. She is founder and head of Hay House, Inc., a self-help publishing company, Carlsbad, California, whose best-selling authors include Wayne Dyer and Joan Borysenko.

Affirmations are statements that reflect our views of who we are and what we want. They can be positive or negative. They influence our feelings and thoughts—and what actually happens in our lives.

Example: I grew up in an abusive family. As a child, I believed that it was natural for men to beat women. As I went though life, I always attracted men who abused me. It wasn't until I learned about self-esteem and self-worth that I let go of that pattern of thinking. As a result, I started to attract men who valued and respected me.

Positive affirmations don't miraculously create a new reality—but they do open the mental channels that can allow good things to happen. People who are happy and self-confident welcome good things into their lives. They attract positive people. They create their own opportunities. *Here's how...*

•**Turn a negative into a positive.** Statements such as, "I don't want to be fat," "I don't like this relationship" or "I don't want to be unhappy" are actually negative affirmations. Dwelling on things that we don't want merely creates more mental space for those things to thrive.

When delivered as positive affirmations, the statements above become "I am slender," "I have a wonderful new relationship" and "I am happy."

•**Train yourself.** Most of us have trained ourselves to be self-critical. We can just as easily train ourselves to be accepting.

Exercise: For the next month, say a few hundred times a day, "I approve of myself." Repeat it out loud or to yourself when you're in the shower, walking to the mailbox, etc.

At first, you'll probably notice that repeating this mantra brings up opposite feelings. You'll find yourself thinking, *I don't believe it* or *Saying this makes me feel silly.*

These are resistance thoughts. Let them pass through your mind. They have no power unless you choose to believe them. Counter them with the original mantra, *I approve of myself.* Your thinking will start to change.

• **Look in the mirror every morning and say, "I really love you."** Do this—and use your name. The universe loves gratitude and appreciation. Appreciating yourself means appreciating the universe.

Imagine that you give someone a gift. If that person is grateful and appreciative, you want to give him/her more presents. But if he is negative about it and says something like, "I don't like the color," you won't want to be so generous again.

When you love yourself, you're thanking the universe for the wonderful gift that is you— and more gifts will come your way.

• **Say "thank you."** I say "thank you" to the universe at least a dozen times a day—when I see the beauty of a tree, a breathtaking sunset, etc. The more grateful you are for the good things in your life, the more life gives you to appreciate.

If you want a joyous life, you must think joyous thoughts.

Example: Some people notice that it's raining and say, "What a lousy day." It's not a lousy day. It's merely a wet day. There are lots of good things to do on rainy days. Why greet it with despair?

• **Eliminate "should" thinking.** Many people force themselves to do things that they dislike, because someone (often a parent) said they should do them—go to a certain school, become a lawyer, marry a particular person, etc.

Better: Replace "should" with "could." The word "could" means that you have choices… that you can follow your own judgment and listen to your instincts.

Exercise: Write the phrase "I should" at the top of a piece of paper, followed by five or six ways to finish the sentence.

Examples: "I should be thin"…"I should be smarter"…"I should have more money now."

You'll probably find that most of the items reflect your own fears and imagined limitations.

Now, instead of writing "I should," substitute it with, "If I really wanted to, I could…"

Examples: "If I really wanted to, I could be thin"…"If I really wanted to, I could be smarter"…"If I really wanted to, I could have more money now."

• **Tell yourself it's easy.** Several times a day, tell yourself how easy it is to do something. "It's easy to have good friends"…"It's easy to find a job I love"…"It's easy to bring good into my life."

This type of affirmation is one of the simplest —and most powerful. We tend to think that things are much more difficult than they really are. The fear of difficulty is really the fear of trying, which keeps us from moving forward.

• **Learn from failure.** The fear of failure can be paralyzing. How many times have you been too afraid to try something new?

We encourage children when they're learning to walk. Every tiny step is a success! Yet we're not so kind to ourselves. We tell ourselves that we're clumsy or stupid…that our initial, halting steps are a failure.

Not true. Every experience that we have is a learning experience. We get better with practice…discover new strengths…and find opportunities.

Exercise: Several times a day, use "success affirmations." Say things such as, "Everything I touch is a success"…"I am blessed beyond my fondest dreams"…and "Golden opportunities are everywhere for me."

Much of life is a rehearsal, a time to make mistakes, try new approaches and learn how to make things better. Everything brings us closer to success.

• **Forgive others and yourself.** We give away our power when we harbor anger toward people and events from the past. Maybe you had an unhappy childhood…an abusive spouse… a job that didn't work out. Let it all go.

Dwelling on old hurts never makes people happy. Worse, it hampers the ability to enjoy the future because you stop believing that you —and only you—can make things better.

Forgiving doesn't mean forgetting or condoning bad behavior. The goal is to free yourself from negativity.

Exercise: Sit with your eyes closed and say, "The person I need to forgive is so-and-so, and I forgive him/her." Repeat it over and over for five to 10 minutes. Then turn your attention inward and take a minute or two to forgive yourself for things you've done.

Repeat this exercise at least once a week. Do it for every injustice or hurt that you still feel. You'll come to realize that the past doesn't control your present...and that you have the inner strength to make yourself happy.

Foods and Supplements That Boost Mood

James S. Gordon, MD, founder and director of the Center for Mind–Body Medicine in Washington, DC. He is a clinical professor in the departments of psychiatry and family medicine at Georgetown University School of Medicine and former chair of the White House Commission on Complementary and Alternative Medicine Policy. He is author of *Unstuck: Your Guide to the Seven-Stage Journey Out of Depression* (Penguin). *www.james gordonmd.com.*

What we eat can affect our mood, making us feel happier. A number of people who suffer from depression, for example, improve significantly when they eat less (or eliminate) processed/sugary foods and consume more complex carbohydrates, such as grains and vegetables. A healthy diet may reduce brain inflammation, important for improving neuron (brain cell) functions and reducing anxiety and depression.

Noted physician James S. Gordon, MD, talks about what other dietary changes can improve mood...

OMEGA-3 FATTY ACIDS

Population studies clearly show that people with a high intake of omega-3 fatty acids have a lower incidence of depression. The membranes that surround brain cells contain significant amounts of fatty acids. When more of these fats consist of omega-3s, the membranes become more flexible and porous—important for absorbing nutrients and receiving/transmitting chemical signals, important in boosting mood.

Recommended: Eat two or three fish meals a week. Cold-water fish, such as sardines, mackerel and herring, are the best food sources of omega-3s. If you don't like fish, try a supplement of 3,000 milligrams (mg) of omega-3 fatty acids, divided into two daily doses. Choose a supplement that provides 180 mg EPA and 120 mg DHA per 1,000-mg capsule.

DIETARY FIBER

Constipation is a common symptom—and possibly a cause—of the blues. People who don't eat enough fiber have smaller, less frequent bowel movements. This means that toxins that are present in the stools can get reabsorbed into the body. This can trigger depression and other mood changes.

Recommended: At least 30 grams (g) of fiber daily—more is probably better. People who mainly eat plant foods automatically get enough fiber. If your diet is short on fiber, add four to five tablespoons of unprocessed oat bran to your morning cereal or smoothie.

Red flag: Having three or fewer bowel movements a week. This is not normal. You should be having one or more bowel movements a day. If you're not, you probably need to consume more fiber (and water, too).

MULTISUPPLEMENT

Everyone who is feeling down should take a daily multisupplement. The majority of Americans are deficient in one or more of the essential micronutrients, including selenium, magnesium and B vitamins.

Why it matters: A deficiency of even one nutrient can impair the body's ability to utilize other nutrients.

Nutritional deficiencies are a common cause of low energy as well as depressed mood.

One study found that people who consumed less than the recommended daily amount of selenium had significant mood improvements when they took supplements.

Magnesium is particularly important for mood because it's used for the production of *serotonin*, the neurotransmitter that increases when people take prescription antidepressants.

Recommended: Start with a daily supplement that provides all of the key vitamins and minerals. You also might want to take a separate B-complex supplement because B vitamins are vital to the metabolism of cells—in particular, the cells of the nervous system.

SAMe

S-adenosylmethionine (SAMe) releases a methyl molecule in the body that is necessary for the production of *dopamine* and serotonin. A review of scientific studies found that SAMe relieves symptoms of depression significantly better than a placebo—and sometimes as well as prescription drugs. SAMe is far less likely than medications to cause significant side effects.

Recommended: I usually advise patients with depression to start with dietary changes, stress-reduction techniques, exercise and sometimes talk therapy. If these aren't effective, it's helpful to take SAMe for several weeks or months—or, in those with chronic depression, sometimes indefinitely.

The starting dose usually is 200 mg at morning and noontime. The amount can be slightly increased after several weeks if the initial dose isn't effective. If you feel agitated, you'll want to decrease the dose.

TRYPTOPHAN/5-HTP

If other approaches don't work, I may recommend *tryptophan*, an amino acid. Both tryptophan and the more easily available *5-HTP* (into which tryptophan is converted) increase the body's production of serotonin. Tryptophan was largely banned in the early 1990s following contamination at a manufacturing plant. The supplement itself is entirely safe.

Both tryptophan and 5-HTP make it easier to fall asleep—important because insomnia and/or disturbed sleep are common in those with depression.

Recommended: Take 500 mg of tryptophan at bedtime. If tryptophan is not available, take 50 mg to 100 mg of 5-HTP twice daily.

PROBIOTICS

Healthy adults have trillions of beneficial intestinal bacteria known as *probiotics*. These organisms facilitate the production of energy within cells, promote the synthesis of B vitamins and other nutrients, and improve digestive health. Many people with depression have lower-than-expected levels of probiotic organisms.

Recommended: One to two capsules daily of a supplement that provides two to three billion organisms. Look for a combination supplement that includes *acidophilus* and *bifidophilus* organisms.

FOOD SENSITIVITIES CAN CAUSE DEPRESSION

An important factor in some people's depression is a sensitivity to one or more foods. I believe that food sensitivity is far more pervasive and far more often a cause of, or contributor to, depression than we know.

Food sensitivity can be caused by the passage of large, reaction-stimulating protein molecules out of an intestine that has been made "leaky." Infections and antibiotics and other drugs may be responsible for these leaky guts, but there may be dietary causes as well, including consumption of refined and processed foods. As large protein molecules pass across the gut into the bloodstream, they are believed to provoke defensive reactions in nearly every system in the body.

This immune reaction can cause depression and may produce a variety of physical symptoms as well, including fatigue.

Many people are sensitive to gluten, a protein found in wheat and some other grains. Other problem foods may include milk, eggs, citrus and soy.

If you suspect that your depression might be linked to diet, you can try an elimination diet…

• **Completely eliminate possible food culprits from your diet.** Begin by saying no to gluten, milk and other dairy products, eggs, soy and sugar. Keep a diary. Every day, note any symptoms…how you're feeling…and whether your energy has increased or decreased.

• **After three weeks, reintroduce the foods one at a time.** For example, eat a slice or two of wheat bread at dinner. See how you feel the next day. If your mood doesn't change, then you probably aren't sensitive to that food. Wait a week, and reintroduce another food.

As Literacy Improves, So Might Happiness

University of Alabama at Birmingham, news release.

Among older adults, the better they're able to read, understand and use health and medical information, the happier they are, suggests a U.S. study.

THE STUDY

Researchers asked 383 people age 50 and older if they could read and answer questions on medical forms without assistance. They also asked them to rate their level of happiness.

Participants who had the most difficulty reading and understanding medical forms were more than twice as likely to report being unhappy as those with higher literacy levels, the study found.

The study was published online in the journal *Social Indicators Research*.

POSSIBLE EXPLANATION

This finding might have to do with a sense of control, explained lead author Erik Angner, PhD, an assistant professor of philosophy and economics at the University of Alabama at Birmingham. Feeling in control—which could be undermined by poor health literacy—has been linked to higher happiness scores.

The researchers suggested that improving health literacy should be a critical part of programs designed to boost health among older adults.

About 90 million Americans have problems understanding and using health information, according to a report from the Institute of Medicine.

How to Express Anger Without Hurting Feelings

Alice Ginott, PhD, a New York City–based clinical psychologist who has conducted workshops with parents and teachers and lectured widely on parent-child relationships. She recently re-released *Between Parent and Child* (Three Rivers), which was written by her husband, Haim G. Ginott, PhD, and first published in 1965.

The best-selling classic *Between Parent and Child* by Haim G. Ginott, PhD, revolutionized the way we relate to children. Earlier child-rearing books had emphasized the primacy of parental authority with little regard for children's feelings. *Between Parent and Child*, which was recently updated by Dr. Alice Ginott and Dr. H. Wallace Goddard, helps people enter into the world of another person in a caring and compassionate way.

Here, Dr. Alice Ginott explains how the principles expressed in the book help all of us, not just parents, acquire a language that is protective of feelings…

NICE TO STRANGERS

Most of us use language that is not critical of behavior with guests and strangers. Do we criticize a guest when he/she breaks an expensive vase? Do we ever say, "What is the matter with you! You're so clumsy! You break everything you touch! Will you ever learn to be more careful?" Of course not. Instead, we say, "Don't worry. It's nothing. I didn't like that vase anyway. Let me help you pick up the pieces."

When we confront people we know well, including family members and coworkers, our first response often is criticism. We are unaware of the emotional hurt we inflict. We need to learn how to criticize without hurting, how to express anger without demeaning and how to praise without judging.

ANGER

We can defuse almost any situation by using the pronoun "I" and talking about what upsets us instead of using the pronoun "you" and telling the other person what is wrong with him/her. Here's how a wife effectively expressed her anger when her repeated calls to her husband were ignored, "I get angry when I call you to dinner and you don't come. I get so angry that I fume inside. I need appreciation, not aggravation." She talked about how she felt instead of criticizing her husband. She didn't call him names. She didn't tell him what was wrong with him. She didn't say, "What is the matter with you? Can't you do anything right?"

Minor squabbles can easily escalate into full-blown fights when people get angry and say the first thing that comes to mind. Insults are met with insults, and the battle is on. Instead, we need to talk about the problem, not the person's shortcomings.

Let's say that an employee hands in an unacceptable report. Using the pronoun "I," the employer could say, "I was upset when I read your report. I was disappointed that it wasn't more detailed, useful and creative." By talking about how the report made him feel, rather than telling the employee how incompetent he was, the employer did not enrage the employee and made a nondefensive discussion possible.

Another example: Sometimes doctors don't honor patients' appointment times. How can a patient effectively express his displeasure? By telling the doctor how it makes him feel to be kept waiting. He could say, "I want to share with you how I'm feeling. I'm angry. I was asked to come at 1:00, and now I have been waiting for more than an hour. I feel that I deserve greater consideration. It would have been easier for me to come at 3:00."

PRAISE AND CRITICISM

When we praise, we should try to say something that will enhance the person's self-image. We need to talk about the accomplishment, not how we feel. For this, we use the pronoun "you."

When your wife comes home from work all excited because she was promoted to vice president, it is helpful to say, "You must be so proud. You have put in such long hours and worked so hard, and this promotion reflects that effort. Isn't that wonderful?"

When it comes to criticism, most of us are so concerned with behavior and accomplishment that we don't pay attention to feelings. It's difficult for any of us to accept advice or con-

structive criticism when we are angry or upset. We need someone to empathize, understand our distress and help us feel better before we can be open to criticism.

Another example: George stormed into his boss's office after a meeting with an important client, "You'll have to get someone else to handle Mr. Smith. He insulted me in a room full of people. He told me I was stupid and incompetent and that I didn't know my business." Aware that he had to take care of George's upset feelings before he could deal with the problem, George's boss answered him sympathetically, "How humiliating to be called names in front of all those people. No wonder you're upset and angry. What do you think we can do to salvage the situation?"

Developing communication skills can help us create a pleasant atmosphere that is conducive to solving problems without causing anger or hurt feelings.

You Can Get Ahead at Work Despite a Chronic Illness

Rosalind Joffe, nationally recognized expert on chronic illness in the workplace and founder of the executive career-coaching firm cicoach.com. She writes a free E-mail newsletter called *Words of Wisdom: The Chronic Illness at Work* and two blogs. She is coauthor of *Women, Work and Autoimmune Disease: Keep Working, Girlfriend!* (Demos Medical). *www.cicoach.com*.

About 40% of working Americans have a *chronic illness*. That means they have a health problem that has lasted longer than a year, requires medical care and limits what they can do. It might be an autoimmune disease, such as rheumatoid arthritis, multiple sclerosis or inflammatory bowel disease…chronic pain, including osteoarthritis or migraines…or a life-threatening illness, such as heart disease, cancer or diabetes.

If you suffer from the pain, fatigue and/or unpredictable symptoms of a chronic illness—and the mental and emotional difficulties that often go with them—you also may find that your work is suffering. Maybe you feel you've missed too many deadlines or that you're "unreliable" and letting your coworkers down. Perhaps you've even decided that career advancement and success aren't possible for you. But chronic illness doesn't have to stop you from getting ahead in the workplace.

Shrewd ways to help you overcome the career obstacles of chronic illness and thrive in the workplace...

WORK HELPS

Why work if you're ill? If you're eligible for disability benefits, wouldn't not working be better? Not necessarily. Work structures your day and gives you a destination. You're focused on goals instead of thinking about your ailing body. Being productive also can improve your self-esteem and mood. You can feel like a competent, "normal" human being—even in the face of extreme physical "abnormality." Studies show that people with chronic illnesses who keep working (in a safe and accommodating environment) experience better long-term health.

HOW TO TALK ABOUT YOUR ILLNESS

If your symptoms do not affect how you do your job, you don't need to discuss your illness with your boss or coworkers. However, talking about your illness with them can have many advantages. When others know about your illness, you're more likely to feel comfortable asking for what you need to get your job done—whether it's more flexible hours or a less demanding schedule of business travel—and getting it. Talking about your illness also sends the message that you're a forthright employee and creates an atmosphere of trust.

What to do: The rule of thumb is KISS—*Keep It Short and Simple*. This will minimize overreactions and misunderstandings, and maximize the comfort levels of your supervisor and coworkers. *To do this...*

• **Stay calm, matter-of-fact and unemotional** when you tell your colleagues about your illness.

Example: "I have been diagnosed with Crohn's disease, but I am confident that I can continue to do my job."

• **Deliver a clear message**—don't use complex medical jargon. Describe the illness in concrete ways that others can understand.

Example: "It's a gastrointestinal disease. Although I'm getting good medical care, it is unlikely to go away completely. One day I might seem fine, but the next day I could feel awful."

• **Emphasize your talents and strengths**—what you can do, not what you can't.

Example: "I am able to think strategically, and manage and motivate the people who work for me, as well as make critical decisions for the department."

• **Talk face-to-face,** rather than via E-mail or a phone call. This will help keep the dialog positive and upbeat and produce the results that you want—understanding, collegiality and support.

• **Ask for the two or three things** that you need most to help you get your job done effectively. *They are likely to be...*

• Backup. If you work on a team, make sure somebody else knows how to do what you do. It's hard to be successful if there are days when you can't do your job and there's no one else to do it. Express appreciation for your teammates' help, and do what you can to help them in return.

• Flexible schedule. You may want to try negotiating a flexible schedule that allows you to come in later on some days than others, go to frequent doctor appointments or even work from home on occasion.

• Options. Are there meetings that you could get briefed on rather than attend? Can you teleconference rather than travel?

POSITIVE ATTITUDE

To succeed at work with the challenge of a chronic illness, it helps to maintain a positive outlook. *To help you do that...*

• **Focus on what you can control.** You may not be able to control the course of your illness, but you can control the direction you take and the choices you make regarding the illness in the workplace. View your chronic illness as a challenge to meet, not an obstacle.

Example: An executive assistant who relied on her flawless recall began to develop memory problems due to her chronic illness. Instead of bemoaning the loss, she came up with ways to compensate for it. No longer able to keep names, dates and information in her head, she used the software in her computer to back herself up. She also put sticky notes everywhere to remind her to double-check her work.

•**Look for the silver lining.** Although you may not believe it at first, workplace success in the face of illness can be transforming. Many people with chronic illness find new strength and confidence.

My story: I was diagnosed with multiple sclerosis almost 30 years ago. Then, 15 years after that diagnosis, I was hospitalized with a second autoimmune disease, ulcerative colitis. Getting my health under control was a major challenge, and there were few resources to guide me.

Eventually, I reached the point where I could thrive in my work. That gave me the confidence to start my own business as a coach helping others cope with chronic illness in the workplace. I also just finished writing a book for women on this topic. I'm convinced that meeting my health challenges gave me the strength to meet these other challenges.

•**Read about how others have coped.** It is instructive and inspiring to read about how to handle change and challenges. *Some of the best books are...*

•*Blindsided: Lifting a Life Above Illness...A Reluctant Memoir* by Richard Cohen (Harper Collins), about a television news producer's struggle with multiple sclerosis.

•*Transitions: Making Sense of Life's Changes* by William Bridges (Persus).

•*I'd Rather Be Working: A Step-by-Step Guide to Financial Self-Support for People with Chronic Illness* by Gayle Backstrom (Amacom).

•*The Chronic Illness Workbook: Strategies and Solutions for Taking Back Your Life* by Patricia A. Fennell (New Harbinger).

Capture Emotional Strength During a Prolonged or Severe Health Crisis

Brenda Shoshanna, PhD, a clinical psychologist in private practice in New York City. She conducts workshops on dealing with illness, loss, life transitions and relationships. She is the "Relationship Saver" on iVillage (*www.ivillage.com*), and author of several books, including *Journey Through Illness and Beyond* (*www.journeythroughillness.com*).

Illness is as much a part of life as health—and brings with it opportunities for personal growth.

It is difficult to remember this in the midst of a crisis, but you do have a say. Instead of giving in to feelings of hopelessness and withdrawing from life, it is possible to actually improve the quality of your life—by repairing fractured relationships, making positive changes and embracing the love of family and friends. *Important steps...*

PUT GUILT ASIDE

Everyone has regrets, which are often magnified during a prolonged or end-of-life illness. Patients may feel guilty because they don't want to be a burden and because they want to maintain self-respect. Some feel that they can no longer contribute to others.

Family members, on the other hand, may experience guilt simply because they're healthy and their loved ones are not. It's difficult to go forward in life while a person they love is no longer able to.

Guilt is a toxic emotion that damages relationships. It can make a patient's final days (or years) less fulfilling than they could be.

Advice for the patient: Every family has regrets from the past. Take this time to ask for apologies and to offer them...tell your loved ones what they've meant to you...and thank them for all they've done and given.

Advice for family members: Don't stop living. By going forward in your life and maintaining a positive attitude, you can uplift your family members and bring more energy and hope to your ill loved one. Those who give up on their lives, who make themselves martyrs, exude a sense of despair, which has a bad effect on everybody.

MAINTAIN YOUR POWER

The fear that accompanies illness can make us feel timid and childlike. When that happens, it's natural to look for an authority figure—usually a doctor—to make decisions for us.

No matter who your doctor is, you're the one in control. You might not be able to change the course of your illness, but you can take charge of the way you respond to it, the decisions you make and the actions you take. It is important to make your own decisions during the course of the illness. If you cannot do this, have a family member ask for details about a treatment and possible alternatives. Those who engage actively with their illness and maintain a sense of control feel less like victims.

Many people live for years with a serious illness. The ways in which you approach the illness, your emotions, beliefs, actions and sense of self-esteem all affect the quality of your days and often the outcome.

REDUCE STRESS

Try meditation and/or visualization. Both techniques help reduce pain as well as stress and depression. *They can also improve the quality of your life—and you can do them on your own, and in all circumstances...*

•**Visualization.** Patients imagine, in as much detail as possible, a scenario in which they're happy and at peace: Sitting by a lake in the woods...walking in a meadow...a moment with special friends, etc.

Other forms of visualization involve picturing the illness dissolving and other parts of the person growing stronger.

•**Meditation.** There are many forms of meditation, all of which develop balance and focus. Concentration on the breath, or on a phrase that is meaningful, or repetition of a prayer, calms the system and quiets turbulent feelings and thoughts.

LISTEN TO YOUR ILLNESS

Research has shown that negative emotions, such as depression and anxiety, can manifest themselves as physical symptoms or even disease. It's common, for example, for a spouse

who has lost a long-term partner to die shortly afterward.

It can be very helpful to look a little more deeply into your life and see what stress might be creating or fueling your illness. Sometimes when we are depressed or feel hopeless, our immune systems are weakened and do not fight disease as well as they might. When some individuals make personal changes in their lives, they notice that the pain and symptoms they experience can decrease or dissolve completely. Illness can be used as an opportunity for emotional healing, and emotional healing can impact illness.

EMBRACE THE CHANGE

Although no one wants to be sick, the more we resist and deny what's happening, the less energy we have available to heal. The more we engage in catastrophic thinking, the worse we feel.

Better: Stay in the present. Rather than dwell on what could or will happen, experience each day as it is.

Helpful: Focus on what is good and enjoyable. Reflect on your life—those things that give you pleasure, what is meaningful, what you would like to do next. Be especially aware of all of the love that you've given and received.

When you are able to, it is beneficial to resume as much of your usual activities as possible. If possible, stay in touch with friends, invite them to visit, and plan outings and trips that are enjoyable and meaningful.

People who view illness as a spiritually transforming experience have more peace of mind and less fear and anger. They often grow to realize that all of life is impermanent and that, ultimately, they're part of that which is greater than themselves. This promotes serenity.

FOR FAMILY MEMBERS

Family members are often afraid to talk honestly with patients. They tend to pretend that everything will be fine...to act cheerful when they are upset and sad. Sometimes they even withhold medical information.

Better: Be real. Patients know intuitively when those around them are "faking it." What they need most is to feel close and connected, to be treated with honesty, which is another way of saying "with respect."

Don't laugh when you feel like crying. It's OK to express feelings of sadness and to share moments of concern. It's also important to allow the patient to say what he/she really thinks and to feel what he really feels. Don't keep trying to cheer someone up if he wants to express doubt and fear. Just be there for him and listen. This will mean a great deal.

It's important to be honest with patients, but this does not mean that you can say everything to everyone. Most patients let you know what they really want to know and what they prefer to have kept from them. It's important to listen and respect where the patient is coming from and to be sensitive to his feelings.

A New Way to Fight Depression Using Only Your Mind

Zindel Segal, PhD, CPsych, the Cameron Wilson Chair in Depression Studies at the University of Toronto, and head of the Cognitive Behavioural Therapy Unit at the Centre for Addiction and Mental Health, both in Toronto, Canada. He is a coauthor of The Mindful Way through Depression: Freeing Yourself from Chronic Unhappiness *(Guilford).*

Suffering from depression is very different from being sad. Sadness is a normal part of life. Depression is a constellation of psychological and physical changes that persist, unrelenting, for a minimum of two weeks—and often much longer.

One of every eight women and one of every five men will suffer at least one bout with serious depression at some point in their lives. Genetics seem to predispose some people to depression, though life events can be a factor as well. Seniors who experience losses in physical functioning and social networks can be especially susceptible to bouts of depression.

For those affected, depression often becomes an ongoing issue—those who have faced it once have a 40% chance of experiencing an episode in the future and those who already have had multiple episodes face up to an 80% chance of additional recurrences.

Depression is most commonly treated with medication that regulates the brain's chemistry and with professional counseling, which helps people take effective action in the face of the low motivation and pessimism that often define depression.

Exciting new tool: In the last decade or so, a new technique has been shown in studies to help sufferers head off depression before it takes hold. The technique is called mindfulness—paying attention to the present moment, without judgment, in order to see things more clearly.

LIFE ON AUTOMATIC PILOT

Mindfulness can prevent depression from taking hold of us because the alternative—our usual state—is that we operate on "automatic pilot." Our minds are elsewhere as we perform mundane activities.

Example: You're taking a shower, but wondering what's waiting in your E-mail.

If we let it, this automatic pilot also will select our moods and our emotional responses to events—and the responses it chooses can be problematic. For instance, if you make a minor misstep in some area of your life, your autopilot might select as your emotional response feelings of anger, failure and/or inadequacy, even though the event might have been completely inconsequential.

Because your mind is not paying full attention to the situation, you might not grasp that the negative feelings are greatly out of proportion to what's really going on. You only know that you feel bad. When these negative feelings persist, they can pull you into the downward spiral of depression.

Example: A friend mentions that one of the stocks in his portfolio has turned a profit. Your investments have not been as successful, and your autopilot selects inadequacy as your primary emotional response. This may sound like an overreaction, but in someone who is prone to depression, these feelings can expand into a full-blown episode.

Mindfulness can be an antidote to automatic pilot. By becoming more aware of the world around us, we experience life directly, not filtered through our minds' relentless ruminations. We learn to see events for what they are rather than what our autopilot might turn them into. That helps us to derail potential episodes of depression before they have a chance to take hold. It typically takes two weeks or longer for depression to fully sink in, so there is often plenty of time to stop the process.

BECOMING MINDFUL

Learning to be mindful involves more than simply paying attention. You must reorient your senses so that you experience a situation with your whole mind and heart and with all of your senses.

Try it out: Pick up a raisin. Hold it, feel it, examine it as if you had never seen anything like it before. Explore the raisin's folds and texture. Watch the way light shines off of its skin. Inhale its aroma. Then gently place it on your tongue. Notice how your hand knows exactly where to put it. Explore the raisin in your mouth before biting. Then chew once or twice. Experience the waves of taste and the sensation of chewing. Notice how the taste and texture change as you chew. Once you swallow, try to feel the raisin moving through your digestive system.

Keep it up: *Practice the following three steps every day to make mindfulness a regular part of your life—and episodes of depression less likely...*

1. Focus on your breath. Focusing your attention on your breath is perhaps the simplest, most effective way to anchor your mind in the moment. You think only of this breath. You can do this anytime, anywhere.

2. Watch your thoughts drift by like clouds. See them, acknowledge them, but do not attempt to reason them away. Some people attempt to use logic to escape depression. They tell themselves, *My life is pretty good—I should be happy.* This just leads to troubling questions like *If my life is good, why am I so unhappy? What's wrong with me?*

It is also tempting to try to push negative thoughts away so that you don't have to deal with them at all. Unfortunately, the thoughts are still there even if you refuse to acknowledge them.

Better: When you feel bad, reflect on what is bothering you. Try to uncover the original thought or event that set off your bad feelings. Then view it as just a thought, something independent from you even though it has popped into your head. Do not dismiss it, though. Even if the thought or the event that caused it was trivial, the feelings it has prompted are real and significant.

Next, notice any physical sensations that you are experiencing. Does your throat feel tight? Is your mouth dry? Are there butterflies in your stomach? Just as you are learning to watch your feelings float by, watch these physical sensations in a detached way. If you can learn to spot the onset of these sensations, you will be able to identify the early signs of depression sooner—and head off the bad feelings before they take root.

3. Take action.

Ask yourself: Does this thought have any merit? Is it connected to negative thoughts that I have had in the past? What can I do to make myself feel better about this issue?

Example: You feel depressed about your work life even though you are doing fine in your job. When you reflect on these negative thoughts, you realize that they began recently, when you learned that your brother received a promotion. You feel left behind because it has been some time since your last promotion.

What actions could you take to allay these negative feelings? Perhaps you could speak with your supervisor about your job performance and your prospects for future promotions...or contact a headhunter to remind yourself that you have other options.

With any problematic thought, identifying it quickly and taking some positive action is often enough to head off depression.

Important: Learning the mindfulness approach can be useful for preventing future bouts of depression—not for combating an episode that is already under way. When people are in the midst of depression, they typically cannot concentrate sufficiently to practice mindfulness. It is better to use the technique between episodes of depression so that it becomes a natural part of your thought process.

Use Your Memories to Improve Your Life

Jefferson Singer, PhD, clinical psychologist in private practice in Waterford, Connecticut, and professor of psychology at Connecticut College, New London. He is author of *Memories That Matter: How to Use Self-Defining Memories to Understand & Change Your Life* (New Harbinger).

Memories are more than just images from our past. They shape how we think of ourselves in the present and affect the direction our lives will take in the future. If you carry around numerous memories of relationships that ended poorly, you might think of yourself as unlovable. If your strongest memories are of scholastic and career successes, you probably consider yourself smart. True or not, these memory-inspired self-evaluations affect your behavior and your happiness.

MEMORIES THAT MATTER

The most powerful remembrances—what I call "self-defining memories"—come back again and again and pack an emotional punch each time. They relate in some way to issues that we're still trying to resolve or goals that we still hope to accomplish.

Example: Ray, a businessman, frequently recalls a memory from his childhood of his father leaning over his shoulder criticizing his homework. This memory is particularly likely to replay when Ray's boss offers him feedback on his job performance.

If we learn to use such self-defining memories to address shortcomings and pursue goals, negative memories lose power and we feel better about ourselves.

Example: When I was a child, it was important to me that I fit in with the crowd. For years, I relived a memory of the time some boys told me I couldn't be in their club. As an adult, one of my goals was to become more confident of my own worth. I realized I had succeeded when this childhood memory became less frequent and was no longer emotional for me when it did recur. The childhood rejection had lost its power to define me.

MAKING CHANGES

Here's how to use our memories to understand and improve our lives...

• **Reevaluate the results.** Caroline lived for years with a recurring memory of the day in divorce court when her marriage ended. The memory brought feelings of shame and failure. When I encouraged Caroline to search for something positive that came from that day, she realized it was then that she gained her freedom from a bad relationship. Now the same recurring memory brings Caroline a sense of liberation.

• **Role-play new endings.** An older couple told me that they hadn't felt close to each other in years. The memory of one particular incident haunted them both—the wife had reached for her husband's hand during an argument, but he had pulled away.

I positioned the couple just as they had been seated during that argument years before and asked them to replay the fight. Only this time, I told them to argue from each other's perspective. The reversed roles changed their take on the situation, and when the wife reached out her hand, her husband didn't pull away. They both still remember that old argument, but now the memory concludes with the more upbeat ending we created in therapy.

• **Surround yourself with objects and images that inspire positive memories.** If the sight of a painting given to you by an ex-wife reminds you of the failed marriage, replace it with a framed copy of an award you won, so you'll instead flash back to that success.

If the picture on your desk of your family at the Grand Canyon brings back negative memories of the bickering on that vacation, select another family photo.

177

I know one woman who hung pictures of her schnauzer around her home because she had only positive memories of the pet.

•**Don't focus on negative memories.** Despite what you might believe, there's little evidence that avoiding bad memories has any downside. Some people find it helpful to wear a rubber band around their wrist to snap when they catch themselves reliving a negative memory—the sharp sensation can yank the mind off the negative path.

Write down a list of positive memories you can turn to when you need a shot of confidence or a way to block out the negative. Specific memories are better than general ones—recall the time that you won a Little League game with a big hit, not just how much you enjoyed playing baseball as a child.

Experiences Bring More Joy Than Possessions Do

Ryan Howell, PhD, assistant professor, psychology, San Francisco State University.
Katherine L. Muller, PsyD, associate director, Center for Integrative Psychotherapy, Allentown, Pennsylvania.
Society for Personality and Social Psychology annual meeting, Tampa, Florida.

Although everyone knows that money can't buy happiness, purchasing life experiences instead of material possessions may increase your well-being, new research suggests.

In a study that asked more than 150 college students to rate a recent purchase intended to make them happy, researchers found that people were more satisfied with purchases of life experiences, such as a trip to the beach or for a meal.

The findings were presented at the annual meeting of the Society for Personality and Social Psychology in Tampa, Florida.

THE STUDY

The study included 154 students from San Francisco State University, average age 25.

About one-third of the group was white, nearly one-quarter were Asian-American, 11% were multi-racial, 15% were Hispanic, and about 4% were black.

The researchers asked each student to rate a recent purchase they made specifically with the intent of increasing their happiness. Half were told to write about a life experience purchase, while the other half was asked to write about a material purchase. According to study co-author Ryan Howell, PhD, an assistant professor of psychology at San Francisco State University, they asked for purchases made with the intent of increasing happiness so they didn't end up comparing a trip to the beach purchase to a box of pencils.

The students reported feeling more alive and invigorated with the purchase of a life experience, said Dr. Howell.

POSSIBLE EXPLANATIONS

There are likely a few reasons this is true, according to Dr. Howell. One may be that purchasing life experiences often brings someone closer to another person and satisfies a natural human need to be connected to others.

Another reason is that experiences provide "memory capital" that you can draw on in less happy times.

"Once you buy something, there's no reason to hold that memory," explained Dr. Howell. "But with a life experience, you can't take anything home. The only thing you can take with you is a memory, and we tend to focus our memories on the intense emotion we felt during the experience or on how it ended. Memories have an inherent bias, and you remember the best parts of life experiences."

IMPLICATIONS

The really good news from his study, given today's economic climate, is that life experience purchases don't have to be expensive to bring happiness, said Dr. Howell.

"A lot of the experiences were physical activities, like paying for park or beach admission," Dr. Howell noted.

However, Dr. Howell said that the findings probably don't apply to everyone. If you can't pay your mortgage, material things might increase your happiness more.

"As people drop closer to the poverty line, they tend to get more satisfaction with material things. The effect of purchasing life experiences probably becomes strong as you become more wealthy," he said.

EXPERT REACTION

"In this economy, being able to buy an item or an experience just for happiness is a luxury. I wonder for those who haven't had their basic needs met, if this would help as well?" said Katherine L. Muller, PsyD, associate director of the Center for Integrative Psychotherapy in Allentown, Pennsylvania.

"But if you do have disposable income, this could be something to consider, and you might want to make a conscious choice to try an experiential purchase," Dr. Muller said. "I think there's real value in the idea that memory is really the only thing you can take with you. And, social connectedness definitely creates more of an imprint, perhaps making the purchase more salient, because you shared it."

Natural Ways To Recover From the Holidays

Jamison Starbuck, ND, naturopathic physician in family practice in Missoula, Montana. She is a past president of the American Association of Naturopathic Physicians and a contributing editor to *The Alternative Advisor: The Complete Guide to Natural Therapies and Alternative Treatments* (Time-Life).

The holiday season is a notorious time for overeating, overdrinking, being stressed and losing sleep. Prevention is, of course, the best treatment for common holiday complaints, such as indigestion, weight gain, constipation, headache, fatigue and insomnia. But for those who find that, despite good intentions, they've had a few too many pieces of pie or haven't gotten a full night's sleep in days, I have developed a postholiday recovery plan that helps reverse the ill effects within three days. *My advice...*

• **Take control of your eating.** For one to three days, eliminate sugars, animal proteins and saturated fats. Limit your diet to fresh fruit …vegetables…and nongluten whole grains, such as rice, millet and quinoa, which are easy to digest. Drink only water (at least eight glasses daily) and herbal tea. To help eliminate toxins, try dandelion root tea. Add one tablespoon of dried dandelion root to eight ounces of boiling water and steep for 10 minutes. Drink two cups daily during this diet. You may also have up to two tablespoons of olive oil daily for energy, to relieve hunger and to add flavor to your foods. Eating this way will give your digestive system a rest. The natural enzymes and fiber content of the foods listed above can correct indigestion and constipation within 24 hours. This eating plan also helps people shed the few pounds they may have gained from holiday eating. When resuming a normal diet, add fish and legumes first.

• **Get moving.** Go outside and play football or basketball instead of watching others play on TV. Take a walk. If you belong to a gym, stop by for a workout or a yoga class. If all else fails, go up and down your stairs 15 times if outdoor activity is impossible.

• **Try homeopathy.** Homeopathy is a type of medicine that uses tiny amounts of natural substances to encourage a healing response by the body. The homeopathic remedy *Nux vomica* can relieve headache caused by hangover or overeating. Purchase the 30C potency at a health-food store. Take two pellets once or twice in a 24-hour period. Hyland's Calms Forté is a marvelous remedy for holiday insomnia. It's manufactured by Standard Homeopathic and available at pharmacies and health-food stores. Take two tablets, under the tongue at bedtime. Calms Forté, which contains minerals (such as magnesium) and herbs (such as passionflower) in homeopathic form, induces sleep by relaxing tired muscles and calming a busy mind. Do not take a homeopathic remedy within 15 minutes of consuming any food or drink.

• **Find a mentally stimulating activity.** Many people experience a letdown the week after major holidays. Feeling blue and/or lethargic certainly doesn't help with your physical recovery. Make time to attend a public lecture, an art museum, a good movie or a class. Anything that's interesting and intellectually challenging helps improve your mood.

Create a Retreat Space in Your Own Home

Mark A. Stengler, NMD, naturopathic medical doctor in private practice, Encinitas, California…adjunct associate clinical professor at the National College of Natural Medicine, Portland, Oregon…author of *The Natural Physician's Healing Therapies* (Bottom Line Books).

How many times have you found yourself exhausted or overwhelmed at the end of the day and wondered, "If only I could escape for just a little while…"

What most people don't realize: You can get away anytime you want with the help of a specially designated retreat space in your home, a space set up so that you can relax…have a few quiet minutes (or longer) to yourself…and recharge. To give you an idea of how to set up your own home retreat and how to use it, Victoria Moran, life coach, motivational speaker and author of *Shelter for the Spirit: Create Your Own Haven in a Hectic World* (Harper), provides details. When you create your home retreat and take time to enjoy it, I think you'll see how it contributes to your feeling of well-being.

SETTING UP YOUR OWN RETREAT SPACE

Retreat spaces are as individual as the people who create them. No one size or one way fits all. *Here are the steps…*

• **Pick a spot.** Depending on the size of your home, you can make your retreat space as large or small as you like. Claim as your own a spare room or guest bedroom—or convert a walk-in closet. A quiet spot is best. Even a corner of the living room can become a retreat space with the help of a partition or by using it when family members are not home. If you and your spouse both want a retreat space, create separate spaces for each of you.

• **Keep the furnishings simple.** Depending on your style, find a comfortable chair. Or if you prefer to sit on the floor, roll out a yoga mat.

• **Decorate.** Use an end table or shelf to hold a few favorite objects that bring happy thoughts or memories, such as a family photo, a shell or trinket from a memorable vacation, or a favorite painting. For a calming effect, light a candle or two (those made from vegetable oil or beeswax are a better choice than paraffin, which is made from petroleum and contains toxins)…play quiet music…or install a small table fountain. If you just want to sit quietly, keep headphones or earplugs nearby to block noise from the rest of the house.

• **Spiff it up!** Keep your retreat space clean and uncluttered so that you won't be distracted by lots of stuff. A simple, well-organized space enables you to relax more easily.

• **Eliminate anything from your space that could cause stress.** This isn't the time or place to pay (or even see) bills or read e-mail. Your retreat space should not include a computer, TV, phone, newspapers or anything that will draw you to the outside world—this is your time to escape!

9

Natural Cancer Care

Optimal Cancer Care

When a person is diagnosed with cancer, conventional doctors typically recommend surgery, chemotherapy and/or radiation. Now a growing body of research shows that complementary and alternative medicine (CAM) therapies benefit cancer patients in a number of ways, such as by reducing the adverse effects of conventional cancer treatments.*

AN ATTACK ON CANCER CELLS

Normal cells divide in a predictable and orderly fashion—for example, in the growth of a fetus. When the DNA within cells is damaged —due to genetic abnormalities, for example, or lifestyle factors, such as smoking or getting too much sun exposure—the cells may become cancerous.

The cornerstone of integrative cancer care is to mobilize the body's natural ability to stimulate *apoptosis*—the selective destruction of cells, including cancer cells. Most patients still require surgery, chemotherapy and/or radiation. The integrative component—including dietary changes and the use of supplements simultaneously with conventional treatments —improves the patient's odds of living a longer and healthier life by altering the body processes closely linked with cancer.

IMPROVED IMMUNITY

The immune system is the first line of defense against cancer. For example, natural killer cells produce an estimated 100 biochemical poisons that attack foreign proteins, including those on the surface of cancer cells.

---

*Integrative cancer centers can be found at major US medical institutions, such as Memorial Sloan-Kettering Cancer Center and M.D. Anderson Cancer Center. To find an integrative medicine program at a National Cancer Institute (NCI)–designated cancer center, contact the NCI (800-422-6237, *www.cancer.gov*...search "designated cancer centers").

Lise Alschuler, ND, past president of the American Association of Naturopathic Physicians. She is a board-certified naturopathic oncologist with a private practice in Scottsdale, Arizona, and is coauthor of *Definitive Guide to Cancer: An Integrative Approach to Prevention, Treatment, and Healing* (Celestial Arts).

Key recommendations...**

• **Load up on antioxidants.** The average cell is subjected to 10,000 daily assaults from free radicals (unstable, negatively charged molecules that can harm DNA), and the resulting damage can overwhelm the ability of immune T cells (including natural killer cells) to destroy cancer cells.

Recommended: Antioxidant-rich fresh produce (at least five servings daily) and supplements, such as vitamin C (1,000 milligrams, or mg to 2,000 mg daily)...selenium (100 micrograms, or mcg to 200 mcg daily)...and zinc (30 mg to 45 mg daily).

• **Take mushroom extracts.** When scientists recently reviewed the results from several randomized clinical trials, they found that the use of mushroom extracts (which contain a chemical compound that stimulates the immune system to destroy tumors) significantly improved survival rates for patients with malignancies of the stomach, colon, esophagus or breast.

A commonly recommended medicinal mushroom is *Coriolus versicolor* (or its chemical compound, PSK).

Typical dose: 3,000 mg daily.

CONTROL HORMONES

All cells have *hormone receptors*, molecular sites where hormones attach and cause biochemical reactions. One of the primary reactions is growth, which can be dangerous if a cell is cancerous.

Hormone-dependent cancers—such as some forms of breast cancer as well as many ovarian and prostate cancers—are most likely to be stimulated by certain hormones. But other cancers, such as malignancies of the lung or pancreas, are also influenced by hormones, particularly estrogen and cortisol, that compromise immunity or directly stimulate the growth of tumor cells. *My advice...*

• **Consume phytoestrogens.** The estrogen-like compounds in plants (phytoestrogens) can reduce the potentially carcinogenic effects of estrogen in the body. Phytoestrogens occupy the estrogen receptor sites, thereby preventing the body's estrogens from binding to those sites. Soy and flaxseed are rich in phytoestrogens.

**Important:* Consult an integrative health-care practitioner before taking any new supplements.

Recommended: One tablespoon daily of ground flaxseed and one to two servings weekly of soy foods.

Caution: Women with a previous or current diagnosis of breast or ovarian cancer should talk to their doctors before consuming high doses of phytoestrogens—in such cases, they may trigger the growth of estrogen-dependent cancer cells.

• **Eat leafy greens.** They promote the health of hormone-producing glands, including the thyroid, and support the liver's detoxification of hormones.

Recommended: At least one cup of dark, leafy greens, such as kale and chard, daily.

• **Eat organic.** Many of the herbicides and pesticides used in commercial produce have strong hormonal and genotoxic (DNA-damaging) effects that can increase the risk of getting or having a recurrence of cancers of the breast, kidney, lung and prostate.

• **Exercise regularly.** It regulates the body's production of insulin as well as cortisol and other stress hormones, which, if elevated for too long, can have cancer-causing effects.

Recommended: Six ½-hour sessions weekly.

REMOVE TOXINS

The body is constantly removing potentially carcinogenic toxins, such as *benzene* (commonly found in gasoline and tobacco).

One of the best herbs for detoxification is green tea. It supports the liver's elimination of toxins. Drink at least five cups of green tea daily.

The Anticancer Diet From a Doctor Who Survived Cancer

The late David Servan-Schreiber, MD, PhD, a neuroscientist and clinical professor of psychiatry at University of Pittsburgh School of Medicine. He is cofounder of the university's Center for Integrative Medicine and author of *Anticancer: A New Way of Life* (Viking). *www.anticancerbook.com.*

A t any given time, the average person might have thousands of cancer cells in his/her body. Individually, these abnormal cells are harmless, but any one of them could potentially proliferate and form a mass of cells (a tumor) that damages normal tissues and can spread to other parts of the body. About one-third of us eventually will get full-fledged cancer.

Often people who get cancer have created impairments in their natural defenses, allowing cancer cells to survive and proliferate. About 85% of all cancers are caused by environmental and lifestyle factors. We can't always control our environments, but we can control what we eat. Diet is one key factor that determines who gets cancer and who doesn't.

Example: Asian men have just as many precancerous microtumors in the prostate gland as American men, yet they are as much as 60 times less likely to develop prostate cancer. It's not a coincidence that their diets are far healthier, on average, than those consumed by men in the US. Asian men eat far more fruits and vegetables than Americans and relatively little red meat. They also tend to eat more fish and soy foods, and they drink more tea, especially green tea. These and other dietary factors allow their immune systems and other natural defenses to prevent cancer cells from proliferating.

My story: I was a physician in Pittsburgh when I was first diagnosed with a brain tumor in 1992. With the benefit of hindsight—and years of research into the origins and development of cancer—I have come to understand that my previous lifestyle, particularly my poor diet, fostered a procancer environment. For example, a typical lunch for me was chili con carne, a plain bagel and a can of Coke.

CAUSES OF CANCER

It can take years for cancer cells to turn into tumors—assuming that they ever do. This lag time means that we have many opportunities to create an anticancer environment in our bodies.

There are three main factors that promote the development of cancer…

• **Weakened immunity.** The immune system normally patrols the body for bacteria and viruses, as well as for cancer cells. When it spots something foreign, it dispatches a variety of cells, including natural killer cells, to destroy the foreign substance. In people who eat an unhealthy diet—not enough produce, too much alcohol, very little fish and so on—the immune system works less efficiently. This means that cancer cells can potentially slip under the radar and eventually proliferate.

• **Inflammation.** Millions of Americans have subclinical chronic inflammation. It doesn't cause symptoms, but it can lead to heart disease and cancer. Chronic inflammation can be caused by infection, a diet low in antioxidant nutrients and even emotional stress. It's accompanied by the release of *cytokines* and other inflammatory chemicals. Inflammation also prevents the immune system from working efficiently.

• **Angiogenesis.** Cancer cells, like other cells in the body, need blood and nourishment to survive. They send out chemical signals that stimulate the growth of blood vessels that carry blood to and from the cancer.

This process is called *angiogenesis*—and it can be strongly influenced by what we eat.

Example: People who eat no more than 12 ounces of red meat weekly can reduce their overall risk for cancer by 30%. Red meat stimulates the release of inflammatory chemicals that inhibit *apoptosis*, the genetically programmed cell death that prevents uncontrolled growth.

CANCER FIGHTERS

The best cancer-fighting foods…

• **Fatty fish.** The omega-3 fatty acids in fish reduce inflammation. Oncologists in Scotland have measured inflammatory markers in the blood of cancer patients since the 1990s. They have found that patients with the lowest levels of inflammation are twice as likely to live through the next several years as patients who have more inflammation.

Laboratory studies indicate that a high-fish diet can reduce the growth of lung, breast, colon, prostate and kidney cancers. And naturally, people who eat more fish tend to eat less red meat.

Important: The larger fatty fish, such as tuna, are more likely to be contaminated with mercury and other toxins. The best sources of omega-3s are smaller fatty fish, such as sardines, anchovies and small mackerel.

• **Low-glycemic carbohydrates.** The glycemic index measures the effects of the carbohydrates in foods on blood glucose levels. Foods with a high glycemic index, such as white bread and table sugar, cause a rapid rise in insulin as well as a rise in *insulin-like growth factor* (IGF). IGF stimulates cell growth, including the growth of cancer cells. Both insulin and IGF also promote inflammation.

Data from the Harvard Nurses' Health Study indicate that people who eat the most high-glycemic foods (these same people tend to be sedentary and overweight) are 260% more likely to get pancreatic cancer and 80% more likely to get colorectal cancer.

Recommended: Unprocessed carbohydrates that are low on the glycemic scale, such as whole-grain breakfast cereals and breads (with whole wheat, barley, oats, flaxseeds, etc.)...cooked whole grains, such as millet, quinoa and barley...and vegetables, such as broccoli and cauliflower.

Also important: Reduce or eliminate refined sugar as well as honey.

Better: Agave nectar, available at most health-food stores. Extracted from cactus sap, it's sweeter than sugar or honey, yet it has a glycemic index four to five times lower. You can use agave nectar just as you would sugar or honey—by adding it to cereals, tea and so on. Because of the liquid content of the syrup, you'll generally want to reduce the amount of other liquids in baked goods. Substitute three-quarter cup of agave nectar per one cup of any other sweetener.

•**Green tea.** Between three and five cups daily can significantly reduce your cancer risk. A chemical in green tea, *epigallocatechin gallate* (EGCG), inhibits angiogenesis. Green tea also contains *polyphenols* and other chemical compounds that reduce inflammation and activate liver enzymes that break down and eliminate potential carcinogens.

In men who already have prostate cancer, consuming five cups or more of green tea daily has been associated with reduced risk of progressing to advanced cancer by 50%. In women with certain types of breast cancer, three cups daily reduced relapses by 30%. Because black tea is fermented, it has a lower concentration of polyphenols and is less protective than green tea.

•**Soy foods.** The isoflavones in tofu, soy milk, edamame (green soybeans) and other soy foods help prevent breast cancer, particularly in women who started eating soy early in life. These compounds, known as *phytoestrogens*, have estrogen-like effects. They occupy the same cellular receptors as the body's estrogen yet are only about one-hundredth as active. This means that they may slow the development of estrogen-dependent tumors.

Recommended: Three servings of soy per week—but only for women who are cancer-free. Avoid soy if you have or had cancer—there's some concern that the estrogen-like compounds in soy might promote tumor growth in women who have a type of breast cancer that is sensitive to estrogen's effects.

•**Turmeric.** No other food ingredient has more powerful anti-inflammatory effects. In laboratory studies, the active ingredient *curcumin* in the spice turmeric inhibits the growth of many different cancers. It helps prevent angiogenesis and promotes the death of cancer cells.

In India, people consume an average of one-quarter to one-half teaspoon of turmeric daily. They experience one-eighth as many lung cancers as Westerners of the same age...one-ninth as many colon cancers...and one-fifth as many breast cancers.

•**Asian mushrooms,** such as shiitake, maitake and enokitake. They're available in most supermarkets and gourmet stores and are one of the most potent immune system stimulants. Among people who eat a lot of these mushrooms, the rate of stomach cancer is 50% lower than it is among those who don't eat them. One to two half-cup servings weekly probably is enough to have measureable effects.

•**Berries.** Berries contain *ellagic acid*, which strongly inhibits angiogenesis. Aim for one-half cup per day.

•**Dark chocolate.** One ounce contains twice as many polyphenols as a glass of red wine and almost as much as a cup of green tea. Laboratory studies indicate that these compounds slow the growth of cancer cells.

Look for a chocolate with more than 70% cocoa. The "lighter" milk chocolates don't contain adequate amounts of polyphenols—and the dairy component of milk chocolate blocks the absorption of polyphenols.

Magical Food Combos That Fight Cancer

Karen Collins, RD, registered dietitian and nutrition adviser to the American Institute for Cancer Research (www.aicr.org). A syndicated newspaper columnist and public speaker, she maintains a private nutrition counseling practice in Washington, DC.

Researchers know that some foods can help prevent cancer. Now there is growing evidence that certain food *combinations* may offer more protection against cancer than any one specific food.

The following combinations of foods are especially beneficial. *Eat them regularly—either at the same meal or separately throughout the week...*

TOMATOES AND BROCCOLI

Results of an animal study presented at the American Institute for Cancer Research International Research Conference showed that rats with tumors that were given a diet of tomatoes and broccoli had significantly smaller tumors than animals fed one of these foods.

The lycopene in tomatoes is an antioxidant. Antioxidants are crucial for preventing cancer because they help prevent unstable molecules, called free radicals, from damaging cell structures and DNA. Broccoli contains chemical compounds known as *glucosinolates*, which may be effective in flushing carcinogens from the body.

Also helpful: Combine broccoli or other cruciferous vegetables, such as brussels sprouts and cabbage, with foods that are high in selenium, such as shellfish and Brazil nuts. A study published by the UK's Institute of Food Research found that the combination of broccoli's glucosinolates and selenium has more powerful anticancer effects than either food eaten alone.

BRUSSELS SPROUTS AND BROCCOLI

These potent cancer-fighting vegetables also are rich in vitamin C and folate, as well as phytonutrients that deactivate carcinogens. When eaten in combination, brussels sprouts and broccoli may provide more protection than either one eaten alone.

Brussels sprouts have the phytonutrient *crambene*, which stimulates phase-2 enzymes, substances that help prevent carcinogens from damaging DNA. Broccoli is high in *indole-3-carbinol*, a phytonutrient that also stimulates phase-2 enzymes—but in a different way.

ORANGES, APPLES, GRAPES AND BLUEBERRIES

Each of these foods is very high in antioxidants. In a recent laboratory analysis, researchers measured the amount of antioxidants in each of these fruits individually. Then they combined them and took additional measurements.

Result: The mixture of fruits was more powerful against free radicals than any one fruit alone.

CURCUMIN AND QUERCETIN

Curcumin is a phytonutrient found in the spice turmeric. *Quercetin* is a phytonutrient that is abundant in yellow onions, especially in the outermost rings. According to a small study in *Clinical Gastroenterology and Hepatology*, people who consumed large amounts of these two phytonutrients had a reduction in the number of colon polyps, growths that may turn into cancer.

The study looked at a small number of people with familial *adenomatous polyposis*, a hereditary condition that increases the likelihood of developing polyps. The phytochemical combination reduced the number of polyps by 60%. It also caused some polyps to shrink.

The researchers used concentrated forms of curcumin and quercetin. You would have to eat two-and-a-half tablespoons of turmeric daily to get a comparable amount. To get the necessary amount of quercetin, you would need to have about two-thirds cup of chopped onions daily.

Recommended: Eat a variety of herbs and spices to get the most phytonutrient protection. Even small amounts used frequently will impact your health over time. Among herbs, rosemary and oregano rank among the best phytonutrient sources. Ginger is another powerful spice.

185

TOMATOES AND FAT

The lycopene in tomatoes is particularly effective against prostate cancer—but only when it's consumed with a small amount of fat. Lycopene, like other members of the carotenoid chemical family, is a fat-soluble substance. The body can't absorb it efficiently in the absence of fat.

It takes only three to five grams of fat (about one teaspoon of oil) to improve the absorption of lycopene from tomatoes. For example, you could have a salad with an oil-based dressing. The type of fat doesn't matter for absorption of lycopene and other carotenoids, but you might as well choose a fat that promotes health. Olive oil and canola oil are good choices.

MORE VARIETY, LESS CANCER

In a recent study published in *The Journal of Nutrition*, researchers divided 106 women into two groups. All of the women were asked to eat eight to 10 servings of fruits and vegetables daily for two weeks. However, one of the groups (the high-diversity group) was told to include foods from 18 different botanical groups, including onions and garlic from the allium family, legumes, cruciferous vegetables, etc. The other group (the low-diversity one) was asked to concentrate all its choices among only five major groups.

Results: Women in both groups showed a decrease in lipid peroxidation—important for reducing the risk of cancer and heart disease. However, only the women in the high-diversity group showed a decrease in DNA oxidation, one of the steps that initiates cancer development.

The ways that chemicals work in the body, known as metabolic pathways, have a rate-limiting effect. This means that beyond a certain point, eating more of a specific food won't provide additional protection. Eating a wide variety of foods brings more metabolic pathways into play, thus bypassing this limiting effect.

Tea Time

Tea may help reduce risk for skin cancer, according to a recent study. Dermatological researchers found that people who drank two or more cups of either black or green tea daily were 30% less likely than people who did not drink tea to suffer squamous cell carcinoma. Moreover, the effect grew over time—those who drank tea for 47 years had a 51% reduced risk. Researchers believe the polyphenols in tea serve as antioxidants that counter free radicals triggered by the sun, helping protect skin from moderate sun exposure.

Judy Rees, MD, PhD, research assistant professor, Dartmouth Medical School, lead author of study.

Let Tea Cool to Reduce Cancer Risk

Among daily tea drinkers, those who consumed the beverage very hot (158°F or higher) were eight times more likely to get cancer of the esophagus (throat) than those who consumed it warm (below 149°F).

Theory: Too-hot liquids injure esophageal cells, causing chronic inflammation that sets the stage for cancer.

Best: Tea may protect against heart disease, diabetes and various cancers—but always let it cool for at least four minutes before drinking.

Farhad Islami, MD, PhD, at the International Agency for Research on Cancer, Lyon, France, and leader of a study of 871 people.

Natural Cancer Treatments That Really Work

Keith I. Block, MD, medical director of Block Center for Integrative Cancer Care in Skokie, Illinois...director of Integrative Medical Education at University of Illinois College of Medicine, Chicago...and scientific director of the Institute for Integrative Cancer Research and Education, Evanston. He is editor of *Journal for Integrative Cancer Therapies*. He is author of *Life Over Cancer* (Bantam).

Many cancer patients augment conventional medical treatment with complementary medicine, such as nutritional or herbal supplements. The newest research and decades of successful clinical use show that some of these natural treatments work very effectively to fight cancer and reduce side effects.

Here are the best science-based complementary treatments for cancer. It's usually fine to take several of these supplements simultaneously, but be sure to talk to your doctor first. For help finding an integrative practitioner, go to *http://nccam.nih.gov/*, then click on "How to Find a Practitoner."

ANTIOXIDANTS

Cancer specialists often advise patients not to take antioxidant supplements, such as vitamin A or vitamin E, during chemotherapy and radiation treatments.

Reason: One way chemotherapy and radiation destroy cancer cells is by causing oxidative stress. According to one theory, antioxidants may be counterproductive because they might have the ability to protect against this oxidative damage.

But new scientific research shows that the opposite is true—antioxidant supplements aren't powerful enough to counter chemotherapeutic medicines or radiation, but they can reduce the side effects of those treatments and also may battle tumors and extend life.

Recent study: Researchers from the University of Illinois at Chicago and the Institute for Integrative Cancer Research and Education analyzed 19 studies involving 1,554 cancer patients who took antioxidants during chemotherapy. They concluded that most cancer patients are better off using antioxidants in conjunction with chemotherapy and radiation than not using them.

Typical doses...

• **Vitamin A.** 7,500 daily international units (IU), which should only be taken under a doctor's supervision—patients should have their liver enzymes monitored on an ongoing basis.

• **Vitamin E.** 400 IU daily, taken under a doctor's supervision (patients should have their platelet counts monitored). It's best to divide the dose, taking half in the morning and half in the evening. Ideally, take it on an empty stomach.

ASTRAGALUS

The herb astragalus has been used in Traditional Chinese Medicine for thousands of years. Scientific studies show that it strengthens the immune system, increasing the activity of cancer-fighting cells and inhibiting the activity of immune cells that increase inflammation and thereby worsen cancer. Research shows that the herb also can boost the power of some types of chemotherapy.

Recent study: Researchers from the School of Public Health at the University of California, Berkeley, analyzed 34 studies involving 2,815 patients with non-small-cell lung cancer who were treated with chemotherapy alone or who were treated with chemotherapy and astragalus. The patients taking astragalus had a 33% lower risk for death after 12 months and a 24%-to-46% better tumor response than those not taking the herb.

Typical dose: 750 milligrams (mg) to 2,500 mg a day of astragalus extract.

GINSENG

Extracts from the root of this herb often are used as a natural stimulant—to boost mental and physical energy, improve athletic performance and relieve fatigue. Ginseng also may boost energy in cancer patients.

Recent study: Doctors from the North Central Cancer Treatment Group at the Mayo Clinic gave either a placebo or ginseng—at daily doses of 750 mg...1,000 mg...or 2,000 mg—to 282 cancer patients. Those taking 1,000 mg or 2,000 mg of ginseng had more energy and vitality and less fatigue. Those taking 750 mg or a placebo had no such improvement. The patients taking the higher doses of ginseng also reported greater physical, mental, emotional and spiritual well-being.

Typical dose: 500 mg to 1,000 mg twice daily of American ginseng (not Asian red ginseng). Medical supervision is needed for the higher dosage, particularly if you are taking blood-thinning medication.

GLUTAMINE

Chemotherapy can damage the mucous lining of the digestive tract, which stretches from the inside of the mouth to the rectum. One common result is *oral mucositis* (OM), a condition in which the mucous lining of the mouth and throat becomes inflamed, painful, ulcerated and prone to infection. The amino acid *glutamine* fuels the daily maintenance of the mucous lining of the digestive tract—and supplemental glutamine helps limit or stop its destruction by chemotherapy.

Recent study: Researchers at the University of Connecticut Health Center gave either glutamine powder or a placebo to 326 cancer patients undergoing chemotherapy who were developing OM. Those taking glutamine experienced a significant reduction in the severity of the condition compared with those taking the placebo. In fact, many of those taking glutamine didn't develop OM at all during their second cycle of chemotherapy.

Typical dose: 5 grams (g) to 10 g, twice daily.

OMEGA-3 FATTY ACIDS

Chronic inflammation is known to fuel the growth of tumors. Omega-3 fatty acids, nutrients abundant in fish oil and flaxseed, are potent anti-inflammatories that slow tumor growth and shrink tumors in animal studies. Recent research shows that omega-3 fatty acids may do the same for men with prostate cancer.

Recent study: Researchers at Duke University Medical Center, the University of Michigan and the University of North Carolina studied 140 men with prostate cancer who were scheduled to undergo prostate surgery in 30 days. They divided the men into four presurgical groups—some took 30 g (about one ounce) of ground flaxseed daily…some ate a low-fat diet and took the flaxseed…some just ate a low-fat diet…and a control group used none of the regimens. After the surgery, researchers found that the tumors of the men who took flaxseed had grown more slowly—at a 30%-to-40% slower rate than those of the other men. The men mixed the ground flaxseed in drinks or sprinkled it on yogurt and other foods. The study was reported at the annual meeting of the American Society of Clinical Oncology.

Typical dose: One ounce of ground flaxseed …or 3 g of fish oil.

ACUPUNCTURE

Acupuncture is a healing technique from traditional Chinese medicine. An acupuncturist inserts tiny needles into the skin along *meridians* (energy channels in the body) in order to restore and enhance *chi*, the fundamental force of health and well-being.

Recent study: Doctors at the Osher Center for Integrative Medicine at the University of California, San Francisco, studied 138 cancer patients undergoing surgery, dividing them into two groups. One group received acupuncture and massage after surgery, along with standard care, such as pain-relieving medications. The other group received standard care only. The acupuncture and massage group had 58% less postsurgical pain and less depression, reported the doctors in an issue of *Journal of Pain and Symptom Management*. It's hard to tell specifically what role acupuncture played and what role massage played, but other studies that look at acupuncture and massage alone show that each technique has benefits, including reducing surgical pain.

Other studies show acupuncture may help prevent or relieve chemotherapy-induced nausea and fatigue…chemotherapy-induced decrease in white blood cell count…radiation-induced dry mouth…shortness of breath …and insomnia and anxiety.

The Key to Healing

Bernie Siegel, MD, a pioneer in mind-body medicine and the founder of Exceptional Cancer Patients (*www. ecap-online.org*), which provides programs based on mind-body-spirit medicine. He is also author of many books and audio programs, most recently *Faith, Hope and Healing; Inspiring Lessons Learned from People Living with Cancer* (Wiley).

Words are powerful tools—especially for people who are dealing with any kind of illness. Doctors often tell cancer patients, for example, that their treatment is designed to "kill," "destroy" or "attack" cancer cells.

All of this is good and well if these words make a patient feel more powerful. But all too often, this approach has the opposite effect and makes those who are ill feel that they are at war with their own bodies—and their health suffers as a result. Why does this happen?

Even if you are "assaulting" an illness—be it cancer, heart disease, diabetes or any other serious ailment—your body is designed to shift into a self-protection mode in the midst of this assault. When threatened, our bodies release stress hormones to fuel a quick escape from whatever is endangering us, and our immune function (one of the keys to overcoming virtually all types of illness) becomes suppressed. Some people feel energized by a good fight, and they approach their health challenge with the precision of a sergeant leading his/her troops. Others, on the other hand, feel completely at odds with such an approach.

This was the case for Dave, a Quaker friend of mine who developed cancer. His oncologist told him, "I am going to kill your cancer." Dave quietly responded, "I am a Quaker. I don't kill anything," and he walked out the door.

Dave ended up consulting a different doctor for his cancer treatment and worked with me on alternative therapies that included imagery and therapeutic drawing. Because the aggressive words used by his initial doctor felt so wrong to Dave, he began a regular practice of visualization that included images of his white cells "carrying away"—rather than destroying—his cancer cells.

I also introduced Dave to drawing, which gave him an opportunity to conceptualize and reproduce images of the healing he sought for his body. You don't need any artistic skill to benefit from therapeutic drawing. It's designed to help patients grapple with questions and fears about their illnesses and their treatment options. Dave lived 12 years after his doctor had given him one to two years to live.

If you think all of this sounds unscientific, I don't blame you. When I first became involved in mind-body medicine more than 30 years ago, I was skeptical, too. I was a surgeon, and I believed that the scalpel was all-powerful.

Then I began examining the evidence and could no longer deny how our minds—and mental well-being—can affect our response to illness. It's been shown that women who have lung cancer or melanoma tend to live longer than men who have the same type of malignancy. We know that this is not a result of female hormones—studies also show that married men who have prostate or bladder cancer generally live longer than single men who have the same cancers. According to my observations, it's all about having positive connections with others. In fact, I am firmly convinced that women are more likely than men to have strong emotional connections that can literally extend their lives.

This point is illustrated by a woman I once knew who was a devoted mother at the time of her cancer diagnosis. "I have nine kids, and I can't die until they are all married and out of the house," she told me. Twenty-three years later, when her last child left the house, her cancer returned and soon proved to be fatal. I have seen similar stories in the hundreds of cancer patients I have known and worked with over the years. What saddened me about the woman with nine children is that she no longer felt that her life had meaning once all of them had left the house.

So before you embark on a new medical treatment, ask yourself two important questions…

1. Does my mind feel at ease with the type of therapy I am considering—or am I simply complying with my doctor's wishes? If the treatment doesn't feel right, is there a way that I can mentally frame it differently? Even a treatment that has potentially unpleasant side effects, such as chemotherapy, can feel "right" if it is undertaken in the spirit of extending a life that has meaning. The treatment becomes a "labor pain of self-birth"—seen in this way, the side effects are diminished when you're undergoing the therapy to give yourself a new life.

2. Is there anything I can do to live my life more fully in the midst of my health challenge? Staying mentally healthy is an invaluable tool. When you heal your life and find peace of mind, your body is much more likely to get the message, too.

Soothing the Side Effects Of Chemotherapy

Matthew D. Bauer, LAc, has practiced acupuncture for more than 20 years. He is a regular contributing columnist to *Acupuncture Today*, and formerly served on the executive committee of the California Acupuncture Association. His practice is in La Verne, California.

Nausea and vomiting are two of the most dreaded side effects of chemotherapy. Considering that the cure can sometimes feel worse than the cancer it is meant to treat, some patients even elect to discontinue treatment. Although recent advances in antinausea and antivomiting medications have helped many cancer patients, the search for additional and more natural methods of relief for these hard-to-tolerate side effects continues. One method that was recently studied is acupuncture.

STUDY PINPOINTS WHAT WORKS

Can acupuncture reduce chemotherapy-induced nausea and vomiting? The Chinese healing method has been successfully used to treat a wide variety of ailments, including temporomandibular joint disorder (TMJ), drug addictions, alcoholism, allergies and back pain. It works by stimulating prescribed anatomical sites on the body.

In a review of 11 studies of acupuncture and its effects on chemotherapy-induced nausea and/or vomiting, the Cochrane Collaboration, an international organization that evaluates medical research, found a mixed bag of results, depending upon which acupuncture method was used and for which side effect.

A REVIEW OF THE FINDINGS

Electro-acupuncture (in which a small electrical current is passed through the needle) helped reduce vomiting during the first 24 hours after chemotherapy.

Traditional manual acupuncture using needles was not shown to be significantly effective for acute vomiting or nausea severity (within 24 hours of treatment).

Based on similar principles, but using (highly trained) fingertip pressure on acupuncture points, "acupressure" was looked at as well. This method showed no benefit for vomiting, but did reduce acute nausea—although it was ineffective for delayed nausea (after 24 hours of treatment).

It is unclear why electro-acupuncture reduced acute vomiting while needles-only acupuncture did not, or why one method was successful with nausea while another was successful for vomiting. Of note is that all participants in all the trials reviewed were taking antivomiting drugs, so additional research is needed to determine whether acupuncture alone is effective, or whether it should be considered an effective adjunct to medications.

EXPERT OPINION

Surprised by these findings? Acupuncturist Matthew D. Bauer, LAc, a former member of the Board of Directors for the California Acupuncture Association and a practicing acupuncturist in La Verne, California with more than 20 years experience, provides some balance. In his view, it's hard to standardize this sort of study enough to make the findings meaningful. "So much depends on the practitioner's skill in placing needles at just the right angle in just the right place," he said. "In looking at this many trials, you're obviously dealing with many practitioners at varying levels of skill and experience, which, of course affects outcomes."

Acupuncture, he says, can be helpful in many ways for people undergoing treatment for cancer. It's worth a try since there's little risk and much potential benefit. It's important to work with a seasoned practitioner who has experience with oncology patients. And, of course, all cancer patients should check with their doctors before adding acupuncture or any other treatment to their cancer protocols.

Wristbands May Lessen Nausea After Radiation

University of Rochester Medical Center, news release.

Acupressure wristbands might help cancer patients experience nearly 25% less nausea during radiation treatments, a new study says.

The finding, published in the *Journal of Pain and Symptom Management*, also discounted the common belief that such non-Western medical treatments act more as a placebo than an effective treatment.

NOT THE PLACEBO EFFECT

"We know the placebo effect exists—the problem is that we don't know how to measure it very well," said study author Joseph A. Roscoe, PhD, a research associate professor at the James P. Wilmot Cancer Center at the University of Rochester Medical Center.

"In this study, we attempted to manipulate the information we gave to patients to see if their expectations about nausea could be changed," Dr. Roscoe explained. "As it turned out, our information to change people's expectations had no effect, but we still found that the wristbands reduce nausea symptoms."

The wristbands put pressure on a "nausea point" identified by traditional Chinese acupuncture. The pressure acts to change the flow of *chi* (energy), according to the Eastern belief.

THE STUDY

The study involved 88 people who experienced nausea after radiation treatments for cancer. Some were given wristbands to wear, and the others were not. And about half of those in the wristband group were also given information that explicitly said the wristbands cut down on nausea, whereas handouts given to the others with wristbands contained more neutral information.

THE RESULTS

Those with wristbands experienced a 24% decrease in nausea, regardless of which set of information they were given before the experiment. The group without wristbands reported just a 5% lessening of nausea.

LEARN MORE

For more information about alternative therapies that stimulate the flow of energy, visit the Web site of the Alternative Medicine Foundation, *www.amfoundation.org/energywork.htm*.

Acupuncture Cuts Dry Mouth in Cancer Patients

University of Texas M.D. Anderson Cancer Center, news release.

Acupuncture reduces severe dry mouth (*xerostomia*) among patients receiving radiation for head and neck cancer, a small pilot study suggests.

BACKGROUND

"The quality of life in patients with radiation-induced xerostomia is profoundly impaired," said study senior author Mark S. Chambers, DMD, a professor in the dental oncology department at the University of Texas M.D. Anderson Cancer Center. "Symptoms can include altered taste, dental decay, infections of the tissues of the mouth, and difficulty with speaking, eating and swallowing. Conventional treatments have been less than optimal, providing short-term response at best."

THE STUDY

This study included 19 patients with xerostomia who'd completed radiation therapy at least four weeks earlier. They were given two acupuncture treatments a week for four weeks. Acupuncture points used in the treatment were located on the ears, chin, index finger, forearm and lateral surface of the leg.

The acupuncture treatments resulted in improvements in physical well-being and xerostomia symptoms, the researchers said.

The study was published online in the journal *Head & Neck*.

LARGER CLINICAL TRIAL PLANNED

A Xerostomia Acupuncture Trial (Phase 3) is currently under way (visit *http://clinicaltrials.gov/show/NCT01266044*).

"Although the patient population was small, the positive results are encouraging and warrant a larger trial to assess patients over a longer period of time," Dr. Chambers said.

To learn more about dry mouth, go to the Web site of the National Institute of Dental and Craniofacial Research, *www.nidcr.nih.gov/OralHealth/Topics/DryMouth*.

Keep Cancer from Coming Back

Julie K. Silver, MD, founder of RESTORE (Recovering Energy and Strength Through Oncology Rehabilitation Excellence), an oncology rehabilitation program at Spaulding Rehabilitation Hospital, and an assistant professor of physical medicine at Harvard Medical School, both in Boston. She is the author of *After Cancer Treatment: Heal Faster, Better, Stronger* (Johns Hopkins).

This year, an estimated 1.4 million Americans will be diagnosed with cancer. The primary cancer therapies—surgery, chemotherapy and/or radiation—are more effective than ever before, but these powerful weapons often leave cancer survivors weak and exhausted.

Until recently, doctors told cancer patients to go home following treatment and wait—sometimes for weeks or months—for their bodies to recover.

Now: Cancer specialists and physiatrists (doctors trained in rehabilitation medicine) have identified the best ways for cancer survivors to achieve a faster, fuller recovery—and perhaps even improve their odds against a recurrence.

As a physiatrist, I have worked with thousands of cancer survivors. But in 2003, when I was diagnosed with breast cancer, I experienced firsthand the debilitating effects of life-saving cancer therapies. Medical research and my personal experience have convinced me that a positive outlook…supportive family and friends…a strong spiritual life…and effective pain relief all aid recovery.

How to have an even greater impact on cancer recovery…

EAT THE RIGHT FOODS

While attacking malignant tumors, chemotherapy and radiation treatments also kill normal cells. Your diet plays a crucial role in helping your body heal and replace lost and damaged tissue. *In addition to eating at least five daily servings of vegetables and fruits…whole grains at most meals…and legumes at least once daily, be sure your diet includes…**

**If your cancer therapy makes you tired or nauseated, it is best to start these practices after your treatment ends.*

- **Protein.** During treatment and for several weeks afterward, increase your intake of protein. It helps prevent infection and repair damaged cells. How much protein do you need? Divide your weight in half and eat that many grams of protein daily.

Example: If you weigh 150 pounds, aim for 75 g daily.

Best protein sources: Fish, poultry, eggs and low-fat dairy products. Protein from plant sources, including most beans, nuts and seeds, also aids healing by providing cancer-fighting phytochemicals.

- **Organic foods.** The potential danger of pesticides is still being debated. But why take a chance? While your body is healing, protect it from potentially toxic pesticides by choosing organic fruits, vegetables and meats. (Look for "certified organic" on the label.)

While increasing your intake of the foods mentioned earlier, it's equally important to avoid…

- **Soy.** Soy and chickpeas, as well as licorice and tea (black and green), are rich sources of plant chemicals known as flavonoids, which may contain components that resemble the hormone estrogen. In many people, these foods help fight a variety of diseases, including some types of cancer, but if you have a hormone-dependent tumor, such as a breast or prostate malignancy, it's best to avoid flavonoid-rich foods.

- **Alcohol.** Relatively small amounts of alcohol have been linked to some types of malignancies, including colon, pancreatic and breast cancer. Limit your intake of alcohol to social occasions, or abstain altogether.

STAY ACTIVE

Exercise improves mood, and there's increasing evidence that it also reduces the risk for breast, colon and possibly prostate cancer—and may help prevent a recurrence of these malignancies. *Your exercise program should include…*

- **Cardiovascular exercise.** Even while you're undergoing treatment, start using a pedometer to track how far you walk. These devices, which cost $15 or more at most sporting-goods stores, record the number of steps you take throughout the day.

Smart idea: Write down your daily step total (a mile equals about 2,000 steps) and aim to increase it by 10% a week until you reach 10,000 steps, or five miles a day.

When you feel strong enough, begin formal workout sessions. Use a treadmill and/or stationary exercise bike—or simply take brisk walks or swim. The American Cancer Society recommends working up to a 30-minute moderate-intensity workout (the equivalent of brisk walking), five days a week. Forty-five minute workouts may be even more beneficial.

Important: If you were active before your cancer diagnosis, aim for your earlier fitness level. If you were sedentary, simply try to exercise regularly for whatever period of time you are able to do so.

Helpful: Several shorter sessions each day—for example, three 10-minute sessions of brisk walking—may be less tiring than a single sustained workout.

• **Strength training.** Lifting weights or using resistance-type exercise machines, such as those made by Nautilus or Cybex, rebuilds muscle mass that is lost during inactivity and treatment, strengthens the bones and immune system, and improves balance.

Strength training should be performed two to three times per week to allow time for your muscles to recover between sessions.

During each workout…

• Focus on all major muscle groups and on strengthening your "core" (middle section of the body)—the core muscles support the rest of your body.

• Find the maximum weight you can lift 10 times—your "10 RM" (repetition maximum). Start by lifting 50% of this amount 10 times. Rest for one to two minutes or longer, then lift 60% of the same weight 10 times. After another one- to two-minute rest, lift 80% of the weight 10 times. Increase the weight as you grow stronger—a reasonable goal is 10% per week until you reach a plateau.

• **Flexibility exercises.** This type of exercise is less important than cardiovascular and strength training, but it will improve comfort and mobility, and make you more resilient and less prone to injury.

Tai chi and yoga are good forms of stretching exercise if you avoid movements that are painful.

Important: Before you start an exercise program, check with your doctor and consider working with a physical therapist or personal trainer. To avoid fatigue and injury, listen to your body. If you feel you're doing too much, cut back.

Although unstructured physical activity—for example, walking from your car to the mall, taking the stairs or gardening—is usually good for health, it provides less benefit than regular, structured exercise. Preserve your energy for exercise sessions by avoiding activities that tire you out.

GET ENOUGH REST

Poor sleep compounds the fatigue that often follows radiation and chemotherapy. Research shows that sleep is vital to the cells and chemicals of the immune system, fortifying the body against infection and cancer growth.

Helpful: Plan for seven to eight hours of sleep a night, and follow the rules of "sleep hygiene"…

• **Avoid heavy meals and limit fluids within two to three hours of going to bed.** Stop drinking caffeine and alcohol (if you drink it) four to six hours before bedtime.

• **To "train" your body to sleep, go to bed and get up at the same time each day—** including the weekend.

• **Keep your bedroom dark and quiet,** at a comfortable temperature.

• **Don't watch television, play computer games or exercise within one to two hours of going to bed.** Allow an hour to unwind with music, reading, quiet conversation or a warm bath.

If worries about your health keep you awake, try meditation or relaxation exercises to lower anxiety. Talk out your concerns with friends and family. Counseling can teach you techniques to ease worrying.

If you find yourself sleeping more than 10 hours a night, tell your doctor—this could indicate depression or an underlying health problem. And if you have trouble falling asleep or staying asleep, ask your doctor about sleep aids (including natural remedies, such as low-dose melatonin).

Six Essential Oils That Help Heal Cancer Patients

Cherie Perez, RN, quality assurance specialist in the department of GU Medical Oncology at M.D. Anderson Cancer Center in Houston.

Like so many New Age practices and beliefs, aromatherapy has ancient roots. The use of essential oils to affect mood and well-being can be found far back in Egyptian, Greek and Roman history. While scientific evidence about aromatherapy is scant, its long-standing role in spirituality and healing, along with anecdotal support of its benefits, gives essential oils an important role as a complementary alternative medicine therapy.

BOOSTING IMMUNE FUNCTION

Cherie Perez, RN, quality assurance specialist in the department of GU (genitourinary) Medical Oncology at M.D. Anderson Cancer Center in Houston, is a strong proponent of aromatherapy, including as an adjunct for cancer treatment. She teaches monthly classes for patients on the topic. Perez shares her thoughts about how aromatherapy can be useful for people who are healthy, as well as those with chronic illnesses. Used properly, Perez says essential oils can indirectly help bolster immune function in cancer patients, strengthening their ability to fight back against the disease by helping to ease pain, depression, sleeplessness and stress. The oils can also help relieve anxiety and improve memory, both frequent problems for people in cancer treatment.

ESSENTIALS ABOUT ESSENTIAL OILS

These essential oils have various scents such as floral, minty, citrus and masculine—and Perez advises using the ones you like best among the choices indicated for a specific treatment, since more than one oil may address the same problem. She explains that the limbic system,

which is triggered by the sense of smell, is the emotional seat of the brain. It's the reason why people often respond strongly to certain scents—positively or negatively. Lavender, for example, might bring back warm memories of a trip to Provence, or sour thoughts about a dour relative who wore it as a fragrance.

DILUTION REQUIRED

All oils are highly concentrated distillations of plant parts, including the flowers, leaves, branches and roots. Because they are so potent (hundreds of times more concentrated than the culinary fresh or dried herb or herbal teas, and therefore easy to overdose on) they should be used only under the supervision of a knowledgeable practitioner, such as a naturopathic physician, registered nurse, massage therapist, clinical herbalist or aromatherapist. Some of the most popular oils include rosemary, eucalyptus, lavender and chamomile. Essential oils can be inhaled (safest with a simple diffuser), enjoyed in your bath or massaged onto your skin (but never directly in their undiluted form…because they can cause a rash or burning sensation).

Oils may come already diluted, and will say so on the ingredient label, but you can also dilute a pure oil yourself, with advice from your practitioner. Add three drops of an essential oil to a half tablespoon of scentless organic vegetable oil (such as sunflower or safflower) or to an unscented body lotion. People with sensitive skin should do a skin test before topical use. How much to dilute an oil depends on the type of oil and your skin's sensitivity. Thyme, for example, is quite irritating to some people, so it should be used more sparingly and with caution. Lavender, on the other hand, is nonirritating to nearly everyone, says Perez. Citrus oils may cause sensitivity to sunlight, so avoid skin application if you are going to be in the sun. Because they're so pretty and fragrant yet highly toxic if ingested, they should be kept where children cannot reach them.

MENU OF OPTIONS

Here's a list of popular oils that address some common problems, as well as those common among people in treatment for cancer…

•**Lavender.** Great as a general relaxant, it also treats migraines and relieves stress. It is excellent for insomnia resulting from cancer treatment.

• **Rosemary.** For muscle pain, low blood pressure (do not use if you have high blood pressure) and cold feet and hands. Rosemary stimulates appetite.

• **Spearmint.** Used to ease nausea and to help digestion. Can help ease gas and other treatment-related digestive problems.

• **Eucalyptus or peppermint.** For rubbing on sore muscles. Eucalyptus may also help joints, including arthritic ones. Eucalyptus may increase the absorption of certain cancer drugs that are applied topically, so use caution and try a patch test first, avoiding application to the same area as the cancer drug.

• **Pink grapefruit or juniper berry.** Used with massage to encourage lymphatic drainage of toxins and waste. Pink grapefruit is one of Perez's favorites for cancer patients, as she believes it helps energize them and raise their spirits. This and all citrus-type oils should be avoided during chemo and radiation—and should not be used until you've spoken with your doctor.

• **Lemongrass, tea tree and orange.** Mix together into two cups of Epsom salts. Use five drops of each oil—a total of 15 drops—to make soothing bath salts (use one-half cup per bath).

WHAT TO LOOK FOR

Aromatherapy has become so popular that essential oils are now widely available, including in health food stores and supermarkets. However, Perez says that it is far better to purchase them from a shop with a staff knowledgeable in aromatherapy. Oils should come in dark blue or brown glass containers, which prevent light or heat damage. Avoid bottles with rubber droppers—the rubber breaks down and contaminates the oil. Finally, the label should feature both the common and the botanical name of the oil (for example, peppermint/ *Mentha piperita*).

HOW TO TRY IT

If you would like to learn more about how to incorporate aromatherapy in your life, Perez recommends *The Complete Book of Essential Oils & Aromatherapy,* by Valerie Ann Worwood (New World Library), which she says is both thorough and easily understood. Again, as in the case with skin sensitivities, people with asthma or allergies need to avoid things that might trigger an attack—for example, chamomile, which is in the ragweed family.

People who want to try inhalation aromatherapy should use only two or three drops of essential oils in a basin of water or diffuser, or on a napkin. And—always consult with your doctor before using aromatherapy or any complementary therapy.

All Natural Cancer Helper —Too Good to Be True?

Andrew L. Rubman, ND, medical director, Southbury Clinic for Traditional Medicines, Southbury, Connecticut.

We are always on the lookout for new, interesting information on alternative or integrative treatments for health conditions, but something that sounds too good to be true can be a scam. That's why, when a report appeared in the highly respected newsletter *Alternatives* about a relatively new adjunct treatment for cancer called Avemar, we decided to check it out.

BACKGROUND ON AVEMAR

First, a bit of background. A defining characteristic of cancer is its uncontrolled metabolism and rampant cell division. Cancer cells really have only one function—proliferation. In the 1950s, a Nobel Prize-winning Hungarian scientist (named Albert Szent-Györgyi) made great strides in cancer research by examining how naturally occurring compounds could help control metabolism in cells, which in turn controls cell profileration.

Another Hungarian doctor built on Szent-Györgyi's work in the 1990s by showing that fermented wheat germ extract could achieve this effect. Avemar is a fermented wheat germ product.

AVEMAR'S EFFECTIVENESS

Avemar appears to have extraordinary abilities against cancer cells. "The pedigree on this stuff is pretty impressive," says Andrew L.

Rubman, ND. "As of now there are more than 18 published studies in peer-reviewed journals, nearly all of them showing positive results. Research at the University of California, Los Angeles (UCLA) has demonstrated that Avemar reduces glucose flow into cancer cells, which inhibits their ability to reproduce."

Although no one is saying Avemar is a cure for cancer, it has been used as an adjunct to conventional therapies. It seems to be especially effective at reducing metastasis, or the spreading of the cancer to other sites throughout the body. "It seems that Avemar boosts immune system function sufficiently to allow the natural process of the body routinely killing cells to succeed much more effectively" Dr. Rubman says. "It's conceivable that its ability to boost the immune system is the reason it is so effective at reducing the spread of cancer."

WHO SHOULD USE IT

Avemar is now being tested on patients with autoimmune conditions.

In Hungary, Avemar is an over-the-counter dietary supplement that is used by cancer patients in conjunction with other drugs. "In one pilot study in Budapest," Dr. Rubman notes, "a group of patients with advanced colorectal cancer were given Avemar and had no disease progression over nine months." And David Williams, MD, editor of *Alternatives*, has been quoted as saying, "There's absolutely no reason that Avemar shouldn't be used with every single cancer patient—particularly in those with severely impaired immune systems and those who are undergoing conventional therapies."

AVAILABILITY

Avemar isn't cheap, but its benefits seem substantial. It's available under the name of Avé-ULTRA, and contains Avemar. It's sold through the Harmony Company, P.O. Box 567, Valley Cottage, New York 10989, at 800-521-0543 or on the Web at *www.theharmonyco.com*. It comes in packets and is taken as a drink once per day or as prescribed by your oncology team. Of course, don't take Avemar without your doctor's consent.

With such great immune-boosting benefits, can non-cancer patients benefit from Avemar, or even just plain wheat germ? Dr. Rubman says

that eating wheat germ as a general immune booster can be good for many. As for taking Avemar prophylactically, if your health-care adviser believes that your immune system could stand improved function, Avemar may be a reasonable choice.

Veggies Lower Risk for Non-Hodgkin's Lymphoma

Linda E. Kelemen, MSc, ScD, formerly with the department of health sciences research, Mayo Clinic College of Medicine, Rochester, Minnesota. She is currently with the Alberta Cancer Board in Calgary, Canada.

As if you needed one more reason to load up your plate with healthful veggies, a recent study indicates that a higher vegetable intake may lower the risk for non-Hodgkin's lymphoma (NHL). According to Linda E. Kelemen, MSc, ScD, formerly lead researcher and assistant professor of epidemiology at the Mayo Clinic College of Medicine in Rochester, Minnesota, disease-fighting antioxidants in foods such as broccoli and Brussels sprouts may have a protective effect against this dangerous lymphatic system cancer that afflicts 65,000 new people each year.

ABOUT THE STUDY

To determine the association between antioxidants in vegetables and fruits and the risk of developing this type of lymphoma, Dr. Kelemen and her Mayo Clinic colleagues examined the diets of more than 800 American adults with and without NHL. Normal, everyday living can create excess free radicals or oxidants that damage cells and may lead to cancer, explains Dr. Kelemen. She compares it with the development of rust on an unprotected car. Fortunately, eating antioxidant-packed vegetables and fruits protect against damage to cells —just like rust-proofing protects your car.

In the study, researchers found that...

•**People who ate the most vegetables a week** (20 or more servings) had a 42% lower risk for NHL than those who ate the fewest (eight or less servings).

- **Leafy greens such as spinach and green salad and cruciferous vegetables** (Brussels sprouts, broccoli, cauliflower, etc.) provided the greatest protection.

- **Two nutrients in particular, lutein and zeaxanthin** (high in leafy greens, spinach and broccoli), were singled out for their potent antioxidant action.

- **The mineral zinc** (common in certain nuts and seeds) also demonstrated a protective effect against NHL.

While researchers did not uncover any strong link between fruit intake and non-Hodgkin's lymphoma risk, Dr. Kelemen points out that the benefits of eating whole fruits to reduce the risk of other diseases is well known.

These findings were published in the *American Journal of Clinical Nutrition*.

EAT YOUR GREENS

When Dr. Kelemen was asked about dietary supplements, she responded that supplements do not contain the more than 100 antioxidants and phytochemicals found in fresh vegetables and fruit. If needed, they could be taken as an addition to—not as a replacement for—a healthy diet.

Are You Getting Enough Sun?

Krispin Sullivan, CN, an Incline Village, Nevada–based clinical nutritionist, works with clients and researches the literature on vitamin D. She is the author of *Naked at Noon: Understanding the Importance of Sunlight and Vitamin D* (Basic Health).

Andrew L. Rubman, ND, medical director, Southbury Clinic for Traditional Medicines, Southbury, Connecticut.

Everyone knows you should avoid midday sun and always wear potent sunscreen. Or not? Numerous health experts are worried that we have turned into a nation (if not a world) of people suffering from deficiency of vitamin D—the sunshine vitamin. That's a serious issue because studies are emerging at a rapid rate that associate insufficient vitamin D with increased risk for many diseases.

The department of family and preventive medicine at the University of California, San Diego, published a study that showed a striking link between vitamin D deficiency and higher rates of cancer, specifically prostate, colon, breast and ovarian cancer. Another study from the Tufts-New England Medical Center in Boston, based on the long-term Nurses' Health Study (from Harvard in Boston), demonstrated that insufficient amounts of vitamin D and calcium may heighten the risk for type 2 diabetes. It also pointed out other studies that linked insufficient vitamin D to insulin resistance.

Nutritionist and writer Krispin Sullivan, CN, has spent the last several years researching the literature on vitamin D, teaching clients how to get vitamin D safely, and has written a book about sunlight and vitamin D. *Her take on this complex nutrient...*

THE CHEMISTRY OF VITAMIN D

Sullivan says that the vitamin D we make from sunlight or get from food and supplements is actually a prohormone from which our bodies produce *calcitriol*, the active form of vitamin D. The hormone calcitriol is one of the controllers of calcium in our bodies, which is why vitamin D is associated with rickets and osteoporosis. Recent research suggests this metabolite of vitamin D has other profound effects within our cells, regulating numerous cellular body functions, in processes in our skin, hair, muscles, bones and glands. Getting enough vitamin D is vital for good health—but there's a catch. Too much vitamin D is dangerous as well. Excess may cause bone loss, soft tissue calcification and other serious problems.

Deficiencies in children and adults can impair normal bone growth or strength (rickets, osteomalacia and osteoporosis). It is also associated with poor development or a decline in health of the jaw and teeth. In fact, getting enough vitamin D and calcium may prevent cavities and periodontal disease in young and old. Low levels of vitamin D are associated with many autoimmune diseases, obesity and many types of cancer, including breast and prostate.

Getting enough vitamin D in later years has been shown to reduce fractures, maintain muscle mass, keep the immune system strong and improve memory and mood.

THE BEST SUN

The best and safest way to get vitamin D is through carefully regulated exposure to the sun, specifically to UVB rays, the rays of light that stimulate production of vitamin D in our skin. However, excess exposure to ultraviolet light, UVB or UVA is harmful. *Safe and effective sun exposure depends on the following factors...*

•**Location.** UVB decreases as latitude increases. Latitudes below 30 degrees (closer to the equator) have stronger UVB rays most of the day and most of the year. For example, Miami is 25 degrees North latitude, providing UVB most of the day and most of the year...New York is 40 degrees North latitude, with little UVB much of the day and year. Altitude also matters. The higher the altitude, the higher the intensity of UVB.

•**Time of year.** Vitamin D production in the skin requires the presence of sufficient UVB-containing sunlight. In most northern latitudes in the US, that's typically from late April or May until mid-August. Only Florida and some parts of Texas and Arizona, and some locations at higher altitudes have significant, nearly year-round, UVB. To make sunning for vitamin D worthwhile, the UV index really needs to reach 8 to 10. Lower UV index ratings require more exposure.

•**Time of day.** In most of the US the sun provides UVB primarily between the hours of 10:00 am and 2:00 pm, precisely the time most people are inside working or avoiding the sun for fear of sun damage. Yet this is when Sullivan recommends people be in the sun.

•**The amount of time exposed**—very fair-skinned people may need as little as five minutes (front and back), four or more times a week, without sunscreen. Melanin, the coloring agent in our skin, protects against UVB damage, but also increases the time needed to make vitamin D, so those with very dark skin or with suntans need more exposure to UVB to make adequate vitamin D (as much as 90 to 120 minutes a day), according to Sullivan. This could be nearly impossible for many busy people. How much is too much? If your skin turns pink, you've stayed too long.

•**The amount of skin exposed.** There is a substance in the skin, called pre-D, that is converted by UVB into *cholecalciferol*. The amount of pre-D is limited and genetically variable such that only so much vitamin D will be produced in any given skin area within a day. The more skin exposed, the more vitamin D produced. This means exposing small patches of skin for longer periods won't produce more vitamin D. Excess UV exposure, staying longer than you need to make your daily vitamin D, may actually begin degrading vitamin D that has already been produced. Sullivan advises exposing as much skin as possible, especially the back.

•**Vitamin A.** It is also important for vitamin D to be in balance with vitamin A (which, like vitamin D, is converted into an active messenger, regulating cell functions), since the two work together in the body. Sunlight exposure depletes levels of vitamin A in the skin, a nutrient important for skin health and repair, so if you decide sun is especially important to get adequate vitamin A in your diet—in effect, sunning increases your need for vitamin A.

Sullivan advises eating liver—preferably beef, buffalo or venison liver—once a week to assure adequate vitamin A intake, but supplements can do the trick. According to Andrew L. Rubman, ND, typically, the 10,000 international units (IU) of vitamin A found in certain fish oil supplements will provide an adequate daily intake, if combined with sun exposure.

HOW MUCH VITAMIN D IS ENOUGH?

Ideally a person will get enough summer sun to meet vitamin D needs throughout the rest of the year simply by spending regular active time outdoors. Of course, in our increasingly active society that spends an increasing amount of time in front of the computer or television, this is not the case for many. And, in reality, it is virtually impossible for most people to get enough vitamin D naturally.

Getting adequate levels of vitamin D is a particularly complex issue because the only food source with significant levels of vitamin D is the fat of fatty cold water fish and there is considerable disagreement among health professionals about how much vitamin D is safe, whether from supplements, food, the sun or in combination. The Dietary Reference Intakes (DRI) for vitamin D is 200 IU for people under age 50…400 IU for ages 51 to 70…and 600 IU for those over age 70. According to Sullivan's review of the literature, a number of medical professionals are now advocating a routine daily intake of 1,000 IUs of vitamin D for everyone except infants.

If supplementation is appropriate, there are several considerations…

•**How much is right?** The highest safe amount (upper limit of safety, or UL, from the DRI group) is currently considered to be 2,000 IU a day. Sullivan firmly disagrees with the higher figure for most people. Vitamin D stores in fat and builds up over time. An initial high dose may be quite safe for many months, even a year or longer, but then rapidly increases blood levels of vitamin D to levels that may contribute to deposition of calcium in soft tissues, bone loss or heart disease. These changes may take place even when blood levels of calcium remain within normal range. She believes a safer dose would be between 800 and 1,200 IU daily.

•**Regular testing.** Tracking levels of 25(OH)D (25-hydroxy vitamin D) should occur on a regular basis over a long period of time. The safest bet is to work with a trained, licensed health-care professional willing to monitor vitamin D and only supplement vitamin D under his/her watchful eye. The challenge is that vitamin D levels move up and down slowly, over time, and it takes having vitamin D levels tested every three or four months for a clear pattern to eventually emerge and give you information about whether your sun exposure or supplementation is producing the vitamin D level you need. Insurance may cover the cost of the first test, but will probably not cover subsequent tests.

How to Tell If That Lump or Bump Is Cause for Concern

Ellen Warner, MD, MSc, medical oncologist, associate scientist, Odette Cancer Centre, Ontario, Canada.

Childhood is full of lumps and bumps as kids jump, climb, leap—and, yes, fall. But as people grow up and slow down, lumps and bumps become more unusual so any appearance of one can be cause for alarm. Why that peculiar lump on my arm? Why do the glands in my throat seem bigger today? What's the bump on the back of my neck? In truth, lumps and bumps are almost never anything to worry about. But that said, some are definite cause for concern and should prompt a call to the doctor because certain lumps and bumps might signal one of several types of cancer. How do you know what's what? When to worry and when to ignore it and wait for it to go away?

LYMPH NODES ARE KEY

Ellen Warner, MD, who is a medical oncologist and researcher at the Odette Cancer Centre in Ontario, Canada, says the type of lump or bump (or in this case actually a swelling) that is the most common cause for concern has to do with lymph nodes. These nodes exist throughout the body and in numerous locations—the head and neck, under the arms, in the chest and abdomen, in the groin area and in the legs. They also appear in approximately the same place on either side of the body. Lymph nodes are part of the body's immune system and swell in response to any type of infection and inflammation as part of their role in helping to fight it off or resolve it.

However, if a node swells and stays swollen on just one side or in several lymph nodes, and if there is seemingly no reason, such as a sore throat or other recent illness, Dr. Warner cautions that it must be checked out. Cancer of the lymph nodes (as opposed to cancer that metastasizes to nodes from another location) can be one of two types—Hodgkin's or non-Hodgkin's lymphoma. Dr. Warner explains that the difference between the two mostly has to do with cellular structure that shows up under the microscope. But they also have different survival rates. Hodgkin's is the more curable of the two with an 85% survival rate while the non-Hodgkin's rate is 60% after five years. This year it is estimated that there will be about 8,200 cases of Hodgkin's lymphoma diagnosed in this country as opposed to approximately 66,120 of non-Hodgkin's lymphoma diagnosed in the same year. Hodgkin's tends to be more common between ages 15 and 34 and at age 60 and over, though non-Hodgkin's is more common in older adults, 50 plus, and people who have compromised immune systems.

What to watch for: A considerable (not slight) swelling in a lymph node that may or may not be tender or possibly painful on one side, or in several lymph nodes, especially in the neck, and less commonly in the armpits or groin, when there has been no recent illness. Usually the swelling is under the chin, along the side of the neck. While there is no way to detect internal swelling of lymph nodes, there are symptoms such as itching, fatigue, coughing, fever, night sweats, weight loss and chest or abdominal pain, says Dr. Warner.

CANCEROUS BUMPS

Another frightening but even less common cause of dangerous lumps and bumps is cancer of connective tissue, a form of sarcoma called soft-tissue sarcoma. Fortunately, this type of cancer is extremely rare, accounting for less than 1% of malignancies diagnosed in this country each year. However, it can appear in numerous places in the body and is subclassified according to which soft tissue it develops. Do not confuse soft tissue sarcoma with fatty nodules called lipomas, which are benign. These are extremely common, usually appearing just under the skin in the arms, legs and trunk of the body.

Dr. Warner says lipomas are generally round and smooth with what she calls a roly-poly feel to them...they grow slowly and can become quite large, even several inches in diameter, and they are not malignant. Soft tissue sarcomas, on the other hand are almost always malignant and the tumor can grow quickly, most often appearing on the limb. But, it can show up on the abdomen or in other parts of the body as well, including the head, neck and trunk.

What to watch for: A sudden swelling that may or may not be tender or painful, beneath the surface of the skin, usually over a fairly large and diffuse area and a lump that does not have distinct borders. Do not hesitate to see a doctor immediately since the survival rate for soft tissue sarcoma that is diagnosed while the tumor is still small and shallow is over 80%.

CANCER PATIENTS PAY ATTENTION

Finally, Dr. Warner says that anyone who already has cancer should be alert for any lump or bump that appears elsewhere on the body seemingly unrelated to the primary site. As is true with any mysterious lump or bump—one that cannot be explained for ordinary, everyday reasons such as a recent infection or fall—go to the doctor and insist on getting it checked, especially if it seems to grow quickly or change character, or becomes itchy.

No need to panic. Just be aware of your body and its changes. Careful observation can make a big difference in the long run.

Natural Treatment for Cervical Dysplasia

Mark A. Stengler, NMD, licensed naturopathic medical doctor in private practice, Stengler Center for Integrative Medicine, Encinitas, California...adjunct associate clinical professor at the National College of Natural Medicine, Portland, Oregon...author of *The Natural Physician's Healing Therapies* (Bottom Line Books).

It's always a concern when Pap test results are abnormal. That's what happened when Samantha, 66 years old, came to me with a diagnosis of *cervical dysplasia*, an abnormal growth of cells on the surface of the cervix that is commonly caused by human papillomavirus (HPV). She had high-grade squamous intraepithelial lesions (HSIL), which indicate advanced precancerous cells. Three different doctors had told her that she'd need a hysterectomy to prevent cancer of the cervix.

Because low-grade cervical dysplasia often goes away on its own, many doctors wait and see what subsequent Pap tests reveal. When dysplasia is more extensive, as in Samantha's case, doctors frequently recommend destroying the abnormal cells with ablative techniques like *cryocauterization* (freezing), laser therapy or surgically removing affected areas of the cervix or the entire uterus (in the most extreme cases).

I've found that even the most extensive cases of dysplasia can usually be cured through nutritional, herbal and hormonal treatments. Over the past 15 years, I've had success using this approach on dozens of patients. *Here is the 12-week protocol...*

• **Stop using birth control drugs and synthetic hormones** such as estrogen, progesterone, and testosterone (excluding bioidentical hormones).

• **Follow a diet rich in cancer-fighting *carotenoids*** (plant pigments abundant in dark green leafy vegetables, carrots, mangoes, canteloupe, yellow squash, peaches, corn, apricots, tomatoes, red cabbage, berries, plums, and legumes). Avoid trans fats and refined sugars and limit red meat (no more than twice weekly).

Take the following supplements...

• **A daily multivitamin.**

• **Additional folic acid and vitamin B-12.** To maximize the levels of both nutrients, take them in injected form, which patients can do at home after instruction from a physician (2,500 micrograms, or mcg, of B-12 twice weekly and 2,500 mcg of folic acid twice weekly) or in sublingual form, tablets dissolved under the tongue (2,500 mcg of B-12 and 1,000 mcg of folic acid) once daily. (Injection is the more effective way to get these nutrients, although sublingual may be easier.)

• *Indole-3-carbinol* and *diindolylmethane (DIM)*. These phytochemicals in supplement form are found in cruciferous vegetables (such as broccoli, cabbage, Brussels sprouts, cauliflower and kale), which appear to have anti-cancer properties. Take 300 to 400 milligrams (mg) daily of indole-3-carbinol and 200 to 400 mg of DIM daily.

• **Green tea,** in supplement form (which is about 10 times stronger than tea). Take 300 mg daily of a product standardized to 55% *epigallocatechin gallate* (EGCG), a phytonutrient.

• **Immune-booster.** This liquid supplement, called Anti-V, is made by Natural Factors (800-322-8704, *www.naturalfactors.com* for a store locator). It contains antiviral herbs, including *lomatium*, echinacea and *astragalus* to neutralize HPV. Take two capsules twice daily.

• *Conium*, a homeopathic therapy that may reverse cancerous changes in the body. Take two pellets of 30C potency twice daily.

Because Samantha's progesterone levels were low, I prescribed a daily application of *natural progesterone cream* of 20 mg concentration to her inner forearms to promote normal cell division in the cervix.

Retested after 12 weeks, Samantha's Pap test was normal and her HPV test, negative (meaning the virus was no longer active). She was overjoyed with the results. I was as well, especially since if her condition hadn't improved, I would have advised that she have one of the surgical procedures. Samantha will continue to follow the protocol for the next year and will be closely monitored by me and her gynecologist over the next two years.

Recommendation: Use this protocol under the supervision of a physician, especially if you have abnormal Pap test results that indicate advanced precancerous cells. *It is very important that your condition be monitored.* If you have low-grade cervical dysplasia, you can follow this protocol on your own (except for the progesterone cream). Use the sublingual form of folic acid and B-12, instead of the injections). Stay on this regimen while your doctor waits to check your Pap test again. This protocol can also be followed by those who want to prevent cervical dysplasia.

Multivitamins Linked to Chromosome Health

Telomeres, the end portions of chromosomes, protect against chromosome damage, that can lead to cancer, according to a recent study.

Telomeres in women who regularly took multi-vitamins were 5.1% longer—equal to 9.8 fewer years of age-related telomere shortening—than telomeres in women who did not supplement with multivitamins.

Honglei Chen, MD, PhD, investigator, epidemiology branch, National Institute of Environmental Health Sciences, Research Triangle Park, North Carolina, and leader of a study of 586 women.

A Nobel Prize Winner In Medicine Discusses Cancer, Age-Related Disease and More

Carol Greider, PhD, the Daniel Nathans Professor and director of molecular biology and genetics in the Institute for Basic Biomedical Sciences at the Johns Hopkins School of Medicine and one of the winners of the 2009 Nobel Prize in Physiology or Medicine for her discovery of telomerase, an enzyme that maintains the length and integrity of chromosome ends.

More often than not, medical break-throughs require years—if not decades—of arduous research.

Carol Greider, PhD, one of the winners of the Nobel Prize in Medicine, explained how her years of scientific research may affect our ability to fight life-threatening diseases, such as cancer, and treat age-related illnesses.

The research conducted by Dr. Greider, director of molecular biology and genetics in the Johns Hopkins Institute for Basic Biomedical Sciences, advances our understanding of the intricate functions of human chromosomes. These strands of gene-carrying DNA, which are found in the nucleus of every human cell, control the life-giving processes of cellular division and replication.

In 1984, Dr. Greider played a key role in the discovery of *telomerase*, an enzyme that maintains the length of structures, known as *telomeres*, that keep chromosomes intact—much the same way a plastic tip at the end of a shoelace stops it from unraveling. Without telomerase, telomeres would shorten every time a cell divides, leading to the death of the cell.

These discoveries, made by Dr. Greider and two of her colleagues with whom she shares the 2009 Nobel Prize in Medicine, have led to new areas of investigation into controlling cancer (cancer cells may depend on telomerase to divide)…treating age-related diseases (telomeres shorten with age)…and understanding several genetic diseases (caused by dysfunctional telomerase and telomeres).

For insights into the ways that these discoveries may affect human health, Dr. Greider answered these questions…

Which diseases are believed to be caused by shorter telomeres?

Telomerase and telomeres may play a role in several genetic disorders. For example, research at Johns Hopkins has shown that genetic mutations in telomerase may contribute to the development of a progressive and often fatal lung disease called *idiopathic pulmonary fibrosis*, which afflicts approximately 50,000 Americans.

A similar mutation may cause *dyskeratosis congenita*, a disorder in which the bone marrow fails to manufacture healthy blood cells, usually leading to severe skin, nail, oral and lung problems and premature aging.

Why is it important to study these less well-known diseases?

Studying patients with telomere-related genetic disorders will help us treat those diseases and understand the consequences of shorter telomere length in everyone. That's important, because there is a wide variability in telomere length among the general population, with many individuals having shorter telomeres.

Research has linked shorter telomere length to an increased risk for coronary artery disease and heart attacks…and to a shorter life span.

As our scientific and medical understanding of these links increases, shorter telomere length may become a recognized risk factor for a variety of diseases and a target for treatment.

What, specifically, is the role of telomeres and telomerase in the battle against cancer?

In the cancer cell, division and replication is not a healthy, regulated function but an uncontrolled disease.

Scientists think that experimenting with telomerase and telomeres—even experimentally shortening telomeres—may have unexpected and positive effects in cancer treatment.

In my laboratory, for example, we bred mice to have nonoperating telomerase and then mated them with mice bred to develop Burkitt's lymphoma, a fast-growing and deadly cancer of the white blood cells.

The first generation of those mice, which developed lymphoma in seven months, had cancer cells containing long telomeres. But by the fifth generation, telomeres in the cancer cells had shortened—and that generation of mice did not develop lymphoma.

Upon investigation, we found that the mice had started to form microtumors in their lymph nodes, but the cancer cells didn't continue to divide.

This study and others have provided the evidence for researchers to begin human trials.

However, cancer is not one disease but many different conditions—and telomerase inhibitors may not work against every cancer.

A recent study in the journal Lancet Oncology showed that lifestyle factors may increase telomerase activity in people with cancer. What can we learn from that research?

Elizabeth Blackburn, PhD, with whom I shared the Nobel Prize, participated in research on 30 men with prostate cancer.

It showed that three months of intensive lifestyle changes, such as a low-fat, plant-based diet, moderate exercise, stress management and social support, increased telomerase activity by almost 30% in a type of immune cell. This increases the cell's ability to maintain telomere length, which may provide protection against cancer progression.

Dr. Blackburn and the other researchers note that this was a small study and a preliminary finding and is not evidence that lifestyle changes affect telomerase or that increasing telomerase affects cancer. This interesting study is the basis for future research but not yet applicable for practical recommendations about lifestyle changes and telomerase levels.

How should people regard supplements or other products that purport to increase telomere length and extend life?

At present, there is no scientific evidence showing that any supplement or nutritional factor can reliably increase the length of telomeres. Until such evidence is produced, I think people should be wary of such supplements and products.

10

Natural Medicine Cabinet

The Best Healing Herbs

Anyone who has taken prescription drugs is well aware that these medications can be not only costly, but they also can cause a variety of uncomfortable or even dangerous side effects, such as excessive bleeding, headache, nausea and dizziness.

Recently reported problem: A study of 150,000 older adults (who are among the heaviest users of prescription medications) found that 29% were taking at least one inappropriate drug—including medications that were ineffective or even dangerous.

Often-overlooked alternative to drugs: Herbal medicine. Herbs should not be substituted for all prescription medications, but the careful use of medicinal plants can improve overall health and reduce or eliminate the need for some medications—as well as the risks for drug-related side effects.*

*See your doctor before using medicinal herbs—especially if you take any medications, have a chronic medical condition or are pregnant or nursing.

Common conditions—and the best herbal treatments…

CHRONIC BRONCHITIS

More than 5% of Americans suffer from chronic bronchitis (a mucus-producing cough that occurs on most days of the month at least three months of the year).

Best herbal treatment: *Horehound* (leaves and flowering tops). It relaxes the bronchi (airways that connect the windpipe to the lungs) and makes it easier to expel mucus.

How to use: Add 1 milliliter (ml) to 2 ml of horehound tincture (concentrated liquid) to one ounce of hot or cold water. Drink this amount three times daily during bronchitis flare-ups.

Important: Most herbs are available in various forms, such as dry leaf, capsules and

David Hoffmann, a clinical medical herbalist based in Sonoma County, California, a fellow of Britain's National Institute of Medical Herbalists and one of the founding members of the American Herbalists Guild. He is the author of 17 books, including *Herbal Prescriptions After 50* (Healing Arts).

powders, but tinctures are convenient, among the quickest to be absorbed and have a long shelf life.

HEARTBURN

When acid from the stomach backs up into the esophagus, the result is often heartburn (a burning pain behind the breastbone).

Best herbal treatment: *Marshmallow root.* It coats and soothes the esophageal lining.

How to use: Make an infusion by adding one heaping teaspoon of powdered marshmallow root to a cup of cold water and letting it sit at room temperature for 12 hours. Drink the entire mixture when heartburn occurs. If you get heartburn more than three times a week, drink one infusion in the morning and another at bedtime until the heartburn eases. If you make more than one cup in advance, you can refrigerate the unused portion for 24 hours.

Important: Do not use hot water. It will provide only about one-fourth of the soothing mucilage (lubricating substance) of a cold-water infusion.

HYPERTENSION

High blood pressure (hypertension) is among the main causes of heart attack and stroke. Prescription medications usually are required for this condition, but herbal therapy can sometimes allow patients to take lower doses of blood pressure–lowering drugs.

Important: Check with your doctor before trying herbs for hypertension. Because the potential complications of hypertension are serious, everyone with this condition should be under a doctor's care.

Best herbal treatment: *Hawthorn* (berries). This herbal therapy dilates arteries (which allows more blood to circulate with less force) …and strengthens the cardiovascular system, in part by enhancing the activity of cells in the heart muscle. In Germany, hawthorn is widely recommended by doctors for cardiovascular disease.

How to use: Add 1 milliliter (ml) to 2 ml of hawthorn tincture to one ounce of hot or cold water. Drink this amount three times daily.

Alternative: Drink hot tea (two to three times daily) that combines hawthorn with linden flowers, an herb that has a mild anti-hypertensive effect. Such tea bags are available at most health-food stores.

INSOMNIA

Stress, poor sleep habits and health problems that cause pain are common causes of insomnia (an inability to fall asleep or remain asleep).

Best herbal treatment: *Passionflower* (leaves or whole plant). Its depressant effect on the central nervous system helps promote restful sleep.

How to use: Add 1 ml to 4 ml of passionflower tincture to one ounce of cold water, or make an infusion by pouring one cup of boiling water over one teaspoon of dried passionflower and letting it sit for 15 minutes. Drink the entire tincture mixture or infusion at bedtime when you suffer from insomnia.

Caution: People who take drugs with sedative effects, such as certain antihistamines, antianxiety medications and insomnia supplements or drugs, should not use passionflower, which can increase these sedative effects.

IRRITABLE BOWEL SYNDROME

Alternating bouts of constipation and diarrhea are characteristic of irritable bowel syndrome (IBS).

Best herbal treatment: *Yarrow* (leaves and other parts that grow above ground) for the diarrhea phase…*mugwort* (leaves) for constipation. These herbs also are effective for episodes of diarrhea and constipation that are not related to IBS.

Yarrow contains *tannins*, substances that reduce the amount of water released by the intestinal lining. Mugwort is a bitter herb that promotes the intestinal contractions needed for bowel movements.

How to use: Add 1 ml to 2 ml of yarrow or mugwort tincture to one ounce of hot or cold water. Drink this amount three times daily when you have diarrhea or constipation.

OSTEOARTHRITIS

Age-related changes in the joints are the primary cause of osteoarthritis. Most patients can get temporary relief with pain relievers, such as *ibuprofen* (Advil), but these drugs often cause side effects, such as gastrointestinal bleeding.

Best herbal treatment: *Black mustard* (for external use) and *meadowsweet* (for internal use). A poultice of black mustard causes mild, temporary inflammation that stimulates circulation—good for muscle and/or joint pain.

How to use: Make a black-mustard poultice by grinding the seeds in a coffee grinder and mixing one-half cup of the mustard powder with one cup of flour. Add enough hot water to make a paste. Spread the mixture on a piece of heavy brown paper, cotton or muslin that has been soaked in hot water, then cover it with a second piece of dry material. Lay the moist side of the poultice across the painful area, leaving it on for 15 to 30 minutes once daily.

Caution: Consult a doctor before using the poultice on a young child, or on anyone who is age 70 or older or seriously ill.

Meadowsweet is a pain reliever that contains aspirin-like chemicals called *salicylates*.

How to use: Add 1 ml to 2 ml of meadowsweet tincture to one ounce of hot or cold water. Drink this amount three times daily until symptoms subside.

PERIODONTAL DISEASE

Bacterial buildup in the spaces between the teeth and gums leads to periodontal (gum) disease—the most common cause of tooth loss in older adults. Gum infection has been linked to an increased risk for heart attack and stroke. Regular dental care and cleanings (at least annually) are essential.

Best herbal treatment: *Goldenseal and/or myrrh*. Goldenseal acts as a topical antibiotic. Myrrh strengthens mucous membranes. Start treatment when you first notice gum tenderness and/or bleeding—the first signs of periodontal disease.

How to use: Mix equal amounts of goldenseal and myrrh tinctures. Use a very fine paintbrush to apply the mixture to the gum line. Leave it on as long as you can—the taste is unpleasant—then rinse your mouth with water and spit it out. Repeat two or three times daily.

SKIN DRYNESS

Declines in the activity of oil-producing glands make skin dryness a common complaint after age 50.

Best herbal treatment: *Gentian*. It's a bitter herb that stimulates the oil-producing exocrine glands in the skin.

How to use: Add 1 ml to 2 ml of tincture to one ounce of hot or cold water. Drink this amount three times daily, until your skin's condition improves.

Must-Have Herbs for Everyday Aches and Pains

Kathy Abascal, RH, a registered herbalist who practices in Vashon, Washington. A member of the American Herbalists Guild, she is coauthor of *Clinical Botanical Medicine* (Mary Ann Liebert).

U ntil recently, if you peeked inside the medicine cabinet of a typical American household, you were likely to find such items as aspirin for headaches…an anti-inflammatory ointment for sore muscles and joints…an antihistamine for colds—and perhaps even a prescription sedative for sleep problems and/or an antidepressant.

Latest development: With the recent economic downturn and rising drug costs, many Americans are turning to medicinal alternatives. In 2008, nationwide sales of herbal supplements totaled $4.8 billion, up more than 4% from the previous year. Perhaps due to the recession, Americans now appear to be trying many of the same herb-based products that have been used for generations in other parts of the world as the front-line treatments for many common conditions.

How herbs can help you: Compared with many medications widely used in the US, herbal therapies tend to have fewer side effects, are generally just as effective—if not more so—and are often less expensive.*

Seven of the most useful herbs to have on hand in your home…

ECHINACEA FOR COLDS

A study reported that echinacea is not effective for the common cold. Then, later research found that it does help. Does it or doesn't it?

*If you have a chronic condition and/or take prescription medication, consult your doctor before taking herbs.

Echinacea stimulates both white blood cells (which attack viruses) and natural killer cells (which destroy virus-infected cells). Most scientific studies of echinacea involve dosing patients every four to six hours. That's not enough.

How to use: Add about one teaspoon of echinacea tincture to one-half cup of water. Drink it *once every waking hour* at the first signs of a cold until symptoms subside.

Helpful: Add to the mixture one-half teaspoon of elderberry tincture—which also helps boost immunity—for additional antiviral effects.

EUCALYPTUS FOR CONGESTION

Used as an essential oil, eucalyptus penetrates the mucous membranes and promotes drainage—helpful for relieving symptoms caused by the common cold and/or sinusitis (inflammation of the sinuses). The oil also has antimicrobial properties that can inhibit viruses and bacteria.

How to use: At the first signs of a cold or sinusitis, put five to 10 drops of eucalyptus essential oil in a large bowl. Add one to two cups of steaming hot water. (The dose is correct if you can smell the eucalyptus.) Put a towel over your head, and lean over the bowl (with your eyes closed) and breathe in the steam for about 10 minutes. Repeat as needed, using fresh eucalyptus oil each time.

Caution: Keep your head far enough from the steaming water to avoid burning yourself.

TURMERIC FOR JOINT PAIN

Studies show that this extremely potent anti-inflammatory herb is about as effective as nonsteroidal anti-inflammatory drugs—such as aspirin and *ibuprofen* (Advil)—for easing joint pain. Unlike these and similar drugs, turmeric (taken at the doses recommended below) rarely causes stomach upset or other side effects.

How to use: Take 400 milligrams (mg) to 500 mg, three times daily. For additional benefits, use powdered turmeric when cooking. As little as one-quarter teaspoon per recipe will have anti-inflammatory effects over time.

Important: When cooking, use turmeric and black pepper. This greatly increases absorption of turmeric into the bloodstream.

Also helpful: Look for a turmeric supplement formula that includes black pepper.

VALERIAN FOR INSOMNIA

Compounds in valerian act on brain receptors to induce drowsiness and relaxation.

How to use: Take one-half teaspoon of valerian tincture, diluted in water according to the instructions on the label, one hour before bedtime and one-half teaspoon at bedtime, as needed. In small doses—about one-quarter to one-half of the insomnia dose—valerian also can help reduce mild anxiety. Most people avoid valerian tea due to its unpleasant odor.

WHITE WILLOW BARK FOR HEADACHES

It contains *salicin*, a chemical that's converted in the body into *salicylic acid*, an aspirin-like substance. Some studies indicate that white willow bark works as well as aspirin (minus the side effects, such as gastrointestinal upset) for headaches and other types of pain, such as osteoarthritis pain and low-back pain.

How to use: Take 200 mg, twice daily with food for headache and other types of pain (described above).

Caution: If you take a blood thinner, such as *warfarin* (Coumadin), consult your physician before using white willow bark, which also has blood-thinning effects.

ST. JOHN'S WORT TO LIFT YOUR MOOD

It's thought to inhibit the activity of enzymes that break down *serotonin*, a neurotransmitter that plays a key role in regulating mood.

Studies have shown that St. John's wort is as effective for mild to moderate depression as some prescription antidepressants.

St. John's wort also is one of the most effective herbs for treating seasonal affective disorder (SAD), a form of depression that tends to occur in winter.

Caution: Consult your doctor before trying St. John's wort if you take a prescription antidepressant or other medication—or drink alcohol.

How to use: The recommended dose is usually 300 mg, three times daily (standardized to 0.3% hypericin). Consult your doctor for advice on treatment duration.

Helpful: If you suffer from SAD, take 1,000 international units (IU) to 2,000 IU of vitamin D along with St. John's wort. A lack of sun and low levels of vitamin D (also associated with infrequent sun exposure) may be related to depression.

ALOE VERA FOR BURNS

Like an antibiotic cream, the gel from aloe leaves has antimicrobial properties. It soothes painful burns.

How to use: Keep an aloe plant in your home. For minor burns, slice open an aloe leaf and squeeze the gel over the affected area. Store-bought aloe gel also is effective.

Helpful: Keep several aloe leaves in the freezer. The gel from the cold leaves will act as a mild anesthetic.

Spices That Lower Cholesterol, Boost the Brain and More

Ann Kulze, MD, primary care physician and founder and CEO of Just Wellness, LLC, which specializes in corporate and group wellness seminars, Charleston, South Carolina. She lectures widely on the topic of nutrition and disease prevention and routinely recommends the everyday use of disease-fighting herbs and spices. She is author of *Dr. Ann's 10-Step Diet: A Simple Plan for Permanent Weight Loss and Lifelong Vitality* (Top Ten Wellness and Fitness, *www.drannwellness.com*).

Spices and herbs not only boost the flavor of your food, they also boost your health. Powerful plant compounds known as *phytochemicals* are found in high concentrations in many spices and herbs. Phytochemicals help fight heart disease, cancer, Alzheimer's, type 2 diabetes, arthritis and other diseases.

Here are the seasonings to add liberally to your food as often as possible. Unless otherwise noted, fresh herbs and spices offer a higher concentration of phytochemicals, but dried still are powerful.

SUPER SPICES...

The following spices have been shown to be particularly beneficial to our health...

• **Cinnamon.** Cinnamon has an almost medicinal power. Recent studies have shown that cinnamon enhances the metabolism of glucose and cholesterol and thus may provide protection from type 2 diabetes and cardiovascular disease.

A study reported in *Diabetes Care* highlighted cinnamon's favorable impact on the blood fat levels of people with type 2 diabetes. After eating one to six grams (about one-quarter to one-and-one-quarter teaspoons) of cinnamon daily for 40 days, overall levels of unhealthy blood fats dropped significantly—up to 26% for total cholesterol and 30% for triglycerides (a type of blood fat).

Even healthy people can benefit from cinnamon's impact on blood sugar, according to a study in *The American Journal of Clinical Nutrition*. Adding cinnamon to rice pudding significantly decreased the test subjects' normal, post-dessert elevations of blood sugar.

Interestingly, at least some of this effect was related to the spice's ability to delay how quickly food leaves the stomach and enters the intestines. In this regard, cinnamon also may be helpful in reducing appetite and hastening weight loss by enhancing satiety (the feeling of fullness).

Suggested uses: Cinnamon can be added to oatmeal, cereal and yogurt...coffee and tea ...pumpkin and apple dishes...and rice and beans for an Indian touch.

• **Turmeric.** *Curcumin* (turmeric's active ingredient) is one of the most potent, naturally occurring anti-inflammatory agents ever identified and thus may be one of the best all-round spices for disease protection and antiaging. Inflammation plays a central role in most chronic diseases.

Turmeric also can be considered "brain health food." Research studies on mice demonstrate turmeric's ability to reduce the buildup of plaque in the brain that is associated with Alzheimer's and cognitive decline. Laboratory research has shown that turmeric also has potent anticancer properties.

Suggested uses: Add turmeric to your favorite bean, poultry, seafood, tofu and rice dishes, as well as to soups and stews. Turmeric often is used in classic Indian dishes, such as curries.

MORE HEALTH HELPERS

• **Cilantro.** Cilantro is high in the vitamins A and K and beta-carotene, and like any dark, leafy green, it is full of beneficial phytochemicals, including a natural antibiotic called *dodecenal*. In a University of California, Berkeley, laboratory study, dodecenal killed the bacteria *Salmonella* more effectively than a powerful prescription antibiotic.

Suggested uses: Add fresh, chopped cilantro to salsa, guacamole, omelets, salads, soups and stews.

• **Ginger.** Ginger is an anti-inflammatory superstar. It suppresses the action of inflammatory *cytokines* and *chemokines*. And for people plagued with motion sickness or morning sickness or experiencing postoperative nausea and vomiting, ginger—fresh or dried—has proved to be an effective and safe option. The phytochemicals in ginger also are valuable for boosting immunity, especially to combat viral infections.

Suggested uses: Dried powdered ginger is even more potent than fresh. Add it to sauces and salad dressings, or sprinkle it on salad, poultry or seafood. You also can add a thumbnail-sized piece of raw ginger to hot tea. Ginger is delicious in its candied form, and pickled ginger is perfect with sushi.

• **Parsley.** One tablespoon of fresh parsley provides more than half of the daily recommended value of vitamin K. It's also rich in vitamin A, lutein and zeaxanthin (which promote eye health) and provides nature's most concentrated source of *flavonoids*, plant pigments that provide health benefits. Parsley is among those plants that may be particularly useful for combatting cancer, allergies and heart disease.

Suggested uses: Add fresh chopped parsley to salads, pasta and rice dishes, soups and stews. Parsley is a main ingredient in the Mediterranean cracked-wheat dish tabouli.

• **Rosemary.** This savory herb contains phytochemicals that can reduce the formation of cancer-causing compounds known as *heterocyclic amines* (HCAs). HCAs can form when the proteins in meat are heated to high temperatures.

Preliminary research also indicates that rosemary may enhance insulin sensitivity, improving the action and efficiency of insulin in the body, aiding in a healthy metabolism and slowing the aging process. And it turns out that Shakespeare's Ophelia wasn't all that far off when she said that rosemary is for remembrance. According to a study in *Journal of Neurochemistry*, rosemary contains the compound *carnosic acid* (CA), which helps protect the brain.

Suggested uses: I always add one teaspoon of dried rosemary or a tablespoon or two of fresh to a pound of ground meat before grilling burgers. Rosemary also is good in lamb and potato dishes, soups and stews.

Natural Remedies for Four Very Common Health Problems

Laurie Steelsmith, ND, a naturopathic doctor and acupuncturist in private practice in Honolulu. She is the author of *Natural Choices for Women's Health* (Three Rivers). *www.naturalchoicesforwomen.com.*

Chances are you have at least one health problem that you experience regularly—perhaps insomnia, constipation, urinary tract infections or another ailment. While it is tempting to pop a pill and hope that whatever it is will go away, that recurring problem is your body's way of telling you that something is out of balance.

Here are five common complaints and how you can treat the underlying causes using natural, common-sense remedies. All of the supplements mentioned here are sold in health-food stores and are safe for most women—but check with your doctor before taking any new supplements.

ENERGY SWINGS

What it could mean: Too many ups and downs in energy generally point to a diet that is too high in simple carbohydrates—such as white potatoes, white rice, white flour and refined sugar—and too low in fiber and lean protein. With little to slow digestion, your body rapidly processes a meal or snack of simple carbohydrates (such as pancakes and hash browns), causing your blood sugar levels to spike and then quickly crash. *Self-defense...*

•**Eat whole grains instead of simple carbohydrates**—brown rice instead of white rice...oatmeal with fresh fruit instead of a sugary breakfast cereal...popcorn instead of potato chips. The additional fiber prolongs digestion and makes your blood sugar levels less prone to fast-paced highs and lows.

•**Eat more lean protein**—from skinless chicken, lean beef and cold-water fish (such as salmon and mackerel), tofu and beans—which helps to stabilize blood sugar levels.

Helpful: Choose organic poultry, meat and wild fish rather than most farm-raised fish to minimize exposure to environmental toxins, such as pesticides and herbicides.

INSOMNIA

What it could mean: Low levels of *progesterone*, a hormone that has a calming effect. High anxiety levels also may contribute to your sleeplessness.

Self-defense: Try one or more of the following sleep inducers...

•**Help your body to produce more *serotonin*,** a brain chemical that affects mood. Supplement with *5-HTP,* a derivative of the amino acid *tryptophan*, which the body uses to manufacture serotonin. Start at 100 milligrams (mg), taken once daily before bed, and work up to 500 mg over two weeks.

Caution: Don't use 5-HTP if you're taking a selective serotonin reuptake inhibitor (SSRI) antidepressant, such as Prozac, Zoloft or Paxil.

•**Reduce anxiety.** Supplement with *L-theanine*, an amino acid derived from green tea that can produce a noticeable calming effect within 30 minutes of ingestion. Take 200

mg every night at bedtime...and again if you wake up in the middle of the night.

•**Increase your progesterone.** If you're still menstruating each month, you also can talk to your doctor about applying natural progesterone cream—enough to provide approximately 25 mg of progesterone (about one-quarter teaspoon)—each night for 14 nights from mid-cycle until your period starts. If you are postmenopausal, you can apply the progesterone cream for 21 days of the month, then take seven days off.

Note: Possible side effects include nausea, headaches and diarrhea.

DIARRHEA OR CONSTIPATION

What it could mean: A diet high in simple carbohydrates may lead to the overgrowth of "unfriendly" bacteria in the digestive tract... and the imbalance can progress into irritable bowel syndrome, a common condition characterized by diarrhea, constipation or both. *Self-defense...*

•**Eliminate simple carbohydrates from your diet**—such as refined sugar, beer, white flour and white potatoes—and eat more vegetables, lean organic protein and fiber-rich beans, brown rice and whole-wheat bread.

•**Eradicate unfriendly bacteria.** If your symptoms are mild, take garlic—the herb's natural antifungal and antibacterial properties target unwelcome residents of your digestive tract. The first week, eat one clove of raw garlic once a day, or take one 900-mg garlic tablet twice a day. Starting the second week, eat two cloves of raw garlic a day, or take one 900-mg garlic tablet two or three times a day. Continue this regimen until symptoms subside.

Note: Take garlic with meals to avoid stomach upset. To prevent bad breath, use garlic tablets labeled "odorless" or "sociable" and/or eat fresh parsley after taking the garlic.

•**Supplement with probiotics.** Two weeks after the garlic treatment is finished, restore balance to your digestive tract by adding "friendly" bacteria. Take a probiotic supplement that provides a total of one billion live organisms per day for at least one month.

Recommended probiotic brands: Natren and Theralac.

CHRONIC YEAST INFECTIONS

What it could mean: Overgrowth of yeast in your digestive tract may cause an overgrowth of yeast in your vagina. Often this is triggered by eating too much sugar—yeast's favorite meal. *Self-defense...*

• **Cut off yeast's food supply.** Follow the previous diet recommendations given for diarrhea or constipation.

• **Use a tea tree oil–based douche** to target vaginal yeast.

Note: Do this only if you know you have a yeast infection. Make your own douche by adding 10 drops of tea tree oil to one pint of water. Using a douche bag (sold at drugstores), douche while sitting on the toilet or standing in the shower twice a day for one week.

• **Reduce unfriendly bacteria and yeast throughout your body.** Take a probiotic supplement that provides one billion live organisms daily for at least one month.

URINARY TRACT INFECTIONS

What it could mean: Dehydration, excessive stress or a low estrogen level due to menopause can allow bacteria to take up residence in the urinary tract. *Self-defense...*

• **Drink water.** Aim for at least 48 ounces of filtered water daily to encourage the elimination of bacteria from the urinary tract.

• **Empty your bladder** as soon as you feel the urge and as completely as possible to evacuate bacteria before they can thrive.

• **Drink 10 ounces of unsweetened cranberry juice daily** to prevent bacteria from attaching to the lining of the urethra (the tube that empties urine from the bladder).

Also: You can take six cranberry capsules daily instead of juice, or follow the label for cranberry extract.

• **Boost your estrogen levels.** If the problem persists, speak to your doctor about using a low-dose prescription vaginal estrogen cream, which strengthens the tissue of the vulva and urethra, making you more resistant to infection.

Cures in Your Cupboard

Joan Wilen and Lydia Wilen, folk-remedy experts, New York City, and coauthors of many books, including *Secret Food Cures* (Bottom Line Books).

We expect to find help for our ailments at the health-food store or the drugstore. But for a surprising number of conditions, help is as near as your kitchen cupboard. Joan Wilen and Lydia Wilen have been collecting, researching and testing folk remedies for more than two decades—and all their remedies have been reviewed for safety by medical doctors, naturopathic doctors and other experts.

Bonus: You might even save a few pennies in the process—having to turn no further than your own kitchen. If you have an existing health condition, check with your physician before trying any of these remedies.

Get help for these minor conditions from the kitchen...

BAD BREATH, GUM DISEASE AND TOOTHACHE
Coconut oil, baking soda

Coconut oil can soothe ailments of the mouth, such as bad breath, gum disease and toothache. For help with any of these conditions, brush your teeth with a mixture of one-eighth teaspoon of baking soda and one-half teaspoon of organic extra-virgin coconut oil (which you can find at a health-food store). Sore gums also are helped when you rub them with coconut oil.

BUMPS AND BRUISES
Lemon

Most bruises that turn black and blue go away on their own, but you can speed the healing process—and reduce both the swelling and the bruising—with this Mayan remedy. Cut a lemon in half, and rub the pulpy side over the bruise once an hour for several hours. Avoid any cuts or breaks in the skin.

CONSTIPATION
Lemon, honey, prune juice, prunes, papaya, apples, dried figs

Drinking water on an empty stomach can stimulate bowel movements. Before breakfast,

211

drink the juice of one-half a lemon in one cup of warm water. If it is too tart, sweeten it with honey. If that doesn't help move your bowels, try one of the following—prune juice (at room temperature, not chilled) or stewed prunes, papaya, two peeled apples or six to eight dried figs. (Soak the figs overnight in water. In the morning, drink the water, then eat the figs.)

DIARRHEA
Milk, allspice, cinnamon, powdered cloves

There are several remedies from other countries that use milk. A West Indian remedy is one cup of milk (or warm water) with a pinch of allspice. The Pennsylvania Dutch recommend one cup of warm milk with two pinches of cinnamon. A Brazilian remedy includes two pinches of cinnamon and one pinch of powdered cloves in one cup of warm milk. (Do not drink milk if you are lactose intolerant. It may cause diarrhea.)

HEADACHE
Green tea, mint

Fatigue, anxiety and stress can trigger headaches. For fast relief, brew one cup of green tea and add sprigs of fresh mint. You can use either spearmint or peppermint. If you don't have fresh mint available, use a peppermint or spearmint tea bag. Combine a bag each of green tea and mint tea to make a powerful brew that will diminish your headache in about 15 minutes.

INDIGESTION
Grapefruit, potato

If you are prone to any of the unpleasant symptoms of indigestion, including stomachache or nausea, you can prepare this remedy in advance to have at the ready. Grate the peel of a grapefruit, and spread the pieces out on a paper towel to dry overnight. Store the dried peel in a lidded jar. When you feel the first signs of indigestion, eat one-half-to-one teaspoon of the grated peel. Chew thoroughly before swallowing.

Another remedy: Raw potato juice can neutralize stomach acid. Grate a potato, and squeeze the gratings through a piece of cheesecloth or a fine strainer to get the juice. Take one tablespoon of potato juice diluted with one-half cup of warm water. Drink slowly.

INSOMNIA
Whole nutmeg, grapefruit juice, yellow onion

Nutmeg can work as a sedative. Crush a whole nutmeg, and steep it in hot water for 10 minutes. Drink it 30 minutes before bedtime. Or drink a glass of pure, warmed grapefruit juice. If you prefer it sweetened, use a little bit of raw honey. Or cut a yellow onion and put it in a glass jar. Keep it near your bed. When you can't sleep, or if you wake up and can't fall back to sleep, open the jar and inhale deeply. Close the jar. Close your eyes, think lovely thoughts and you'll fall back to sleep.

MEMORY PROBLEMS
Carrot juice, milk, fresh ginger, sage tea, cloves

For mild memory problems, try this memory-improving drink. Mix one-half glass of carrot juice with one-half glass of milk—and drink daily. Or use daily doses of fresh ginger in cooking or in tea. Ginger is known to improve memory. Or brew one cup of sage tea, and add four cloves. Drink daily. Sage and cloves are believed to strengthen memory.

POISON IVY/OAK/SUMAC
Banana skin, lemon, garlic, tofu

These remedies can help ease the itching and redness of poison ivy. Rub the inside of a banana skin directly on the affected skin. Use a fresh banana skin every hour for a day. (Freeze the leftover banana pieces to use in smoothies or to eat on hot days.)

Or slice one or two lemons, and rub them on the area. This helps to stop the itching and clears the skin. Or chop up four cloves of garlic, and boil them in one cup of water. When the mixture is cool, apply it with a clean cloth to the area.

Another remedy: Apply mashed up pieces of tofu directly on the itchy area—and hold them in place with a cloth or bandage. This should cool off the area and help any poison ivy flare-up.

SINUS PROBLEMS
Tomato juice, garlic, cayenne pepper, lemon juice

When your sinuses feel clogged and uncomfortable, this bracing drink can help. Combine one cup of tomato juice, one teaspoon of freshly chopped garlic, one-quarter-to-one-half teaspoon of cayenne pepper (according to your tolerance for spicy food) and one teaspoon of lemon juice. Heat the mixture until it is warm but not too hot to drink. Drink it slowly, and it should help clear up sinuses quickly.

KITCHEN CURES SHOPPING LIST

Keep your kitchen stocked with these ingredients—and you'll have homemade remedies and cures at the ready!

- **Allspice**
- **Apples**
- **Baking soda**
- **Banana** (skin)
- **Carrot juice**
- **Cayenne pepper**
- **Cinnamon**
- **Cloves**
- **Cloves** (powdered)
- **Coconut oil**
- **Figs** (dried)
- **Garlic**
- **Ginger**
- **Grapefruit**
- **Grapefruit juice**
- **Green tea**
- **Honey**
- **Lemon**
- **Lemon juice**
- **Milk**
- **Nutmeg** (whole)
- **Onion** (yellow)
- **Papaya**
- **Potato**
- **Prune juice**
- **Prunes** (stewed)
- **Spearmint or peppermint**
- **Sage tea**
- **Tomato juice**
- **Thyme**
- **Tofu**

Improve Your Health With Honey

Jamison Starbuck, ND, naturopathic physician in family practice in Missoula, Montana. She is a past president of the American Association of Naturopathic Physicians and a contributing editor to *The Alternative Advisor: The Complete Guide to Natural Therapies and Alternative Treatments* (Time-Life).

As a physician, I've long known of the medicinal benefits of honey. Even though skeptics dismiss honey's beneficial effects as little more than a placebo, current research supports its medicinal properties. For example, studies conducted at the University of Illinois and the University of California confirm that honey is a potent source of antioxidants—those much-touted healthful substances found in some foods, such as fruits and vegetables, that defend against disease-causing free radicals. Typically, the darker the honey, the higher the antioxidant content, according to these scientists. Buckwheat honey is among the best. However, high levels of antioxidants are also present in light honey, depending on the crop. I recommend adding one to two tablespoons daily to tea or hot cereal—or eat it directly off a spoon.

Caution: If you are diabetic, eat no more than one teaspoon daily. Do not give honey to children under age one. Honey can contain trace amounts of deadly *botulinum toxin*, which cannot be eliminated by an infant's digestive system.

Honey also can be used as a topical antiseptic for cuts, scrapes, surgical incisions and fungal infections, such as athlete's foot or a red, flaky, fungal inflammation of the ears or eyelids. Honey is acidic and does not provide the nutrients that bacteria and fungi need for growth. Clinical studies focusing on honey derived from the flowers of the New Zealand/Australian manuka tea tree (*Leptospermum scoparium*) show that it is effective even against antibiotic-resistant *Staphylococcus aureus*. If you want to use honey as a topical antiseptic, apply it three times daily as you would an antibiotic or antifungal cream. Always monitor skin lesions for any sign of infection, such as swelling, redness, discharge, heat or pain. If any of these occur, see your doctor.

Because of its antiseptic properties, honey is an excellent remedy for upper respiratory ailments, such as sore throat or laryngitis. You can speed your healing from these conditions —even strep throat—by drinking tea liberally dosed with honey, which also has a soothing effect. Add two tablespoons of honey to a cup of tea and drink at least three cups daily throughout the course of a sore throat or upper respiratory ailment.

Eating local honey is an effective treatment for pollen allergies. Start by eating one tablespoon of honey daily in early March (or six weeks before pollen season in your area) and continue throughout the allergy season.

213

Honey also can be used to naturally preserve the nutritional value of food. For example, researchers have found that honey extends the storage time of meats and slows the browning of cut fruit. Substitute honey for sugar when you make a fruit salad, or add it to green salad or veggie dressings. Use honey glazes on roast meats.

And don't worry about gaining weight from honey use. Because it is rich in enzymes and nutrients, it is a very satisfying food. My patients find that when they regularly use honey instead of sugar, a little bit goes a long way.

The Buzz About Apis

Mark A. Stengler, NMD, naturopathic medical doctor in private practice, Encinitas, California…adjunct associate clinical professor at the National College of Natural Medicine, Portland, Oregon…author of *The Natural Physician's Healing Therapies* (Bottom Line Books).

Apis (pronounced aye-pis) is a remedy that is derived from the honeybee—the stinger as well as the whole bee. Think of the symptoms that a bee sting causes such as stinging, burning, swelling and itching. These are all the symptoms for which apis is beneficial. So a homeopathic doctor may recommend it for bee stings, allergic reactions including hives, arthritis, urinary-tract infections, kidney disease, herpes, sore throat and ovarian pain.

Apis is indicated when symptoms include a lack of thirst, a negative response to heat, and a positive response to cold applications.

Recommendations for…

•**Allergic reactions.** Allergic reactions that cause hives or burning and stinging pains that move around the body can be improved quickly with apis. Apis also improves other symptoms of allergic reaction such as swelling of the throat and eyes. These could be allergic reactions to food or to drugs.

Note: Seek emergency medical treatment for allergic reactions, especially if you start to have trouble catching your breath.

•**Arthritis.** If you have swollen joints that burn or sting—and if your joints feel better after applying cold compresses—then the condition can probably be alleviated with apis.

•**Bee stings.** Apis quickly relieves the pain of a bee sting. This is proof of the homeopathic principle that "like cures like." Take it as soon as possible after getting stung to prevent swelling and other symptoms from getting severe. It is a remedy that should be in your home first-aid kit.

•**Herpes.** Apis is a common remedy for herpes infections. Herpes of the mouth—cold sores that sting and burn and that have a vesicle formation—improves quickly with apis. This also applies to the acute treatment of genital herpes.

•**Kidney disease.** Apis is used in acute kidney disease such as glomerulonephritis or nephritic syndrome where there is protein loss in the urine and edema of the body.

•**Meningitis.** Symptoms include a stiff neck, high fever and dilated pupils. Homeopathic apis is most effective in patients whose symptoms are made worse when heat is applied. This remedy can be used in conjunction with conventional treatment.

•**Ovarian pain.** Apis is specific for right-sided ovarian cysts where there is burning and stinging pain. It not only reduces the pain, but also stimulates dissolving of the cysts.

•**Shingles.** Apis is one of the primary homeopathic medicines for shingles, especially when there is stinging or burning. Apis helps to relieve the pain and heal the shingles.

•**Sore throat.** Apis is very effective for relieving a sore and swollen throat, especially when the sore throat has specific characteristics. Those characteristics include a burning pain (that feels better when you have a cold drink) and a bright red, swollen uvula (the flap of tissue in the middle of the mouth).

•**Toxemia in pregnancy.** Apis is a good remedy for toxemia in pregnancy where there is protein in the urine, high blood pressure and lots of body swelling.

• **Urinary-tract infections.** Urinary-tract infections can be helped by apis. This is particularly true for bladder infections that cause scalding pain during urination. If you have a right-sided kidney infection, it's another indication that this remedy will probably work well.

Dosage: For acute conditions such as a bee sting or allergic reaction, I recommend taking the homeopathic formulation with a 30C potency every 15 minutes for two doses. Then wait and see if the remedy is helping. The other option is to take one dose of a higher potency such as a 200C.

For skin rashes, sore throats and other conditions that are not so acute, I recommend taking a 6C, 12C, or 30C potency twice daily for three to five days, or as needed for continued improvement.

What are the side effects? Side effects are not an issue with apis. It either helps or there is no effect at all. It is also safe to use for children.

Comfort in a Cup: Healing Herbal Teas

Brigitte Mars, adjunct professor of herbal medicine at Naropa University in Boulder, Colorado. She is a professional member of the American Herbalists Guild, host of the radio show *Naturally* and author of *Healing Herbal Teas* (Basic Health). *www.brigittemars.com.*

Herbal teas help soothe pain, ease stress and treat disease—more economically and with fewer side effects than drugs.

For convenience: Use tea bags.

For potency: Use loose organic herbs (sold in health-food stores).

Instructions: Boil eight ounces of water. Remove from heat. Stir in one heaping tablespoon of dried herbs or three level tablespoons of fresh herbs. Steep 10 minutes. Remove tea bag or strain off loose herbs. Drink hot or iced. Have two to three cups daily until symptoms subside...then one cup every few days to maintain health.*

CHAMOMILE TEA EASES...

• **Insomnia**
• **Gastrointestinal upset**
• **Inflammation**

How it works: It has mild sedative properties to calm nerves...stimulates production of digestive fluids...and may inhibit metabolism of *arachidonic acid*, an inflammatory omega-6 fatty acid.

Keep in mind: Steep no longer than three to five minutes to prevent bitterness. Discontinue two weeks before any surgery. Do not use if you are allergic to ragweed, celery or onion or take blood-thinning drugs.**

GINGER TEA EASES...

• **Nausea, motion sickness, and morning sickness**
• **Colds and flu**
• **Pain** (sore throat, arthritis, migraine)

How it works: It stimulates secretion of digestive fluids...reduces congestion and inflammation...and bolsters the immune system. It also reduces risk for blood clots.

Keep in mind: Steep it in hot (but not boiling) water. Discontinue two weeks before any surgery. Do not use if you have heartburn, ulcers or gallbladder problems or take blood-thinning or diabetes drugs.

GINSENG TEA EASES...

• **Low energy**
• **Low libido**

How it works: It boosts the immune system ...increases the body's resistance to stress... and contains *phytosterols* (steroid-like plant chemicals) that may promote proper hormone function.

Keep in mind: For best effect, drink between meals. Discontinue two weeks before any surgery. Do not use if you take blood-thinning or diabetes medication...or have a history of breast cancer.**

*Some herbs can interact with drugs or cause allergic reactions. Always consult your doctor before using herbal tea, *especially* if you have heart disease, diabetes, ulcers, gallbladder problems, a bleeding or seizure disorder, or a kidney or liver disorder, or if you are anticipating surgery.

**Do not use if you are pregnant or breast-feeding.

NETTLE TEA EASES...

- **Arthritis pain**
- **Bloating**
- **Allergies, asthma**

How it works: It reduces inflammation... acts as a *diuretic*...and may deactivate *mast cells* (which release histamine, a chemical that provokes mucous membrane hyperactivity).

Keep in mind: It is best to use *dried* nettle —the fresh plant can cause a stinging rash. Discontinue if it causes gastrointestinal upset. Do not use if you have any problems with blood sugar.**

PASSIONFLOWER TEA EASES...

- **Anxiety**
- **Stress**
- **Drug or alcohol withdrawal**

How it works: It may slow the breakdown of calming neurotransmitters...and it has sedative effects.

Keep in mind: It is slightly bitter, so add honey or agave nectar for a sweeter taste. Do not use with blood-thinning drugs or with sedating medication (sleeping pills, certain antihistamines, or painkillers).**

PEPPERMINT TEA EASES...

- **Stomach upset**
- **Bad breath**

How it works: It increases circulation to the digestive tract...improves flow of digestive fluids...calms intestinal spasms...suppresses mouth chemicals that contribute to bad breath.

Keep in mind: It is safe to use when pregnant or breast-feeding. Do not use if you have a hiatal hernia or gallbladder problems.

**Do not use if you are pregnant or breast-feeding.

A Soothing Cup to Fight Your Cold

Chamomile tea is great for colds and other ailments. Drinking at least five cups a day increases *phenolics*, which help the body fight colds...and boosts levels of *glycine*, which helps soothe muscle spasms and fights stress. Chamomile tea also may help relieve menstrual and other cramps.

Caution: Chamomile can cause a severe reaction in people who are allergic to ragweed.

Andrew L. Rubman, ND, medical director, Southbury Clinic for Traditional Medicines, Southbury, Connecticut.

Scents that Heal

Alan Hirsch, MD, founder and neurological director of the Smell & Taste Treatment and Research Foundation in Chicago. A neurologist and psychiatrist, he has published more than 300 articles on smell and taste disorders and is author of eight books, including *Life's a Smelling Success* (Authors of Unity). *www.smellandtaste.org*.

Aromatherapy safely eases many ailments, my research shows, by triggering release of brain chemicals that affect physical and emotional well-being.

Best: Hold a food, flower, essential oil or naturally scented toiletry one-half inch away from your face and level with your lips. Inhale for three minutes...take a five-minute break... repeat up to two dozen times.

ANXIETY

Try: Lavender.

It may work by: Increasing the alpha brain waves that promote a relaxed, meditative state.

To use: Inhale lavender essential oil...light a lavender-scented candle...or place a lavender eye pillow over your eyes.

FATIGUE

Try: Jasmine.

It may work by: Boosting the beta brain waves that improve alertness.

To use: Close one nostril with a finger and deeply inhale a jasmine oil or jasmine-scented toiletry...repeat with other nostril. Continue alternating for five minutes. This single-nostril technique prolongs the effects.

HEADACHE

Try: Green apple (sliced).

It may work by: Triggering the release of brain chemicals, such as endorphins and serotonin, that inhibit pain sensations and alleviate tension.

To use: To reduce migraine or tension-headache pain and duration, inhale the apple scent as soon as you feel a headache coming on. This seems to work best for people who like the smell of green apple.

LOW LIBIDO

Try: Good & Plenty candies plus cucumber or banana.

It may work by: Stimulating the arousal centers of the female brain, reducing inhibitions and promoting alertness.

To use: Best results are achieved by simultaneously smelling the candy and either of the other foods—so hold both up together.

MENOPAUSE-RELATED MEMORY PROBLEMS

Try: Flowers.

It may work by: Acting on the connection between the olfactory nerve and the parts of the brain involved in memory.

To use: Whenever you want to retain new information, smell mixed scents to increase learning speed. Try a bouquet of fragrant mixed flowers or a floral-scented perfume.

MENSTRUAL CRAMPS

Try: Green apple (sliced) plus any personal favorite scent.

It may work by: Easing muscle contractions (the apple)…and lifting mood.

To use: Select an aroma you particularly enjoy—a favorite scent helps to banish the blues by distracting you from pain.

OVEREATING

Try: Banana or green apple (sliced) or peppermint essential oil.

It may work by: Stimulating the satiety center of the brain that registers when your stomach is full.

To use: To reduce food cravings, deeply inhale three times in each nostril, alternating sides. Alternate among fragrances monthly to help prevent weight-loss plateaus.

SADNESS

Try: Baked goods.

It may work by: Evoking happy memories of childhood.

To use: Bake or buy a favorite pie, cake or other fragrant treat—the aroma alone will help you feel better. If your diet permits, take a few bites for an extra boost in mood.

Herbs that Boost Your Immunity

Kathy Abascal, RH, a registered herbalist who practices in Vashon, Washington. A member of the American Herbalists Guild, she is coauthor of *Clinical Botanical Medicine* (Mary Ann Liebert).

While scientists are furiously working to develop a vaccine and/or drug treatment to help protect us against the world's next major influenza outbreak, many herbalists believe that potentially effective natural medicines already exist.

Within the last century, three influenza pandemics—in 1918, 1957 and 1968—killed millions of people worldwide. Medical science has changed dramatically since the outbreaks, but a little-known yet highly effective approach to treating the flu of 1918 may prevent people from contracting the illness during a future outbreak—or help aid in recovery if they do become sick.

NEW LESSONS FROM OLD RESEARCH

In 1918 and 1919, a strain of influenza dubbed "the Spanish flu" (in part because it received the most press coverage in Spain, which was not preoccupied with World War I) circled the globe and resulted in not just one, but two (and in some places three) waves of deadly illness. The Spanish flu and its associated complications, including pneumonia and pleurisy (inflammation of the covering of the lungs), killed as many as 50 million people worldwide.

Some people received what were then believed to be the most progressive and scientific conventional treatments available—mercury, strong laxatives, aspirin, arsenic, quinine and a mixture of ipecac and opium called Dover's powder. According to the Centers for Disease Control and Prevention, more than 2.5%, or 25 out of every 1,000 people treated conventionally, died.

Surveys from the period show that patients given herbal remedies used by a nationwide group of physicians who called themselves the "Eclectics"—because they practiced "eclectic" medicine (what we today might call herbal or alternative medicine)—died at a rate of 0.6%, meaning that six out of every 1,000 who received these botanical treatments died.

Who documented this huge disparity? At the onset of the Spanish flu outbreak, John Lloyd was a respected pharmacist, plant extract researcher, past president of the American Pharmaceutical Association, and owner, with his brothers, of Lloyd Brothers, a Cincinnati, Ohio–based distributor of pharmaceutical botanicals.

In 1919—when the Spanish flu pandemic was on the wane—Lloyd conducted a survey of 222 physicians who had purchased his company's herbal products, asking which ones they had used to treat influenza and pneumonia, how the products were administered and which of the treatments they considered to be the most effective.

Respondents listed more than 40 botanical treatments, including *gelsemium* (the dried root and rhizome of the yellow jasmine plant native to the Southeastern US), *echinacea* (purple coneflowers that are native to Midwestern North America), aconite (a bluish flowered herb of the buttercup family) and boneset (a white-flowered plant native to Eastern North America).

Most of the Eclectics practiced "specific medication," treating the flu by addressing each individual patient's specific symptoms —respiratory illness, fever, coughs, vomiting, fatigue, etc. This approach differed from that of conventional doctors, who treated every influenza patient basically the same with purgatives, quinine, aspirin and Dover's powder, regardless of the individual's symptoms.

INCREASE YOUR IMMUNITY

A number of herbal medicines can be used to strengthen the immune system.

The herbs listed below are generally safe and are widely available at health-food stores.* Good manufacturers that offer these herbs include Herbalist & Alchemist (*www. herbalist-alchemist.com*) as well as HerbPharm (*www.herb-pharm.com*).

Adaptogens are herbs used to balance the immune system. They work slowly, so they should be started six to eight weeks before the flu season (typically November to April) and continued throughout that period. Also, adaptogens can be used as needed for general immunity strengthening to help fight colds and other respiratory ailments.

Take one of the following…

•**Ginseng.** Chinese or Asian ginseng (*Panax ginseng*) and American ginseng (*Panax quinquefolium*) have been used for centuries to fight fatigue and increase immunity. Siberian ginseng, or eleuthero (*Eleutherococcus senticosus*), has similar properties but is not a member of the ginseng family.

Immune-boosting dosage: Chinese or Asian ginseng: 5 milliliters (ml) to 10 ml of tincture daily…*American ginseng:* 3 ml to 5 ml of tincture three times daily…*Siberian ginseng:* 3 ml of tincture three times daily.

•**Ashwagandha** (*Withania somnifera*). Ashwagandha has been used for more than 4,000 years in India to treat and fight infectious diseases and immune system disorders.

Immune-boosting dosage: 3 ml of tincture three times daily.

•**Astragalus** (*Astragalus membranaceus* and related plants). Though little research has been conducted on this herb in the West, it has been used here since the 1800s to strengthen the immune and respiratory systems.

Immune-boosting dosage: 4 ml to 8 ml of tincture three times daily.

THE ECLECTICS' FLU TREATMENT

Herbs used by the Eclectics to treat influenza included echinacea (*Echinacea purpurea*,

*Check with your health-care provider before using these herbs, especially if you are taking prescription medications, such as blood thinners or drugs to treat high blood pressure or diabetes. Pregnant and nursing women, in particular, should be especially careful to consult a professional before using herbs.

Echinacea angustifolia and *Echinacea pallida*) and boneset (*Eupatorium perfoliatum*). Echinacea traditionally is used to boost immune functioning at the onset of a cold or flu, while boneset is used to reduce fever and relieve aches and pains caused by the flu.

Dosage: For echinacea, mix one ounce of tincture in four ounces of water and take one teaspoon every waking half hour for up to 14 days. For boneset, mix 1 ml to 2 ml in one ounce of warm water and take every one to two waking hours.

USING HERBS SAFELY

The American Herbalists Guild (617-520-4372, *www.americanherbalistsguild.com*) and the American Association of Naturopathic Physicians (866-538-2267, *www.naturopathic.org*) can help you find a qualified practitioner of herbal medicine in your area. Like all medicines, some herbs can be harmful if taken in the wrong quantities or combinations.

Amazing Folk Remedies for Colds, Coughs, Flu, More

Joan Wilen and Lydia Wilen, folk-remedy experts, New York City, and coauthors of many books, including *Bottom Line's Healing Remedies: Over 1,000 Astounding Ways to Heal Arthritis, Asthma, High Blood Pressure, Varicose Veins, Warts and More!* (Bottom Line Books), from which this article is adapted.

Not every winter illness requires a trip to the doctor's office. The following time-tested folk remedies offer effective, inexpensive treatments for minor health complaints.

Important: Consult your doctor if your condition persists or grows worse.

COLDS

The average adult contracts between two and four colds each year, mostly between September and May. *Medical science has no cure for these highly contagious viral infections, but the following folk remedies can help* ward off colds, ease symptoms and possibly shorten a cold's duration...

• **Garlic.** Garlic contains *allicin*, which has been shown to reduce the severity of a cold. Eat four cloves of freshly crushed raw garlic three times a day until you have recovered.

• **Cinnamon, sage and bay.** Cinnamon contains compounds believed to reduce congestion. Sage can help sooth sore throats. Some Native American cultures have used bay leaves to clear breathing passages. Steep one-half teaspoon each of cinnamon and sage with a bay leaf in six ounces of hot water. Strain and add one tablespoon of lemon juice. Lemon helps reduce mucus buildup. If you like your tea sweet, add honey.

• **Chicken soup.** The Mayo Clinic has said in its health newsletter that chicken soup can be an excellent treatment for head colds and other viral respiratory infections for which antibiotics are not helpful.

FLU

Influenza is a potentially serious viral infection. People often mistake colds for the flu. Colds take hold gradually and are not usually accompanied by severe aches or a fever. The onset of the flu is sudden, and symptoms include fever, severe muscle aches and fatigue.

• **Garlic and cognac.** A shot of cognac is a popular flu remedy in Germany, where it's thought to ease symptoms and help the body cleanse itself. Garlic helps clear mucus, among other potential benefits. Peel and dice a half-pound of garlic. Add one quart of 90-proof cognac, and seal the mixture in an airtight bottle. Store in a cool, dark place for two weeks. Strain out the garlic, and rescal the liquid in the bottle. Prepare a new batch each year.

To treat the flu: Add 20 drops to eight ounces of water. Drink three glasses a day, one before each meal.

For prevention: Use 10 to 15 drops, instead of 20, per glass in flu season.

Important: This treatment is not advisable for people who have drinking problems or for children.

• **Sauerkraut.** Sauerkraut's concentration of lactic acid bacteria may weaken infections. Have two tablespoons of sauerkraut juice or about one-half cup of sauerkraut each day during flu season to reduce the chances of infection.

SORE THROATS

Experiment with these remedies until you find what works best for you...

•**Apple cider vinegar.** Vinegar is a powerful anti-inflammatory, and its acidity might help kill the bacteria that cause some sore throats. Add two teaspoons of apple cider vinegar to six ounces of warm water. Gargle with a mouthful, spit it out, then drink a mouthful. Continue this until the mixture is gone. Rinse your mouth with water to prevent the vinegar from eroding your teeth. Repeat the vinegar gargle every hour for as long as your sore throat persists.

•**Sage.** Sage is an anti-inflammatory. Add one teaspoon of dried sage to one six-ounce cup of boiling water. Steep for three to five minutes, strain, then gargle and swallow.

•**Lemon and honey.** Honey coats the throat, while lemon can temporarily reduce the mucus buildup that often accompanies a sore throat. Squeeze one lemon, add a teaspoon of honey and drink. Repeat every two hours.

•**Tongue stretching.** Stick out your tongue for 30 seconds, relax it for a few seconds, then repeat four times. This is believed to increase blood flow to the throat, speeding the healing process.

COUGHS

Try these folk remedies to figure out which works best for you...

•**Lemon, honey and olive oil.** Honey and olive oil coat and soothe, while lemon reduces mucus. Heat one cup of honey, a half cup of olive oil and the juice of one lemon over a medium flame for five minutes. Turn off the heat, and stir for two minutes to blend the ingredients. Consume one teaspoon of the mixture every two hours.

•**Vinegar and cayenne pepper.** Cayenne pepper contains *capsaicin*, a proven painkiller, while vinegar serves as an anti-inflammatory. Add a half cup of apple cider vinegar and one teaspoon of cayenne pepper to one-half cup of water. Add honey if desired. Take one tablespoon when your cough acts up and another tablespoon before bed.

•**Horseradish and honey.** Horseradish can help loosen mucus, while honey coats the throat. Grate one teaspoon of fresh, peeled horseradish into two teaspoons of honey. Consume one teaspoon every two to three hours.

•**Ginger.** Ginger is an anti-inflammatory that contains gingerols, which provide pain-reducing and sedative benefits. Chew a piece of fresh, peeled gingerroot when you feel the cough acting up, usually in the evening before bed. Chew until the ginger loses its kick.

•**Licorice root tea.** Licorice relieves the pain of irritated mucous membranes. Drink licorice root tea as long as your cough persists.

Note: Don't try licorice root if you have high blood pressure or kidney problems.

Meet the Amazing Medicinal Mushroom

Mark Blumenthal, founder and executive director, American Botanical Council, Austin, Texas, and editor, *HerbalGram* and *HerbClip. www.herbalgram.org.*

Many mushrooms have strong healing powers. Compounds in various mushrooms have been shown to enhance immunity, fight off infections and cancer, and lower blood sugar and blood pressure. Among the most popular "medicinal mushrooms" is the maitake (*Grifola frondosa*), which is not only tasty but prized—particularly in Asian cultures—for its healing abilities.

To learn more about this versatile fungus, we consulted Mark Blumenthal, founder and executive director of the American Botanical Council in Austin, Texas. He tells us that maitake can be used by healthy people as well as those with health issues such as a compromised immune system, with no significant risk of adverse side effects. While incorporating mushrooms into the diet is always a good idea, maitake in the form of dietary supplements packs considerably more punch.

IMMUNE ENHANCEMENT AND MORE

The number-one use for maitake lies in boosting immune system function, though it has also been used for certain specific ailments. According to Blumenthal, some cancer patients use maitake-based preparations as part of their natural treatment regimens in order to reduce the adverse effects of chemotherapy drugs. Additionally, maitake has demonstrated the ability to increase *apoptosis*, the natural programmed death of old, worn-out cells that acts as a check against their becoming cancerous. (Cancer cells proliferate instead of undergoing apoptosis.) Maitake also has been shown to improve cardiovascular-related parameters such as blood pressure, cholesterol and glucose (blood sugar) levels.

HOW TO TAKE MAITAKE MUSHROOMS

Maitake preparations can be taken with vitamins and certain other dietary supplements, usually in the morning and evening or with meals. They are typically sold as liquid extracts, capsules or tablets containing dried maitake extract powder, says Blumenthal. Blumenthal recommends taking the "D-fraction standardized maitake," so indicated on the packaging, because it has the most powerful immune-stimulating activity, according to much of the published research.

Dosage depends on the intended use and the form of the product, notes Blumenthal. Given the power of maitake and the potentially severe conditions that it can be used for, it is best to work with a holistic physician, herbalist or other trained professional when starting a supplementation regimen. *Blumenthal notes that research shows that maitake can be used as an adjunct therapy for...*

•**High blood pressure and/or cholesterol levels.**

•**High blood sugar levels** associated with diabetes or metabolic syndrome.

•**Increased immune function** to help prevent colds and flu.

•**Supplementation to chemotherapy.**

NO SIDE EFFECTS BUT...

To Blumenthal's knowledge, there are no significant adverse side effects or drug interactions associated with the use of maitake mushroom preparations when used as directed. Still, as noted above, with serious diseases such as diabetes or cancer or high blood pressure, it is always best to add a trained alternative or conventional physician to your treatment team before taking dietary supplements. This is especially important if you are taking prescription medications for any of the above conditions.

Cranberry as Effective As an Antibiotic

Mark A. Stengler, NMD, naturopathic medical doctor in private practice, Encinitas, California...adjunct associate clinical professor at the National College of Natural Medicine, Portland, Oregon...author of *The Natural Physician's Healing Therapies* (Bottom Line Books).

Researchers in Scotland looked at the effectiveness of cranberry extract compared with the antibiotic *trimethoprim*, which is commonly used to prevent recurring urinary tract infections (UTIs). Participants, who had had at least two antibiotic-treated UTIs in the previous 12 months, were given a daily dose of either 100 milligrams (mg) of trimethoprim or 500 mg of cranberry extract.

Result: Those who took the cranberry extract had a recurrent UTI infection 84.5 days (following the last one), on average, while those taking trimethoprim had their next infection 91 days later. Those taking trimethoprim had more adverse effects, including rash and itching.

My view: For women prone to UTIs, taking cranberry extract makes more sense than antibiotic therapy. Long-term use of antibiotics contributes to antibiotic resistance. It also rids the body of healthful bacteria. This study used a cranberry extract known as Cran-Max, available at drugstores and select retailers in the US (*www.cranmaxinfo.com*). You may not get the same results with other cranberry juices or supplements.

Home Remedies for Vaginal Yeast Infections

Elizabeth G. Stewart, MD, assistant professor of obstetrics and gynecology, Harvard Medical School, Boston.

To make your vagina less hospitable to yeast, swallow one capsule daily of a probiotic with *lactobacillus* bacteria, such as Culturelle (800-722-3476, *www.culturelle.com*).

Also: Use one of the following remedies for one to two weeks. Wrap one peeled garlic clove in a two-by-two-inch piece of grade-10 cheesecloth. Insert it into your vagina and leave it there for 24 hours, then remove with your fingers and replace with a fresh clove and cloth.

Or: At a pharmacy or online, buy empty size-00 capsules and boric acid powder. Fill capsules with powder. Insert one capsule daily *into the vagina*—it will dissolve within an hour. Do *not* swallow it—boric acid is toxic if taken orally.

Immediately discontinue any home remedy that worsens irritation. If itching or discharge persists after two weeks, see your doctor.

11

Natural Mind Boosters

The Most Powerful Brain-Building Nutrients & Herbs

You open your cupboard but then can't recall what you wanted... you're introducing two friends and suddenly draw a blank on one's name.

Such instances of "brain fog" are common, but they are not an inevitable part of aging. Many people remain remarkably sharp all their lives—and the right nutritional strategies can help you be one of them.

Cognitive declines can result from hormonal changes and reductions in neurotransmitters, chemicals that help brain cells communicate with each other. Increasing your intake of certain nutrients helps balance hormones and protect neurotransmitters. *You can get these nutrients from...*

• **Foods.** Eating brain-boosting foods is an ideal way to get needed nutrients.

Reasons: The body is designed to absorb nutrients from foods rather than from isolated or manufactured chemicals (such as in supplements)...and foods contain complementary components that enhance nutrient absorption.

• **Herbs.** The healthful aromatic oils are most active when herbs are fresh, but dried herbs also will do.

• **Supplements.** These are an option if you cannot find the foods that provide certain nutrients, or if you need specific nutrients in quantities beyond what you typically get from food. Unless otherwise noted, the following supplements generally are safe, have few side effects and may be used indefinitely. All are sold at health-food stores.

Maoshing Ni ("Dr. Mao"), PhD, DOM (doctor of oriental medicine), LAc (licensed acupuncturist), chancellor and cofounder of Yo San University in Los Angeles, and codirector of Tao of Wellness, a clinic in Santa Monica, California. He is author of 12 books, including *Second Spring: Dr. Mao's Hundreds of Natural Secrets for Women to Revitalize and Regenerate at Any Age* (Free Press). *www.taoofwellness.com.*

223

Important: Ask your doctor before supplementing, especially if you have a health condition…use medication…or are pregnant or breast-feeding. To reduce the risk for interactions, do not take supplements within 30 minutes of medication…and limit your use of these supplements to any four of the following.

NUTRIENTS YOUR MIND NEEDS

For the foods recommended below, one serving equals four ounces of meat, poultry, fish, or soy products…eight ounces of milk…two ounces of nuts…two eggs (with yolks)…one-half cup of vegetables or fruit…and one cup of leafy greens.

•**Choline.** The neurotransmitter *acetylcholine* plays a key role in learning and memory. Choline is a precursor to acetylcholine that is produced in the liver. Production of choline declines with age, as does the body's ability to efficiently use the choline that remains.

Brain boost: Eat one or more servings daily of choline-rich broccoli, cauliflower, eggs, kidney beans, navy beans, liver, milk or peanuts.

Supplement option: 1,200 milligrams (mg) daily.

•**DMAE** (*2-dimethylaminoethanol*). The body uses fatty acids to create brain cells and neurotransmitters. DMAE, a chemical in fatty acids, helps produce acetylcholine.

Brain boost: Have two servings weekly of DMAE-rich anchovies or sardines. If fresh fish is not available, have canned water-packed sardines or anchovies and rinse before eating to reduce salt.

Supplement option: 500 mg twice daily after meals.

•**L-carnitine.** Mitochondria are the engines of cells. The amino acid *L-carnitine* transports fatty acids to mitochondria for use as fuel and provides nutrients to brain cells.

Brain boost: Have two weekly servings of lamb or poultry, which are rich in L-carnitine.

Supplement option: 500 mg to 1,000 mg before breakfast and again in the afternoon.

•**Vitamin B-12.** This is key to red blood cell formation and nerve cell health. The body's ability to absorb vitamin B-12 diminishes with age—about 10% to 15% of people over age 60 are deficient in it.

Brain boost: Have two servings weekly of beef or lamb…halibut, salmon, sardines or sea bass…eggs…or vitamin B-12–enriched soybean products (miso, tempeh).

Supplement option: 500 micrograms (mcg) to 1,000 mcg daily.

THE MOST HELPFUL HERBS

An easy way to get the benefits of mind-sharpening herbs is to brew them into a *tisane*, or herbal infusion—more commonly called herbal tea.

To brew: Pour eight ounces of very hot water over one heaping tablespoon of fresh herbs or one teaspoon of dried herbs. Steep for five minutes, strain and drink.

Convenient: To reduce the number of cups needed to meet the daily recommendations below, brew two or more herbs together.

•**Chinese club moss.** This herb contains the chemical *huperzine A*, which helps conserve acetylcholine.

Brain boost: Drink one to two cups of Chinese club moss tea each day.

Supplement option: 50 mcg of huperzine A twice daily (discontinue if supplements cause gastric upset or hyperactivity).

•**Ginkgo biloba.** This herb increases blood flow to the brain's tiny capillaries and combats DNA damage caused by free radicals.

Caution: Do not use ginkgo if you take blood-thinning medication, such as *warfarin* (Coumadin).

Brain boost: Drink three cups of ginkgo tea daily.

Supplement option: 120 mg daily.

•**Kitchen herbs.** Oregano, peppermint, rosemary and sage have oils that may increase blood flow in the brain and/or support neurotransmitters, promoting alertness.

Brain boost: Use any or all of these herbs to brew a cup of tea for a pick-me-up in the morning and again in the afternoon.

Also: Use herbs liberally when cooking.

Supplement option: About 150 mg each of any or all of these herbs daily, alone or in combination.

•**Mugwort (wormwood).** This herb improves circulation, aiding delivery of nutrients to brain cells.

Brain boost: Twice a week, drink one cup of mugwort tea...add a half-dozen leaves of fresh mugwort to salad...or sauté leaves with garlic or onions.

Supplement option: 300 mg daily.

Caution: Avoid mugwort during pregnancy —it may stimulate uterine contractions.

DON'T FORGET: GREEN TEA

Strictly speaking, an *herb* is a flowering plant whose stem above ground does not become woody. In that sense, the leaf of the *Camellia sinensis shrub*—otherwise known as tea—is not an herb. Yet green tea (which is less oxidized than black) is so helpful that it must be listed among the top brain boosters.

Along with antioxidant *polyphenols*, green tea provides the amino acid *theanine*, which stimulates calming alpha brain waves and improves concentration. Green tea also has been linked to a reduced risk for Alzheimer's disease.

To brew: Pour eight ounces of very hot water over one teaspoon of loose, fresh green tea leaves (or a tea bag if fresh is not available) and steep for three to five minutes. You needn't strain the tea. As you empty your cup, you can add more warm water to the remaining leaves—as long as the water turns green, the tea still contains polyphenols.

Brain boost: Drink three cups of green tea (caffeinated or decaffeinated) daily.

Supplement option: 350 mg of green tea extract daily.

Natural Ways to Power Up Your Brain

Daniel G. Amen, MD, psychiatrist, brain-imaging specialist and CEO and medical director of Amen Clinics, Inc., headquartered in Newport Beach, California. *www.amenclinics.com*. He is assistant clinical professor of psychiatry and human behavior at University of California, Irvine School of Medicine. Dr. Amen is author of 23 books, including *Magnificent Mind at Any Age* (Harmony).

Y ou can improve your memory, energy, productivity and general well-being throughout your entire life by developing everyday habits that are good for your brain...

• **Get exercise that requires quick movements.** Exercise increases blood flow to the brain, ensuring a healthy supply of oxygen and the nutrients on which the brain depends. Insufficient blood flow can lead to poor coordination and difficulty processing complex thoughts.

Exercise also increases the supply of *brain-derived neurotrophic factor* (BDNF), a protein that helps with the creation of new cells.

A recent study of people in their 70s found that those who exercised moderately or vigorously at least once a week were 30% more likely to maintain their cognitive skills than people who exercised less often.

Any type of exercise is good, but the ideal exercise for a healthy brain combines an aerobic workout with complex movements requiring quick reactions.

Examples: Dancing, tennis, table tennis, racquetball and juggling.

• **Eat berries, beans and salmon.** *Be sure that your diet includes...*

• Fruits and vegetables. Antioxidants in fruits and vegetables fight damage from free radicals—unstable molecules that damage cells, contribute to aging and promote inflammation, which is a factor in Alzheimer's disease. Berries are particularly rich in antioxidants.

• Complex carbohydrates—such as cooked dried beans and whole grains. The brain uses sugar as its main energy source. Complex carbohydrates release sugar slowly. In contrast, white bread and other refined starches and sugars cause dramatic spikes and drops in blood sugar, leading to concentration problems and fatigue.

• Cold-water fish. Any lean protein, including chicken and lean pork, helps build neurons. Salmon, cod and other cold-water fish have the added benefit of providing omega-3 fatty acids, which play an important role in maintaining nerve cell membranes. Other sources of these healthy fats are avocados, nuts and olive oil.

• **Boost vitamin D.** Vitamin D is believed to play a role in mood and memory. A recent study published in *Journal of Geriatric Psychiatry and Neurology* found a possible association between dementia and low levels of vitamin D.

The best source of vitamin D is sunlight—at least 15 minutes a day without sunscreen. If you spend most of the day indoors or live in a northern latitude, take a supplement with 400 international units (IU) of vitamin D daily.

•**Avoid food additives,** such as *monosodium glutamate*, and artificial sweeteners, such as *aspartame*. Though studies are inconclusive, anecdotal evidence suggests that these additives may have a hyperstimulating effect, causing confusion and/or mood swings.

•**Limit caffeine and alcohol.** Caffeine and alcohol reduce blood flow to the brain, depriving cells of nutrients and energy. Both can interfere with sleep, which is essential to healthy brain activity.

Both also can be dehydrating—the brain is 80% water, so anything that dehydrates has the potential to cause problems in thinking.

One or two cups of coffee or tea a day are harmless and enhance alertness, but heavy caffeine consumption—more than 500 milligrams (mg) to 600 mg a day, or about four to seven cups of coffee—should be avoided.

Alcohol has additional dangers—it blocks oxygen from reaching cells' energy centers and reduces the effectiveness of neurotransmitters involved in learning and memory. Heavy drinkers—people who consume four or more alcoholic drinks a day—have a higher risk for dementia.

Some people drink wine daily because of evidence that it may be good for the heart. However, there are other ways to help the heart—such as exercise and diet—that don't put the brain at risk. If you are accustomed to having a drink every day, consider cutting back to one or two drinks a week.

•**Avoid airborne toxins.** Fumes from paint, pesticides and other chemicals have been associated with brain damage. If you are exposed to strong fumes—for example, while painting the interior of your house or having your nails done—be sure that the area is well-ventilated.

•**Don't smoke, and avoid being in rooms where others are smoking.** Oddly, smoking can make you feel smarter by stimulating the release of neurotransmitters that improve reaction reaction time, but nicotine constricts blood vessels, reducing blood flow and depriving the brain of nutrients.

•**Don't overdo electronic interaction.** Computers, mobile devices and other electronic tools can interfere with optimal brain function in several ways. They have an addictive quality, stimulating release of the neurotransmitter *dopamine*, which acts on the brain's pleasure centers. Over time, greater amounts of dopamine are required to get the same pleasurable feeling.

E-mail and text-messaging can interfere with concentration, encouraging a state of mind that is alert to the next distraction, rather than focused on the task at hand. One study at London University found a temporary IQ loss of 10 points in people who constantly checked for messages during the day.

Best: Process e-mail and text messages at set times of day, not as each message comes in. Take frequent breaks away from the computer.

•**Protect your skull.** The brain is very soft. The hard skull that covers it has many ridges that can damage the brain during trauma. Yet people are astonishingly careless with this precious organ.

Take precautions to protect yourself from head injury. Stabilize ladders carefully. Use nonslip mats in the bathtub and shower. Keep the floor in your house and the pathways outside it clear of debris that could cause you to trip and fall. If you bicycle or ski, be sure to wear a helmet.

•**Manage stress.** Long-term exposure to high levels of the stress hormone *cortisol* is associated with a smaller-sized *hippocampus* —the brain area involved with memory—and with poor performance on memory tests.

Cope with stress by finding daily activities that calm you, such as exercise, meditation, prayer or yoga. During difficult times, focus on what you are grateful for and talk things out with someone who can help you keep an optimistic perspective.

Memory Loss Linked to Low Levels of "Good" Cholesterol

When 3,673 men and women were followed for seven years, researchers found that those with low levels of high-density lipoprotein (HDL) "good" cholesterol (less than 40 milligrams per deciliter) at age 60 were 53% more likely to experience memory loss than those with high HDL levels (60 mg/dL or higher).

To increase HDL levels: Exercise regularly ...do not consume trans fats...and replace saturated fats with monounsaturated fats, such as olive oil, whenever possible.

Archana Singh-Manoux, PhD, senior research fellow, French National Institute for Health and Medical Research, Saint-Maurice, France.

Mediterranean Diet Aids the Aging Brain Says Study

Nikolaos Scarmeas, MD, associate professor, neurology, Columbia University Medical Center, New York City.
Gary Kennedy, MD, director, geriatric psychiatry, Montefiore Medical Center, New York City.
Alice Lichtenstein, DSc, Gershoff Professor of Nutrition Science and Policy, Tufts University, Boston.
Archives of Neurology.

Chalk up another endorsement for the so-called Mediterranean diet: The eating regimen, which is rich in fruits, vegetables, fish and olive oil, may help the brain stay sharp into old age, a new study suggests.

Following the healthful diet reduced the risk of getting mild cognitive impairment—marked by forgetfulness and difficulty concentrating. And it also cut the risk of developing Alzheimer's disease if cognitive impairment was already present, said study lead author Nikolaos Scarmeas, MD, an associate professor of neurology at Columbia University Medical Center in New York City.

The study was published in the *Archives of Neurology.*

Previous research has found that people who follow the Mediterranean diet are at less risk of developing a variety of diseases, including heart disease, cancer and Parkinson's disease.

THE STUDY

The Columbia researchers evaluated nearly 1,400 people without cognitive impairment and 482 people with mild cognitive impairment, and then followed them for an average of 4.5 years. The participants—average age 77—also completed a food frequency questionnaire, detailing what they had eaten during the past year.

The researchers divided the participants into three groups—those who adhered regularly to the Mediterranean diet, those who adhered moderately to it, and those who adhered somewhat or not at all. Then they evaluated the participants' cognitive functioning.

STUDY RESULTS

The researchers found that the diet helped prevent both mild cognitive impairment and also the risk of further decline, even if people weren't entirely strict in their adherence to the diet.

"As compared to the group that ate very little or not at all of the Mediterranean diet, those who ate it to a moderate degree had 17% less risk of developing mild cognitive impairment," Dr. Scarmeas said. "Those who adhered a lot had a 28% less risk of developing mild cognitive impairment."

The diet also helped those who already had mild impairment. "Compared to those who adhered not at all or very little, those who ate the Mediterranean diet to a moderate degree had a 45% reduction in risk of going from mild cognitive impairment to Alzheimer's disease. Those who adhered a lot had a 48% reduction in risk of going from mild cognitive impairment to Alzheimer's," he said.

Dr. Scarmeas said previous research he conducted found that a greater adherence to the Mediterranean diet was associated with a lower risk of Alzheimer's disease.

THEORY

It's not known exactly how the diet may help keep the brain healthy, Dr. Scarmeas said. One possibility is that it might reduce inflammation, which plays a role in brain disease. Or it might work by improving cardiovascular risk factors, such as high cholesterol, he said.

EXPERT PERSPECTIVES

"You see what is called a dose response. The more stringently you follow the Mediterranean diet, the better the outcome," noted Gary Kennedy, MD, director of geriatric psychiatry at Montefiore Medical Center in New York City.

Alice Lichtenstein, DSc, Gershoff Professor of Nutrition Science and Policy at Tufts University in Boston, said, "It's encouraging to see the results—those reporting the healthier dietary pattern seem to do better." What remains to be seen, she added, is whether it was the specific diet that helped people avoid cognitive decline or if those people who ate properly had other healthy habits that decreased their risk.

All three experts agreed: Until more evidence is in that the Mediterranean diet keeps brains sharp, there are plenty of other reasons to follow it, including heart health.

To learn more about the Mediterranean diet, visit the Women's Heart Foundation Web site, *www.womensheart.org/content/nutrition/medi terranean.asp*.

Leafy Greens Help Your Mind Stay Sharp

People who eat lots of green vegetables, such as spinach, kale and collard greens, have a 40% slower rate of mental decline than people who eat less than one serving per day.

Best: Aim for at least three one-cup servings of leafy green vegetables every day to protect memory and thinking speed.

Martha Clare Morris, PhD, associate professor, department of internal medicine, Rush University Medical Center, Chicago, and leader of a study of 3,718 people ages 65 and older, published in *Neurology*.

How to Streamline Your Life

Leo Babauta, author of *The Power of Less* (Hyperion). He created and runs the popular Internet blog ZenHabits (*www.zenhabits.net*), which has more than 137,000 subscribers and two million visitors a month. *Time* magazine selected the blog as one of the 25 best of 2009.

When you imagine what it means to have "a full life," what comes to your mind? Is a full life about being busy all the time, with ever-increasing choices and complexity? If so, you must be very happy in today's culture, where on any given day, there are an infinite number of places to go, things to do, messages to absorb and objects to buy.

Or do you think a full life is something else—something simpler, but maybe something that you can't immediately put your finger on?

What you may be sensing, instinctively, is that slowing down has its benefits. In fact, most people would be more content if they streamlined their lives, figuring out how to live with less (fewer commitments, fewer possessions, less worry) and instead spent their time, money and energy on what's most satisfying to them.

Streamlining your life does not mean just sitting around and getting little done. In simplicity, there is profound power. When you set limits this way—focusing on what is essential and meaningful to you and eliminating the rest—you stop letting others decide what your life should be. You make life move at your pace without feeling frustrated, old or deprived. *To streamline your life and become happier...*

• **"Audit" your daily life to figure out your true priorities.** Start by making a list of all your ongoing commitments—large ones and small ones—to people, activities, possessions and goals. *Examples...*

• You've committed to a weekly night out with friends.

• You're on a planning committee for an upcoming event.

• You wash your car once a week and maintain it once a month.

• You go walking for 40 minutes each weekday in order to lose weight.

For each of the commitments you list, ask yourself…

• How important is it to me?

• Is it in line with my life priorities and values?

• How would it affect my life if I dropped it?

These are sometimes tough questions, and the answers may not be apparent until you experiment—try eliminating an activity for a couple of weeks, and see how you feel.

Example: I used to spend nights watching TV, justifying this activity by saying that it relaxed me. When I stopped, I realized that all the advertisements on TV had actually been making me discontented and pushing me to spend money on frivolous items.

• **Say "no" more often.** Accepting new social commitments to family, friends and organizations takes up more time than we realize. They add up and up until we're allowing other people's priorities to run our lives. Even when a commitment will bring you little joy, it's difficult to say no because you feel obligated and imagine feeling guilty if you don't do it. *To break out of this trap…*

• Get perspective on your guilt. Most requests that you turn down would only minimally inconvenience other people. Truly important requests, of course, you are always free to commit to.

• Validate the other person's request if you turn it down. Be honest but gracious, and the other person is less likely to feel hurt. For example, say, "I appreciate you thinking of me. Unfortunately, I just can't do it—I have other priorities and I don't want to commit to something I can't follow through on."

• **Make a to-do list each day, but keep it short.** I used to make long lists of what I "had" to accomplish each day. I wound up doing the fun, easy tasks first in order to check off as many items as possible but usually ran out of time before completing the most important, time-sensitive or challenging tasks. The result? I did a lot of things…but never felt productive.

Much better: Now, I limit myself to three critical tasks daily and I do them early in the morning. I get fewer things done every day, but I am far more productive because the things I do are much more important to do on that day.

For example, my three critical tasks today are: 1) Write my daily post for my Web site. 2) Customize the design for a new Web site that I'm launching. 3) Help a nonprofit organization redesign its Web site.

Of course, I still do less time-sensitive tasks if I have time left over, but I try to save them up and do similar ones in batches to be more efficient, including returning phone calls… reading and responding to e-mails…running general errands…and house chores.

• **Do one thing at a time.** These days, people assume that doing several things at once—so-called multitasking—is the best way to get things done. In fact, it is a horrible way to get things done.

Example: I used to talk on the phone with a friend while eating my lunch and paying bills at the same time.

Result: I did a poor job at all these tasks—my friend could sense my lack of interest in the conversation, I didn't really enjoy or savor my food and I would make mistakes writing checks.

Much better: Bring your full concentration to one task at a time. If it's an enjoyable activity, you'll really enjoy it. If it's just a chore, you'll get it done quickly and accurately. Your life will be less complicated and less stressful.

• **Use the time you free up to do what's important to you**—otherwise, you'll fritter away the time. For instance, since I no longer watched TV at night, I decided to go to bed much earlier and rise before dawn each day to engage in a morning ritual I love—reading a book in the quiet and solitude before the rest of the family rises. Cutting down on my work projects has also allowed me to spend more time with my kids. And I've taken the time I used to commit to after-work projects, such as serving on various committees, to have regular dates with my wife.

More from Leo Babauta…

No-Stress Way to Pay Bills

It's amazing how people let the simple, predictable chore of paying monthly bills create so much stress, with paperwork getting lost, deadlines being missed and mad dashes to the post office.

I used to think that waiting to pay all my bills once a month was efficient and financially advantageous, since it allowed my money to sit in an interest-bearing account a bit longer each month.

Reality: Whenever you create such a "system" to simplify your life, it's important to do what's easiest in practice, not theory. For me, the longer a bill sits around, the easier it is to forget about or lose. And just one late-payment penalty can negate several years of extra interest you might earn by waiting until the last minute to pay.

So now, I keep my checkbook and stamps handy and pay each new bill with the next day's mail. It's quick and easy—and there's never any stress.

Breakthrough Jellyfish Treatment Makes You Smarter Within Days

Mark A. Stengler, NMD, naturopathic medical doctor in private practice, Encinitas, California...adjunct associate clinical professor at the National College of Natural Medicine, Portland, Oregon...author of *The Natural Physician's Healing Therapies* (Bottom Line Books).

S cientists have found that a naturally occurring protein in one of the planet's oldest sea creatures—the jellyfish—might hold the key to improved memory and comprehension. The substance, *apoaequorin* (a-poh-ee-kwawr-in), found in the *Aequorea victoria* jellyfish species, has a unique way of working in the brain that is different from other natural memory enhancers. Many of my patients already are benefiting from it. Apoaequorin not only seems to reverse some of the effects of aging on the brain but also might help alleviate the effects of serious neurodegenerative diseases such as Alzheimer's

disease, Parkinson's disease and ALS (Lou Gehrig's disease).

THE JELLYFISH CONNECTION

Scientists first discovered apoaequorin and its companion molecule, *green fluorescent protein* (GFP), in the Aequorea jellyfish, found off the west coast of North America, in the 1960s. The natural glow of GFP enables researchers to observe microscopic processes within cells that were previously invisible, such as how proteins are transported or how viruses enter cell membranes. Apoaequorin, which binds to calcium and becomes luminescent once it does, has been used since the 1990s in a similar way to track the activity of calcium in the body's cells. In 2008, three researchers who played key roles in developing these chemical markers were awarded the Nobel Prize in Chemistry.

Apoaequorin's value as a memory-boosting supplement also depends on its calcium-binding properties but in a different way. In the brain, calcium plays an important role in the chemical process that allows nerve cells to recharge before firing. It has to be present in just the right amounts. If too much calcium builds up inside a nerve cell, it interferes with the nerve-firing process and causes the cell to die. One of the key roles of calcium-binding proteins is to prevent the toxic buildup of calcium by removing excess calcium from the nerve cells.

In the normal course of aging, beginning at around age 40, the number of calcium-binding proteins in our brain cells starts to decline, resulting in the gradual buildup of toxic calcium inside these cells. This leads to impaired cellular function and eventually brain damage as the toxic calcium kills off brain cells. The symptoms of this age-related deterioration start slowly but then accelerate as we get older.

Because apoaequorin is similar to the naturally occurring calcium-binding proteins in the brain, the theory is that by taking daily supplements, you can replace the calcium-binding proteins that are lost through the aging process—allowing your brain cells to function optimally again while also preserving them from the long-term toxic effects of excess calcium.

A "EUREKA" MOMENT

The jellyfish protein went from "scientific" discovery to "supplement for the brain" because of the efforts of Mark Underwood, cofounder of the biotech firm Quincy Bioscience, the company that makes Prevagen (888-565-5385, *www.prevagen.com*), the only commercially available form of apoaequorin. Underwood's "eureka" moment came when he was reading about an Australian swimmer who developed multiple sclerosis–like symptoms after being stung by a jellyfish. Underwood wondered what protected the jellyfish from its own venom…and whether apoaequorin's calcium-binding abilities could have neuroprotective properties.

His company conducted a number of studies in conjunction with the University of Wisconsin–Milwaukee that found that apoaequorin did seem to have a powerful protective effect on brain cells. In one study, 56 people ranging in age from 20 to 78 showed significant improvements in memory after taking 10 mg of Prevagen daily for 30 days. More than half the group reported gains in general memory and information retention…two-thirds did better at word recall…and 84% showed improvement in their ability to remember driving directions.

Most of my patients and others report that taking Prevagen helps them feel mentally sharper, improves their memory and gives them more mental energy. Some even say that their mood is enhanced and that they sleep more soundly.

HOW TO USE IT

Prevagen is best taken in the morning (because cognitive function is more important during the day than at night), with or without food. I recommend it for anyone over age 40 who wants to improve memory and focus. While 10 mg daily is the recommended starting dose, apoaequorin also is safe at higher doses. I recommend that my own patients who have suffered a noticeable decline in cognitive function start out with 10 mg daily for four weeks. If they don't notice an improvement in memory and focus, they can increase to 20 mg daily. Most of my patients benefit from taking 10 mg or 20 mg daily. Research has shown that Prevagen is safe to take with other memory-enhancing supplements, such as omega-3 fish oils, or medications, such as *donepezil* (Aricept). People with allergies to fish or shellfish can use it because jellyfish is neither. The manufacturer of Prevagen is exploring apoaequorin's potential as a medical treatment for conditions such as Alzheimer's disease and Parkinson's disease. I plan to stay informed, but for now, it's a good choice for those who need safe, natural memory support.

Eating Fish Improves Memory

According to a recent study, men and women between the ages of 70 and 74 who ate an average of more than 10 grams (0.35 ounces) of fish daily scored better on memory, visual conception, attention, orientation and verbal fluency tests. The effect was stronger as fish consumption increased to as high as 80 grams (2.8 ounces) per day.

A. David Smith, PhD, professor emeritus of pharmacology, University of Oxford, England.

Common Herb Can Make You Alert

Rosemary improves alertness and memory, according to master aromatherapist, Suzanne Catty.

What to do: Put one or two drops of rosemary essential oil on top of each foot. Blood returns to the lungs from the feet, then delivers rosemary molecules to the brain, including a portion that is responsible for memory and alertness.

Caution: Epileptics, people with high blood pressure and pregnant women should not use rosemary oil.

Suzanne Catty, chief executive officer and master aromatherapist, New World Organics, Toronto.

Iron Deficiency Reduces Mental Acuity

Iron helps deliver oxygen to the body's cells and improves memory, attention and learning. Women who are pregnant or have heavy menstrual periods are at high risk for iron deficiency.

Caution: Before taking iron supplements, check with your doctor. Some people can develop hemochromatosis, in which excess iron builds up in the blood and can damage the heart and liver.

Laura E. Murray-Kolb, PhD, adjunct assistant professor, international health, Johns Hopkins University, Baltimore, and author of a study of 113 women, published in *The American Journal of Clinical Nutrition.*

Vitamin B-12 Key to Aging Brain

Jonathan Friedman, MD, associate professor, surgery and neuroscience and experimental therapeutics, Texas A&M Health Science Center College of Medicine, and associate dean, College of Medicine, Bryan-College Station campus, and director, Texas Brain and Spine Institute, College Station, Texas.

Anna Vogiatzoglou, RD, doctoral candidate, department of physiology, anatomy and genetics, University of Oxford, England.

Shari Midoneck, MD, associate professor of clinical medicine, Weill Cornell Medical College, and internist, Iris Cantor Women's Health Center, New York City.

Neurology.

Low levels of vitamin B-12 may increase the risk for brain atrophy or shrinkage, new research suggests. Brain atrophy is associated with Alzheimer's disease and impaired cognitive function.

THE STUDY

The research involved 107 volunteers, ages 61 to 87, who were cognitively normal at the beginning of the five-year study. All participants underwent annual clinical exams, MRI scans and cognitive tests, and had blood samples taken.

Individuals with lower vitamin B-12 levels at the start of the study had a greater decrease in brain volume. Those with the lowest B-12 levels had a sixfold greater rate of brain-volume loss compared with those who had the highest levels of the vitamin.

Interestingly, none of the participants were deficient in vitamin B-12. They just had low levels within a normal range.

"They all had normal B-12 levels, yet there was a difference between the higher levels and the lower levels in terms of brain shrinkage. This is new information which could potentially change what we recommend to people in terms of diet," said Jonathan Friedman, MD, an associate professor of surgery, neuroscience and experimental therapeutics at Texas A&M Health Science Center College of Medicine and associate dean of the College of Medicine, Bryan-College Station campus.

IMPLICATIONS

Although the study, published in *Neurology*, can't confirm that lower levels of B-12 actually cause brain atrophy, they do suggest that "we ought to be more aware of our B-12 status, especially people who are vulnerable to B-12 deficiency [elderly, vegetarians, pregnant and lactating women, infants], and take steps to maintain it by eating a balanced and varied diet," said study coauthor Anna Vogiatzoglou, a registered dietitian and doctoral candidate in the department of physiology, anatomy and genetics at the University of Oxford, in England.

Not only might B-12 levels be a modifiable risk factor for cognitive decline, it might also be a clue to help clinicians assess cognitive problems earlier on.

"It's worth looking at B-12 levels. It's a simple blood test," affirmed Shari Midoneck, MD, an internist at the Iris Cantor Women's Health Center in New York City. "It doesn't hurt to take B-12."

According to the study authors, vitamin B-12 deficiency is a public health problem, especially among older people.

Good sources of the vitamin include meat, fish, milk and fortified cereals.

NEW B-12 CLINICAL TRIAL

Right now, it's not clear what the biological mechanisms behind the link might be, nor is it clear whether added B-12 would avert brain atrophy.

"We are doing a clinical trial in Oxford in which we are giving B vitamins [including B-12] to elderly people with memory impairment," Vogiatzoglou said. "In this trial, we are doing MRI scans at the start and the end, and so, we will be able to find out if taking B vitamins really does slow down the shrinking of the brain."

To learn more about vitamin B-12, go to the National Institutes of Health Web site, *http:// ods.od.nih.gov/factsheets/vitaminb12.asp*.

Antioxidant Improves Memory

In a study of 6,000 men, half took pills containing 50 milligrams (mg) daily of the antioxidant beta-carotene (roughly the amount in four carrots), and the others took a placebo.

Result: Those who took beta-carotene for at least 15 years scored higher on memory tests than those who took a placebo.

Theory: Beta-carotene protects against oxidative stress, which can lead to brain aging.

If you're concerned about memory loss: Ask your doctor about taking 50 mg daily of a beta-carotene supplement.

Francine Grodstein, ScD, associate professor of medicine, department of epidemiology, Brigham and Women's Hospital, Boston.

Age-Proof Your Brain

Mark A. Stengler, NMD, naturopathic medical doctor in private practice, Encinitas, California...adjunct associate clinical professor at the National College of Natural Medicine, Portland, Oregon...author of *The Natural Physician's Healing Therapies* (Bottom Line Books).

Slowed learning. Misplaced glasses. A sudden blank where a good friend's name used to be. These brain glitches, or "senior moments" as they're sometimes called, are all too common as we age. But with proper care, your brain can carry on its marvelous work, ensuring that you feel alert and active.

A substance that I consider one of the best for boosting memory and brain power can help. It's called *phosphatidylserine* (pronounced fos-fa-TIdal-sare-een) or simply PS. Derived from soy, it is a type of *phospholipid*, a molecule containing both the amino acid serine and essential fatty acids found in all cell membranes. When we are young, we have all the PS we need in our cells. As we age, though, our PS level decreases. Studies have shown that PS is beneficial for cognition in general, but in particular for the parts of the brain affected by age-related decline in memory, ability to learn, vocabulary skills and concentration. In addition, PS can relieve symptoms of depression ...dementia, including Alzheimer's disease (AD)...and the negative effects of stress.

HOW IT WORKS

PS improves the fluidity of the cell membranes, making it easier for cells to communicate with one another. Studies show that PS increases brain levels of *acetylcholine, serotonin, dopamine* and other neurotransmitters. In animal studies, supplementing with PS prevented age-induced loss of brain matter in the basal forebrain, an area that is partly responsible for learning and memory.

PS CAN HELP IN MANY WAYS

• **Boosts motivation.** Many studies have found that PS seems to improve overall brain function in older people. In a study of elderly patients without dementia, those who took PS showed improvement in motivation, initiative and interest in the world around them. They also were more social and had boosts in memory and learning compared with the placebo group.

• **Depression.** Studies on the effect of PS on depression in elderly patients have had positive results. An Italian study of older women with major depressive disorder found improvement in both behavior and cognitive performance in the PS group, compared with the placebo group. There are no known drug interactions with PS, and some patients take both PS and an antidepressant medication. If you are on an antidepressant medication, tell your doctor that you also are taking PS.

•**Alzheimer's disease.** Studies have shown that PS improves AD patients' memory, motivation and cognition. It also reduces anxiety, a problem in patients with AD. In a study of 425 people with moderate-to-severe cognitive loss, the PS group showed significant improvement.

Note: PS is not a cure for AD (none exists), and these patients' improvements did not last indefinitely. When my patients take both PS and an AD medication, I consult with their neurologists. More study is needed.

•**Stress.** PS appears to relieve the negative effects of stress on the body because of its effect on levels of *cortisol*, a hormone that is elevated during times of stress. After measuring cortisol levels of healthy volunteers following exercise, researchers found that PS modulated release of the hormone. Cortisol levels increase in depressed people, which is why PS also seems to help with depression. PS can be prescribed to alleviate the effects of stress in people of all ages.

MY VIEW

In my practice, I see many patients with age-related cognitive impairment ranging from mild cognitive decline to dementia. After taking 300 mg of PS for two months, the majority shows a noticeable improvement in cognitive functioning. Because PS is not a blood thinner, it is particularly beneficial for people who take blood-thinning medication, such as *warfarin* (Coumadin). PS supplements are safe for almost everyone except those who are allergic to soy.

For patients with age-related cognitive decline and for those who simply want to improve their memory, I recommend supplementing with two 200-milligram (mg) doses of PS during the day and 100 mg each evening, for a total of 500 mg daily. I also prescribe this amount of PS for older people who are depressed, overly stressed or who lack motivation. PS can be taken with or without food. There are no reported side effects. Look for products with 100 mg of PS per capsule. I don't recommend the 100-mg formulas that contain a PS complex in which PS is only a percentage of the 100 mg. Products

that I have found to be good include those made by KAL (800-669-8877, *www.nutraceutical.com*) and Natural Factors (800-322-8704, *www.naturalfactors.com*).

•**PS for children.** I have found that PS is safe for children as young as four years old. I prescribe 300 mg to 500 mg daily for children with attention deficit hyperactivity disorder (ADHD). Preliminary studies show it to be effective, especially when used in combination with fish oil. In addition, I regularly use PS with children who have problems with focus, attention and learning. I recommend 300 mg daily of PS. When it continues to help, I keep them on it indefinitely.

•**Another memory-boosting supplement.** *Phosphatidylcholine* (pronounced fos-fa-TIdal-ko-lean), or PC, is another brain-boosting phospholipid. It provides the body with *choline*, a chemical similar to B vitamins and the precursor to the neurotransmitter *acetylcholine*. PC is a major component of *lecithin*, a fat found naturally in animal and plant tissues and isolated for supplement use from either soy or egg yolks. Lecithin is a good source of PC, which studies have associated with improved memory. (Lecithin and PC often are referred to interchangeably.) A study with 61 healthy volunteers showed that ingesting two tablespoons of lecithin daily improved memory test scores compared with the placebo group.

To prevent memory loss, you can boost your lecithin levels by consuming foods such as sunflower seeds, mustard, oatmeal and cauliflower. But I recommend lecithin supplements for those who already have memory decline. For memory improvement, I recommend two tablespoons of lecithin granules daily added to a fruit smoothie or juice.

For patients who have early-stage dementia who have tried PS and lecithin and need a more aggressive approach, I recommend both PS and lecithin.

MORE WAYS TO BOOST BRAIN POWER

When speaking to my patients about boosting brain function, I often mention the following brain boosters…

•**Exercise.** We have known for many years that regular exercise contributes to improved cognitive function in older adults. Recently, a study showed that exercise increases blood circulation to the brain, which seems to be the reason for the cognitive benefit. This is yet another reason to go for a long walk…take a bike ride…or go to the gym for a workout.

• **Try something new.** Studies have shown that taking on a new challenge, such as a ballroom dancing class, or having a new experience, perhaps volunteering in a school, boosts brain power.

• **Play video games.** A new study from the University of Illinois, Urbana-Champaign, found that certain types of video games improved the brain's "executive function" skills, such as planning, decision making and impulse control, in men and women in their late 60s.

The best brain-boosting games: Turn-taking strategy games that involve task switching, memory, visual short-term recall and reasoning.

Examples: The computer games *Rise of Nations* (Microsoft) and the *Civilization* series (Microprose).

Rejuvenate Your Mind With Acupressure

Applying pressure to certain areas of the body opens energy pathways by increasing blood circulation.

How to do it: Gently place your thumb and middle finger of one hand on your forehead above each eyebrow, making a bridge. Meanwhile, with your other hand, reach around to the back of your head and apply firm pressure just below the base of the skull on either side of the spine. Use light pressure in front and firm pressure in back for three minutes to refresh your mind.

More information: *www.acupressure.com.*

Michael Reed Gach, PhD, founder, Acupressure Institute, Berkeley, California.

Exercise May Help Prevent Age-Related Memory Loss

American Medical Association, news release.

Exercise may help treat memory problems in adults, according to new research from Australia.

The study found that a home-based physical activity program led to modest improvements in cognitive function in adults with memory difficulties.

THE STUDY

The participants—138 people age 50 and older who had memory problems but didn't meet criteria for dementia—were randomly assigned to do a 24-week home-based physical activity program or to receive usual care.

Those in the exercise group were encouraged to do at least 150 minutes of moderate-intensity physical activity per week in three 50-minute sessions. Walking was the most frequently recommended type of activity. Participants in the exercise group did an average of 142 minutes more physical activity per week, or 20 minutes more per day, than those in the usual care group.

Over 18 months, participants in the exercise group had better Alzheimer Disease Assessment Scale-Cognitive Subscale (ADAS-Cog) scores and delayed recall, and lower Clinical Dementia Rating scores, than those in the usual care group. The ADAS-Cog consists of a number of cognitive tests.

The findings were published in *The Journal of the American Medical Association*.

"To our knowledge, this trial is the first to demonstrate that exercise improves cognitive function in older adults with subjective and objective mild cognitive impairment. The benefits of physical activity were apparent after six months and persisted for at least another 12 months after the intervention had been discontinued," said Nicola T. Lautenschlager, MD, of the University of Melbourne.

IMPLICATION

"Unlike medication, which was found to have no significant effect on mild cognitive impairment at 36 months, physical activity has the advantage of health benefits that are not confined to cognitive function alone, as suggested by findings on depression, quality of life, falls, cardiovascular function, and disability," the researchers added.

They noted that the number of older adults with Alzheimer's disease (AD) could increase from the current 26.6 million to 106.2 million by 2050. If AD onset could be delayed by 12 months, there would be 9.2 million fewer cases of AD worldwide.

EXPERT COMMENTARY

Exercise and other lifestyle factors may benefit older adults at risk for Alzheimer's disease, said Eric B. Larson, MD, MPH, of the Group Health Research Institute Seattle.

"Health advances of the past century have led to more individuals surviving to extreme old age, when their risk of Alzheimer disease and related dementias increases substantially," Dr. Larson added. "Exercise—and possibly other lifestyle factors—appears to affect vascular risk and late-life brain health."

For more information on memory loss, visit the National Institute on Aging's Web site, *www. niapublications.org.*

Dr. Gary Small's Secrets For Getting Your Memory Back in Gear

Gary Small, MD, professor of psychiatry and biobehavioral sciences, and director, University of California, Los Angeles, Memory & Aging Research Center. Dr. Small is one of the world's leading physician/scientists in the fields of memory and longevity. He is author of *The Memory Bible* and *The Longevity Bible* (both from Hyperion). *www.drgarysmall.com.*

Age is the biggest factor for memory loss. We all have memory problems of some sort by age 60, such as momentarily forgetting someone's name, or briefly wondering why we just walked into a room. We can't stop the effects of aging, but we can slow them down.

At the University of California, Los Angeles, Center on Aging, where I am director, we find that using very simple techniques and lifestyle changes—such as reading regularly and playing board games—can have a positive impact on memory retention. Scientific research shows that whenever we push ourselves to solve problems in a new way, we may be strengthening the connections between our brain cells.

MEMORY TECHNIQUES

Some people are so good at memorizing things that they test their talent in competitive matches involving knowledge of trivia or the recall of remarkably large numbers. Scientists have found that those people are no different from the rest of us. There is nothing out of the ordinary in their brain structure nor are there any indications of unusual intelligence. They simply often tap into a memory technique used since antiquity called the Roman Room method.

This method is simple. Visualize yourself walking a familiar route, such as the rooms of your home. Mentally place images of the items to be remembered on specific points on the route. It may be helpful to place items where they may logically be—if you want to remember to buy coffee beans, perhaps they're best mentally placed on the kitchen counter. When you want to recall them, mentally retrace your steps.

Over time, you can add more objects to the rooms. If one day you want to remember to pick up the newspaper, add it next to the coffee beans on the counter. If it's airline tickets, visualize them taped to the fridge door. You can also extend your route or even add other familiar locations for certain kinds of memory tasks.

The Roman Room method is a very useful technique. Orators back in Ancient Rome would remember lengthy speeches this way, imagining each progression of a speech by mentally walking through rooms where they had placed objects to remind themselves of lines. *Yet since today we have much more clutter coming at us, I also teach my patients an additional memory technique that I call Look, Snap, Connect…*

• **Look** reminds us to focus our attention. The most common explanation for memory loss is that the information never gets into our minds in the first place. Because we are distracted, we don't take in the information or don't allow ourselves to absorb it. Simply reminding ourselves to focus our attention will dramatically boost memory power.

• **Snap** stands for creating a mental snapshot or visual image in your mind's eye of the information to be remembered. For most people, visual images are much easier to remember than other forms of information.

• **Connect** means we need to link up the visual images from *snap* in meaningful ways. These associations are key to recalling memories when we want them later. When linking your mental images, create a story that has action and detail.

Example: Say that you want to remember five words on your "to do" list: Mail, gasoline, grandson, sweater, airline. Come up with a story linking them. For instance, I imagine a grandson knitting a sweater on a plane, then mailing it at the airport, when the plane lands to refuel.

Whatever the story ends up being, having detail, action and, for me, humor, all help to imprint the information.

This linking technique works very well with everyday memory tasks, such as grocery lists or errands to run.

When trying to remember faces and names, create an image either linked to the person whose name you need to remember or a distinguishing feature of his/her face. A redhead named Lucy could be remembered by noting that the red hair reminds you of Lucille Ball. You could remember the last name of a woman named Potvin by imagining that she landscaped her yard with pots full of vines.

MENTAL AEROBICS

It's never too late to improve your memory. Recent studies show that even people in the early stages of Alzheimer's can be taught significant face and name retention under the guidance of a professional. For those of us looking to overcome the common forgetfulness in daily life, we can tackle much of that ourselves by doing activities that involve *lateral thinking*.

Lateral thinking means that we are trying to solve a problem from many angles instead of tackling it head on. Here are some mental aerobic exercises to get you started and, hopefully, suggest further how to invoke lateral thinking in your life.

QUIZ TIME

A lot of memory loss is simply being too busy to absorb what people are saying. These exercises are meant to remind you to slow down, pay attention and consider what is at hand. *In doing so, your memory will improve…*

1. Brush your hair using your nondominant hand. You may find it awkward at first, but over a few days notice how much easier it gets. This and other exercises don't directly help your memory (after all, how often will any of us need to remember to brush with the opposite hand?). What these mental aerobics do is challenge your mind to think differently and examine tasks we often do without thinking, and which lead to our minds getting "flabby."

2. Fill in a grid so that every row, column and two-by-two box contains the numbers 1, 2, 3 and 4.

3. Say "silk" six times. Then answer the following question: What do cows drink?

This exercise will help you be more thoughtful about things, which in turn is conducive to better memory.

4. See how many words you can spell from these letters:

LIGOBATE

No letter may be used twice in any given word, and each word must contain the letter L.

5. How many months have 28 days?

6. All of the vowels have been removed from the following saying. The remaining consonants are in the correct sequence, broken into groups of two to five letters. What is the saying?

STRK WHLTH RNS HT

How well did you do? Regardless, this is just a start to remembering more and living better.

ANSWERS TO QUIZ

Q2: Across row 1: 1, 2, 3, 4 or 1, 2, 4, 3. Row 2: 4, 3, 1, 2. Row 3: 2, 1, 4, 3 or 2, 1, 3, 4. Row 4: 3, 4, 2, 1.

Q3: Cows drink water. If you said "milk," you need to focus your attention.

Q4: agile, ail, aale, bagel, bail, bale, blog, boil, el, Gail, gale, gel, glib, glob, globe, goal, goalie, lab, lag, lea, leg, lib, lie, lob, lobe, log, loge, oblige.

Q5: All of them. (If you say only one month has 28 days, it's an example of not paying attention to the matter at hand—all months have 28 days, after all.)

Q6: Strike while the iron is hot.

How to Make Better Decisions in Less Time

Barry Schwartz, PhD, Dorwin Cartwright Professor of Social Theory and Social Action, department of psychology, Swarthmore College, Swarthmore, Pennsylvania. He is author of *The Paradox of Choice: Why More Is Less* (Ecco).

At work and home, we make hundreds of decisions every day, some trivial, some important—which soap to buy, which political candidate to vote for, how to plan for retirement. These days, high-tech communications only add to the difficulty. We need to make decisions even more quickly when we respond to E-mail or answer our cell phones.

The result? We choose haphazardly or, worse, we become paralyzed by information overload and end up making no decision.

Example: Employees complain that their 401(k) plans offer too few investment options —but research shows that the more mutual funds an employer makes available, the less likely employees are to participate in the plan at all, even if it means passing up thousands of dollars in employer-matching contributions.

Here are strategies I've learned from my own and other social scientists' studies into decision making…

• **Learn to accept "good enough."** We all sometimes misuse our time and energy by trying to make the best choice. For instance, we might devote an hour or more to relatively frivolous decisions, such as choosing a restaurant, but spend just a few minutes picking a lawyer or doctor, often relying on just one friend's recommendation.

Better: Ask yourself how significantly a choice will affect your life. The more minor and short-term the impact, the less time you should spend making the decision.

The concept of "good enough" is difficult to embrace because it feels like you're settling for mediocrity—but "settling" often increases overall satisfaction.

Examples: You decide to write a heartfelt letter to your spouse on your anniversary. You want to choose just the right words—but after several drafts, you give up in frustration and buy a card at a store. Yet even an imperfect letter would have been much more meaningful to your spouse.

Or you find a movie that you're interested in at the video store. Instead of taking it home and enjoying it, you think there must be another that would better suit your mood. You spend 45 minutes scouring the aisles without success. By the time you leave—with your original selection in hand—you have wasted a good chunk of your precious leisure time.

• **Deliberately reduce the options when a decision is not critical.** Base your decision criteria on your past experience.

Examples: You have to hire a summer intern at work. If you've been able to find someone suitable in previous years by interviewing four candidates, set that as your limit.

You can apply the same technique to choosing a hairdresser, dog groomer or dry cleaner. Spend enough time to find someone who is adequate, then get on with your life.

• **Spend a lot of time and energy on a decision only if the extra effort can yield significantly better results.** Say you have a choice of three long-distance phone service providers, any of which will meet your needs. You're tempted to figure out which company's plan gives you a slight advantage, but the time-consuming and confusing process will save you no more than a few dollars a month.

You shouldn't choose blindly, but give yourself only a specific amount of time to review the plans or a deadline to make a choice.

Even spending enormous amounts of time on critical decisions, such as buying a home or helping your child choose a college, may not be worth the effort. Decisions such as these often involve more uncertainty than you ever can resolve in advance.

●**Don't let marketers play you.** Companies today are brilliant at seeding dissatisfaction in consumers to get them to buy more expensive products. This applies to everything from laundry detergent to such big-ticket items as cars. Computer software makers are notorious for this, pushing *Acme Software* version 7 or 8 when version 6 still is adequate for your needs. Most "enhancements" are minimal or tangential to a product's main purpose.

Smart: Stick with an older product or service until you experience shortcomings that really compromise your satisfaction. You'll save money and gain time.

●**Don't keep researching products and services after you have made a decision.** Have you ever bought a new car or computer, then scanned the newspapers each week to check the current price? This behavior just creates postpurchase misgivings.

If the car's price drops below what you paid, you will feel like you were ripped off. If the car's price rises, you will wonder what was wrong with your particular vehicle that allowed you to get such a good deal.

People derive only modest pleasure from confirming that they got a good deal and substantial dissatisfaction from finding out that they could have done better.

●**Make your decisions irreversible.** It makes sense to want to know about a return policy when you make a purchase, but being allowed to change your mind only increases the chance that you will.

On the other hand, when a decision is final, you engage in a variety of powerful psychological processes that enhance your satisfaction about your choice relative to the alternatives.

Example: The proliferation of no-fault divorces and prenuptial agreements has influenced many people to stop treating the selection of a life partner as a sacred decision. During the course of a marriage, you are likely to encounter many people who might seem better-looking, smarter or more understanding than your spouse.

Always wondering whether you could have done better is a prescription for misery. You're better off thinking, *I've made my decision, so this other person's qualities have nothing to do with me. I'm not in the market.*

Brain Adjusts to Cope With Life's Upsets

Roberto Cabeza, PhD, professor of psychology and neuroscience, Duke University, Durham, North Carolina.
Paul Sanberg, PhD, distinguished university professor and director, Center of Excellence for Aging and Brain Repair, University of South Florida College of Medicine, Tampa.
Psychological Science.

New evidence suggests that the brains of older women process negative images differently than young women, a sign that the human brain seems to learn to cope with the slings and arrows of life.

"Older adults seem to be able to show a reduced response to negative emotions," said Roberto Cabeza, PhD, a coauthor of the study and a professor of psychology and neuroscience at Duke University.

Researchers have long suspected that the brains of older people deal with emotions differently, Dr. Cabeza said. "There have been reports that there's a shift in the bias, perhaps an attenuation of negative emotions and an emphasis on processing positive emotions," he said.

THE STUDY

For the new study, Dr. Cabeza and his colleagues put those theories about brain activity to the test in 15 young women (average age 25) and 15 older women (average age 70). All the women were healthy.

The women were shown photos chosen to elicit positive, neutral and negative responses. Later, the women took part in a test designed to reveal which photos they remembered. The researchers also scanned the brains of the women using functional magnetic resonance imaging (fMRI) technology, which measures neural activity.

While both groups of women were more likely to remember negative images, the older ones remembered fewer of them than the young women, Dr. Cabeza said. Older female brains also showed less activity between different neural areas.

THEORY

The results "fit in with the theory that older adults are down-regulating or somehow suppressing a processing of negative information," he said, perhaps in response to "adapting" to the demands of life. "They may try to emphasize positive information and process less negative information," he added.

Why would older people do that? "They're having negatives like sickness and death of friends, relatives and spouses," Dr. Cabeza said. "It's possible that in this change and shift, by paying less attention and processing fewer negative events, we're protecting ourselves from these negative events."

IMPLICATIONS

In the larger picture, the findings, published online in the journal *Psychological Science*, suggest that the brain changes over time and doesn't simply go into decline as people age, he said.

Paul Sanberg, PhD, director of the University of South Florida College of Medicine's Center of Excellence for Aging and Brain Repair, is a neuroscientist who's familiar with the study findings. He said the brain rewires itself over time as people learn new things, and young people, of course, have had less time for that process to work.

"Younger people aren't experienced in the world, they haven't seen as many negative things in their lives," Dr. Sanberg said. "They haven't learned to cope with those things as much."

MORE RESEARCH IN MEN AND MIDDLE-AGED PEOPLE

Dr. Sanberg noted that the new study only included women and said there could be a difference between the genders. He said future research could look at middle-aged people and seek out signs that their reactions to images lie somewhere between those of young and old people.

To learn more about how the brain functions, visit the Web site of the U.S. National Institutes of Health, *www.ninds.nih.gov/disorders/ brain_basics/know_your_brain.htm.*

You're Only as Old as You Think You Are

Becca Levy, PhD, associate professor of epidemiology and psychology at Yale School of Public Health in New Haven, Connecticut. She was the lead author of a study on stereotypes and aging, published in *Journal of Gerontology: Psychological Science.*

Some people lose strength and vitality when they get older, while others remain robust. The same disparity exists when it comes to eyesight, hearing and mental faculties.

Genetics and lifestyle can play a part, but to a surprising extent, what you *think* about aging does as well. *Yale psychologist Becca Levy, PhD, discusses how stereotypes affect aging…*

● **How do stereotypes affect how we age?** There are numerous ways, but let's look at hearing loss as an example. Most people consider it an inevitable fact of growing older, but there's more to it than biology.

In a study conducted at Yale, we measured the hearing of more than 500 adults age 70 and older and asked them what five words or phrases first came to mind when they thought of an old person.

Three years later, the people who associated aging with stereotypes like "feeble" and "senile" had suffered significantly more hearing loss than those who had answered with positive words like "wise" and "active." In other studies, negative thoughts or beliefs about aging were linked to poorer memory as the years passed.

•Can one's recovery from serious physical ailments, such as heart disease, also be affected? Apparently so. In one study, we interviewed 62 heart attack patients (ages 50 to 96) about their stereotypes of aging within two weeks after their heart attacks.

Seven months later, patients who expressed more positive stereotypes had experienced better physical recoveries—as measured by tests involving balance and timed walking—than those who expressed more negative stereotypes.

•Could a person's views on aging even affect his/her life span? One of our studies showed just that. It involved 660 people, ages 50 to 94, who were asked questions that explored the ways they perceived their own aging.

For example, the study participants, all of whom lived in Oxford, Ohio, were asked how much they agreed with statements, such as "Things keep getting worse as I get older" and "I am as happy now as I was when I was younger."

Nearly 25 years later, researchers tracked those participants who were still alive and how long the others had lived. Those who had expressed a more positive view when surveyed lived a median of seven years longer, even after differences in their ages and health at that time were taken into account. It held true for both men and women who were over age 60 as well as those who were younger.

•How do researchers explain this phenomenon? There is no definitive explanation, but we think that several mechanisms are involved. Some are physiological and might well involve the harmful effects of stress on bodily systems.

Another piece is likely to be behavioral—people who believe that aging means unavoidable memory decline, for example, quite possibly won't try as hard or as long to remember, and won't bother to apply strategies that could help. Similarly, people who think there's nothing that can be done about hearing loss probably aren't as quick to seek medical attention if they develop hearing trouble.

In the longevity study, we found that views on aging can affect an older person's will to live—this explained, at least in part, the difference in survival. When you don't believe that the benefits of a long life will outweigh the hardships, you're less likely to follow a healthful lifestyle and seek treatments that prolong life.

•What's the source of these stereotypes? Negative depictions of aging can be found everywhere—from greeting cards to bestselling books to the media. We think television, in particular, has a major effect. We surveyed a group of people ages 60 to 92, who watched an average of 21 hours of television per week, and found that the more TV they watched, the more negative their beliefs were about aging.

The negative stereotyping most likely starts early—for example, wicked witches in fairy tales are gnarled and wrinkled—and sinks in deeply. Then, as aging occurs, some individuals start applying these negative beliefs to themselves.

•Is it possible to change these beliefs? We've been able to show in the lab that they change quite readily in the short term. In one recent study, we tested how fast elderly people could walk—a key measurement of frailty (a condition that includes exhaustion and weight loss as well as loss of muscle mass and strength).

Participants were randomly assigned to either a positive or negative age-stereotype group. We subliminally flashed words with positive connotations about aging, such as "wise," "alert" and "mature," to one group, and showed negative words, such as "senile" and "decrepit," to the other group.

Participants in the positive stereotype group walked significantly faster and demonstrated better balance than those in the negative stereotype group.

To a great extent, we don't question these stereotypes because we've absorbed them so completely that we're not even conscious of them. Becoming aware of their presence in everyday life is a first step toward questioning their validity.

•What, specifically, can people do to fight these stereotypes? In the TV study, we asked participants to keep a journal describing the

241

way that older people were represented. The participants were shocked to discover how often they were made the target of jokes, and that they were frequently omitted from programming. "It's like we're nonexistent," wrote one study participant.

In your own life, make a point to pay attention to more positive images of aging—active, effective people in politics, the arts and the community, for example. I don't mean "superstars" who are jumping out of planes at age 80. It's too easy to write them off as exceptions that have nothing to do with you. Also, spend time with older role models, such as relatives and residents of your community, and learn about their strengths and contributions.

•**Doesn't this promote a falsely optimistic view?** Not necessarily. It's more a matter of accepting that aging will involve a range of changes—some are positive, some are negative …some are inevitable and some are malleable. It is important to recognize the many places where a realistic attitude and positive action can make a real difference.

Editor's note: More and more organizations are now promoting the accomplishments of older adults. One such program is the Purpose Prize, which provides $100,000 awards to people over age 60 who make significant contributions to society.

To learn more, contact Encore.org, a non-profit think tank that promotes the achievements of older adults, 415-430-0141, *www. encore.org*.

Puzzled by a Problem?

"Sleeping on it" works only if you reach the *rapid eye movement* (REM) stage of slumber.

Study: Participants were tested on their ability to find links between words (for example, given cookie, heart and sixteen, they had to come up with sweet). Next they rested quietly or napped, then tested again. Those who rested or slept without reaching REM did not improve…those whose naps included REM improved almost 40% on average.

Try it: Think of a problem you're having—a song you're struggling to write, a relationship conflict. Nap for 60 to 90 minutes to reach REM. Wake and write down your thoughts—you may have your solution!

Sara Mednick, PhD, assistant adjunct professor of psychiatry, University of California, San Diego School of Medicine, coauthor of a study of 77 people and author of *Take a Nap! Change Your Life* (Workman).

12

Natural Relief for PMS and Menopause

What to Do When Your Period Is a Question Mark

Maybe your thinking isn't as clear, your concentration isn't as focused and your memory isn't as sharp. Maybe you're more irritable, depressed and tense. Maybe you've developed back pain, a headache or pelvic cramps. Maybe your body has become bloated and your breasts tender. Maybe you've started to crave sweets and salty food. What's happening to you?

PREMENSTRUAL SYNDROME, OR PMS

"PMS is an array of symptoms—emotional, cognitive, physical, behavioral—that occur cyclically during the premenstrual phase of the cycle and are followed by relief during the menses," says Lori Futterman, RN, PhD, director of the San Diego Premenstrual Syndrome Clinic, an assistant professor at University of

California, San Diego, and author of *PMS, Perimenopause, and You* (Lowell House).

An estimated 70% to 90% of women experience PMS, with 10% to 40% saying the symptoms interfere with daily life—one or more of the 150 distressful symptoms linked to the syndrome. Why so many?

"The reason that PMS can have such far-reaching effects is that people have receptors for estrogen and progesterone—two of the hormones that are involved in PMS—throughout their entire bodies," explains Diana Taylor, RN, PhD, professor emerita at the School of Nursing at the University of California, San Francisco (UCSF), and coauthor of *Taking Back the Month: A Personalized Solution for Managing PMS and Enhancing Your Health* (Perigee).

Bill Gottlieb, health educator and author of six books, including *Alternative Cures* (Ballantine), *Breakthroughs in Drug-Free Healing* and *Speed Healing* (Bottom Line Books) and *The Natural Fat-Loss Pharmacy* (Broadway). Former editor-in-chief of Rodale Books and Prevention Magazine Health Books, he lives in northern California.

"That's why PMS can affect how a woman feels from literally head to toe."

But she can also feel better from head to toe.

"I have seen women with PMS overcome their symptoms with vitamins, minerals, herbs and lifestyle and nutritional changes," says Linda Woolven, a herbalist and acupuncturist in Toronto, Canada, and author of *Smart Woman's Guide to PMS and Pain-Free Periods* (Wiley).

Here's what she and other experts say can help clear up your month-to-month symptoms in three months or less…

•**Take a multivitamin-mineral and PMS supplement.** "In my research with the UCSF PMS Symptom Management Program, vitamin and mineral supplements were the most frequently used strategy for PMS, and for most women helped relieve PMS severity within three months—particularly fluid retention, constipation, concentration problems and mood swings," says Dr. Taylor.

Recommended: "I recommend a general multivitamin-mineral supplement that is taken for half the month, from the first day of the period to mid-cycle," she says. "Then stop taking the multivitamin-mineral supplement and start taking a PMS formula supplement, and take it every day from mid-cycle until the start of the period.

"If you continue to have PMS symptoms a few days into your period, it's fine to continue taking the PMS formula for a few more days," says Dr. Taylor. "Just be sure to switch back to the regular multivitamin-mineral formula, and stop taking the PMS formula by the end of your period."

Suggested intake: Dr. Taylor suggests a multivitamin-mineral formula with approximately these levels of nutrients: Vitamin A, 15,000 international units (IU); vitamin D, 400 IU; vitamin E, 600 IU; vitamin C, 1,000 milligrams (mg); folic acid, 50 mg; thiamine (vitamin B-1), 50 mg; riboflavin (vitamin B-2), 50 mg; niacin, 50 mg; vitamin B-6, 200 micrograms (mcg); vitamin B-12, 50 mcg; biotin, 30 mcg; pantothenic acid, 50 mg; calcium, 150 mg; magnesium, 300 mg; iodine, 150 mcg; iron, 15 mg; zinc, 25 mg; manganese, 10 mg; potassium, 100 mg; selenium, 25 mcg; chromium, 100 mcg.

Product: "The PMS supplement I recommend most often is the Schiff PMS 1 Nutritional Supplement," she says. "It's well-tolerated by most women and requires taking no more than eight small gelatin capsules a day."

•**Chasteberry for PMS.** "Chasteberry—*Vitex agnus-castus*—is the most important herb for normalizing and regulating the menstrual cycle," says Woolven. "In Europe, it is a standard treatment to relieve PMS symptoms, including depression, cramps, mood swings, water retention and weight gain."

Study: Researchers in Germany asked more than 1,600 woman with PMS to take a chasteberry supplement. After three cycles, 93% of the women reported a decrease or complete cessation of PMS symptoms. Less depression. Less anxiety. Less food cravings. Less bloating. Less breast tenderness. The study was reported in the *Journal of Women's Health and Gender-Based Medicine*.

Suggested intake: 175 to 225 mg daily of a tablet standardized for 0.5% agnuside, the active ingredient. Or 30 drops of a tincture, three times a day.

Also helpful: Woolven suggests you consider the following treatments for PMS symptoms if dietary changes and chasteberry haven't worked after three months…

•**Water retention.** Take 50 mg of B-6 three times a day with food. It acts as a diuretic.

•**Depression.** Add 50 to 100 mg of 5-HTP, three times a day. It boosts serotonin, a brain chemical that regulates mood.

•**Anxiety.** Add a tincture of passionflower—40 drops, three or four times a day.

•**Insomnia.** Add valerian, 150 to 300 mg, standardized for 0.8 percent valeric acid, 30 minutes before bed.

•**Acne.** Add zinc, 25 to 50 mg, once a day.

Important: Use these herbs and nutritional supplements with the approval and supervision of a qualified health practitioner, says Woolven.

•**Foot reflexology for menstrual cramps.** Reflexology is a healing modality that says the feet (and the hands and the outer ears) are "maps" of the rest of the body, with specific points that correspond to organs and areas, explains Bill Flocco, director of the American Academy of Reflexology in Burbank, California.

By applying therapeutic pressure to those points, you can help your body heal from a wide range of health problems. *Including menstrual cramps…*

The study: Women with PMS were divided into three groups. One group received reflexology for several months, one group received "placebo" reflexology (pressure on points that weren't linked to PMS) and one group didn't receive any treatment. The group receiving reflexology had a 47% reduction in symptoms, including menstrual cramps. The study appeared in the journal *Obstetrics and Gynecology.*

What to do: The primary point for menstrual cramps is the "uterine reflex" on the back lower corner of the inside of the foot, says Flocco. To work the area, place your left foot on your right knee. With the thumb of your right hand, apply pressure to the area below the protruding anklebone, between the ankle and the back of the heel bone. "Start off lightly, gradually increasing the pressure," says Flocco.

Use a technique Flocco calls the "thumb roll"—place the tip of your thumb directly on the skin and then roll it forward, applying pressure. Then move the tip of the thumb slightly forward, and perform the maneuver again. (It is like the movement of an inchworm.) Repeat until the entire area is covered.

After working on your right foot, switch to your left.

Work the left and right foot for a total of 10 to 15 minutes a day, four to five days before your period starts, says Flocco. "Usually within a month or two, women report a dramatic reduction in or elimination of their menstrual cramps," he says.

Caution: Since this technique stimulates the uterus, do not perform it if you are in the first trimester of pregnancy.

Rapid resource: The Web site *www.americanacademyofreflexology.com* offers reflexology charts, books about reflexology, dates of reflexology classes and other information about the modality. Address: American Academy of Reflexology, Bill Flocco, Director, 725 E. Santa Anita Ave., #B, Burbank, CA 91501, call 818-841-7741 or e-mail *aareflex@aol.com.*

Premature Menopause

Mark A. Stengler, NMD, naturopathic medical doctor in private practice, Encinitas, California…adjunct associate clinical professor at the National College of Natural Medicine, Portland, Oregon…author of *The Natural Physician's Healing Therapies* (Bottom Line Books).

Susan, a 42-year-old construction consultant, had not menstruated in three years. Her premature menopause (cessation of periods before age 40) was due to a car accident that had injured her pelvis and damaged her ovaries. By the time she consulted me, she was having severe hot flashes every two hours, day and night. She also had low energy, headaches, sciatic pain (nerve pain in the lower back, buttock and thigh), constipation, mild incontinence, insomnia, restless leg syndrome (uncontrollable urge to move the legs while at rest) and low libido. Formerly an upbeat person, Susan had become anxious and depressed.

Susan's blood tests came back normal except for a slight deficiency of vitamin B-12, which suggested poor digestive absorption. Saliva testing showed deficiencies of the female hormones estrogen and progesterone and the antistress hormone *dehydroepiandrosterone* (DHEA), plus elevated levels of the stress hormone cortisol.

To relieve Susan's hot flashes and other menopausal symptoms, I prescribed natural estrogen and progesterone in skin cream form, plus DHEA capsules to boost sex drive. (Progesterone and DHEA do not require prescriptions but are best used under a doctor's supervision to ensure proper dosages.) To raise her energy levels, I advised Susan to take a daily sublingual (under the tongue) B-12 tablet, since this nutrient is involved in cellular energy production. Sleep problems obviously can exacerbate low energy, so I recommended the amino acid *5-hydroxytryptophan* (5-HTP), which increases levels of *serotonin*, a relaxing brain chemical (5-HTP should not be used by patients who take drugs for insomnia, anxiety or depression). I told Susan to drink a protein shake each morning, because she said she was too rushed to sit down for breakfast. And I outlined a workout program of walking and light weight lifting three times weekly, because exercise increases energy and improves mood by balancing blood sugar and stress hormone levels.

Six weeks later, Susan reported that she was sleeping better than she had in years and that her restless leg symptoms were much improved. Her headaches had continued for two weeks after she started my recommended therapies but then disappeared. Her incontinence and constipation were gone—which also reduced her sciatic pain by alleviating the pressure on her sciatic nerve. Best of all, she said, her hot flashes had vanished, and her energy, mood and libido all had improved significantly.

Follow-up tests showed that Susan's cortisol levels had dropped. Because she was experiencing mild water retention, I decreased her estrogen dose slightly to correct the problem. Our goal now is to maintain proper hormonal balance with natural hormone therapy until she reaches age 50 or so (the typical age of menopause) and then wean her off the hormones.

More from Mark A. Stengler, NMD...

Fibrocystic Breast Disease

Forty-four-year-old Pauline suffered from fibrocystic breast disease (FBD), a non-cancerous condition characterized by lumpy breasts that are tender or painful. Symptoms often intensify before or during menstruation. This condition affects approximately 60% of all women, commonly between the ages of 30 and 50. Having lived with FBD for years, Pauline was searching for natural approaches to relieve her symptoms. Conventional doctors offered her pain medicine or birth control pills, but neither was a good option in her mind, because they did not address the underlying cause.

I explained to Pauline that most women who have FBD also have a hormone imbalance—specifically, progesterone levels that are lower than what is optimal during the last two weeks of their menstrual cycles. Or I find that their progesterone levels are normal, but estrogen levels are elevated, leading to a high level of estrogen relative to progesterone. Some women also develop FBD as a result of low thyroid function. In Pauline's case, testing showed mildly low levels of thyroid and progesterone hormones. Since these hormone levels were only slightly low, I recommended a thyroid "glandular" supplement that supports thyroid function. I also prescribed homeopathic Pulsatilla, a great hormone balancer that treats FBD symptoms, including breast tenderness. I often prescribe natural progesterone for the treatment of FBD, since it works so well. But in Pauline's case, I felt the use of nutritional supplements and dietary changes would be all she needed.

As we spoke more, I learned that Pauline sometimes consumed two foods that are associated with FBD due to their caffeine content—coffee and chocolate.

Also high in caffeine: Black tea and colas (diet and regular), as well as some over-the-counter drugs, such as headache and menstrual cramp medications, and some pain relief and cold remedies. Some studies have shown that the complete avoidance of caffeine-containing foods is helpful for FBD. I also recommended the herb chasteberry, which has been shown to relieve premenstrual breast pain. Chasteberry increases progesterone production by the ovaries. When two capsules (240 mg each) are taken every morning, reduced breast pain is usually noted within two to three menstrual cycles.

Finally, I asked Pauline to take fish oil and evening primrose oil—each contains a blend of essential fatty acids, important for reducing inflammation and regulating hormones. Fish oil contains *eicosapentaenoic acid* (EPA), which has anti-inflammatory effects. Evening primrose oil contains *gamma linoleic acid* (GLA), which reduces pain and inflammation. After two months, Pauline reported that her breast tenderness had decreased significantly. When I saw her again four months later, she reported no breast tenderness or swelling. The lumpiness of her breasts was reduced significantly as well.

Also from Mark A. Stengler, NMD...

Do You Have Problem Periods?

Excessive bleeding during menstruation is a common problem that many women experience.

Achieving a better hormone balance should help. The herb chasteberry (sold in health-food stores) helps the ovaries to produce *progesterone*, which promotes better regulation of the menstrual cycle. Take 40 drops of chasteberry tincture or 240 mg in capsule form every morning for several months (do not use if you take birth control pills).

Also helpful: One-quarter teaspoon of natural progesterone cream, totaling 20 mg of progesterone, applied twice daily to the skin of the inner forearm, during the two weeks preceding your period. Although progesterone cream is sold over the counter in pharmacies, it is best used under a doctor's supervision because excessive doses can cause irregular menstrual cycles.

Iron-deficiency anemia may be caused by (and paradoxically, may contribute to) heavy periods. Have your doctor run a blood test for *ferritin* (a protein marker of the body's stored iron levels). If your level is below 20 nanograms per milliliter (ng/ml), take 50 mg to 100 mg daily of chelated iron (which is chemically bound to another substance for easier absorption), under a doctor's supervision, until your ferritin level returns to normal.

Daily Tampon?

It is not a good idea to use a tampon all day, every day.

If you are tempted to use tampons between periods to absorb heavy discharge, see your doctor to check for a yeast infection, sexually transmitted disease or other problem. With treatment, discharge should diminish.

The normal hormonal changes that occur after menopause can increase discharge. But because vaginal tissues become thinner, daily tampon use could cause irritation that further increases discharge.

Better: Experiment with different panty liners to find a brand that is comfortable for you.

Karen Deighan, MD, associate professor of obstetrics and gynecology, Loyola University Medical Center, Maywood, Illinois.

What You Don't (But Should) Know About Hysterectomy

JoAnn E. Manson, MD, DrPH, professor of medicine and women's health at Harvard Medical School and chief of the division of preventive medicine at Brigham and Women's Hospital, both in Boston. Dr. Manson is coauthor of *Hot Flashes, Hormones & Your Health* (McGraw Hill).

More than half of the American women who undergo hysterectomy (surgical removal of the uterus) opt to have their ovaries removed at the same time to reduce ovarian cancer risk.

But: New research casts doubt on the wisdom of this.

Reasons: Ovarian cancer, though potentially deadly, is relatively rare...and ovary removal increases other health risks, especially for women who have not yet reached natural menopause.

Recently, my colleagues and I published results from a study of 29,380 women who had undergone hysterectomy. Compared with women who had intact ovaries, those who'd had their ovaries removed were 25% less likely to get breast cancer and rarely if ever got ovarian cancer—but they were 17% more likely to develop heart disease and 12% more likely to die during the 24-year follow-up. Among women who never took estrogen, ovary removal before age 50 was associated with double the risk for heart disease and stroke and a 40% increased risk for death.

Also: A Mayo study of 4,748 women found a 44% higher risk of dying from cardiovascular disease and a 67% higher overall mortality rate in those whose ovaries had been removed before age 45 than in women who had intact ovaries. Additional research found that ovary removal before menopause increased the risk for bone fracture, cognitive impairment, tremors and declines in sexual function. Estrogen therapy appeared to prevent many, but not all, of these negative outcomes (though estrogen use carries its own risks).

And: Analysis of data from several studies found that ovary removal before age 65 increased a woman's chance of dying before age 80 by 8.5%.

Revealing: Researchers estimated that, in a hypothetical group of 1,000 women whose ovaries were removed at ages 50 to 54, compared with a similar group of women with intact ovaries, 84 more women would die from heart disease and 16 more would die from complications of hip fracture by age 80...only five fewer would die from ovarian cancer.

Why: After menopause, ovaries continue to produce hormones (at lower levels), including androgens that convert to estrogen in fat and muscle cells. Loss of these hormones may contribute to the negative effects of ovary removal.

Recommended: It may be prudent to remove ovaries if genetic testing and/or family history suggest a high risk for ovarian cancer or types of breast cancer linked to ovarian cancer. Otherwise, if facing hysterectomy, consider keeping your ovaries—especially if you are premenopausal.

What if your ovaries already were removed? Talk to your doctor about the pros and cons of estrogen therapy, as well as ways to minimize your risk for heart disease and osteoporosis.

Consider Keeping Your Ovaries

Women undergoing hysterectomy may not have to have their ovaries removed, says Esther Eisenberg, MD, MPH.

Recent study: Ovary retention may improve survival in women over age 40 who are not at increased risk for ovarian cancer. Even small amounts of hormones produced by the ovaries

reduce the risk for heart disease, hip fractures and other problems. Discuss the pros and cons of ovary removal with your physician.

Esther Eisenberg, MD, MPH, medical officer, Reproductive Sciences Branch, National Institute of Child Health & Human Development, Bethesda, Maryland, and coauthor of *Hysterectomy: Exploring Your Options* (Johns Hopkins).

When Your Insides Don't Stay Inside

John O.L. DeLancey, MD, professor of obstetrics and gynecology and director of pelvic floor research at the University of Michigan Medical School in Ann Arbor.

As women age, they often experience weakening of the *pelvic floor*—a network of muscles, ligaments and tissues that keeps the pelvic organs in place. For up to one-third of women, this weakening leads to *pelvic organ prolapse*, a condition in which the uterus, vaginal wall, bladder, rectum and/or small bowel drop and protrude outside the vaginal opening. The condition can be embarrassing, uncomfortable and sometimes painful —but there is no need to suffer in silence.

PROLAPSE: A PRIMER

Pelvic organ prolapse most often affects women over age 50 who have had one or more vaginal births, but it can occur in younger women, too. At the University of Michigan, we have uncovered a strong connection between muscle damage during vaginal births and pelvic organ prolapse. Vaginal muscle weakness may be especially common after a difficult labor and delivery, particularly if forceps were required.

Other factors that can contribute to pelvic organ prolapse include obesity or respiratory problems with a chronic cough (both of which put extra strain on the abdomen and/or pelvis)...chronic constipation, which increases pressure from the bowel on the vaginal wall, leading to shifting of organs within the pelvis...or a genetic tendency toward weak pelvic tissues.

In my experience, pelvic organ prolapse results in a protrusion that can range from grape-size to grapefruit-size. If the bulge remains tiny and unobtrusive, your physician can simply monitor the problem. However, if you feel an uncomfortable lump in the vaginal opening or a sensation that something is falling out of the vagina, treatment should be considered. Additional symptoms may occur sporadically, especially during physical activity. These include low back pain…a pulling or aching sensation in the pelvis or lower abdomen…an uncomfortable feeling of pressure or fullness in the vagina…urinary incontinence…and/or pain during intercourse.

NONSURGICAL THERAPIES

To relieve symptoms and/or prevent them from worsening…

• **Get fitted with a pessary.** This soft, flexible plastic device comes in various shapes and sizes. It is worn in the vagina to support and correct the position of the pelvic organs. When a pessary fits properly, you probably won't even feel that it is there and it will not limit your activities. A pessary may be worn for up to three consecutive months between cleanings, or it may be removed nightly to minimize risk of irritation. Most pessaries are removed before sex. A pessary does not significantly increase the risk for toxic shock syndrome (a dangerous infection that can start in the vagina).

• **Lose weight if necessary** to avoid putting pressure on pelvic organs.

• **Choose the right workout.** Stick with low-impact aerobic exercise, such as swimming, cycling or walking. For weight training (and at all other times), avoid lifting anything over 25 pounds. Don't strain when using exercise machines. Avoid abdominal exercises, such as crunches.

• **Do Kegel exercises** to strengthen the pelvic floor.

How: Tighten your pelvic muscles as if to halt the flow of urine, hold for several seconds and relax. Repeat 15 times three times daily, squeezing as tightly as possible. You can do Kegels sitting or standing.

• **Control constipation.** Straining during bowel movements puts pressure on pelvic muscles and ligaments.

Helpful: Eat high-fiber foods, such as whole grains, fruits and vegetables, and drink plenty of water. Light exercise—even a quick walk around the block—often helps get things moving. If the problem persists, consider an over-the-counter fiber supplement, such as Metamucil or Citrucel.

Estrogen Overload Is a Big Problem

Mark A. Stengler, NMD, naturopathic medical doctor in private practice, Encinitas, California…adjunct associate clinical professor at the National College of Natural Medicine, Portland, Oregon…author of *The Natural Physician's Healing Therapies* (Bottom Line Books).

A little-known yet increasingly common health problem—for men and women —is excess estrogen. Though estrogen usually is thought of as a female hormone, men also produce it. When a person's estrogen levels are too high, the condition is called hyperestrogenism. This hormonal imbalance affects one in five people. It most commonly develops after age 50 but can affect younger adults and even children. Hyperestrogenism contributes to numerous and disparate health problems, from headaches to weight gain to cancer.

CAUSES: BIOLOGICAL

In women, estrogen is produced primarily in the ovaries. It plays many roles in the reproductive process, cognition and bone formation. Production drops dramatically at menopause. In men, small amounts of estrogen are created as a by-product of the metabolism of *testosterone*, a hormone produced in the testes. Estrogen's main role in men is to strengthen bones.

Various biological factors are known to contribute to hyperestrogenism…

• **Excess weight.** Fat cells contain the enzyme *aromatase*, which stimulates estrogen production. Being just 5% over an appropriate weight increases hyperestrogenism risk.

• **Impaired liver function.** When the liver's detoxifying capabilities are compromised—by poor diet, excessive alcohol use, genetics or exposure to pollutants—the organ can't properly metabolize estrogen.

•**Sluggish bowel activity.** Normally, about 80% of excess estrogen is eliminated via stool. When bowel function is slow—for instance, due to insufficient dietary fiber—waste products linger in the colon, so estrogen is reabsorbed into the bloodstream.

•**Hormone therapy.** Birth control pills or estrogen therapy (in women) or testosterone therapy (in men, since testosterone can convert into estrogen) can increase hyperestrogenism risk.

•**Low thyroid hormone.** If the thyroid gland does not function well, metabolism slows.

•**Prescription medications.** The breast cancer drug *tamoxifen* binds with cells' estrogen receptors, leaving estrogen stranded in the bloodstream. The ulcer medication *cimetidine* (Tagamet) interferes with estrogen metabolism and increases estrogen activity.

•**Nutritional deficiencies.** The liver needs sufficient amounts of vitamins B-6, B-12, C and E as well as magnesium to function well and eliminate excess estrogen.

•**High sugar consumption.** Eating excess sweets raises blood sugar, causing the body to excrete more magnesium. Because this mineral is involved with estrogen detoxification, less magnesium means more risk for hyperestrogenism.

•**Dairy foods.** Cow's milk—even organic—contains naturally occurring estrogen. Watch high dairy consumption.

•**Stress.** The hormone *cortisol*, released at times of stress, makes cells more receptive to estrogen. It also interferes with the estrogen-modulating hormone *progesterone*, allowing estrogen to dominate.

CAUSES: ENVIRONMENTAL

Man-made substances that have estrogen-like effects are called *xenoestrogens*. These include benzene in car exhaust...*phthalates* in some plastics...*polychlorinated biphenyls* (PCBs) in electrical equipment...polybrominated biphenyls (PBBs) in flame retardants ...and pesticides, such as *dichloro-diphenyl-trichloroethane* (DDT). Though PCBs and DDT were banned in the 1970s, they degrade slowly and still exist in water, plants and animals.

Estrogen-like hormones often are added to livestock feed to fatten up the animals—when we eat this meat, we ingest the hormones. When estrogen-elevating drugs are excreted by patients, they enter our drinking water supply and accumulate over time.

It is naive to believe that environmental pollutants do not affect humans. *Examples...*

•**One study investigated girls born in the 1970s in Puerto Rico.** Participants who showed signs of early breast development —as young as age seven—had higher blood levels of phthalates than did girls whose breasts budded at the normal age of 10.

•**Emory University researchers found that girls breast-fed by mothers who had high blood levels of PBBs during pregnancy began to menstruate 12 months earlier,** on average, than did girls whose mothers had lower PBB levels during pregnancy.

SELF-DEFENSE STRATEGIES

Excess estrogen can contribute to myriad health problems, from the bothersome to the life-threatening. It even may be linked to cognitive problems. A recent study of 2,974 Japanese-American men, ages 70 to 91, revealed that high levels of *estradiol* (an estrogen) were associated with an increased risk for cognitive decline and Alzheimer's disease.

To diagnose hyperestrogenism, a doctor may order tests of saliva and/or urine samples collected over 24 hours, to detect "active" estrogen (the amount attached to cell receptor sites and therefore problematic). Blood tests may be used—but they are less accurate, because they do not measure active estrogen.

If you are diagnosed with hyperestrogenism —or if you want to lower your risk for developing it—follow the guidelines below.

•**Eat a high-fiber diet.** Get at least 30 grams of fiber each day to improve liver and bowel function.

Good choices: Broccoli, cauliflower, brussels sprouts, buckwheat, brown rice, flaxseeds and whole grains.

•**Choose organic produce and grains,** which are largely free of pesticides. They ease the workload on the liver, helping it get rid of excess estrogen.

●**Select meats from grass-fed livestock.** These animals were not given feed laced with hormones, so their meat is free of added estrogen.

●**Opt for plant milks,** such as organic almond milk and rice milk, instead of cow's milk.

●**Drink purified water.** To remove xenoestrogens, install an under-sink reverse-osmosis water-filtration system (sold at home-improvement stores) at home.

Economical: Faucet filters, such as those from Brita or Pur.

●**Consume alcohol only in moderation,** if at all, to optimize liver health.

●**Take daily multivitamin/mineral supplements.** Teens and adults should use a formula that includes magnesium at 400 milligrams (mg) to 500 mg...vitamin B-6 at 25 mg to 50 mg...vitamin B-12 at 50 micrograms (mcg) to 2,000 mcg...vitamin C at 500 mg to 1,000 mg...and vitamin E at 200 international units (IU). Children should take an age-appropriate formula.

People who test positive for, or have many symptoms of, hyperestrogenism also should...

●**Supplement with *indole-3-carbinol*.** This phytonutrient, extracted from broccoli, supports liver function.

Daily dosage: 400 mg in capsule form.

●**Take calcium d-glucarate.** Found naturally in apples, cherries, grapefruit, broccoli and alfalfa, this nutrient helps the liver.

Daily dosage: 2,000 mg.

Supplements are sold in health-food stores. Indole-3-carbinol and calcium d-glucarate have not been studied in children and should not be used by women who are pregnant or breast-feeding—otherwise they are safe and can be taken indefinitely.

Estrogen overload contributes to numerous health problems. If you have any of the conditions below, ask a holistic doctor if hyperestrogenism could be to blame.

IN WOMEN...

●**Endometriosis** (uterine lining overgrowth)

●**Fibrocystic breast disease**
●**Hair loss**
●**Menstrual cycle irregularities**
●**Premenstrual symptoms** (moderate, even severe)
●**Ovarian cysts or ovarian cancer**
●**Uterine fibroids or uterine cancer**

Omega-3s May Fight Hot Flashes

In a study of 120 menopausal women, one group took omega-3 fatty acid supplements three times daily for eight weeks, while another group took placebos.

Result: Among women who had hot flashes before the study began, those who took omega-3 supplements had an average of 1.6 fewer hot flashes daily, compared with a decrease of 0.50 in the placebo group.

Theory: Omega-3s may play a role in regulating the interaction of brain chemicals that have been linked to hot flashes.

If you have hot flashes: Ask your doctor about trying an omega-3 supplement.

Michel Lucas, PhD, R.D., epidemiologist and nutritionist, Harvard School of Public Health, Boston, Massachusetts.

Keep Your Weight Down With Calcium and Vitamin D

Combat postmenopausal weight gain by taking daily supplements of calcium (1,000 milligrams) and vitamin D (400 international units).

Recent study: Among 36,282 women ages 50 to 79, those who took these supplements over a seven-year period were less likely to gain weight than those who did not.

Theory: These nutrients may stimulate breakdown of fat cells and reduce absorption of fat by the intestines.

Important: Diet and exercise still are key to maintaining a healthy weight.

Bette Caan, DrPh, senior research scientist, Kaiser Permanente, Oakland, California, and leader of a study published in *Archives of Internal Medicine*.

Exercise Improves Quality of Life During Menopause

Exercise can improve mood and boost a woman's quality of life during menopause. Aerobic exercise, such as walking, and nonaerobic activities, such as yoga, help reduce menopause symptoms, including lack of energy, irritability and, in some women, severity of hot flashes and night sweats.

Steriani Elavsky, PhD, assistant professor of kinesiology, Penn State University, University Park, Pennsylvania, and leader of a four-month study of 164 women, published in *Annals of Behavioral Medicine*.

Ease Menopausal Anxiety

Emotional symptoms of menopause are eased by exercising.

Recent finding: Anxiety, stress and depression are significantly lower among postmenopausal women who work out regularly.

But: Physical activity does not alleviate hot flashes.

Deborah B. Nelson, PhD, associate professor, Temple University College of Health Professions, Philadelphia, and co-investigator of a study of 380 women, published in *Medicine & Science in Sports & Exercise*.

Ten-Minute Stress Cure— How You Can Elicit the Relaxation Response

Herbert Benson, MD. Dr. Benson is director emeritus of the Benson-Henry Institute for Mind/Body Medicine at Massachusetts General Hospital and Associate professor of medicine at Harvard Medical School. He is a pioneer in mind–body medicine.

Medical researchers are connecting more and more dots in their understanding of the insidious ways stress harms our health. No question it's important to learn all we can about this important topic, but sometimes it seems as though we are chasing our own tails trying to find new solutions when simple ones are already known to be effective. One such simple solution is known as the Relaxation Response, which has been around since the 1960s—and in fact has roots in virtually every religious tradition. Developed in 1968 by Harvard professor Herbert Benson, MD, this straightforward approach to stress relief has amassed an impressive resume of research demonstrating its efficacy at improving a wide range of problems, from premenstrual syndrome (PMS) to menopausal symptoms to poor academic performance.

Dr. Benson is widely recognized as one of the foremost researchers in the field of stress management. Director Emeritus of the Benson-Henry Institute for Mind/Body Medicine at Massachusetts General Hospital, he explains that "scores of diseases and conditions are either caused by or made worse by stress." He says that 60% to 90% of all doctor visits are for complaints related to or impacted by it, including anxiety, mild or moderate depression, anger, hostility, menopausal hot flashes, infertility, PMS, high blood pressure and heart attacks. To some extent, he said, "every one of those can be caused by stress or exacerbated by it."

TURNING THE HORMONES "OFF"

We now know that stress is more than just a mild feeling of being under the gun, but rather a complicated series of biochemical and hormonal processes in the body. Also known as the "fight or flight" response, the stress response activates stress hormones, including cortisol and adrenaline. While cortisol has an important role in our health and is required for survival, research has demonstrated its ill effects, including (in the lab) that high levels cause shrinkage in a part of the brain called the hippocampus, central to memory and thinking. High levels of cortisol also contribute to accumulation of abdominal fat. "The fact that for most of us these stress hormones are constantly in the 'on' position to varying degrees has significant health consequences," said Dr. Benson.

The Relaxation Response is the exact opposite of the stress response. It mitigates the stress reaction by slowing metabolism, lowering heart rate and decreasing blood pressure. During the relaxation response, levels of nitric oxide, an important biochemical involved in circulation and the improvement of blood flow, are elevated. This calming biochemical response enables the muscles to relax and breathing to slow down to a more normal rate.

HOW DOES IT WORK?

The Relaxation Response is based on repetition of a simple word or phrase, just like prayer and other forms of meditation, Dr. Benson pointed out. "Prayer generally consists of repetitive words sometimes in a chant-like rhythm," he noted, and in fact his early research on the Relaxation Response used repetitive phrases like "Hail Mary, full of grace" for Roman Catholic research subjects, and "shalom" or "echad" for Jewish ones. Today research on the Relaxation Response typically uses the word "one" or "peace" to elicit the effect, Dr. Benson says, since he finds it useful for the widest variety of people.

Research on the short and long-term health benefits of the Relaxation Response is convincing. Published research going back to 1973 has demonstrated that use of the technique can lower blood pressure, anxiety, the symptoms and pain of headache and irritable bowel syndrome, the discomfort of PMS, as well as bring down stress hormone levels, improve insomnia and modify a number of risk factors for myocardial infarction (heart attacks). Most recently, educational research has demonstrated that incorporating use of the Relaxation Response into the school curriculum at the middle school, high school and college levels led to higher grade point averages, increased self-esteem, decreased psychological distress, better attendance and less aggression.

DO-IT-YOURSELF RELAXATION

The Relaxation Response has often been compared to Transcendental Meditation (TM), the technique taught by Maharishi Mahesh Yogi and popularized in this country by the Beatles in the mid-1960s. However, whereas it can cost thousands of dollars to learn TM from an authorized program, the Relaxation Response can be mastered on your own, for free.

HOW TO ELICIT THE RELAXATION RESPONSE*:

Set aside 10 to 20 minutes to try this technique once or twice daily, perhaps before breakfast and before dinner…

1. Sit quietly in a comfortable position.

2. Close your eyes.

3. Deeply relax all your muscles beginning at your feet and progressing up to your face. Keep them relaxed.

4. Breathe comfortably. Become aware of your breathing. As you breathe out, say the word "ONE" silently to yourself. For example, breathe IN…OUT ("ONE"), IN…OUT ("ONE"), etc. Breathe easily and naturally.

5. Other thoughts will come to mind. This is normal and should be expected. When other thoughts occur, simply say "Oh, well" and return to repetition.

You may open your eyes to check the time, but don't use an alarm. When you finish, sit quietly for several minutes—first keeping your eyes closed, then slowly opening them. Wait a few minutes before standing.

Don't worry about whether you are "successful" in achieving a deep level of relaxation. Maintain a positive and passive attitude, permitting relaxation to occur at its own pace. When distracting thoughts occur—and they will—don't be critical of yourself. Try instead to ignore them by not dwelling upon them, and just return to your breathing and repeating of the word "ONE."

*From *The Relaxation Response*, used with permission from the author.

Note: With practice, says Dr. Benson, this response will come with very little effort. He suggests practicing the technique once or twice a day, but also suggests not doing it within a couple of hours of eating, as the digestive process seems to interfere with eliciting the Relaxation Response.

Menopause Does Not Impair Memory

In a study conducted over a five-year period, yearly follow-ups did not show a decline among 803 menopausal women who took memory tests, such as repeating a list of numbers backward. Menopausal changes do not cause forgetfulness.

Peter M. Meyer, PhD, associate professor and director, section of biostatistics, preventive medicine department, Rush University Medical Center, Chicago.

Change for the Better

Bill Gottlieb, health educator and author of six books, including *Alternative Cures* (Ballantine), *Breakthroughs in Drug-Free Healing* and *Speed Healing* (Bottom Line Books) and *The Natural Fat-Loss Pharmacy* (Broadway). Former editor-in-chief of Rodale Books and Prevention Magazine Health Books, he lives in northern California.

Forty-three million American women are postmenopausal—and they'll be joined by 17 million of their sisters by 2020. In fact, by 2015, nearly 50% of women in the US will be menopausal.

Perimenopause (the time immediately before menopause) usually starts in a woman's 40s, when the length of the menstrual cycle starts to change and then there are missed menses. You're "officially" menopausal 12 months after your final period—on average, that's around the age of 51.

But whenever you enter menopause—you're not dealing with a disease that requires a cure, says Tori Hudson, ND, medical director of A Woman's Time clinic in Portland, Oregon, and author of *Women's Encyclopedia of Natural*

Medicine: Alternative Therapies and Integrative Medicine for Total Health and Wellness (McGraw-Hill).

"Except when triggered by surgery, medications or radiation, menopause is a normal, natural event of aging," she says. "It is not a disease process. It is not a sign of impending disability or frailty. It can be—and often is—the beginning of a new phase of life, with new options, new learning opportunities and new adventures."

However: "Even though it is a normal process of aging, the natural transition from the reproductive years to the postmenopausal years is not necessarily a smooth one," says Dr. Hudson.

As the hormones estrogen and progesterone fluctuate and drop with perimenopause, you can start to have hot flashes, insomnia, mood swings, poor concentration and other symptoms. The intensity of those symptoms can range from the mild (one hot flash per month, for example) to the severe (one hot flash per hour).

For 75% to 90% of women, symptoms last four to seven years and then disappear. For 10% to 25%, they persist. *For 100%, relief is within reach…*

• **Cool off your hot flashes.** About 85% of perimenopausal and menopausal women in the US report hot flashes—a wavelike sensation of heat over the body, particularly the upper torso, face and head. (When they happen at night, drenching you in perspiration, they're called *night sweats*.)

Experts still don't know what causes hot flashes. But they do know safe, self-care methods that can reduce their intensity and severity or even stop them completely.

• **Black cohosh.** This is the best-researched herb for hot flashes and night sweats, with the most positive therapeutic results, says Dr. Hudson.

Recent study: Chinese doctors studied 244 menopausal women for three months, giving them a black cohosh extract or *tibolone*, a synthetic steroid with estrogen-like effects. (Tibolone is used in 70 countries to treat the symptoms of menopause, but has not been approved by the FDA for use in the US.)

After three months, the women taking the black cohosh extract had an average 68% drop in their "Kupperman Score," a standard measurement of menopause symptoms.

That means after taking black cohosh extract, they had fewer and less intense hot flashes…fewer and less intense night sweats…were less nervous and irritable…were less depressed…and their concentration improved. Tibolone produced similar benefits. But it also produced vaginal bleeding, breast pain and abdominal pain.

"The efficacy of black cohosh is as good as tibolone for the treatment of menopausal complaints, even for moderate to severe symptoms," say the researchers. "Black cohosh is an excellent option for treatment of menopausal conditions."

Product: This study used the form of black cohosh that has been tested successfully in more than 90 scientific studies—Remifemin, from Enzymatic Therapy. It's available at *www. enzymatictherapy.com*, or call 800-783-2286.

Suggested intake: Follow the dosage recommendation on the label, says Holly Lucille, ND, a naturopathic physician in Los Angeles —one tablet in the morning and one in the evening, with water.

Why it works: For many years, doctors theorized that black cohosh extract reduced hot flashes because it contained *phytoestrogens*—estrogen-like plant compounds. But black cohosh does not appear to be estrogenic whatsoever, say researchers at the University of Illinois in Chicago, who analyzed the estrogenic properties of the herb. Now, that same team of researchers, led by Z. Jim Wang, PhD, has discovered the way that black cohosh might work.

Your brain has opiate receptors—chemical sensors that respond to opiates such as morphine, Dr. Wang explains. When the opiates attach to their receptors, they trigger key brain functions, such as the regulation of pain, appetite and body temperature.

"We found that elements in black cohosh extract bind to the 'mu' opiate receptor," says Dr. Wang. "This particular opiate receptor system affects several aspects of female reproductive neuroendocrinology, such as the levels of sex hormones and neurotransmitters that are important for temperature regulation."

In other words, black cohosh might work to correct the drop in neurotransmitters that disrupts your personal thermostat.

Caution: In rare cases, black cohosh may affect the liver. If you have a known liver disease such as chronic hepatitis C, or you consume three or more alcoholic drinks a day, you probably shouldn't use black cohosh, says Dr. Hudson—or, if you do, a doctor should regularly test your liver enzymes to check that the herb is not starting to cause damage.

•**Pycnogenol.** Doctors in Taiwan studied 155 menopausal women, dividing them into two groups. One group took Pycnogenol—a potent antioxidant derived from pine bark. The other group took a placebo.

After six months, there was no change in the placebo group. But the women taking Pycnogenol had an average decrease in the severity and frequency of hot flashes—and also an overall reduction in other symptoms of menopause, such as insomnia, fatigue, headache, vaginal dryness, memory and concentration problems, and low libido. (There was also a drop in blood pressure and "bad" LDL' cholesterol—important benefits for menopausal women, who have an increased risk for heart disease.)

Why it works: Pycnogenol increases circulation and decreases inflammation, both of which could help ease menopause symptoms, say the researchers.

Suggested intake: The women in the study used 100 milligrams (mg), twice daily.

•**Sleep through the night.** If you're tossing and turning at night, you should turn toward help. "It's crucial to stop insomnia as soon as it starts in perimenopause or menopause, because poor sleep leads to fatigue and depression, which quickly worsens a woman's quality of life," says Dr. Hudson. *There are several types of insomnia that can bother a menopausal woman…*

•**Waking up with night sweats.** If that's the case, try black cohosh, says Dr. Hudson.

Also helpful: Another possible product to use is Women's Phase II, from Vitanica. It contains ingredients a study shows can reduce hot flashes and night sweats *and* improve sleep—

dong quai root, licorice root, burdock root, motherwort leaf and wild yam root. It's available at *www.vitanica.com*, or call 800-572-4712.

●**Difficulty falling asleep.** This kind of insomnia is easy to clear up, says Dr. Hudson.

She recommends that about 30 minutes before bedtime you try either valerian (1 to 2 capsules, or 1 to 2 teaspoons of a liquid extract) …melatonin (start at 2 mg and increase up to 10 mg)…*L-tryptophan* (1,000 mg)…or *5-HTP* (100 to 300 mg, 45 minutes before bedtime).

"It's a trial-and-error process," she says. "Usually one of them will do the trick."

●**For insomnia and depression.** 5-HTP and L-tryptophan boost mood-elevating serotonin levels, so either supplement is a good choice if you have insomnia and depression, says Dr. Hudson.

●**For insomnia and anxiety.** Valerian is calming and is a good choice if you have insomnia and anxiety.

●**Difficulty staying asleep or waking early and not being able to go back to sleep.** If you wake up and can't fall back to sleep, you might try an over-the-counter medication such as Tylenol PM or Benadryl.

If you're chronically anxious or depressed, you might take an herbal preparation during the day, such as kava,* which a study shows can help alleviate these emotions in perimenopausal women. Dr. Hudson recommends 100 to 210 mg of an extract standardized to 70% kavapyrones. (Kava should not be used long term. Talk to your doctor.)

However: These two types of insomnia are difficult to treat with self-care and require medical attention, says Dr. Hudson.

She sometimes uses hormonal replacement therapy…sometimes tests neurotransmitters and then treats with specific amino acids that balance neurotransmitters…and sometimes tests levels of the stress hormone cortisol, and, if it's high at night, uses intensive natural treatments to lower it.

"These aren't self-care methods, but they can really work," she says.

●**The best treatment for vaginal dryness.** "Vaginal dryness, vaginal thinning—with

*Kava should not be used long term. Please consult your doctor before taking Kava.

irritation, itching and pain with vaginal sex— are very common problems for menopausal women, but they usually don't become troublesome until several years after menopause," says Dr. Hudson.

What happens: When estrogen levels decline, the vulva loses its collagen, fat and water-retaining ability and becomes flattened, thin and dry, and loses tone. The vagina also shortens and narrows, and the vaginal walls become thinner and less elastic.

Best: "The remedy that works the quickest and the best is prescription vaginal estrogen— it's a miraculous medicine," says Dr. Hudson. It comes in creams, gels, suppositories and vaginal rings. Dr. Hudson favors bioidentical estriol, which she says has more affinity to vaginal tissue than other estrogens. "A common prescription is one milligram of estriol per one gram of cream. One gram of cream is inserted in the vagina daily as a loading dose, then twice a week as a maintenance program." Talk to your doctor about this treatment.

A possible alternative—particularly for breast cancer survivors concerned about exposure to estrogen—is the over-the-counter product Replens, a vaginal moisturizer. "It has less of an effect than vaginal estrogen, but still significantly improves the elasticity and integrity of vaginal tissue," says Dr. Hudson. Replens is widely available.

Another possible choice is an all-natural vaginal moisturizer—the Personal Moisturizer, from Emerita, available at *www.emerita.com*, or call 800-888-6041.

●**Lift depression, ease anxiety.** "Depression and anxiety are very common during perimenopause, especially in women with a history of depression," says Dr. Hudson. Irritability and mood swings are also common.

What happens: Fluctuating hormones impact brain chemistry, causing more intense emotional ups and downs.

An herbal formula with both the antidepressant herb St. John's Wort and black cohosh is a "perfect combo" for a woman with hot flashes and mild depression, says Dr. Hudson.

Product: Woman's Passage, from Vitanica, which includes hops extract (shown to reduce hot flashes and help with sleep), St. John's

Wort extract (for depression) and black cohosh extract (for hot flashes).

Another possible treatment, says Dr. Hudson, is SAMe (*S-adenyosyl-methionine*), a natural compound that helps produce neurotransmitters (brain chemicals that regulate mood) and phospholipids (crucial factors in strong, well-functioning brain cells).

Suggested intake: 1,600 mg a day, in 800 mg or 400 mg doses.

For anxiety, Dr. Hudson suggests black cohosh and one or more of several anti-anxiety compounds, including…

• **GABA** (gamma-aminobutyric acid), a calming biochemical, which works in a few days to a week or two, at a dose of 750 mg, twice a day.

• **Kava,*** a calming herb, which works in a day, with a maximum daily intake of 210 mg (see your doctor).

• **Magnesium,** a mineral that balances the nervous system, at 300 mg a day.

• **B-complex vitamins,** which also balance the nervous system, using a B-50 or B-100 supplement.

• **Fish oil,** which has been shown to be effective for many emotional difficulties, including depression, anxiety and hostility—1 to 2 grams a day.

*Kava should not be used long term. Please consult your doctor before taking Kava.

The Super Food That Helps with Menopause and More

Mark A. Stengler, NMD, naturopathic medical doctor in private practice, Encinitas, California…adjunct associate clinical professor at the National College of Natural Medicine, Portland, Oregon…author of *The Natural Physician's Healing Therapies* (Bottom Line Books).

An ancient crop long cultivated by farmers in the highlands of Peru is now being touted as an amazing super food.

Maca (pronounced MACK-uh)—a root-vegetable cousin of the common radish—was a nearly extinct crop as late as 1992. Now, however, it is eagerly sought after for its healthful properties.

SOOTHES MENOPAUSAL SYMPTOMS

For women, maca has a long-standing reputation for soothing menopausal symptoms. A study published in 2006 in the *International Journal of Biomedical Science* details research at five sites in Poland, focusing on 124 women, ages 49 to 58, who were in the early stages of menopause.

During the study, the women took varied combinations of either a placebo or 2,000 milligrams (mg) of maca every day.

Results: Compared with placebo users, those taking maca experienced significant reductions —84%, on average—in the frequency and severity of menopausal symptoms, particularly hot flashes and night sweats. The participants also reported that maca reduced nervousness, mood swings, fatigue, stress, headaches and depression, as well as improved sleep patterns and libido.

Bonus: In a substudy of the trial, researchers found that the women taking maca had a notable increase in bone density.

HOW TO TAKE MACA

I recommend organically grown maca products from Natural Health International, or NHI (888-668-3661, *www.naturalhi.com*, available online or through naturopathic doctors). The company sells a blend for women called Femenessence™ MacaPause™ (the same blend used in the study of Polish women, who experienced significant improvement in their menopausal symptoms) and another for men, Revolution Macalibrium, formulated to enhance energy and vitality in men as they age.

Cost: $38 for 120 capsules of 750 mg each. The average dosage of maca supplements is 1,000 mg to 2,000 mg daily, which you can take anytime. You can also sprinkle maca powder into your favorite foods and drinks. The powder costs about $18/pound and is available online from *www.navitasnaturals.com*, *www.superorganicfoods.com* and *www.iherb.com*. Maca has a slightly nutty flavor, so I recommend mixing it with almond milk.

13

Pain Free Naturally

For Pain Relief That Won't Harm You— Four Natural Herbs

As a naturopathic physician, there is nothing more satisfying than helping patients alleviate pain with natural pain relievers— especially since these have few of the adverse effects of pharmaceutical medications.

More than 30 million Americans take conventional painkillers *daily* for a variety of ailments, including arthritis, headaches, sore muscles and back or neck pain. While these drugs are good at temporarily relieving pain, they all have unhealthful side effects, particularly when used over time for chronic conditions. They can irritate the stomach, cause stomach and intestinal ulcers and increase heart disease risk.

Fortunately, there are natural pain relievers that work as well as, or better than, these drugs, and they are much gentler on your body.

I prescribe the herbs described on the next pages for patients with a variety of ailments. I believe that they can help you, too.

Caution: Women who are pregnant or breast-feeding should not take these remedies, because they have not been studied in these populations.

Strategy: For chronic pain involving any of the conditions in the table at the end of this article, take the first painkiller listed for that condition for four weeks. If you notice an improvement, stay with it. If not, try the next one (if there is one).

Try the following herbs—which are all available at health-food stores or online—for the conditions listed…

DEVIL'S CLAW

Devil's claw (*Harpagophytum procumbens*), a shrub found in southern Africa, works

Mark A. Stengler, NMD, naturopathic medical doctor in private practice, Encinitas, California…adjunct associate clinical professor at the National College of Natural Medicine, Portland, Oregon…author of *The Natural Physician's Healing Therapies* (Bottom Line Books).

258

similarly to many pharmaceutical pain relievers —by blocking the action of pain-promoting compounds in the body—but without damaging the digestive tract. In studies involving people with chronic low back pain, devil's claw extract proved as effective as prescription pain relievers.

Dose: Devil's claw extract is available in capsules. Look for 1.5% to 2.0% *harpagoside*, one of the active ingredients. Take 1,000 milligrams (mg) three times daily of a standardized extract.

Recommended brand: Nature's Way Standardized Devil's Claw Extract (800-962-8873, *http://naturesway.com*). The only significant potential side effect is diarrhea.

CURCUMIN

Curcumin (*diferuloylmethane*), a constituent of turmeric, is the pigment compound that gives the spice its distinctive yellow coloring. In one study of rheumatoid arthritis patients, 1,200 mg daily of curcumin extract improved morning stiffness and joint swelling.

Dose: Take 500 mg of standardized turmeric extract (containing 90% to 95% curcumin) three times daily.

Recommended brands: New Chapter Turmeric force (800-543-7279, *www.newchapter. com*) and Life Extension Super Curcumin (888-771-3905, *www.lifeextensionvitamins.com*). It has blood-thinning properties, so do not take curcumin if you take blood-thinning medication, such as *warfarin*, unless monitored by a physician.

Avoid this: If you have gallstones, because curcumin can cause gallstones to block bile ducts.

WHITE WILLOW BARK

This pain reliever has anti-inflammatory and blood-thinning benefits similar to those of aspirin, but unlike aspirin, it doesn't appear to damage the stomach lining. For centuries, the bark of the white willow (*Salix alba*), a tree found in Europe and Asia, was noted for its pain-relieving qualities. Its active ingredient is salicin, which the body converts to *salicylic acid*, a close cousin to aspirin (*acetylsalicylic acid*).

Dose: Take 120 mg daily of white willow bark extract capsules. If this amount does not reduce pain, try 240 mg.

Recommended brand: Solaray White Willow Bark (for product information, call 800-579-4665 or visit *www.nutraceutical.com*).

Avoid this: If you have an aspirin allergy and for one week before undergoing surgery. White willow bark is a blood thinner, so take it only while being monitored by a physician if you take blood-thinning medication.

BOSWELLIA

Part of India's Ayurvedic healing tradition, boswellia (*Boswellia serrata*) comes from a tree found in India, Northern Africa and the Middle East. The tree yields a milky resin containing *boswellic acids*, substances that inhibit the body's synthesis of inflammatory *leukotrienes*. A study of patients with knee arthritis found that boswellia extract relieved pain and stiffness as well as daily doses of the prescription drug *valdecoxib* (Bextra). And boswellia's benefits persisted for one month longer than those of Bextra.

Dose: Take 750 mg of a standardized extract containing 60% to 65% boswellic acid two to three times daily for as long as symptoms last.

Recommended brand: Solgar Boswellia Resin Extract (877-765-4274, *www.solgar.com*). While generally safe, boswellia has been known to cause occasional mild digestive upset.

NATURAL PAIN RELIEVERS

Condition	Pain Relievers to Try*
Headache (tension or migraine)	White willow bark
Inflammatory bowel disease	Boswellia, Curcumin
Low back pain	Devil's claw, White willow bark, Curcumin
Muscle aches and pain	White willow bark, Curcumin
Menstrual pain	White willow bark

*Take the first painkiller listed for your condition for four weeks. If it doesn't work, try the next one (if there is one).

Osteoarthritis	Boswellia, White willow bark, Devil's claw
Rheumatoid arthritis	Boswellia, Curcumin, Devil's claw
Tendonitis	Devil's claw, Curcumin, White willow bark

Qigong Eases Arthritis

Kevin W. Chen, PhD, MPH, associate professor, Center for Integrative Medicine, University of Maryland, Baltimore, and coauthor of a study of 106 arthritis patients, published in *Clinical Rheumatology*.

Practitioners of *qigong* use traditional Chinese medicine techniques—such as mind–body breath work, acupressure, therapeutic touch and focused attention—to stimulate the healing flow of *qi* (energy).

New study: Among patients with knee osteoarthritis, those who participated in five or six qigong sessions reported 13% to 26% greater reduction in pain and 13% to 28% more improvement in function than patients who got placebo treatments.

Results vary depending on the practitioner —so look for an experienced practitioner when starting out, then take classes to learn to practice qigong on your own.

Resources: National Qigong Association, 888-815-1893, *www.nqa.org*…Qigong Research Society, 856-234-3056, *www.qigongresearch society.com*.

Any Old Cane Won't Do

American Geriatrics Society, news release.

When it comes time to use a cane to walk or support you after an injury, don't grab any old stick, advises the American Geriatrics Society.

Getting a cane tailored to your body and needs, and using it properly, is vital to its success and your health, according to the society's past president, John Murphy, MD.

"A common use of canes is for arthritis in the hip," said Dr. Murphy. "For patients using a cane for pain in one hip, the cane should be held in the hand opposite the affected leg. The cane should then move forward with the affected leg."

Dr. Murphy offered several tips for selecting a cane…

• **Check the tip.** A rubber tip is a must for traction. Check the tip often, and replace it when the tread is worn.

• **Get a grip.** Find one that feels comfortable when held. A person who has arthritis or an injury that affects the fingers and hands might need a specialized grip.

• **Adjust for your body.** When standing, the elbow should be at a 30-degree angle when the cane is held next to the leg. When your arm is at your side, the cane's top should be parallel with your wrist.

What Relief! Natural Ways to Curb Your Pain

Mark A. Stengler, NMD, naturopathic medical doctor in private practice, Encinitas, California…adjunct associate clinical professor at the National College of Natural Medicine, Portland, Oregon…author of *The Natural Physician's Healing Therapies* (Bottom Line Books).

Not long ago, a 60-year-old woman came to my office suffering from severe arthritis pain in both hands. I gave her a bean-sized dab of a homeopathic gel that she applied directly to the skin on her hands. After a few applications in the span of 30 minutes, her pain was reduced by 90%. She did not need to apply the gel again for two weeks.

I witnessed a similar result with a retired National Football League player. He had severe chronic hip pain from past injuries. With one application of the gel, his pain was relieved by 70% for two full days.

The relief that these people experienced has given them each a new lease on life. *But here's the best news*—unlike pharmaceutical pain relievers, which often cause gastrointestinal upset or damage to internal organs, natural therapies can reduce pain without adverse effects.

WHAT ARE YOU TAKING
FOR PAIN?

Most Americans take too many pharmaceutical pain relievers. An estimated 175 million American adults take over-the-counter (OTC) pain relievers regularly. About one-fifth of Americans in their 60s take at least one pain-killer for chronic pain on a regular basis.

There has been a lot written about the life-threatening risks of anti-inflammatory medications such as *rofecoxib* (Vioxx) and *celecoxib* (Celebrex), two pain relievers that had been heavily prescribed by conventional doctors to treat the chronic pain of arthritis and similar conditions. Vioxx was pulled off the market by its manufacturer, Merck, following research that linked it to increased risk of heart attack and stroke. Celebrex is undergoing post-marketing clinical trials to determine whether it poses similar risks and now carries warnings about adverse effects, such as abdominal pain, diarrhea and edema (water retention).

Of course, pain-relieving drugs can be a blessing in the event of injury, severe acute migraines or diseases, such as terminal cancer. A number of years ago, when I had a wisdom tooth extracted, I received a local anesthetic. Afterward, I went to an acupuncturist for pain relief so I wouldn't need any painkillers. For about one hour after the acupuncture, I was fine—but then the pain-relieving endorphins wore off. I tried a few natural remedies, but when the pain became excruciating, I resorted to the OTC pain reliever *acetaminophen* (Tylenol). That did the trick.

But many people use painkillers on a regular basis for several months or even years, which increases the risk of dangerous side effects. For instance, people who rely on acetaminophen increase their risk of developing stomach ulcers, liver disease and kidney disease. If you regularly take Celebrex or an OTC nonsteroidal anti-inflammatory drug (NSAID), such as aspirin or *naproxen* (Aleve), you run the risk of kidney and stomach damage. Regular use of NSAIDs also increases risk of heart attack, according to the FDA.

BETTER RESULTS,
FEWER RISKS

Before you take any remedy, it's important for your doctor to identify what is causing your pain. Remember, pain is your body's distress signal that something is being irritated or damaged. Sometimes we protect ourselves by reacting instinctively. If you touch something hot, for example, you eliminate the pain by quickly pulling back your hand.

But what if your back hurts? You may need a pain reliever—but back pain also can be a signal that you're harming your body by bending or sitting the wrong way. You may need to address the underlying cause to prevent further injury. Pain receptors are found in the skin, around bones and joints—even in the walls of arteries. If a muscle is torn, for example, a pain signal is released from fibers in the shredded tissue.

In light of the dangers from prescription and OTC drugs, what safe alternatives are available to you? There are many natural supplements that I recommend.

NATURE'S PAIN RELIEVERS

If you take prescription or OTC pain medication, work with a naturopathic physician, holistic medical doctor or chiropractor who will incorporate natural pain fighters into your treatment regimen. With his/her help, you may be able to reduce your dosage of pain medication (natural pain relievers can be used safely with prescription or OTC painkillers)—or even eliminate the drugs altogether.

Natural pain-fighting supplements are even more effective when combined with physical therapies, such as acupuncture, chiropractic, magnet therapy or osteopathic manipulation (a technique in which an osteopathic physician uses his hands to move a patient's muscles and joints with stretching, gentle pressure and resistance). Physiotherapy (treatment that uses physical agents, such as exercise and massage, to develop, maintain and restore movement and functional ability) also is helpful.

Here are—in no special order—the best natural pain relievers, which can be taken alone or in combination...

261

•**White willow bark extract** is great for headaches, arthritis, muscle aches and fever. In Europe, doctors prescribe this herbal remedy for back pain, and recent research supports this use. One study conducted in Haifa, Israel, involved 191 patients with chronic low-back pain who took one of two doses of willow bark extract or a placebo daily for four weeks. Researchers found that 39% of patients taking the higher dose of willow bark extract had complete pain relief, compared with only 6% of those taking a placebo. The participants who benefited the most took willow bark extract that contained 240 milligrams (mg) of the compound *salicin*, the active constituent in this herbal remedy. (Aspirin is made from *acetylsalicylic acid*, which has many of the chemical properties of salicin.) However, aspirin can cause gastrointestinal ulceration and other side effects, including kidney damage. Willow bark extract is believed to work by inhibiting naturally occurring enzymes that cause inflammation and pain.

I recommend taking willow bark extract that contains 240 mg of salicin daily. In rare cases, willow bark extract can cause mild stomach upset. Don't take willow bark if you have a history of ulcers, gastritis or kidney disease. It also should not be taken by anyone who is allergic to aspirin. As with aspirin, willow bark extract should never be given to children under age 12 who have a fever—in rare instances, it can cause a fatal disease called Reye's syndrome. Willow bark extract has blood-thinning properties, so avoid it if you take a blood thinner, such as *warfarin* (Coumadin). For low-back pain, you may need to take willow bark extract for a week or more before you get results.

•*Methylsulfonylmethane* (MSM) is a popular nutritional supplement that relieves muscle and joint pain. According to Stanley Jacob, MD, a professor at Oregon Health & Science University who has conducted much of the original research on MSM, this supplement reduces inflammation by improving blood flow. Your cells have receptors that send out pain signals when they're deprived of blood. That's why increased blood flow diminishes pain.

MSM, a natural compound found in green vegetables, fruits and grains, reduces muscle spasms and softens painful scar tissue from previous injuries. A double-blind study of 50 people with osteoarthritis of the knee found that MSM helps relieve arthritis pain.

Start with a daily dose of 3,000 mg to 5,000 mg of MSM. If your pain and/or inflammation doesn't improve within five days, increase the dose up to 8,000 mg daily, taken in several doses throughout the day. If you develop digestive upset or loose stools, reduce the dosage. If you prefer, you can apply MSM cream (per the label instructions) to your skin at the painful area. This product is available at health-food stores and works well for localized pain. MSM has a mild blood-thinning effect, so check with your doctor if you take a blood thinner.

•*S-adenosylmethionine* (SAMe) is a natural compound found in the body. The supplement is an effective treatment for people who have osteoarthritis accompanied by cartilage degeneration. SAMe's ability to reduce pain, stiffness and swelling is similar to that of NSAIDs such as ibuprofen and naproxen, and the anti-inflammatory medication Celebrex. There's also evidence that SAMe stimulates cartilage repair, which helps prevent bones from rubbing against one another. A 16-week study conducted at the University of California, Irvine, compared two groups of people who were being treated for knee pain caused by osteoarthritis. Some took 1,200 mg of SAMe daily, while others took 200 mg of Celebrex. It took longer for people to get relief from SAMe, but by the second month, SAMe proved to be just as effective as Celebrex.

Most patients with osteoarthritis and fibromyalgia (a disorder characterized by widespread pain in muscles, tendons and ligaments) who take SAMe notice improvement within four to eight weeks. Many studies use 1,200 mg of SAMe daily in divided doses. In my experience, taking 400 mg twice daily works well. It's a good idea to take a multivitamin or 50-mg B-complex supplement daily while you're taking SAMe. The vitamin B-12 and folic acid contained in either supplement help your body metabolize SAMe, which means that the remedy goes to work faster.

•**Kaprex** is effective for mild pain caused by injury or osteoarthritis. It is a blend of hops, rosemary extract and *oleanic acid*, which is derived from olive leaf extract. Rather than blocking the body's pain-causing enzymes, these natural substances inhibit pain-causing chemicals called *prostaglandins*.

In a study sponsored by the Institute for Functional Medicine, the research arm of the supplement manufacturer Metagenics, taking Kaprex for six weeks reduced minor pain by as much as 72%. I recommend taking one 440-mg tablet three times daily. Kaprex is manufactured by Metagenics (800-692-9400, *www.metagenics.com*), the institute's product branch. The product is sold only in doctors' offices. To find a practitioner in your area who sells Kaprex, call the toll-free number. Kaprex has no known side effects and does not interact with other medications.

•**Proteolytic enzymes,** including *bromelain*, *trypsin, chymotrypsin, pancreatin, papain* and a range of protein-digesting enzymes derived from the fermentation of fungus, reduce pain and inflammation by improving blood flow. You can find these natural pain fighters at health-food stores in products labeled "proteolytic enzymes." Take as directed on the label. Bromelain, a favorite of athletes, is available on its own. Extracted from pineapple stems, bromelain reduces swelling by breaking down blood clots that can form as a result of trauma and impede circulation. It works well for bruises, sprains and surgical recovery. If you use bromelain, take 500 mg three times daily between meals.

Repair is a high-potency formula of proteolytic enzymes that I often recommend. It is manufactured by Enzymedica (to find a retailer, call 888-918-1118 or go to *www. enzymedica.com*). Take two capsules two to three times daily between meals. Don't take Repair or any proteolytic enzyme formula if you have an active ulcer or gastritis. Any enzyme product can have a mild blood-thinning effect, so check with your doctor if you take a blood thinner.

•**Pain Med** is the homeopathic gel that gave such quick relief to the patients I described at the beginning of this article. It is remarkably effective for relieving the pain of arthritis, muscle soreness and spasms, sprains, strains, stiffness, headaches (especially due to tension) as well as injuries, including bruises.

Pain Med is a combination of nine highly diluted plant and flower materials, including *arnica, bryonia, hypericum* and *ledum*. Like other homeopathic remedies, it promotes the body's ability to heal itself. A bean-sized dab works well for anyone who has pain. It should be spread on the skin around the affected area. Following an injury, use it every 15 minutes, for a total of up to four applications. As the pain starts to diminish, apply less often. Do not reapply the gel once the pain is gone. Pain Med does not sting, burn or irritate the skin. It is clear, has no odor, does not stain and dries quickly. Because it has so many uses and works so rapidly, Pain Med is a good first-aid remedy to have on hand. To order, contact the manufacturer, GM International, Inc., at 800-228-9850 or *www.gmipainmed.com*.

Foods that Help Reduce Arthritis Pain

Vegetables, fruits and whole grains provide antioxidants that may ease the pain and swelling of arthritis, an inflammation of the joints. Also helpful are omega-3 fatty acids (found in cold-water fish, flaxseed and other foods), which the body converts to anti-inflammatory compounds. Eat eight to 12 ounces weekly of fish rich in omega-3s, such as salmon, mackerel and sardines. Limit polyunsaturated fats, such as corn oil and safflower oil, which are high in omega-6 fatty acids, substances converted in the body into compounds that promote inflammation. Also limit your intake of saturated fat, found primarily in meat and dairy products, because these unhealthy fats may increase inflammation.

Karen Collins, RD, CDN, nutrition adviser, American Institute for Cancer Research, Washington, DC.

Arthritis—Easy Ways to Beat the Pain

Peter Bales, MD, board-certified orthopedic surgeon and member of the clinical staff in the department of orthopedic surgery at the University of California at Davis Health System. A research advocate for the Arthritis Foundation (*www.arthritis.org*), he is the author of *Osteoarthritis: Preventing and Healing Without Drugs* (Prometheus).

Osteoarthritis has long been considered a "wear-and-tear" disease associated with age-related changes that occur within cartilage and bone.

Now: A growing body of evidence shows that osteoarthritis may have a metabolic basis. Poor diet results in inflammatory changes and damage in cartilage cells, which in turn lead to cartilage breakdown and the development of osteoarthritis.

A recent increase in osteoarthritis cases corresponds to similar increases in diabetes and obesity, other conditions that can be fueled by poor nutrition. Dietary approaches can help prevent—or manage—all three of these conditions.

Key scientific evidence: A number of large studies, including many conducted in Europe as well as the US, suggest that a diet emphasizing plant foods and fish can support cartilage growth and impede its breakdown. People who combine an improved diet with certain supplements can reduce osteoarthritis symptoms—and possibly stop progression of the disease.

A SMARTER DIET

By choosing your foods carefully, you can significantly improve the pain and stiffness caused by osteoarthritis. *How to get started…*

•**Avoid acidic foods.** The typical American diet, with its processed foods, red meat and harmful trans-fatty acids, increases acidity in the body. A high-acid environment within the joints increases *free radicals*, corrosive molecules that both accelerate cartilage damage and inhibit the activity of cartilage-producing cells known as *chondrocytes*.

A Mediterranean diet, which includes generous amounts of fruits, vegetables, whole grains, olive oil and fish, is more alkaline. (The body requires a balance of acidity and alkalinity, as measured on the pH scale.) A predominantly alkaline body chemistry inhibits free radicals and reduces inflammation.

What to do: Eat a Mediterranean-style diet, including six servings daily of vegetables… three servings of fruit…and two tablespoons of olive oil. (The acids in fruits and vegetables included in this diet are easily neutralized in the body.) Other sources of healthful fats include olives, nuts (such as walnuts), canola oil and flaxseed oil or ground flaxseed.

Important: It can take 12 weeks or more to flush out acidic toxins and reduce arthritis symptoms after switching to an alkaline diet.

•**Limit your intake of sugary and processed foods.** Most Americans consume a lot of refined carbohydrates as well as sugar-sweetened foods and soft drinks—all of which damage joints in several ways. For example, sugar causes an increase in *advanced glycation endproducts* (AGEs), protein molecules that bind to *collagen* (the connective tissue of cartilage and other tissues) and make it stiff and brittle. AGEs also appear to stimulate the production of cartilage-degrading enzymes.

What to do: Avoid processed foods, such as white flour (including cakes, cookies and crackers), white pasta and white rice, as well as soft drinks and fast food. Studies have shown that people who mainly eat foods in their whole, natural forms tend to have lower levels of AGEs and healthier cartilage.

Important: Small amounts of sugar—used to sweeten coffee or cereal, for example—will not significantly increase AGE levels.

•**Get more vitamin C.** More than 10 years ago, the Framingham study found that people who took large doses of vitamin C had a *threefold* reduction in the risk for osteoarthritis progression.

Vitamin C is an alkalinizing agent due to its anti-inflammatory and antioxidant properties. It blocks the inflammatory effects of free radicals. Vitamin C also decreases the formation of AGEs and reduces the chemical changes that cause cartilage breakdown.

What to do: Take a vitamin C supplement (1,000 milligrams, or mg, daily for the prevention of osteoarthritis…2,000 mg daily if you have osteoarthritis).* Also increase your intake of vitamin C–rich foods, such as sweet red peppers, strawberries and broccoli.

• **Drink green tea.** Green tea alone won't relieve osteoarthritis pain, but people who drink green tea *and* switch to a healthier diet may notice an additional improvement in symptoms. That's because green tea is among the most potent sources of antioxidants, including *catechins*, substances that inhibit the activity of cartilage-degrading enzymes. For osteoarthritis, drink one to two cups of green tea daily. (Check with your doctor first if you take any prescription drugs.)

• **Eat fish.** Eat five to six three-ounce servings of omega-3–rich fish (such as salmon, sardines and mackerel) weekly. Omega-3s in such fish help maintain the health of joint cartilage and help curb inflammation. If you would prefer to take a fish oil supplement rather than eat fish, see the recommendation below.

SUPPLEMENTS THAT HELP

Dietary changes are a first step to reducing osteoarthritis symptoms. However, the use of certain supplements also can be helpful.

• **Fish oil.** The two omega-3s in fish—*docosahexaenoic acid* (DHA) and *eicosapentaenoic acid* (EPA)—block chemical reactions in our cells that convert dietary fats into chemical messengers (such as prostaglandins), which affect the inflammatory status of our bodies. This is the same process that's inhibited by nonsteroidal anti-inflammatory drugs (NSAIDs), such as *ibuprofen* (Motrin).

What to do: If you find it difficult to eat the amount of omega-3–rich fish mentioned above, ask your doctor about taking fish oil supplements that supply a total of 1,600 mg of EPA and 800 mg of DHA daily. Look for a "pharmaceutical grade" fish oil product, such as Sealogix, available at FishOilRx.com, 877-387-4564 *www.fishoilrx.com*…or RxOmega-3 Factors at *www.iherb.com*.

If, after 12 weeks, you need more pain relief—or have a strong family history of osteoarthritis—add…

*Check with your doctor before taking any dietary supplements.

• **Glucosamine, chondroitin *and* MSM.** The most widely used supplements for osteoarthritis are glucosamine and chondroitin, taken singly or in combination. Most studies show that they work.

Better: A triple combination that contains *methylsulfonylmethane* (MSM) as well as glucosamine and chondroitin. MSM is a sulfur-containing compound that provides the raw material for cartilage regrowth. Glucosamine and chondroitin reduce osteoarthritis pain and have anti-inflammatory properties.

What to do: Take daily supplements of glucosamine (1,500 mg)…chondroitin (1,200 mg)…and MSM (1,500 mg).

Instead of—or in addition to—the fish oil and the triple combination, you may want to take…

• **SAMe.** Like MSM, *S-adenosylmethionine* (SAMe) is a sulfur-containing compound. It reduces the body's production of *TNF-alpha*, a substance that's involved in cartilage destruction. It also seems to increase cartilage production.

In one study, researchers compared SAMe to the prescription anti-inflammatory drug *celecoxib* (Celebrex*). The study was double-blind (neither the patients nor the doctors knew who was getting which drug or supplement), and it continued for four months. Initially, patients taking the celecoxib reported fewer symptoms—but by the second month, there was no difference between the two groups.

Other studies have found similar results. SAMe seems to work as well as over-the-counter and/or prescription drugs for osteoarthritis, but it works more slowly. I advise patients to take it for at least three months to see effects.

What to do: Start with 200 mg of SAMe daily and increase to 400 mg daily if necessary after a few weeks.

*Please check with your doctor before taking Celebrex.

Fruit Therapy

Eating pineapple may relieve arthritic pain. It may also help other inflammation, such as sunburn and joint pain.

Why: Pineapple contains *bromelain*, an enzyme that new research shows has anti-inflammatory benefits.

Bromelain can also be purchased in supplement form, with a recommended dose of about 100 milligrams a day for sore joints. Check with your own doctor to be sure it is OK for you.

Michael Roizen, MD, chief wellness officer, Cleveland Clinic, and Mehmet Oz, MD, vice-chair of surgery and professor of cardiac surgery at Columbia University, coauthors of *You: On a Diet* (Free Press).

Craniosacral Controversy

Mark A. Stengler, NMD, naturopathic medical doctor in private practice, Encinitas, California...adjunct associate clinical professor at the National College of Natural Medicine, Portland, Oregon...author of *The Natural Physician's Healing Therapies* (Bottom Line Books).

For such a gentle type of hands-on bodywork, craniosacral therapy (CST) has sparked some hard criticism. Some doctors describe it as flat-out worthless, citing the lack of scientific studies verifying its effectiveness. Yet in the US, practitioners of CST include osteopathic doctors, naturopathic doctors, dentists, physical therapists and nurses —and many thousands of their patients say that the therapy has helped them.

CST is used to treat pain from head, neck and back injuries...constipation...hypertension ...headache...chronic fatigue...fibromyalgia (chronic pain in muscles, ligaments and tendons)...temporomandibular joint, or TMJ, syndrome (jaw joint inflammation)...Parkinson's disease...Bell's palsy...vertigo and instability...and depression. CST also is used for children with behavior problems, learning disorders, attention deficit/hyperactivity disorder (ADHD) or autism.

How it is done: The practitioner places his/her hands on the patient's head and gently manipulates the bones of the skull. The basis of CST is the concept that the membrane encasing the brain and spinal cord fluid oscillates at a certain frequency, independent of the heartbeat. Accidents, illnesses and emotional trauma can restrict this oscillation. Specific manipulations of the skull (and sometimes near the tailbone) release membrane restrictions, freeing the cerebrospinal fluid to flow more efficiently throughout the cerebrospinal system. CST does not heal directly, but rather starts the body on a path toward self-healing. Because all bodily systems are interconnected, CST may indirectly benefit all tissues and organs.

CST sessions typically last 30 to 60 minutes. The frequency and number of treatments depend on the practitioner and ailment. Generally, patients go once or twice weekly for a month or more, then have occasional maintenance sessions. Cost varies depending on the region and type of practitioner. Health insurance, including Medicare, usually covers CST performed by a doctor of osteopathy (DO) and sometimes by other practitioners.

Although I did not take CST training in medical school, I did receive CST myself just to check it out. I believe it can be useful, especially for people with back or neck injuries ...patients who do not like or cannot receive chiropractic adjustments...newborns who suffered neck torsion (twisting) during delivery ...and children with behavior disorders. I also recall a seven-year-old patient whose very enlarged tonsils shrank by 30% after two CST treatments—and thus far, she has not needed surgery. CST may be particularly helpful when used along with chiropractic care, physical therapy and/or massage therapy.

Caution: If you have a history of stroke, ask your cardiologist before trying CST—in theory, it could increase stroke risk.

First devised by an osteopathic doctor in the 1930s, CST was further developed by the late John E. Upledger, DO, formerly a professor of biomechanics at Michigan State University. For more information or to find a practitioner near you, visit the Web site of the Upledger Institute of Palm Beach Gardens, Florida (800-233-5880, *www.upledger.com*).

Headache Relief from Acupuncture Plus Drugs

When combined with painkiller medication, acupuncture reduced the number of days people had migraine or tension headaches by 40% or more, compared with painkiller use alone.

Referrals: American Association of Acupuncture and Oriental Medicine, 866-455-7999, *www.aaaomonline.org.*

Klaus Linde, MD, senior researcher, Technical University of Munich, Germany, and lead author of two analyses of studies involving about 6,800 people.

Say Good-Bye to Your Chronic Headaches

Alexander Mauskop, MD, neurologist and director of the New York Headache Center in New York City (*www.nyheadache.com*). He is the author of *What Your Doctor May Not Tell You About Migraines* (Warner).

Of all the medical conditions that send patients to their doctors, chronic headaches (including migraines) are among the least likely to be treated effectively.*

Problem: Most chronic headache sufferers would like to simply pop a pill to relieve their pain. Although there are many helpful medications, each can have side effects and is designed to *reduce* headache pain rather than *prevent* it.

Solution: After treating thousands of headache patients, I devised a natural "triple therapy" that helps prevent migraines from developing in the first place.

Latest development: Now that I've prescribed this therapy for more than 15 years, I have added other treatments that complement the original program.

What you need to know...

*To find a headache specialist or headache support group near you, contact the National Headache Foundation (888-643-5552, *www.headaches.org*).

WHEN THE PAIN WON'T GO AWAY

Approximately 15 million Americans have chronic headaches (occurring on at least 15 days a month).

The most common forms, in order of prevalence, are *tension-type headaches* (head pain caused by tight muscles—for example, in the neck—often due to stress)...and *migraines* (throbbing head pain accompanied by other symptoms, such as nausea or dizziness, and sometimes preceded by light sensitivity and visual disturbance known as an "aura").

MY NATURAL THERAPY

Doctors don't know the exact cause of migraines, but the most popular theory focuses on disturbances in the release of pain-modulating brain chemicals, including the neurotransmitter *serotonin.*

In reviewing the medical literature, I found several references to the mineral *magnesium,* which has been shown to prevent migraines by helping open up blood vessels in the brain. Studies indicate that half of all migraine sufferers are deficient in this mineral.

Within a short time, I also discovered several references that supported the use of *riboflavin* (vitamin B-2), which plays a role in energy production in brain cells...and the herb *feverfew,* which promotes the health of blood vessels.

My advice: Each day, take a total of 400 milligrams (mg) of magnesium (as magnesium oxide or in a chelated form—if one form causes diarrhea, try the other)...400 mg of riboflavin... and a total of 100 mg of feverfew, divided in two doses with meals. Many people take this therapy indefinitely. Ask your doctor about the appropriate duration of treatment for you.

Caution: Feverfew may interfere with your blood's ability to clot, so consult your doctor before taking this herb. Riboflavin may turn your urine bright yellow, but the change is harmless.

FOR EVEN MORE PAIN RELIEF

Coenzyme Q10 (CoQ10) is a substance that, like riboflavin, is believed to fight migraines by boosting energy production in brain cells. Research has shown that 100 mg of CoQ10 three times a day reduces migraine frequency.

My advice: Take a total of 300 mg of CoQ10 daily, in one or two doses.

An extract from the root of the butterbur plant is another supplement that has shown promise as a remedy for migraines. In one study, 75 mg of butterbur taken twice daily for four months helped reduce the frequency of migraine attacks.

Although the exact mechanism of action is unclear, the herb might help reduce inflammatory substances in the body that can trigger headaches. Butterbur is sold in the US under the brand name Petadolex (888-301-1084, *www.petadolex.com*).

My advice: Take a total of 150 mg of butterbur daily, in one or two doses.

OTHER HELPFUL STRATEGIES

All the natural therapies described earlier help prevent migraines, but you're likely to achieve even better results if you adopt a "holistic" approach that includes the following steps. These strategies also help guard against chronic tension headaches but are overlooked by many doctors. *My advice...*

•**Get regular aerobic exercise.** Exercise supplies more blood to the brain and boosts levels of feel-good hormones known as *endorphins*, which help fight migraines. Physical activity also helps release muscle tension that contributes to tension-type headaches.

Scientific evidence: In data collected from 43,770 Swedes, men and women who regularly worked out were less likely to have migraines and recurring headaches than those who did not exercise.

Helpful: Do some type of moderate-intensity aerobic activity for at least 30 minutes five times a week.

•**Use relaxation techniques.** A mind-body approach, such as progressive muscle relaxation (deliberately tensing then releasing muscles from toe to head)...guided imagery (in which you create calm, peaceful images in your mind)...or breathing exercises (a method of slow inhalation and exhalation), can ease muscle tension and relax blood vessels to help prevent migraines and tension headaches.

Also helpful: Biofeedback, which involves learning to control such involuntary functions as skin temperature, heart rate or muscle tension while sensors are attached to the body, helps prevent migraines and tension headaches. Biofeedback usually can be learned in about eight sessions and should be practiced daily by migraine and tension headache sufferers. To find a biofeedback practitioner near you, consult the Biofeedback Certification Institute of America (866-908-8713, *www.bcia.org*).

•**Try acupuncture.** There's good evidence that this centuries-old needling technique can reduce the severity and frequency of migraines and tension headaches.** It typically requires at least 10 sessions to see benefits. Ask your health insurer whether acupuncture is covered. If not, each session, typically an hour long, will cost $50 to $100, depending on your location.

If you feel that you are developing a migraine or tension headache: Perform a simple *acupressure* treatment on yourself to help relieve headache pain.

What to do: Place your right thumb on the webbing at the base of your left thumb and index finger, and your right index finger on the palm side of this point. Gently squeeze and massage this area, using small circular motions, for one to two minutes. Repeat on the right hand.

**To find an acupuncturist near you, go to the National Certification Commission for Acupuncture and Oriental Medicine Web site (*www.nccaom.org*) and click on "Find a Practitioner."

Illustration by Shawn Banner.

Warmer-Than-Average Temperatures Raise Migraine Risk

Kenneth J. Mukamal, MD, internist, Beth Israel Deaconess Medical Center, Boston.
Richard Lipton, MD, director, Montefiore Headache Center, Montefiore Medical Center, New York City. *Neurology.*

If you think changes in the weather bring on migraines, it might not be all in your head.

Harvard researchers report in a new study that people are more likely to visit emergency rooms with migraines if the outside temperature is above normal. Barometric pressure has an effect, too, although it is not as significant.

The findings do not definitively prove that the weather causes migraines. Nor are they "a reason to stay indoors or move to a different part of the country," said study author Kenneth J. Mukamal, MD, an internist at Beth Israel Deaconess Medical Center in Boston.

"But this does tell us that when we identify migraine triggers, we need to keep temperature in mind," he said.

BACKGROUND

An estimated 28 million Americans suffer from migraine headaches, perhaps as many as 17% of women and 6% of men. The headaches can disable sufferers, forcing some to flee to quiet, darkened rooms for relief.

Treatments include painkillers, biofeedback and a newer class of drugs called triptans.

Many people report "triggers" that cause their migraines, including red wine, chocolate, menstrual cycles and lack of sleep. Others blame changes in the weather, and previous studies have suggested they're on to something.

THE STUDY

In the new study, researchers examined the records of 7,054 emergency room patients who were treated for migraines at Beth Israel Deaconess Medical Center between 2000 and 2007.

The researchers tried to find links between the number of headache cases and levels of temperature, barometric pressure and humidity. They also looked at air pollution levels.

The study was published in *Neurology*.

THE RESULTS

The researchers found that the number of emergency visits for headaches would rise by an average of 7.5% within 24 hours if the temperature rose by 9 degrees Fahrenheit above the expected temperature.

In a hypothetical example, the hospital would expect to see 7.5% more headache patients 24 hours after the temperature was 90 degrees instead of a typical 81 degrees.

High temperatures alone, such as those in the summer, were not as much of a trigger. The most influential factor was whether a particular day was hotter than expected.

"Warmer days were associated with higher risk, even in the winter," Dr. Mukamal said.

The researchers also found that drops in barometric pressure made headache visits more likely 48 to 72 hours later. Pollution did not seem to have an effect on headaches.

POSSIBLE EXPLANATION

Why might the weather affect migraines? Barometric pressure could affect the layer of fluid that protects the brain inside the skull, said Richard Lipton, MD, director of the Montefiore Headache Center at Montefiore Medical Center in New York City. But the effect of temperature, he said, is mystifying.

WHAT TO DO

"If someone knows that they're vulnerable to changes in temperature, what they might do is be particularly cautious about the things they can control," he said. "If you know the temperature is changing, that might be a good day to make sure you get your regular amount of sleep, avoid red wine, chocolate and the other triggers."

The National Institute of Neurological Disorders and Stroke Web site, *www.ninds.nih. gov*, has more information on migraine. Under "Health Information," click on "M" and then choose "Migraine."

Ozone/Oxygen Shot Helps Heal Herniated Disk

Society of Interventional Radiology, news release.

A shot of ozone and oxygen may prove to be a safe, effective and less invasive way to relieve the pain of a herniated disk, U.S. researchers say.

BACKGROUND

Small spongy disks normally act as shock absorbers between the vertebrae, but when one is damaged, it may bulge or break, putting pressure on spinal nerves. The standard treatments for severe pain caused by herniated disks are either open diskectomy or microdiskectomy, surgeries that require the removal of disk material through an incision.

STUDY FINDINGS

But one study of more than 8,000 patients found that injecting a gas mixture of oxygen and ozone into a herniated disk significantly relieves the pressure put on the nerves, easing patients' pain. A second study showed that the oxygen/ozone treatment works by reducing disk volume through ozone oxidation; the reduced volume eases disk pressure on the nerves.

The findings were presented at the Society of Interventional Radiology's annual meeting in San Diego.

STUDY DETAILS

In the study of more than 8,000 patients, those who had the oxygen/ozone treatment reported their pain lessening by an average of nearly 4 points, based on a 10-point scale (with 0 being no pain and 10 representing the worst pain experienced). The patients' ability to conduct everyday tasks—such as washing and dressing themselves or even just standing up—also improved by more than 25% based on the rating scale used.

"Oxygen/ozone treatment of herniated disks is an effective and extremely safe procedure. The estimated improvement in pain and function is impressive when we looked at patients who ranged in age from 13 to 94 years with all types of disk herniations," said Kieran J. Murphy, MD, an interventional neuroradiologist and vice chair and chief of medical imaging at the University of Toronto in Canada.

COMPARISON TO SURGICAL TREATMENT

"Equally important, pain and function outcomes are similar to the outcomes for lumbar disks treated with surgical diskectomy, but the complication rate is much less (less than 0.1 percent)," Dr. Murphy said. "In addition, the recovery time is significantly shorter for the oxygen/ozone injection than for the diskectomy."

Much of the research into oxygen/ozone therapy has been done in Italy, where it is

believed as many as 14,000 individuals have been treated in the past five years.

"There are millions of people with back pain who suffer and who can't work because of their pain. Undergoing invasive surgical diskectomy puts you on a path where you may be left with too little disk. Taking out a protruding disk may lose the shock absorption that naturally resides between them in the spine," said Dr. Murphy. He predicts that this procedure will become standard in the United States within the next five years.

The U.S. Department of Health & Human Services has more information on how to prevent back pain at *www.healthfinder.gov*. Search "prevent back pain."

A Simple 5-Step Plan— Get Rid of Back Pain... For Good

Miriam E. Nelson, PhD, associate professor and director of John Hancock Center for Physical Activity and Nutrition at the Gerald J. and Dorothy R. Friedman School of Nutrition Science and Policy at Tufts University, Boston. A fellow of the American College of Sports Medicine, she is coauthor, with Lawrence Lindner, of *Strong Women, Strong Backs* (Putnam).

As many as 90% of all adults suffer back pain at some point in their lives. Back pain—lower back pain, in particular—ranks fifth among the most frequent reasons for hospitalizations.

Worse for women: Their musculoskeletal systems—ligaments, vertebrae, spinal disks, etc.—are more delicate than men's and more vulnerable to injury. Women also tend to be less active, on average, than men, and a sedentary lifestyle is a common cause of back pain.

Most back problems are caused by prolonged sitting or by lifting heavy objects the wrong way, but other factors contribute to back pain, including excess body weight, stress and depression. Even smoking is a factor for reasons that aren't exactly clear.

Simple lifestyle measures—maintaining a healthy weight, not smoking and controlling stress and depression—can prevent many cases of back pain. Most important, though, are exercises that strengthen muscles in the back, chest, abdomen, hips and sides. These are the core muscles—the scaffolding that supports the spine and enables the back to flex and twist without injury. Strengthening these muscles can relieve pain and also prevent it.

A FIVE-STEP PLAN

The following workout, which takes no more than 20 minutes, targets all of the core muscles. It can be done three to five times weekly (unlike most strength-training workouts, which should be done no more than three times a week, because muscles need time to recover between sessions). These exercises can be done more often because the intensity is lower —and they're less likely than traditional workouts to cause back pain or other injuries.

For each of the following exercises…

• **Complete 10 repetitions,** rest for one minute, then complete another 10 reps. If you can complete only five or six reps, the intensity is too high and you should do only what you can comfortably manage.

• **Work up to an advanced progression.** This is a way to increase the exercise intensity by making the movements more difficult.

• **Always warm up**—by taking a brisk walk around the block or stepping quickly in place —for five minutes before doing the exercises.

STEP 1: ABDOMINALS

Most people's abdominal muscles are weaker than they should be. Strengthening the abdominals is among the best ways to prevent back pain.

Starting position: Lie on your back on the floor with your knees bent and the soles of your feet flat on the floor. Lightly rest your hands on the lower part of the stomach.

The movement: Contract the abdominal muscles until you feel the small of the back pushing toward the floor. Imagine that you're pulling your belly button downward. Hold the "tense" position for three seconds, then relax.

Progression: Do almost the same exercise as above, with this difference. While the abdominal muscles are tight, raise the still-bent right leg a few inches off the floor and hold it up for three seconds, then place that leg down and raise the left leg for three seconds. The entire move will take 10 to 12 seconds.

STEP 2: CHEST MUSCLES

Along with abdominal exercises, chest workouts protect the back by strengthening the "front" of the core muscle groups.

Starting position: Stand facing a wall or a counter, about an arm's length away, with your feet hip-width apart and knees slightly bent. Put your palms on the wall (or lightly hold the edge of the counter).

The movement: Holding your body straight, bend at the elbows until you are leaning forward toward the wall or counter about 30 degrees. Pause in this position for a moment, then push with your arms until you're back in the starting position.

Progression: Work the same muscles with more intensity with a modified push-up. Lie facedown on the floor, with your palms directly next to your shoulders, elbows bent.

Keeping your knees on the floor, slowly push up only your chest. Keep your trunk in a straight line from your head to your knees. Push up until your shoulders are over your hands, but don't lock the elbows. Pause for a moment, then lower back down until your nose is about four inches from the floor. Keep your trunk in a straight line throughout the movements.

STEP 3: MIDBACK

Many exercises target the upper/lower back, but relatively few target the middle back—a common area for problems.

Starting position: Lie facedown on an exercise mat or carpet, with your arms straight out to the sides, perpendicular to the body.

The movement: Contract your shoulder blades to lift the arms up and slightly back. Hold the arms in the lifted position, and make four figure eights with the hands. Then lower your arms to the starting position.

Progression: Make the figure eights with the thumbs down or up…or while holding a balled-up sock in each hand…or with the little finger up or down. Varying the movement works different parts of the muscles.

STEP 4: UPPER BACK

This exercise increases shoulder strength as well as back strength.

Starting position: Tie a knot in the middle of an elastic exercise band (available at sporting-goods stores for $2 to $3). Place the knot over the top of a door, and then close the door to anchor the band in place. The two ends should be hanging down on the same side of the door. Sit in a chair facing the door, with your toes against the door. Hold one end of the band in each hand.

The movement: Slowly pull your hands down and in toward your chest. Keep your elbows pointed down and close to your body. Pause for a moment, then slowly let your arms extend back to the starting position.

Progression: When the exercise starts feeling easy, change to a higher-resistance band.

STEP 5: LOWER BACK

This is the area that gives most people problems.

Starting position: Lie facedown on an exercise mat or carpet. Reach your right hand in front of you,  palm down. The left arm should be down alongside your body, with the palm up.

The movement: Slowly raise your right arm, chest and left leg about five inches off the floor. Keep your face down, so your spine is in a straight line. Keep your right leg and left hand on the ground. Pause for a moment, then return to the starting position.

Reverse the movement, raising your left arm, chest and right leg, and keeping the left leg and right hand on the floor.

Progression: Kneel on all fours. Raise your right arm straight in front of you while simultaneously raising the left leg straight behind. Keep the abdominal muscles contracted. Pause, return to the starting position. Then reverse the movement.

272

OPTIONAL EXERCISE: THIGHS, HIPS AND MORE

This optional exercise is a complex move that targets the upper legs as well as the trunk. It is good for improving stability and balance. The exercise requires the use of a stability ball, available at sporting-goods stores for about $20.

Starting position: Stand with your back to 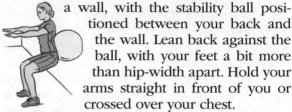 a wall, with the stability ball positioned between your back and the wall. Lean back against the ball, with your feet a bit more than hip-width apart. Hold your arms straight in front of you or crossed over your chest.

The movement: While keeping light pressure on the ball with your lower back, bend at the knees and slowly squat down—the ball will roll with the movement. Squat down as far as you comfortably can. The ball will then be positioned at about the midback.

Keeping pressure on the ball, contract the buttocks and slowly "roll" yourself up and back to the starting position.

Illustrations by Shawn Banner.

Alleviate Neck And Back Pain With Fish Oil

In a new finding, when neck and back pain sufferers took a fish-oil supplement (1,200 milligrams daily) for 75 days, 60% reported significant pain relief that allowed them to decrease or discontinue use of painkillers.

Theory: The omega-3 fatty acids found in fish oil block the inflammation that can lead to neck and back pain. Fish oil also may help relieve joint pain.

If you have neck or back pain: Ask your doctor about taking fish oil. Do not use fish oil if you take *warfarin* (Coumadin) or another blood thinner.

Joseph Maroon, MD, vice chairman of neurological surgery, University of Pittsburgh.

How to Prevent a Stiff Back

Take a break at least every half hour to stretch out your back—walk around for two minutes, then assume a squatting position for 15 seconds to decompress the cushiony disks between the vertebrae of the spine. Slouching puts added strain on the lower back, so I recommend using an ergonomic chair (sold at office-supply stores) designed to provide back support and promote proper posture. Also, get regular exercise to keep the back muscles toned and flexible—aim for at least three sessions of 15 to 30 minutes weekly, being sure to include some stretching. In addition, supplement once or twice daily with 500 milligrams (mg) of calcium and 250 mg of magnesium to help prevent muscle tightness.

Mark A. Stengler, NMD, naturopathic medical doctor in private practice, Encinitas, California...adjunct associate clinical professor at the National College of Natural Medicine, Portland, Oregon...author of *The Natural Physician's Healing Therapies* (Bottom Line Books).

Ergonomic Garden Tools Prevent Aches and Pains

Walter Reeves, host of DIY's *Garden Sense* on the DIY Network. He is author of nine books on gardening, including *The Georgia Gardener's Guide* (Cool Springs). He lives in Decatur, Georgia. *www.walterreeves.com.*

Gardening is one of the leading causes of repetitive stress injuries, such as carpal tunnel syndrome. Gardeners also are prone to muscle and ligament strains.

Ergonomic garden tools are designed to lessen the toll that gardening takes on the body. *My favorites...*

•**Pruning shears.** Select shears with swivel handles or levers or gears to reduce the amount of force required to cut. Lefties should buy left-handed shears (many manufacturers make them). *Examples of ergonomic shears...*

•Felco offers several pruners with swivel handles, including the Felco 7 Pruner, the Felco 10 Pruner for left-handers and the Felco 12 Pruner for people with small hands. $40 to $80. Available at garden centers or *www.felcostore.com.*

•Fiskars offers a wide range of well-made ergonomic pruners. The PowerGear Large Bypass Pruner features both a rotating handle and gears. $29.99. 866-348-5661, *www.fiskars.com.*

•Florian 701 Ratchet-Cut Hand Pruner uses levers. $38.75. 800-275-3618, *www.floriantools.com.*

•**Shovels.** The top of the handle should be above your waist but no higher than your chin. The shaft should feel comfortable in your hand—if it's too narrow, gripping it will cause hand pain. The "step," or nondigging end of the head, should be at least as wide as your shoe so that you can comfortably apply pressure with your foot. If foot pain is an issue, choose a shovel that has a flat step. A lightweight fiberglass or ash shaft will reduce the stress on your arms and back, but a heavier, stronger head will require less force to drive into the earth.

Example: Ames True Temper (800-393-1846, *www.ames.com*) offers a range of quality shovels for less than $25.

•**Trowels.** A traditional trowel puts the wrist at an unnatural angle. Neutral grip trowels allow the wrist to remain in a more natural knuckles-forward position (as if aiming a handgun). People with leg or back problems should consider a long-handled trowel that can be used from a standing position.

Examples: Peta's Easi-Grip Trowel and Arm Support Cuff together significantly reduce wrist strain. Trowel and cuff are available for $11.95 and $9.95, respectively. Peta's Long Reach Trowel ($34.95) can be used while standing. *www.peta-uk.com/.* Also available from *www.arthritissupplies.com*, 877-750-0376.

•**Rakes and hoes.** Use of a rake or hoe generally means turning the leading hand (the one lower on the shaft) to an awkward angle, creating stress on the wrist. There are devices available that allow a safer, more natural grip.

•**Kneelers and stools.** Getting up and down in the garden can be challenging. Step2's Garden Kneeler and Seat can be used as a low stool for sitting or, when flipped over, as a kneeling bench with support handles. $23.50. Available at garden centers, The Home Depot and online at Amazon.com.

Heartburn Relief

Ara DerMarderosian, PhD, professor of pharmacognosy (the study of natural products used in medicine) and Roth chair of natural products at the University of the Sciences in Philadelphia. He also is the scientific director of the university's Complementary and Alternative Medicines Institute.

Many people who suffer from heartburn take over-the-counter antacids or expensive prescription medication, such as *esomeprazole* (Nexium) and *lansoprazole* (Prevacid). These treatments can help but often cause side effects, such as diarrhea and dry mouth.

Heartburn, a sharp, burning pain under the rib cage, occurs when stomach contents "back up" (reflux) into the esophagus.

Chamomile, ginger and deglycyrrhizinated licorice have long been used (in tea, extract and tincture) to relieve heartburn as well as indigestion and intestinal irritation. Their effectiveness is supported by anecdotal evidence.

For relief proven in clinical studies, try pectin, a substance found in the outer skin and rind of fruits and vegetables. Apples and bananas are among the best sources of pectin. If you suffer from heartburn, try eating an apple (do not choose green or other tart varieties) or a banana to see if it relieves your symptoms.

Pectin supplements, which are available at most health-food stores, are another option. Take at the onset of heartburn until it subsides. For dosage, follow label instructions. Pectin supplements are generally safe but may interfere with the absorption of some medications, so check with your doctor before trying this supplement.

Caution: Chronic heartburn (more than twice a week) may indicate gastroesophageal reflux disease (GERD), a condition that should be treated by a gastroenterologist.

Natural Therapies for Ulcers

James N. Dillard, MD, DC, former assistant clinical professor at Columbia University College of Physicians and Surgeons and past clinical director of Columbia's Rosenthal Center for Complementary and Alternative Medicine, both in New York City.

If you've got an ulcer, chances are you're taking an over-the-counter (OTC) antacid and/or prescription medication to neutralize gastric acid or inhibit its production. These medications include proton pump inhibitors (PPIs), such as *esomeprazole* (Nexium) and *lansoprazole* (Prevacid), and H2-blocking drugs, such as *cimetidine* (Tagamet) and *ranitidine* (Zantac).

What most people don't realize: There are several natural, complementary remedies that help reduce ulcer symptoms and promote healing while conventional treatment is under way. Some of these treatments also can help prevent ulcers in some patients.

WHAT CAUSES ULCERS

It's been more than 20 years since doctors learned that an infectious disease—rather than emotional stress—was the primary cause of most ulcers.

A screw-shaped bacterium, *Helicobacter pylori*, or *H. pylori*, burrows through the protective mucous lining in the small intestine and/or stomach, allowing harsh digestive fluids to accumulate and ulcerate the lining. About 50% of Americans over age 60 are infected with H. pylori. The bacterium doesn't always cause ulcers—but about 60% of patients with ulcers harbor H. pylori.

The remainder of ulcers are caused by regular use of stomach-damaging nonsteroidal anti-inflammatory drugs (NSAIDs), such as aspirin, *ibuprofen* (Advil) and *naproxen* (Aleve) …alcohol…and/or smoking. Excessive alcohol wears down the lining of the stomach and intestines. Nicotine causes the stomach to produce more acid.

Best complementary treatments…*

*Check with your doctor before taking supplements. They can interact with prescription medications.

NONDRUG THERAPIES

●**Probiotics.** The intestine contains up to four pounds of "friendly" bacteria, which aid digestion. There's some evidence that maintaining adequate levels of beneficial bacteria helps create an inhospitable environment for H. pylori and makes it harder for this ulcer-causing bacterium to thrive.

Self-defense: Take a probiotic supplement that contains *Lactobacillus acidophilus* and *Bifidobacterium bifidus*. These organisms create a healthful mix of bacteria and can inhibit the growth of harmful organisms. Probiotics are helpful if you've taken antibiotics, which can kill off some beneficial bacteria.

The optimal dose for probiotics hasn't been determined. Preliminary research cites a daily dose of up to 10 billion organisms—the amount usually included in one to two capsules. Probiotics are available at health-food stores.

●**Cabbage juice.** This folk remedy has some evidence to support it. Cabbage is high in vitamin C, which seems to inhibit growth of H. pylori. It also contains *glutamine*, an amino acid that may strengthen the protective lining in the stomach.

A small Stanford University School of Medicine study found that ulcer patients who drank about a quart of cabbage juice daily healed significantly faster than those who didn't drink it.

Self-defense: If you have an active ulcer, consider drinking a quart of cabbage juice (about the amount in half a head of cabbage) once daily for up to two weeks.

●**Deglycyrrhizinated licorice (DGL).** Herbalists often recommend fresh licorice root to heal ulcers. Licorice contains *mucin,* a substance that protects the stomach lining, and antioxidants that may inhibit H. pylori growth.

However, natural licorice can increase the effects of *aldosterone*, a hormone that promotes water retention and can increase blood pressure in some people. DGL supplements (available at health-food stores) are a better option, because the substances that increase blood pressure have been removed.

Self-defense: Take one DGL tablet before meals, and another before bed. DGL may be effective for people with ulcers whose H. pylo-

ri has been successfully treated with antibiotics but who still have some stomach irritation.

●**Vitamin A.** Vitamin A helps repair damaged mucous membranes. A report in the British medical journal *The Lancet* suggests that ulcers heal more quickly in patients given supplemental vitamin A.

Caution: High-dose vitamin A therapy can be toxic, so get your vitamin A from dietary sources along with a daily multivitamin—*not* from a separate vitamin A supplement.

Self-defense: Get 10,000 international units (IU) of vitamin A daily if you're undergoing ulcer treatment. (A multivitamin typically contains 3,500 IU to 5,000 IU of vitamin A.)

Good food sources: Beef liver (one-and-one-half ounces contains 13,593 IU)…carrots (one raw carrot contains 8,666 IU)…and spinach (one cup of raw spinach contains 2,813 IU).

●**Zinc.** Like vitamin A, zinc is involved in tissue healing. In Europe, a drug compound made with zinc plus an anti-inflammatory is often used for treating ulcers. Early studies indicate that zinc alone can speed ulcer healing and possibly even help prevent some ulcers.

Self-defense: Don't exceed the recommended daily intake—15 milligrams (mg)—of zinc. Take a daily multivitamin that includes zinc… and get adequate intake from dietary sources (five medium fried oysters, 13 mg…3/4 cup fortified breakfast cereal, 15 mg…three-ounces lean beef tenderloin, 5 mg).

ANOTHER WAY TO FIGHT ULCERS

NSAIDs alleviate pain by inhibiting the production of pain-causing chemicals called *prostaglandins.* However, the body produces several kinds of prostaglandins, including some that protect the stomach lining. That's why NSAIDs, which block the production of pain-causing *and* stomach-protecting prostaglandins, make people who regularly use the drugs more susceptible to ulcers.

Self-defense: If you require regular pain relief, start with *acetaminophen* (Tylenol). It relieves pain without depleting stomach-protecting prostaglandins.

Caution: Taking more than the recommended dosage or drinking alcohol with acetaminophen can cause liver damage.

Also helpful: Ask your doctor about taking Arthrotec, a prescription drug combination that includes the NSAID *diclofenac* along with *misoprostol*, which protects the stomach and intestinal lining. One study found that patients taking Arthrotec experienced up to 80% fewer ulcers than those taking an NSAID alone.

The Healing Powers of Touch

Tiffany M. Field, PhD, director of the Touch Research Institute (*www.miami.edu/touch-research*) at the University of Miami School of Medicine. She has participated in more than 100 studies on the effects of massage therapy on many medical and psychological conditions. She is the author of *Touch* (MIT Press).

Nearly 60% of doctors in the US recommend massage for some patients —almost twice as many as recommended it five years ago.

Why the dramatic increase?

For years, therapeutic massage was recommended primarily for musculoskeletal conditions, such as arthritis, low back pain and muscle tension. Now, credible research shows that massage has benefits that most doctors never expected. *What we now know...*

WHY MASSAGE HELPS

Scientists now have evidence that massage affects virtually every major body function— from immunity to lung and brain function— and confers health benefits through a variety of mechanisms.

Even though massage therapists are usually trained in one or more massage techniques, such as Swedish, Shiatsu and deep tissue massage, there is no evidence that one technique is better than another for most conditions.

Studies indicate that the application of moderate pressure—firm enough to make an indentation in the skin—is the key to massage's health benefits. By stimulating *pressure receptors* under the skin, massage activates different branches of the *vagus nerve*, which regulates blood pressure, heart rate and many other physiological functions.

Massage also...

• **Reduces levels of stress hormones,** such as cortisol. This is important for pain relief, easing depression and increasing energy levels. Reductions in cortisol also enhance immune function, including the ability of natural killer cells to target viruses and cancer cells.

• **Enhances deeper sleep stages** (known as *delta sleep*), which helps reduce levels of a brain chemical, known as *substance P*, that is related to the sensation of pain.

Massage is now used to treat...

HIGH BLOOD PRESSURE

Patients with elevated blood pressure often have high levels of stress hormones. Massage not only lowers levels of these hormones but also stimulates the branch of the vagus nerve that leads to the heart. Stimulating the nerve decreases heart rate and lowers blood pressure.

In one study, adults with hypertension were given 10 half-hour massages over five weeks. They showed a statistically significant decrease in diastolic (bottom number) blood pressure and reported less depression and anxiety— common problems in patients being treated for hypertension.

CARPAL TUNNEL SYNDROME

The *median nerve* in the wrist passes through a narrow opening (the carpal tunnel) on the palm side of the wrist. Swelling or inflammation of the nerve, usually caused by repetitive movements such as typing or using a screwdriver, can result in chronic tingling, numbness and/or pain in the thumb as well as the index and middle fingers. Researchers at Baylor University Medical Center have recently reported that even gripping the steering wheel of a car for long hours may lead to carpal tunnel syndrome.

A daily self-massage can reduce pain and promote an increase in *nerve-conduction velocity*, a measure of nerve health.

15-minute self-massage: Using moderate pressure, stroke from the wrist to the elbow and back down on both sides of the forearm. Next, apply a wringing motion to the same area. Using the thumb and index finger, stroke the entire forearm and the hand in a circular or back-and-forth motion. Finish by rolling the skin with the thumb and index finger, moving across the hand and up both sides of the forearm.

BURNS

Serious burns are among the most painful wounds. The standard treatments—including brushing away debris and cleaning the area—can be excruciatingly painful. Massage done before the skin is brushed appears to elevate the pain threshold of burn patients—perhaps by increasing levels of the brain chemical *serotonin.*

Example: If one hand is burned, another person can vigorously rub the patient's other hand. This activation of skin receptors, in effect, blocks the feeling of pain related to the burn.

PAIN

Studies show that massage curbs back pain, migraine and cancer pain. It may do this by reducing the pain-promoting chemical substance P as well as the stress hormone cortisol.

Key findings: In three separate studies, patients with back pain were treated either with massage or a sham treatment (a massage with insufficient pressure to provide any benefit). Patients in both groups were treated twice weekly for 20 minutes. Those in the massage group consistently had less pain and better range of motion than patients in the sham group.

Massage also seems to help post-surgical pain. In a pilot study, researchers at Cedars-Sinai Medical Center in Los Angeles found that patients who received massages after heart-bypass surgery had less pain and fewer muscle spasms than those who didn't get massages.

To find a massage therapist, consult the American Massage Therapy Association, 877-905-0577, *www.amtamassage.org.*

Fibromyalgia Relieved by Water Exercise

In an eight-month study of 33 women with fibromyalgia (which is characterized by painful muscles, ligaments and tendons), those who participated in a supervised exercise program in a heated swimming pool for 60 min-utes three times weekly experienced fewer symptoms than nonexercisers.

Theory: Warm water induces relaxation, which helps fight pain. Ask your doctor if water workouts are an option for you.

Narcís Gusi, PhD, professor, University of Extremadura, Cáceres, Spain.

A Simple Solution to Aches and Pains

Roger Herr, PT, a Seattle–based physical therapist, past president of the American Physical Therapy Association's Home Health section and member of the board of the Physical Therapy Association of Washington.

If you wake up feeling achy, tired or sore, it could be a sign that you need a new mattress. But some mattresses are far better than others —especially if you have a chronic condition, such as arthritis or varicose veins.

TIME FOR A NEW MATTRESS?

About one-third of Americans sleep on mattresses that are at least eight years old. That's not necessarily a problem—age alone is not always the best way to determine whether it's time to replace a mattress. Some high-quality mattresses last 10 or more years.

WHAT TO LOOK FOR

When shopping for a mattress, consider these features...

• **Density.** For years, the standard recommendation has been an extra-firm mattress for people with back pain and/or arthritis, and a firm mattress for everyone else. But there's no independent research to support this recommendation—most studies are conducted by mattress manufacturers—and this advice actually can be harmful for some people. For example, if you have fragile skin (a common problem among older adults), a firm mattress can cause painful pressure.

There is no perfect density for everyone—you must try out mattresses to see which is most comfortable for you and best supports the natural "S" curve of your back.

My advice: Go mattress shopping at night, when you are likely to be tired. That way, you'll get a more realistic assessment than you would if you went first thing in the morning, when you are apt to feel refreshed. Wear loose clothing, such as a T-shirt and sweatpants, and lie on mattresses in your preferred sleeping position. If you have a bed partner, lie together on mattresses to see how they respond to your body weights. Be sure that the mattress seller offers you a trial period (14 to 30 days), so that you will have a chance to try out the product with an option to return or exchange it.

• **Height.** Contrary to popular belief, a taller bed is usually safer than a shorter one. The standard height of most mattresses is 14 inches. Some additional height can be a significant help if you must get in and out of bed with chronically painful muscles or joints—or after an injury.

My advice: Your sleeping surface (including the bed frame, box spring—if any—and the mattress when you are sitting on it) should be 20 to 25 inches above the floor.

• Material. There are a handful of materials that comprise virtually all the mattresses sold in the US.

• Coil-spring mattresses are owned by the majority of Americans. The most flexible coil-spring (usually made of steel) mattresses have smaller coils—at least 680 coils per mattress is most comfortable for many people. For people who weigh more than 250 pounds, however, larger-coil mattresses (about 400 coils per mattress) typically last longer and provide better support. *Examples:* Sealy and Shifman (Bloomingdale's house brand). *Price range:* $350 to $5,000.

• Memory-foam mattresses, which use heat- and pressure-sensitive material that adjusts to the contours of your body, are the most popular foam mattresses. These mattresses provide support at all the pressure points of your body but may feel too hot for people who experience night sweats or for women who have hot flashes. *Examples:* Tempur-Pedic and Dormia. *Price range:* $400 to $7,500.

• Latex (rubber-based) mattresses mold to the contours of the body. *Examples:* King Koil, Sealy and Stearns & Foster. *Price range:* $700 to $4,000.

• Air beds contain inflatable chambers that provide support. These mattresses are adjustable, so each bed partner can select a desired level of firmness for his/her side of the bed. Air beds are a good choice if one bed partner is significantly heavier than the other. *Examples:* Select Comfort and Spring Air. *Price range:* $400 to $4,100.

THE BEST MATTRESS FOR YOU

Consider the following if you have a chronic medical condition…

• **Allergies.** Natural latex mattresses (such as Vivètique) are designed to be hypoallergenic, antimicrobial and resistant to dust mites. To be labeled as "natural latex," they must be composed of at least 50% natural rubber from rubber-tree sap.

• **Arthritis.** If you suffer joint pain due to osteoarthritis or rheumatoid arthritis, flexible support—from a coil-spring or memory-foam mattress—helps prevent potentially painful pressure points.

• **Back pain.** A coil-spring mattress with or without a pillow-top (an extra layer of padding on top) or a memory-foam mattress usually helps support the natural curve of your back. If you sleep on your back, also consider placing one or two pillows under your knees to relieve the pressure on your back.

• **Pulmonary complications.** If you suffer from congestive heart failure or chronic obstructive pulmonary disease (COPD)—chronic bronchitis and/or emphysema—a firm-density mattress (such as coil spring) is best because it provides needed support to the back and torso, to facilitate breathing. Elevating the upper body by sleeping on extra pillows also helps prevent shortness of breath and other breathing difficulties.

• **Varicose veins.** This condition, which usually occurs as a result of blood pooling in veins close to the surface of the skin, responds best to a medium-density mattress (such as latex). Whenever possible, prop pillows beneath your calves to elevate your legs at or above the level of your heart. This helps prevent blood from pooling in the lower legs.

Apple Cider Vinegar

Mark A. Stengler, NMD, naturopathic medical doctor in private practice, Encinitas, California…adjunct associate clinical professor at the National College of Natural Medicine, Portland, Oregon…author of *The Natural Physician's Healing Therapies* (Bottom Line Books).

Patients often tell me that apple cider vinegar has helped them with a variety of ailments. This intrigued me because, until recently, there was little research to back up these claims.

CURE-ALL?

Apple cider vinegar has been singled out as beneficial for a variety of conditions, including leg cramps, stomach upset, sore throat, sinus problems, high blood pressure, obesity, osteoporosis and arthritis. It also has been used to help rid the body of toxins, improve concentration, slow aging, reduce cholesterol and fight infection.

It is used topically to treat acne, sunburn, shingles and insect bites…as a skin toner… and to prevent dandruff. Many women add it to bathwater to treat vaginitis. Two of its most common uses are for weight loss and arthritis.

THE SCIENTIFIC EVIDENCE

Recent studies have found that consuming apple cider vinegar can improve insulin resistance, a condition in which muscle, fat and liver cells have become resistant to the uptake of the hormone *insulin* and the blood sugar *glucose* needed to provide fuel for energy.

This is common among people who have diabetes as well as in some people we consider prediabetic—that is, their blood glucose and insulin levels are approaching the numbers that define diabetes. People with insulin resistance are more likely to be overweight and have increased cholesterol and triglyceride levels as well as high blood pressure.

A 2004 study at the University of Arizona examined the effects of apple cider vinegar on 29 participants (10 had type 2 diabetes, 11 had signs that they could become diabetic and eight were healthy, or "insulin sensitive"). All participants fasted and were randomly asked to drink either a vinegar solution (two tablespoons or 20 g of apple cider vinegar, some water and a bit of saccharin for flavor) or a placebo drink. The drinks were followed by a high-carbohydrate meal of one white bagel, butter and orange juice.

Researchers found that postmeal spikes of insulin and glucose in the vinegar group were significantly lower in those who had insulin resistance and slightly lower in those who had diabetes, compared with those in the placebo group. Other research has shown that apple cider vinegar helps control insulin and glucose spikes in healthy people.

HOW IT WORKS

Researchers theorize that the *acetic acid* in any vinegar, including apple cider vinegar, interferes with the enzymes that digest carbohydrates, so carbs pass through the digestive tract without being absorbed. Acetic acid also has been shown to affect enzymes that alter glucose metabolism in liver and muscle cells, reducing insulin spikes.

Because high levels of insulin promote inflammation, taking vinegar to maintain better insulin levels will control any inflammatory response in the body. This may explain why vinegar eases arthritis pain.

DOSAGE

People can try apple cider vinegar for weight loss, blood sugar balance and other traditional uses, including arthritis relief. Dilute one to two tablespoons (some people use as little as two teaspoons to start with) in an equal amount of water, and drink it at the beginning of a meal.

Sometimes it is more convenient to take it in supplement form. A good product is Apple Cider Vinegar Plus, which is made by Indiana Botanic Gardens (800-644-8327, *www. botan icchoice.com*). Take one capsule with each meal for a total of three capsules a day. Ninety capsules cost $29.99.

Apple cider vinegar can cause digestive upset in some people. If you have active ulcers, use caution when taking apple cider vinegar.

Got Pain in Your Heel, Knee or Elbow?

Sabrina M. Strickland, MD, orthopedic surgeon and specialist in sports medicine at the Hospital for Special Surgery and an assistant professor at Weill Cornell Medical College, both in New York City. She is also chief of orthopedics at the Bronx Veterans Affairs Medical Center in Bronx, New York.

Virtually all adults suffer a bone or joint (orthopedic) injury at some point in their lives. Often complicated by damage to nearby muscles or ligaments, orthopedic complaints can severely limit movement and sometimes cause excruciating pain.

Although surgery is available to correct most orthopedic injuries, about 80% of cases can be treated with appropriate home care, such as rest, anti-inflammatory drugs and applications of ice and/or heat.

Best treatments for some of the most common orthopedic complaints…

BONE SPURS

Bone spurs (*osteophytes*) are bony outgrowths that can form on the spine or a joint—in your knees, hips, elbows, fingers or feet. Although no one knows what causes bone spurs, people with osteoarthritis have a higher risk of getting them, so it's possible that they're a normal part of aging.

If bone spurs cause pain, try nonsteroidal anti-inflammatory drugs (NSAIDs). You may want to consider surgery if the spurs interfere with your ability to perform everyday activities (the specific type of surgery would depend on the location of the bone spur).

Heel spurs, which form where the connective tissue of the foot (*fascia*) joins the heel bone (*calcaneus*), are one of the most common types of bone spur.

Important: Plantar fasciitis, inflammation of the plantar fascia (the arch tendon of the foot), is an injury that often occurs as a result of overuse. This condition, which causes heel pain that may radiate forward into the foot, differs slightly from a heel spur, which can result from repetitive pulling of the plantar fascia.

Main treatment: For heel spurs, place a silicone heel cup, available at pharmacies for $5 to $10, in your shoe. It cushions the heel and reduces pain. Use the heel cup daily—especially when wearing hard shoes—then gradually taper off its use. This approach, along with physical therapy, relieves the pain within a few months. A heel cup may also improve symptoms of plantar fasciitis.

Surgical option: Plantar fasciotomy, in which all or part of the fascia is separated from the heel bone, is performed when the pain from heel spurs or plantar fasciitis is intense and doesn't improve within nine months with other treatments. In rare cases, nerve injury to the foot or infection can occur.

KNEE PAIN

The meniscus is a C-shaped piece of cartilage that helps stabilize the knee. People who suddenly twist or rotate the knee can tear a meniscus. In younger adults, a torn meniscus is usually caused by traumatic injury—from playing sports, for example. In people who are middle-aged and older, it's more likely to be caused by age-related degeneration of the cartilage.

Symptoms: A "popping" sensation in the knee, followed by pain and swelling within a day. Magnetic resonance imaging (MRI) studies in knee patients show that about one-third have meniscal tears that don't cause discomfort or loss of mobility. These tears do not require treatment.

Main treatment: Patients with mild symptoms, such as pain and/or swelling, are often given an injection of cortisone and/or assigned to physical therapy. This approach often eliminates symptoms within four to six weeks, even if the meniscus doesn't completely heal.

Also helpful: The supplements glucosamine (1,500 milligrams, or mg, daily) and chondroitin (1,200 mg daily) may improve symptoms in people who also have arthritis. Combination formulas are available. I tell patients to use glucosamine and chondroitin for three months while trying other nonsurgical treatments.

Caution: Glucosamine supplements may not be safe for people with seafood allergies.

Surgical option: Between 25% and 35% of patients with a torn meniscus will require surgery to regain normal knee motion and stability. In some cases, the meniscus can be repaired. More often, the torn portion is trimmed away. People who have had the surgery usually regain all or most of their normal knee function within four to six weeks. Risks, though rare, include infection and injury to nerves or blood vessels in the knee.

TENNIS ELBOW

About 90% of patients who get tennis elbow (*lateral epicondylitis*) do not play tennis. The condition is caused by overuse of the extensor tendon, which runs from the wrist to the elbow. People who flex the wrist repeatedly—from prolonged hammering or painting, for example, or from poor tennis form—are at greatest risk.

Symptoms: Pain that radiates from the elbow to the forearm and/or wrist…pain when bending the wrist…or tenderness on the outside of the elbow.

Medical experts used to think that tennis elbow was mainly due to inflammation.

New finding: The real problem is a condition in the cells of the tendon, known as *tendonosis*, in which wear and tear is thought to cause degeneration of the tendon. Experimental treatments, such as injecting platelet-rich plasma, are meant to promote tissue repair rather than fight inflammation.

Main treatment: About 90% of people with tennis elbow recover with rest and the use of ice. Also, patients should use a counterforce brace, which limits stress on the proximal part of the tendon (near the elbow). Avoid painful activities for two weeks, then gradually resume them with use of the brace.

Helpful: An exercise that lengthens the muscle and accelerates healing.

What to do: While keeping the wrist straight, hold a hammer in the hand of the affected arm. With the palm facing down, slowly bend the wrist downward. At the bottom of the movement, switch the hammer to the other hand to avoid lifting the weight with your bad arm. Repeat eight to 10 times, a few times a day.

Surgical option: Fewer than 10% of patients with tennis elbow will require surgery. The goal is to remove dead tissue from the area to encourage the formation of new blood vessels and healthy tissue.

Patients typically are able to resume most activities in four to six weeks, and to resume tennis and other sports in four to six months. In rare cases, nerve and/or ligament damage may occur.

Illustration by Shawn Banner.

No More Foot Pain!

Sherri Greene, DPM (doctor of podiatric medicine). She has practiced conventional and holistic podiatric medicine in New York City for the past 16 years. Her treatment modalities include reflexology, herbal medicine and essential oils.

Many people downplay the significance of foot problems. But that's a big mistake.

What a foot problem may really mean: You could have an undetected medical condition. For example, numb or painful feet can be a red flag for the damaged blood vessels and nerves that can occur with diabetes or peripheral arterial disease (a circulatory problem that causes reduced blood flow to the limbs). Foot problems also may be associated with seemingly unrelated ailments, such as hip or back pain.

An effective way to identify the root cause of foot pain is to take a whole-body (holistic) approach that often can replace conventional treatments. *Holistic approaches to everyday foot problems…*

●**Go barefoot.** After spending day after day confined in tight or ill-fitting shoes, the muscles of the foot can weaken—the same way an arm loses muscle tone when encased in a cast. Going barefoot in your home allows your feet to stretch, strengthen and find their natural alignment.

Caution: People with diabetes should *never* go barefoot—this medical condition commonly causes nerve damage in the feet, which makes it difficult to feel cuts or other injuries. Also, do not walk barefoot on marble or other potentially slippery floors or if you have balance or vision problems. In all of these cases, wear sturdy slippers or similar footwear that protect your feet and provide good traction.

• **"Open" your toes.** This gentle form of stretching can improve flexibility of the tendons, release tension and stimulate blood flow to the feet and the rest of the body.

It can help prevent foot ailments, such as hammertoe (in which the end of a toe curls downward) and Morton's neuroma (inflammation of a nerve between the toes that causes pain in the ball of the foot), and is useful for people suffering from painful foot conditions such as *plantar fasciitis* (described below).

What to do: Lace your fingers between each toe (imagine holding hands with your foot)…or use physical separators, such as pedicure toe dividers (available at drugstores) or gel-filled YogaToes (available at YogaPro, 877-964-2776, *www.yogapro.com*). Open your toes for five to 30 minutes at least five days per week.

Caution: People with rigid bunions should not use YogaToes—they may strain the ligaments and cause additional pain.

FOR COMMON FOOT PROBLEMS

If your suffer from frequent foot pain, you may have one of these foot problems…

• **Bunion.** No one knows exactly what causes this swollen, painful outgrowth of bone at the base of the big toe. Heredity plays a role, but podiatrists also suspect excess body weight and ill-fitting shoes.

Holistic therapy: To relieve inflammation, massage the foot with peppermint, lemongrass, wintergreen or lavender oil. To make your own massage oil, start with a half teaspoon of a "carrier," such as almond oil or vitamin E oil, and add two to three drops of the healing oil. Warm the oil mixture in the palm of your hand before massaging your feet for five to 10 minutes daily.

• **Plantar fasciitis.** This condition is inflammation of the thick band of tissue that connects the heel to the base of the toes. The pain—often excruciating—is most pronounced under the heel.

Anything that stresses the bottom of the foot can cause plantar fasciitis, including being overweight, suddenly increasing the amount of exercise you do or wearing shoes without arch support.

Holistic therapy: Massage the arch of the foot by rolling a squash ball (a tennis ball is too large) on the floor from heel to toes. Use pressure that is firm enough to move the tissues without causing pain.

This massage reduces inflammation by moving accumulated acids out of tissues. Perform it daily until symptoms resolve. *For plantar fasciitis, also perform this stretch twice daily on a regular basis…*

What to do: Take one large step forward and bend your forward knee. Press the heel of the back leg onto the floor. Hold for 10 to 30 seconds, then switch leg positions. For added stretch, bend the back knee, as well.

Important: If your foot problems affect your ability to walk or don't heal or improve after two weeks of home care, see a podiatrist.

Illustration by Shawn Banner.

Natural Pain Busters

Mark A. Stengler, NMD, naturopathic medical doctor in private practice, Encinitas, California…adjunct associate clinical professor at the National College of Natural Medicine, Portland, Oregon…author of *The Natural Physician's Healing Therapies* (Bottom Line Books).

When something hurts, you want to feel better quickly. Often that means reaching for an over-the-counter or prescription drug. But there are *natural* pain stoppers that offer the same relief—without the risks.

Aspirin and *ibuprofen* (Advil) can both cause intestinal bleeding…*acetaminophen* (Tylenol) can lead to liver damage…powerful prescription pain relievers, such as *acetaminophen-hydrocodone* and acetaminophen with codeine, may make you drowsy and can be addictive.

Despite the dangers, these medications are valuable for treating occasional severe (long-lasting) or acute (sudden, but stopping abruptly) pain. But for many chronic conditions that need ongoing relief, such as osteoarthritis, natural pain stoppers work just as well with a much lower risk for side effects.

Caution: Severe pain, or mild pain that gets suddenly worse, can be a sign of a serious injury or other medical problem.

Best: Seek medical attention immediately.

HOW TO USE
NATURAL REMEDIES

For each common pain problem discussed here, I give more than one treatment. You may have more success with, or simply prefer, a particular treatment. If something has worked for you in the past, start there. If you don't get much relief from a treatment, try another option. If you get only partial improvement, try adding another supplement. Because natural remedies have a very low risk for serious side effects, it's usually safe to use them in combination with prescription or nonprescription medications, such as for high blood pressure—and over the long run, they can help reduce the need for these drugs entirely. Check with your doctor before starting a natural regimen or changing your drug regimen.

Natural remedies also work well in combination with pain-relieving "body work," such as chiropractic, physical therapy and acupuncture.

HELP A HEADACHE

Migraines and other headaches are often set off by food sensitivities—most commonly, to red wine, caffeine, chocolate and food additives, such as monosodium glutamate. Other triggers, such as lack of sleep or hormonal fluctuations, can also leave you with headache pain.

Best: Pay attention to patterns and avoid your triggers.

Fortunately, headaches are usually very responsive to natural remedies…

•**Mild (tension) headaches.** First, try acupressure. This ancient Chinese technique uses gentle pressure and light massage on specific points.

In traditional Chinese medicine, *chi* (chee) is the vital energy of all living things. Your chi flows along 12 meridians that run through your body and nourish your tissues. Each meridian is associated with a particular organ, such as the liver or gallbladder. Along each meridian are specific points, designated by numbers, that are the spots where the flow of chi can be affected. *For headaches, the standard acupressure points are…*

•Gallbladder 20—the small indentation below the base of the skull, in the space between the two vertical neck muscles. Push gently for 10 to 15 seconds, wait 10 seconds, then repeat five to 10 times.

•Large intestine 4—located in the webbing between the thumb and index finger. Push gently for 10 to 15 seconds (as described above). Do this on one hand, then switch to the other.

•Yuyao—the indentation in the middle of each eyebrow (straight up from the pupil). Push gently for 10 to 15 seconds (as described above) on both points simultaneously.

If you don't feel relief within several minutes after trying a particular pressure point, move on to a different one.

Another option for mild headaches: A cup of peppermint tea, or a dab of peppermint oil on the temples, can banish a mild headache quickly.

Note: Peppermint essential oil is highly concentrated—don't take it internally.

To brew peppermint tea, make an infusion using one to two teaspoons dried peppermint leaf in eight ounces of boiling water. Let steep for five minutes. You may find relief after one cup. Drink as much and as often as necessary.

•**Migraine headaches.** The herb feverfew has been used effectively for centuries to treat migraines. Take a feverfew capsule standardized to contain 300 micrograms (mcg) of the active ingredient *parthenolide* every 30 minutes, starting at the onset of symptoms.

Maximum: Four doses daily or until you feel relief.

Prevention: Take a feverfew capsule standardized to contain 300 to 400 mcg of parthenolide—or 30 drops of a standardized tincture, either in a few ounces of water or directly on your tongue, every day. In about three months, you should notice dramatically fewer migraines, and/or less severe symptoms.

Note: Feverfew may thin blood, so consult your doctor if you are taking a blood thinner, such as *warfarin* (Coumadin).

SOOTHE SORE MUSCLES

Natural remedies can help an aching back or sore, cramped muscles. Here, too, acupressure is valuable. Zero in on the points that are most tender and then gently press on them and release, or massage for 10 to 15 seconds, at 10-second intervals, five to 10 times. If you can't reach a spot, have someone do it for you.

For some people, an ice pack on the affected area helps. Others prefer warmth from a hot compress or heating pad. For acute injuries, use cold (within 24 hours). Otherwise, use warmth or alternate warmth and cold. *Other remedies that help sore muscles...*

● **Herbal arnica cream or tincture** can soothe sore muscles and is also great for bruises. It reduces swelling, which helps lessen pain. Rub a small amount on the affected area. Repeat as needed.

Caution: Don't use on broken skin because it is not intended for internal use.

● **Homeopathic *Rhus toxicodendron*** is especially helpful in relieving low back pain. Take two pellets of 30C potency twice daily for two or three days.

EASE ARTHRITIC JOINTS

The stiff, swollen joints of osteoarthritis are a major cause of doctors' visits for people over age 45. *But with natural remedies, the pain and joint damage can be kept to a minimum...*

● **Glucosamine sulfate** helps rebuild damaged cartilage in arthritic joints and works as well as or better than many of the drugs doctors recommend. It can take several weeks to feel the benefits. Begin by taking 1,500 to 2,000 milligrams (mg) daily for three months. After that, cut back to 500 to 1,000 mg daily. If symptoms worsen, go back to the higher dose. It's OK to continue with anti-inflammatory drugs, but be sure to tell your doctor about your regimen.

● **Boswellia,** an herb used in Ayurveda, traditional medicine from India, is a powerful anti-inflammatory that's very helpful for arthritis. Take 1,200 to 1,500 mg of a standardized extract containing 60% to 65% boswellic acids, two to three times daily.

● **Bromelain,** an enzyme derived from pineapple stems, is very effective at reducing pain and swelling. Bromelain supplements come in two designations—MCU (milk-clotting units) and GDU (gelatin-dissolving units). Use either formula, choosing a product that's standardized to either 2,000 MCU per 1,000 mg or 1,200 GDU per 1,000 mg. Take 500 mg three times daily between meals.

Caution: If you take a blood-thinning medication such as warfarin, skip the bromelain—it could thin your blood too much.

Any of these supplements can be used alone or in combination. Natural pain stoppers can be effective alternatives to drugs, but pain is also your body's way of telling you that something is wrong. If your pain is very sudden or severe, and/or accompanied by other symptoms—such as weakness, nausea, redness and swelling in the painful area, shortness of breath or fever—get medical attention immediately.

Licorice Licks Pain

A dissolving oral patch shrinks painful canker sores by 90%, while untreated sores often get bigger. The patch, CankerMelts, releases licorice root extract for two to six hours—and eases pain in about 10 minutes.

Ivanhoe Newswire.

Index

V

Vaginal dryness, 256
Valerian, 161, 207, 244, 256
Vegetables. *See* Fruits and vegetables
Vicodin (*acetaminophen-hydrocodone*), 283
Vinegar, 35, 220, 279
Vioxx (*rofecoxib*), 261
Vision, vitamin A benefiting, 146
Visualization, 174, 236. *See also* Guided imagery
Vitamin, daily. *See* Multivitamins; Supplements
Vitamin A, 144, 146, 187, 198, 275
Vitamin B. *See also* Niacin
  for brain health, 224, 232–233
  in cervical dysplasia treatment, 201
  in cholesterol management, 70
  for healthy aging, 144
  for liver function, 146–147
  for menopause symptoms, 257
  as MS treatment, 155–156
  for numbness in fingers or toes, 145
  for skin health, 145
  in treating depression, 160
  for water retention, 244
Vitamin C
  for arthritis pain, 264–265
  kidney stone risk and, 144
  for oral health, 145
  for skin health, 28, 30
  in treating depression, 160
  as wrinkle fighter, 30
Vitamin D
  benefits of, 149–150, 197–199
  for brain health, 225–226
  breast cancer and, 149, 150–151
  children's diabetes risk and, 150
  as depression treatment, 160
  for healthy aging, 144
  for lung health, 151
  MS link to, 155–156
  PAD link to, 151
  for rejuvenation, 94
  from salmon, 151
  for weight control, 251–252
Vitamin E, 143, 144, 160, 187
Vitamin K, 153–154
Volunteering, 165

W

Walking, 60–61. *See also* Exercise
Water. *See also* Food and drink
  arsenic in, 50
  in detox diet, 83
  for energy boost, 93, 96
  for skin health, 26, 30, 35
  urinary tract health and, 211
Water retention, 244
Watermelon, 123–124
Weight control. *See also* Obesity
  aromatherapy for, 217
  calcium for, 148
  in carbohydrate-depression cycle, 158

detoxification and, 88–90
in diabetes management, 45–46, 52
estrogen level affected by, 249
supplements helping with, 251–252
triglycerides and, 72
Whey protein, 134
White willow bark, 207, 259, 260, 261–262
Whole-health care, 3–5. *See also* Natural treatments
Winter cherry. *See* Ashwagandha
Withania. See Ashwagandha
Wormwood. *See* Mugwort
Wrinkles, 31, 32–33. *See also* Skin health
Wristbands, as nausea treatment, 191

X

Xerostomia, 191. *See also* Oral health

Y

Yarrow, 205
Yeast infections, 211, 222
Yoga, 3. *See also* Exercise
Yogurt, 132, 133. *See also* Probiotics

Z

Zantac (*ranitidine*), 274
Zinc, 113–114, 145, 244, 275
Zocor (*simvastatin*), 68
Zoloft (*sertraline*), 158, 210